# Ar-Raheeq Al-Makhtum

# Biography of the Prophets

(Book Series Volume 1)

# Ibn Kathir

Copyright ©
TX C. of Hope
1979

All rights reserved. No part of this book may be reproduced or transmitted in any form or by any means, electronic or mechanical, including photocopying, recording, or by any information storage and retrieval system, without written permission from the Publisher.

All proceeds (100%) are donated to fight hunger for both humans and animals

To Hope

وإذا سألوك عن فلسطين فقل لهم:
وفيه شهيد
يرعاه شهيد،
تصوير شهيد,
أرسله شهيد
وصلى عليه شهيد

# Contents

ربي إني أسألك صدق التوكل عليك وحسن الظن بك

| | | |
|---|---|---|
| 1. | Prophet Adam and Eve (Hawwa) | 07 |
| | The Father of Mankind | |
| 2. | Prophet Idris (Enoch) | 28 |
| | A High Ranking Prophet | |
| 3. | Prophet Nuh (Noah) | 30 |
| | A Faithful Servant | |
| 4. | Prophet Hud | 39 |
| | A Trusting Servant | |
| 5. | Prophet Salih | 47 |
| | A Wise and Trustworthy Servant | |
| 6. | Prophet Ibrahim (Abraham) | 51 |
| | The Friend of God | |
| 7. | Prophet Isma'il (Ishmael) | 59 |
| | Truthful in his promise | |
| 8. | Prophet Ishaq (Isaac) | 67 |
| | Generous at heart | |
| 9. | Prophet Yaqub (Jacob) | 68 |
| | A patient servant | |

| | | |
|---|---|---|
| 10. | Prophet Lut (Lot) | 76 |
| | A Righteous and Wise Servant | |
| 11. | Prophet Shuaib | 81 |
| | The Orator of the Prophets | |
| 12. | Prophet Yusuf (Joseph) | 84 |
| | A Truthful and Forgiver | |
| 13. | Prophet Ayoub (Job) | 112 |
| | A Patient and Faithful servant | |
| 14. | Prophet Dhul-Kifl (Isaiah) | 117 |
| | A calm-natured servant | |
| 15. | Prophet Yunus (Jonah) (Dhan-Nun) | 119 |
| | A Repentant and Faithful Servant | |
| 16. | Prophet Moses and Aaron | 124 |
| | Faithful and Noble Servants | |
| 17. | Prophet Hizqeel (Ezekiel) | 164 |
| | A Prophet of Fortitude | |
| 18. | Prophet Elyas (Elisha) | 165 |
| | An Obedient Servant | |
| 19. | Prophet Shammil (Samuel) | 166 |
| | A revered prophet | |
| 20. | Prophet Dawud (David) | 170 |
| | A Wise and Valiant Servant | |
| 21. | Prophet Sulaiman (Soloman) | 176 |
| | Knowledgeable and Gifted Servant | |

| | | |
|---|---|---|
| 22. | Prophet Shia (Isaiah)<br>A humble servant | 182 |
| 23. | Prophet Aramaya (Jeremiah)<br>An eloquent preacher | 184 |
| 24. | Prophet Daniel<br>A wise and gifted servant | 191 |
| 25. | Prophet Uzair (Ezra)<br>A gifted teacher | 193 |
| 26. | Prophet Zakariyah (Zechariah)<br>A True Worshipper | 195 |
| 27. | Prophet Yahya (John)<br>A Compassionate and Righteous Servant | 196 |
| 28. | Prophet Isa (Jesus) and Mary<br>The Healer | 198 |
| 29. | Prophet Muhammad<br>The Seal of the Prophets | 215 |

# Prophet Adam and Eve (Hawwa)

*Allah the Most Exalted says in the Holy Qur'an:* "We relate to you, [O Muhammad], the best of stories in what We have revealed to you of this Qur'an although you were, before it, among the unaware." [12:3]

نَحْنُ نَقُصُّ عَلَيْكَ أَحْسَنَ ٱلْقَصَصِ بِمَا أَوْحَيْنَآ إِلَيْكَ هَٰذَا ٱلْقُرْءَانَ وَإِن كُنتَ مِن قَبْلِهِۦ لَمِنَ ٱلْغَٰفِلِينَ ۝

And [mention, O Muhammad], when your Lord said to the angels, "*Indeed, I will make upon the earth a successive authority.*" They said, "*Will You place upon it one who causes corruption therein and sheds blood, while we declare Your praise and sanctify You?*" Allah said, "*Indeed, I know that which you do not know.*" [2:30]

وَإِذْ قَالَ رَبُّكَ لِلْمَلَٰٓئِكَةِ إِنِّي جَاعِلٌ فِى ٱلْأَرْضِ خَلِيفَةً قَالُوٓا۟ أَتَجْعَلُ فِيهَا مَن يُفْسِدُ فِيهَا وَيَسْفِكُ ٱلدِّمَآءَ وَنَحْنُ نُسَبِّحُ بِحَمْدِكَ وَنُقَدِّسُ لَكَ قَالَ إِنِّىٓ أَعْلَمُ مَا لَا تَعْلَمُونَ ۝

**Teaching Adam**

Allah granted Adam the power to know the natures of all things and to summarize them by names; that is a bird, and that is a star, and that is a tree, etc. Allah implanted in Adam an insatiable need for and love of knowledge and a desire to bequeath knowledge to his children. This was the reason for his creation and the secret of his glorification. The angels realized that Adam was the creature who knew what they did not know and that his capacity to learn was his noblest quality. His knowledge included knowledge of the Creator which we call faith or Islam, as well as the knowledge he would need to inhabit and master the earth. All kinds of worldly knowledge which are included in this. Adam knew the names of everything.

*Allah He taught Adam the names - all of them. Then He showed them to the angels and said, "Inform Me of the names of these, if you are truthful." [2:31]*

وَعَلَّمَ ءَادَمَ ٱلْأَسْمَآءَ كُلَّهَا ثُمَّ عَرَضَهُمْ عَلَى ٱلْمَلَٰٓئِكَةِ فَقَالَ أَنۢبِـُٔونِى بِأَسْمَآءِ هَٰٓؤُلَآءِ إِن كُنتُمْ صَٰدِقِينَ ﴿٣١﴾

*They said, "Exalted are You; we have no knowledge except what You have taught us. Indeed, it is You who is the Knowing, the Wise." (2:32)*

قَالُوا۟ سُبْحَٰنَكَ لَا عِلْمَ لَنَآ إِلَّا مَا عَلَّمْتَنَآ إِنَّكَ أَنتَ ٱلْعَلِيمُ ٱلْحَكِيمُ ﴿٣٢﴾

*He said, "O Adam, inform them of their names." And when he had informed them of their names, He said, "Did I not tell you that I know the unseen [aspects] of the heavens and the earth? And I know what you reveal and what you have concealed." [2:33]*

قَالَ يَٰٓـَٔادَمُ أَنۢبِئْهُم بِأَسْمَآئِهِمْ ۖ فَلَمَّآ أَنۢبَأَهُم بِأَسْمَآئِهِمْ قَالَ أَلَمْ أَقُل لَّكُمْ إِنِّىٓ أَعْلَمُ غَيْبَ ٱلسَّمَٰوَٰتِ وَٱلْأَرْضِ وَأَعْلَمُ مَا تُبْدُونَ وَمَا كُنتُمْ تَكْتُمُونَ ﴿٣٣﴾

And [mention] when We said to the angels, *"Prostrate before Adam"*; so they prostrated, except for Iblees (Satan). He refused and was arrogant and became of the disbelievers. [2:34]

وَإِذْ قُلْنَا لِلْمَلَٰٓئِكَةِ ٱسْجُدُوا۟ لِـَٔادَمَ فَسَجَدُوٓا۟ إِلَّآ إِبْلِيسَ أَبَىٰ وَٱسْتَكْبَرَ وَكَانَ مِنَ ٱلْكَٰفِرِينَ ﴿٣٤﴾

And We said: "*O Adam, dwell, you and your wife, in Paradise and eat therefrom in [ease and] abundance from wherever you will. But do not approach this tree, lest you be among the wrongdoers.*" [2:35]

وَقُلْنَا يَٰٓـَٔادَمُ ٱسْكُنْ أَنتَ وَزَوْجُكَ ٱلْجَنَّةَ وَكُلَا مِنْهَا رَغَدًا حَيْثُ شِئْتُمَا وَلَا تَقْرَبَا هَٰذِهِ ٱلشَّجَرَةَ فَتَكُونَا مِنَ ٱلظَّٰلِمِينَ ﴿٣٥﴾

But Satan betrayed them. And We said, "*Go down, [all of you], as enemies to one another, and you will have upon the earth a place of settlement and provision for a time.*" [2:36]

فَأَزَلَّهُمَا ٱلشَّيْطَٰنُ عَنْهَا فَأَخْرَجَهُمَا مِمَّا كَانَا فِيهِ ۖ وَقُلْنَا ٱهْبِطُوا۟ بَعْضُكُمْ لِبَعْضٍ عَدُوٌّ ۖ وَلَكُمْ فِى ٱلْأَرْضِ مُسْتَقَرٌّ وَمَتَٰعٌ إِلَىٰ حِينٍ ﴿٣٦﴾

Then Adam received from his Lord [some] words, and He accepted his repentance. Indeed, it is He who is the Accepting of repentance, the Merciful. [2:37]

فَتَلَقَّىٰٓ ءَادَمُ مِن رَّبِّهِۦ كَلِمَٰتٍ فَتَابَ عَلَيْهِ ۚ إِنَّهُۥ هُوَ ٱلتَّوَّابُ ٱلرَّحِيمُ ﴿٣٧﴾

We said, "*Go down from it, all of you. And when guidance comes to you from Me, whoever follows My guidance - there will be no fear concerning them, nor will they grieve.*" [2:38]

قُلْنَا ٱهْبِطُوا۟ مِنْهَا جَمِيعًا ۖ فَإِمَّا يَأْتِيَنَّكُم مِّنِّى هُدًى فَمَن تَبِعَ هُدَاىَ فَلَا خَوْفٌ عَلَيْهِمْ وَلَا هُمْ يَحْزَنُونَ ﴿٣٨﴾

Almighty Allah also revealed: "*And surely, We created you (your father Adam) and then gave you shape (the noble shape of a human being), then We told the angels, 'Prostrate to Adam,' and they prostrated, except Iblis (Satan), he refused to be of those who prostrate.*" [7:11]

$$\text{وَلَقَدْ خَلَقْنَـٰكُمْ ثُمَّ صَوَّرْنَـٰكُمْ ثُمَّ قُلْنَا لِلْمَلَـٰٓئِكَةِ ٱسْجُدُوا۟ لِـَٔادَمَ فَسَجَدُوٓا۟ إِلَّآ إِبْلِيسَ لَمْ يَكُن مِّنَ ٱلسَّـٰجِدِينَ ﴿١١﴾}$$

Allah said, "*What prevented you from prostrating when I commanded you?*" Satan replied, "*I am better than him. You created me from fire and created him from clay.*" [7:12]

$$\text{قَالَ مَا مَنَعَكَ أَلَّا تَسْجُدَ إِذْ أَمَرْتُكَ ۖ قَالَ أَنَا۠ خَيْرٌ مِّنْهُ خَلَقْتَنِى مِن نَّارٍ وَخَلَقْتَهُۥ مِن طِينٍ ﴿١٢﴾}$$

Allah said, "*Descend from Paradise, for it is not for you to be arrogant therein. So get out; indeed, you are of the debased.*" [7:13]

$$\text{قَالَ فَٱهْبِطْ مِنْهَا فَمَا يَكُونُ لَكَ أَن تَتَكَبَّرَ فِيهَا فَٱخْرُجْ إِنَّكَ مِنَ ٱلصَّـٰغِرِينَ ﴿١٣﴾}$$

[The arrogant Satan] said, "*Reprieve me until the Day they are resurrected.*" [7:14]

$$\text{قَالَ أَنظِرْنِىٓ إِلَىٰ يَوْمِ يُبْعَثُونَ ﴿١٤﴾}$$

Allah said, "*Indeed, you are of those reprieved.*" [7:15]

$$\text{قَالَ إِنَّكَ مِنَ ٱلْمُنظَرِينَ ﴿١٥﴾}$$

Satan said, "Because You have put me in error, I will surely sit in wait for them on Your straight path." [7:16-17]

$$\text{قَالَ فَبِمَآ أَغْوَيْتَنِى لَأَقْعُدَنَّ لَهُمْ صِرَٰطَكَ ٱلْمُسْتَقِيمَ ﴿١٦﴾}$$

"Then I will come to them from before them and from behind them and on their right and on their left, and You will not find most of them grateful [to You]."

$$\text{ثُمَّ لَءَاتِيَنَّهُم مِّنۢ بَيْنِ أَيْدِيهِمْ وَمِنْ خَلْفِهِمْ وَعَنْ أَيْمَٰنِهِمْ وَعَن شَمَآئِلِهِمْ ۖ وَلَا تَجِدُ أَكْثَرَهُمْ شَٰكِرِينَ ﴿١٧﴾}$$

Allah said, "Get out of Paradise, reproached and expelled. Whoever follows you among them - I will surely fill Hell with you, all together." [7:18]

$$\text{قَالَ ٱخْرُجْ مِنْهَا مَذْءُومًا مَّدْحُورًا ۖ لَّمَن تَبِعَكَ مِنْهُمْ لَأَمْلَأَنَّ جَهَنَّمَ مِنكُمْ أَجْمَعِينَ ﴿١٨﴾}$$

Adam and Eve said, "Our Lord, we have wronged ourselves, and if You do not forgive us and have mercy upon us, we will surely be among the losers." [7:23]

$$\text{قَالَا رَبَّنَا ظَلَمْنَآ أَنفُسَنَا وَإِن لَّمْ تَغْفِرْ لَنَا وَتَرْحَمْنَا لَنَكُونَنَّ مِنَ ٱلْخَٰسِرِينَ ﴿٢٣﴾}$$

Satan misled Adam and Eve with deception. Then when they ate the forbidden apple, that which was hidden from them of their shame (private parts) became manifest to them and they began to stick together the leaves of Paradise over themselves (in order to cover their shame).

When Allah decided to create Adam: Allah told his angels that He was going to create a vicegerent on the earth who would have children and grandchildren, and who would corrupt the earth and shed each other's blood. That is the reason the angels said: *"Will You place upon it one who causes corruption therein and sheds blood, while we declare Your praise and sanctify You?"* Allah said, *"Indeed, I know that which you do not know."* [2:30]

وَإِذْ قَالَ رَبُّكَ لِلْمَلَٰٓئِكَةِ إِنِّى جَاعِلٌ فِى ٱلْأَرْضِ خَلِيفَةً قَالُوٓا۟ أَتَجْعَلُ فِيهَا مَن يُفْسِدُ فِيهَا وَيَسْفِكُ ٱلدِّمَآءَ وَنَحْنُ نُسَبِّحُ بِحَمْدِكَ وَنُقَدِّسُ لَكَ قَالَ إِنِّىٓ أَعْلَمُ مَا لَا تَعْلَمُونَ ﴿٣٠﴾

The angels were informed about the creation of Adam by the Jinn who lived before Adam. The Jinn had existed for over 2000 years before Adam, and then killed and shed blood. Therefore, Allah sent on them an army of angels that sent them out to the depths of the oceans. The angels knew that no one would be created on earth who would not shed blood. The angels did understand that Allah would mold him and blow His spirit into him. Adam was created from a handful of dust taken from different lands, so the children of Adam were created like the composition of the land. Therefore, we have white people, red, black and yellow ones; we have good and evil, ease and sorrow, and everything that comes in between them.

And [mention] when We said to the angles: *"Prostrate to Adam,"* and they prostrated, except for Iblis (Satan). He said, *"Should I prostrate to one You created from clay?"* [17:61]

وَإِذْ قُلْنَا لِلْمَلَٰٓئِكَةِ ٱسْجُدُوا۟ لِءَادَمَ فَسَجَدُوٓا۟ إِلَّآ إِبْلِيسَ قَالَ ءَأَسْجُدُ لِمَنْ خَلَقْتَ طِينًا ﴿٦١﴾

Allah created Adam from dust and made into the clay. After that Allah left Adam until he became as potter's clay. Allah told us in the Quran that He created man (Adam) from clay like the clay of pottery. When the time drew near to breathe the spirit into Adam, as Allah decreed, He commanded the angels: When I breathe My spirit into him prostrate before him. Allah breathed His spirit into Adam and when it reached his head Adam sneezed. The angels said: "*Say all praise belongs to Allah.*" Adam repeated: "*All praise belongs to Allah.*" Allah said to him: "*Your Lord has granted you mercy.*"

Satan (Iblis) used to go past Adam saying, "*You have been created for a great purpose.*"

After that Allah breathed His spirit into Adam. The first thing into which the spirit passed was Adam's eyes and then his nose. Adam then sneezed.

Allah said: "*May your Lord have mercy upon you!*" Adam go to the angels and see what they would say."

Adam went and greeted them. The angels replied by saying: "*Peace be upon you and the mercy and blessings of Allah.*"

Allah said to Adam: "*This is your greeting and that of your offspring.*" (Bukhari)

When the spirit reached Adam's eyes, Adam looked at the fruits of Paradise. When it reached his abdomen Adam felt an appetite for food. So Adam jumped hurriedly before the spirit could reach his legs, so that he could eat from the fruits of Paradise.

So Allah said: "Man was created of haste." [21:37]

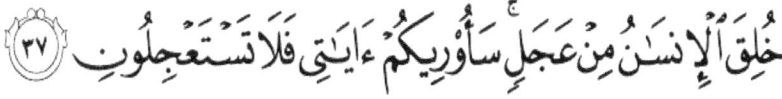

The command of Allah is coming, so be not impatient for it. Exalted is He and high above what they associate with Him. [16:1]

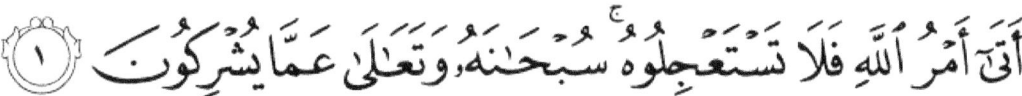

And [mention, O Muhammad], when We took from the prophets their covenant and from you and from Noah and Abraham and Moses and Jesus, the son of Mary; and We took from them a solemn covenant. [33:7]

$$وَإِذْ أَخَذْنَا مِنَ ٱلنَّبِيِّـۧنَ مِيثَـٰقَهُمْ وَمِنكَ وَمِن نُّوحٍ وَإِبْرَٰهِيمَ وَمُوسَىٰ وَعِيسَى ٱبْنِ مَرْيَمَ ۖ وَأَخَذْنَا مِنْهُم مِّيثَـٰقًا غَلِيظًا ﴿٧﴾$$

## Similarity between Adam and Jesus (peace be upon them)

Indeed, the example of Jesus to Allah is like that of Adam. He created Him from dust; then He said to him, "Be," and he was. [3:59]

$$إِنَّ مَثَلَ عِيسَىٰ عِندَ ٱللَّهِ كَمَثَلِ ءَادَمَ ۖ خَلَقَهُۥ مِن تُرَابٍ ثُمَّ قَالَ لَهُۥ كُن فَيَكُونُ ﴿٥٩﴾$$

The Messiah, son of Mary, was not but a messenger; [other] messengers have passed on before him. And his mother was a supporter of truth. They both used to eat food. Look how We make clear to them the signs; then look how they are deluded. (5:75)

$$مَّا ٱلْمَسِيحُ ٱبْنُ مَرْيَمَ إِلَّا رَسُولٌ قَدْ خَلَتْ مِن قَبْلِهِ ٱلرُّسُلُ وَأُمُّهُۥ صِدِّيقَةٌ ۖ كَانَا يَأْكُلَانِ ٱلطَّعَامَ ۗ ٱنظُرْ كَيْفَ نُبَيِّنُ لَهُمُ ٱلْـَٔايَـٰتِ ثُمَّ ٱنظُرْ أَنَّىٰ يُؤْفَكُونَ ﴿٧٥﴾$$

They have certainly disbelieved who say that Allah is Christ, the son of Mary. Say, "Then who could prevent Allah at all if He had intended to destroy Christ, the son of Mary, or his mother or everyone on the earth?" And to Allah belongs the dominion of the heavens and the earth and whatever is between them. He creates what He wills, and Allah is over all things competent. (5:17)

لَقَدْ كَفَرَ ٱلَّذِينَ قَالُوٓا۟ إِنَّ ٱللَّهَ هُوَ ٱلْمَسِيحُ ٱبْنُ مَرْيَمَ قُلْ فَمَن يَمْلِكُ مِنَ ٱللَّهِ شَيْـًٔا إِنْ أَرَادَ أَن يُهْلِكَ ٱلْمَسِيحَ ٱبْنَ مَرْيَمَ وَأُمَّهُۥ وَمَن فِى ٱلْأَرْضِ جَمِيعًا ۗ وَلِلَّهِ مُلْكُ ٱلسَّمَـٰوَٰتِ وَٱلْأَرْضِ وَمَا بَيْنَهُمَا ۚ يَخْلُقُ مَا يَشَآءُ ۚ وَٱللَّهُ عَلَىٰ كُلِّ شَىْءٍ قَدِيرٌ ﴿١٧﴾

## The Meaning of the Angel's Prostration

Adam opened his eyes and saw all the angels prostrating before him except one creature who was standing at a distance. Adam did not know what kind of creature it was nor did he know its name. Iblis (Satan) was standing with the angels so as to be included in the command given to them but he was not one of them. He was a Jinn, and as such he was supposed to be inferior to the angels. What is clear is that this prostration was to show respect and did not mean that the angels were worshipping Adam. Iblis truly believed that he was more honorable than Adam. Therefore he abstained from prostrating even though Allah had commanded him to do so, just as He had commanded the angels. If an analogy is made we see that Iblis is vain. For indeed clay is better than fire. In clay can be found the qualities of calmness, clemency, perseverance and growth; whereas in fire can be found heedlessness, insignificance, haste, and incineration. Iblis tried in vain to justify his refusal: He said: "*Shall I prostrate to one whom You created from clay?*" [17:61]

وَإِذْ قُلْنَا لِلْمَلَـٰٓئِكَةِ ٱسْجُدُوا۟ لِـَٔادَمَ فَسَجَدُوٓا۟ إِلَّآ إِبْلِيسَ قَالَ ءَأَسْجُدُ لِمَنْ خَلَقْتَ طِينًا ﴿٦١﴾

And surely, We created you (your father Adam) and then gave you shape (the noble shape of a human being), then We told the angels, "Prostrate to Adam", and they prostrated, except Iblis (Satan), he refused to be of those who prostrate. [7:11]

$$\text{وَلَقَدْ خَلَقْنَـٰكُمْ ثُمَّ صَوَّرْنَـٰكُمْ ثُمَّ قُلْنَا لِلْمَلَـٰٓئِكَةِ ٱسْجُدُوا۟ لِـَٔادَمَ فَسَجَدُوٓا۟ إِلَّآ إِبْلِيسَ لَمْ يَكُن مِّنَ ٱلسَّـٰجِدِينَ ۝}$$

Adam was following what was happening around him and had feelings of love, awe, and astonishment. Deep love of Allah, Who had created and glorified him and Who had made His angels prostrate before him. Awe of the Creator's wrath when He excluded Iblis from His mercy. Adam was surprised by this creature, Iblis who abhorred him without even knowing him and who imagined himself better than Adam without having proved that he was worthier. What a strange creature Iblis was, and how strange was his excuse for not prostrating!

Iblis imagined that fire is better than clay, but how did he get such an idea? Such knowledge is exclusive to Allah Who created fire and clay and Who knows which is the better of the two. From the dialogue Adam realized that Iblis was a creature characterized by cunning and ingratitude. He then knew that Iblis was his eternal enemy.

Adam was greatly astonished at Iblis's audacity and Allah's tolerance. Immediately after his creation Adam witnessed the large amount of freedom that Allah gives to His commissioned creatures. Allah could have totally annihilated Iblis or turned him into a handful of dust or stifled the refusal in his mouth. Yet, Allah gives His commissioned creatures absolute freedom even to the extent that they can refuse Allah the Almighty's commands. Allah grants everyone the freedom of denial, disobedience, and even disagreement with Him. His kingdom will not diminish if the disbelievers do not believe in Him nor will it be extended if many people believe in Him. On the contrary, the disbelievers will lose, and the believers will gain but Allah is above all of that.

There were many traditions about Iblis at the time of Prophet Muhammad (pbuh). Ibn Masud, Ibn Abbas and a group of the companions of the Prophet Muhammad (pbuh) said that Iblis had been the head of the angels in the worldly heavens. Ibn Abbas said in one narration that his name had been Azazil and in another narration he said it had been Al-Harith.

Ibn Abbas also said that Iblis was a Jinn and that they had once been the keepers of Paradise, with Iblis the most honorable and the most learned and the most pious of them. Another tradition says that he had been one of the famous four possessors of wings (angels), before Allah transformed him into the accursed Satan. Adam realized that Iblis was the symbol of evil in the universe. However Adam did not yet know anything about himself. Then Allah made him perceive his true identity and the reason for his creation, and the secret of his glorification.

## Adam Sees Eve (Hawwa)

Ibn Abbas and a group of companions of the Prophet (pbuh) narrated that when Iblis was sent out of Paradise and Adam was accommodated therein, Adam was alone in Paradise and did not have a partner from whom he could get tranquility. Adam slept for some time and when he woke up, he saw a woman whom Allah had created from his ribs. So he asked her: "Who are you?" She replied, "A woman." He asked: "Why have you been created?" She said: "So that you could find tranquility in me."

The angels, trying to find out the extent of his knowledge, asked him: "What is her name, O Adam?" He replied, "Eve (Hawwa)."

They asked: "Why was she so named?"

He replied, "Because she was created of me and I am a living being."

## Eve's Creation

Muhammad Ibn Ishaaq and Ibn Abbas related that Eve was created from the shortest left rib of Adam while he was sleeping and after a while she was clothed with flesh. That is why Allah said: "O Mankind! Be dutiful to your Lord, He created you from one soul and created from it its mate and dispersed from both of them many men and women." [4:1]

يَٰٓأَيُّهَا ٱلنَّاسُ ٱتَّقُوا۟ رَبَّكُمُ ٱلَّذِى خَلَقَكُم مِّن نَّفْسٍ وَٰحِدَةٍ وَخَلَقَ مِنْهَا زَوْجَهَا وَبَثَّ مِنْهُمَا رِجَالًا كَثِيرًا وَنِسَآءً وَٱتَّقُوا۟ ٱللَّهَ ٱلَّذِى تَسَآءَلُونَ بِهِۦ وَٱلْأَرْحَامَ إِنَّ ٱللَّهَ كَانَ عَلَيْكُمْ رَقِيبًا ﴿١﴾

Allah also said: It is He who created you from one soul and created from it Adam and Eve, in order that he might enjoy the pleasure of living with her. [7:189]

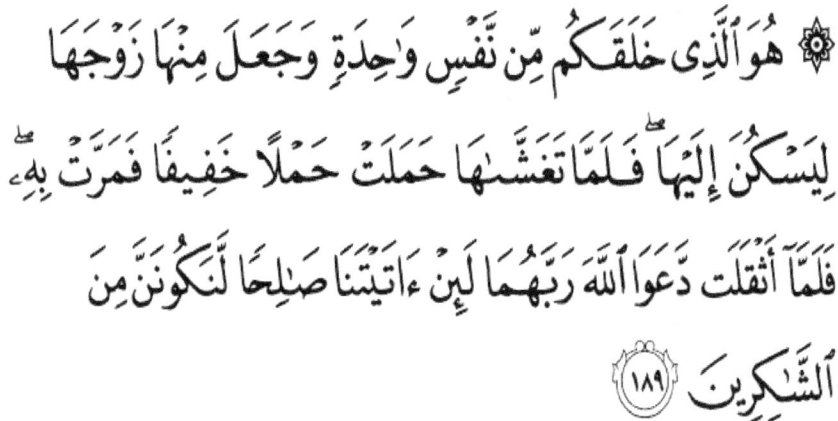

### Establishing the Greeting

Abu Hurairah narrated that the Prophet Muhammad (peace be upon him) said: "O Muslims! I advise you to be gentle with women, for they are created from a rib, and the most crooked portion of the rib is its upper part. If you try to straighten it, it will break and if you leave it, it will remain crooked, so I urge you to take care of the women." (Sahih Bukhari).

### The Location of Adam and Eve's Paradise

The location of this Paradise is unknown to us. The Quran did not reveal it, and the commentators had five different opinions. Some said that it was the paradise of our refuge and that its place was heaven.

Others regretted that statement because if it was the paradise of refuge Iblis would have been forbidden admission and disobedience would have been forbidden as well. Still others said that it was another paradise that was created by Allah for Adam and Eve.

A fourth group said it was a paradise on the earth located in a high place. Another group of commentators accept what was in the Quran without questioning where this paradise was located.

## Allah's Warning to Adam and Eve

Adam and Eve were admitted to Paradise and there they lived the dream of all human beings. Allah permitted them to enjoy everything except one tree that might have been the Tree of Pain or the Tree of Knowledge. And We said, "O Adam, dwell, you and your wife, in Paradise and eat therefrom in [ease and] abundance from wherever you will. But do not approach this tree, lest you be among the wrongdoers." [2:35]

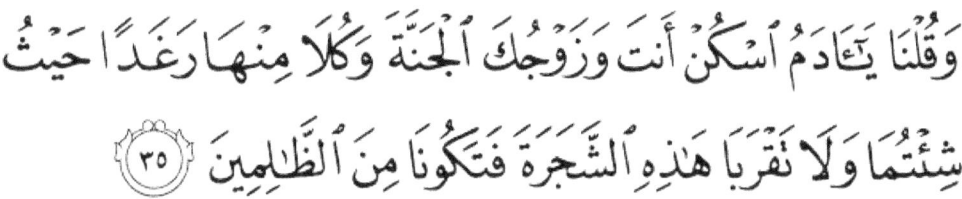

## Adam's Weakness

Adam and Eve understood that they were forbidden to eat the fruit of that tree. Adam was however a human being and man tends to forget. His heart changes and his will weakens. Satan summoned all the envy within him and took advantage of Adam's humanity to exploit him. Satan then whispered to Adam day after day, coaxing him: "Shall I guide you to the Tree of Immortality and the Eternal Kingdom?"

He whispered to them to make apparent to them that which was concealed from them of their private parts. He said, "Your Lord did not forbid you this tree except that you become angels or become of the immortal." And he swore [by Allah] to them, "Indeed, I am to you from among the sincere advisors." [7:20-22]

فَوَسْوَسَ لَهُمَا ٱلشَّيْطَٰنُ لِيُبْدِىَ لَهُمَا مَا وُۥرِىَ عَنْهُمَا مِن سَوْءَٰتِهِمَا وَقَالَ مَا نَهَىٰكُمَا رَبُّكُمَا عَنْ هَٰذِهِ ٱلشَّجَرَةِ إِلَّآ أَن تَكُونَا مَلَكَيْنِ أَوْ تَكُونَا مِنَ ٱلْخَٰلِدِينَ ﴿٢٠﴾

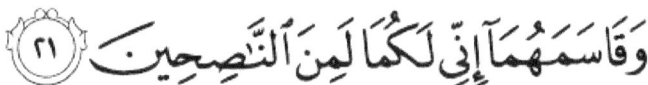

Adam asked himself: "What will happen if I eat from this tree? It might truly be the Tree of Immortality." His dream was to live forever in Paradise. Years went by, and Adam and Eve were preoccupied with thoughts of that tree. Then one day they decided to eat of its fruit. Adam stretched out his hand, picked one of the fruits and offered it to Eve.

So he made them fall, through deception. And when they tasted of the tree, their private parts became apparent them, and they began to fasten together over themselves from the leaves of Paradise. And their Lord called to them, "Did I not forbid you from that tree and tell you that Satan is to you a clear enemy?"

فَدَلَّىٰهُمَا بِغُرُورٍ فَلَمَّا ذَاقَا ٱلشَّجَرَةَ بَدَتْ لَهُمَا سَوْءَٰتُهُمَا وَطَفِقَا يَخْصِفَانِ عَلَيْهِمَا مِن وَرَقِ ٱلْجَنَّةِ وَنَادَىٰهُمَا رَبُّهُمَا أَلَمْ أَنْهَكُمَا عَن تِلْكُمَا ٱلشَّجَرَةِ وَأَقُل لَّكُمَا إِنَّ ٱلشَّيْطَٰنَ لَكُمَا عَدُوٌّ مُّبِينٌ ﴿٢٢﴾

According to the Old Testament, Eve was tempted by the serpent to eat of the forbidden tree. She ate because of the words of the serpent and fed Adam some of it. At that moment, their eyes were opened to the fact that they were naked, and they took the leaves of the fig tree to cover themselves. Their clothing (before their sin) was made of light on the private parts of both of them. This story in the Old Testament is not accurate. Allah the Almighty revealed: "O Children of Adam, let not Satan tempt you as he removed your parents from Paradise, stripping them of their clothing to show them their private parts. Indeed, he sees you, Satan and his tribe, from where you do not see them. Indeed, We have made the devils allies to those who do not believe." [7:27]

يَٰبَنِىٓ ءَادَمَ لَا يَفْتِنَنَّكُمُ ٱلشَّيْطَٰنُ كَمَآ أَخْرَجَ أَبَوَيْكُم مِّنَ ٱلْجَنَّةِ يَنزِعُ عَنْهُمَا لِبَاسَهُمَا لِيُرِيَهُمَا سَوْءَٰتِهِمَآ إِنَّهُۥ يَرَىٰكُمْ هُوَ وَقَبِيلُهُۥ مِنْ حَيْثُ لَا تَرَوْنَهُمْ إِنَّا جَعَلْنَا ٱلشَّيَٰطِينَ أَوْلِيَآءَ لِلَّذِينَ لَا يُؤْمِنُونَ ﴿٢٧﴾

Adam had hardly finished eating when he felt his heart contract, and he as filled with pain, sadness and shame. The surrounding atmosphere had changed and the internal music had stopped. He discovered that he and his wife were naked, so they both started cutting tree leaves with which to cover themselves. Allah commanded two angels to remove Adam from His holy proximity. Gabriel stripped him of the crown on his head, and Michael took the diadem from his forehead. Adam thought that his punishment had been hastened and bowed down in pain crying; "Forgiveness! Forgiveness!" Allah asked: "Are you running away from Me?" Adam replied, "No, my Lord, but I am shy of You."

Adam spent 100 years in Paradise. In another narration it was said he spent 60 years. Adam wept for 60 years for his loss of Paradise and 70 years for his mistake, and he wept for another 70 years when his son was killed. Allah told them that the earth would be where they would live and die and whence they would come on the Day of Judgment.

## Commentary: Why Adam and Eve Descended

Some people believe that the reason why mankind does not dwell in Paradise is that Adam was disobedient and that if it had not been for this sin, we could have been there all along. These are naive fictions because when Allah wanted to create Adam, He said to the angels, "I shall make a vicegerent on the *earth*." He did not say, "I shall make a vicegerent in Paradise." Adam's descent on earth, then, was not due to degradation but rather it was dignified descent. Allah knew that Adam and Eve would eat of the tree and descend to earth. He knew that Satan would rape their innocence. That experience was essential for their life on earth; it was a cornerstone of their vicegerency. It was meant to teach Adam, Eve, and their progeny that it was Satan who had caused them to be expelled from Paradise and that the road to Paradise can only be reached by obedience to Allah and enmity to Satan.

## Commentary: Adam's Free Will

Could it be said that Adam and the rest of mankind were predestined to sin and to be expelled from Paradise and sent to the earth? In fact, this fiction is as naive as the first one. Adam had complete *Free Will*, and he bore the consequences of his deed. He disobeyed by eating of the forbidden tree, so Allah dismissed him from Paradise. His disobedience does not negate his freedom. On the contrary, it is a consequence of it. The truth of the matter is that Allah knew what was going to happen, as He always knows the outcome of events before they take place. However Allah does not force things to happen. He grants free will to His human creatures. On that He bases, His supreme wisdom in populating the earth, establishing the vicegerents, and so on. Adam understood the lesson. Allah accepted Adam's repentance. And sent him to the earth as His first Messenger.

## Encounter between Adam and Moses – Hadith

Abu Hurairah narrated that the Messenger (peace be upon him) said: Adam and Moses argued with each other (peace be upon them). Moses said to Adam: "Your sin expelled you from Paradise." Adam said: "You are Moses whom Allah selected as His messenger and as the one to whom He spoke directly. Yet you blame me for a thing which had already been written in my fate before my Creation?"

Prophet Muhammad (peace be upon him) said twice, "So Adam outclassed Moses." (Sahih Bukhari)

Omar Ibn Al Khattab also narrated that the Prophet Muhammad (peace be upon him) said: "Moses (pbuh) said: My Lord! May I see Adam who removed us and himself from the Paradise?" So Allah made him see Adam and he said to him: "Are you Adam?"

Adam said: "Yes!" And he said to him: "You are the one in Whom Allah breathed His spirit and before whom He bowed His angels and to whom He taught the names of all things?"

Adam answered: "Yes!" So Moses said: "What made you remove us and yourself from Paradise?"

Adam said: "Who are you?" Moses said: "I am Moses." Adam said: "So you are Moses the prophet of the Children of Israel. Were you the one Allah spoke to directly?" Moses answered: "Yes!"

Adam said: "Why do you blame me for a matter which Allah had predestined?" So Prophet Muhammad (peace be upon him) said twice: "Adam outclassed Moses." (Sahih al Bukhari)

## Variation of Where Adam, Eve, and Iblis Descended

There are many traditions concerning the place of Adam's descent upon earth. Ibn Abi Hatim narrated that Ibn Abbas said: "Adam descended on land 'Dihna' between Mecca and Taif." Al-Hassan said that Adam descended in India and Eve in Jeddah (Saudi Arabia), Iblis in Bodistiman (Iraq), and the serpent in Ashahan (Iran). Ass'ady related that Adam descended with the Black Stone (the black stone that is set into the wall of the Ka'bba. It came from Paradise), and he had a handful of the seeds of Paradise. Adam planted them in India and they grew into the fragrant tree therein.

Evolutionary scientists coined the phrase, abominable mystery. The mystery centers on the rise of the flowering plants. In the fossil record they appear very suddenly, and there is nothing that looks like an angiosperm before them and then they suddenly appear and in considerable diversity. The answer to this mystery is simple. Allah made flowers and plants in a variety of shapes, sizes, and colors as a blessing from Him. Prophet Adam planted them in India. Four other plants were sent for Adam from paradise, date trees, grapes, olive, and pomegranate.

Ibn Omar said that Adam descended on As-Safa and Eve on Al Marwa (names of two mountains in the vicinity of the sacred house in Mecca. Part of the rites of pilgrimage (Hajj) includes pacing between these two hills in commemoration of Hajar's search for water). This was also reported by Ibn Hatim. Abdul Razzaq reported that Abi Musa Al-shari said that when Allah ordered Adam to descend from Paradise to earth, He taught Adam the making of everything and provided him with the crops from Paradise. Abu Hurairah narrated that the Prophet Muhammad (peace be upon him) said: "The best of days on which the sun has risen is Friday. On this day Adam was created, and on this day he was descended to earth." (al-Bukhari).

## Adam's Life on Earth

Adam knew he bade farewell to peace when he left Paradise. On earth he had to face conflicts and struggle. No sooner had one ended than another began. Adam also had to toil to sustain himself. He had to protect himself with clothes and weapons and to protect his wife and children from the wild beasts. Above all, he had to struggle with the spirit of evil. Satan, the cause of his expulsion from Paradise, continued to beguile him and his children in an effort to have them thrown into the eternal hellfire. The battle between good and evil is continuous, but those who follow Allah's guidance should fear nothing while those who disobey Allah and follow Iblis will be damned along with him.

Adam grasped all of this and with the knowledge of this suffering he started his life on the earth. The only thing that allowed his grief was that he was master of the earth and had to make it yield to him. Adam was the one who had to cultivate and construct and populate the earth. He was also the one who had to procreate and raise children who would change and improve the world. The pinnacle of earthly bliss was reached when Adam and Eve witnessed the birth of their first children, a set of twins.

Adam was a devoted father and Eve a contented mother. The twins were Cain (Qabil) and his sister. Later Eve gave birth to a second set of twins, Abel (Habil) and his sister. The family enjoyed the bounties and fruits of the earth provided by their Lord. The children grew up to be strong and healthy young adults. Cain tilled the land while Abel raised cattle.

## Cain's Disobedience

The time arrived when the two young men desired life partners. This was part of Allah's plan for mankind, to multiply and form nations with different cultures and colors. Allah revealed to Adam that he should marry each son to the twin sister of the other. Adam instructed his children according to Allah's command, but Cain was displeased with the partner chosen for him, for Abel's twin sister was not as beautiful as his own.

It appears that since the beginning of time, physical beauty has been a factor in the attraction between men and women. This attraction caused Cain to envy his brother Abel. He rebelled against Allah's command by refusing to accept his father's advice. At first glance Cain's rebellion might appear strange, but we should remember that although man has a pure nature, the potential for dichotomy exists. In other words, he had both good and bad qualities. He can become greedy, covetous, possessive, selfish and even destructive. Man is, therefore capable of seeking self-satisfaction even if it leads to failure in this life and in the hereafter. Allah tests us through our divided nature.

## Cain's Jealousy of Abel

Adam was in a dilemma. He wanted peace and harmony in his family, so he invoked Allah for help. Allah commanded that each son offer a sacrifice, and he whose offering was accepted would have right on his side. Abel offered his best camel while Cain offered his worst grain. His sacrifice was not accepted by Allah because of his disobedience to his father and the insincerity in his offering.

And recite to them the story of Adam's two sons, in truth, when they both offered a sacrifice [to Allah], and it was accepted from one of them but was not accepted from the other. Said [the latter], "I will surely kill you." Said [the former], "Indeed, Allah only accepts from the righteous [who fear Him]." [5:27]

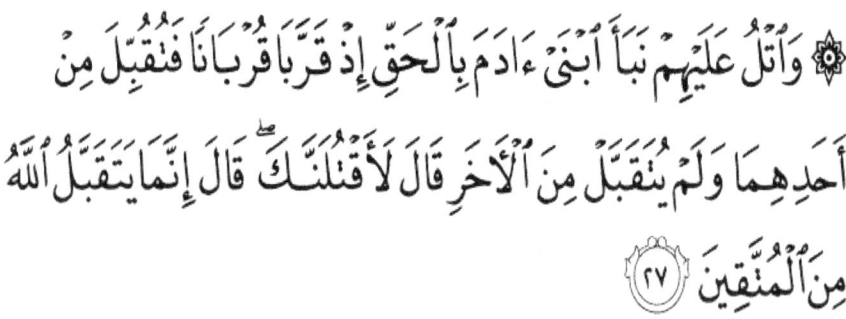

This enraged Cain even further. Realizing that his hopes marrying his own beautiful sister were fading, he threatened his brother. "I will kill you! I refuse to see you happy while I remain unhappy!" Abel feeling sorry for his brother, said: "It would be more proper for you, my brother, to search for the cause of your unhappiness and then walk in the way of peace. Allah accepts the deeds only from those who serve and fear Him, not from those who reject His Commands."

## The First Death

Abel was intelligent, obedient, and always ready to obey the will of Allah. This contrasted sharply with his brother who was arrogant, selfish and disobedient. Abel did not fear his brother's threats, but neither did he want his brother to be hurt. Allah had blessed Abel with purity and compassion. Hoping to allay the hatred seething in his brother Abel said, "My brother, you are deviating from the right path and are sinful in your decisions. It is better that you repent to Allah and forget about your foolish threat. But if you do not then I will leave the matter in the hands of Allah. You alone will bear the consequence of your sin, for the Fire is the reward of the wrong-doers." This brotherly plea did nothing to lessen the hatred in Cain's heart, nor did he show fear of Allah's punishment. Even familial considerations were cast aside. Cain struck his brother with a stone killing him. This was the first criminal act committed by man on earth. When Abel had not appeared for some time, Adam began to search for him but found no trace of his beloved son. He asked Cain about Abel's whereabouts. Cain insolently replied that he was not his brother's keeper nor his protector. From these words his father understood that Abel was dead and Adam was filled with grief.

## The First Burial

Cain did not know what to do with his brother's corpse. He carried it on his back wandering from place to place trying to hide it. His anger had now subsided and his conscience was saddled with guilt. He was tiring under the burden of the corpse which had started to have a stench. As a mercy, and to show that dignity must be retained even in death, Allah sent two birds (ravens). The birds began to fight, causing the death of one. The victorious bird used its beak and claws to dig a hole in the ground, rolled its victim into it and covered it with sand.

**Quranic**: Then Allah sent a raven scratching up the ground, to show him how to hide his brother's naked corpse. He said: Woe unto me! Am I not able to be as this raven and so hide my brother's naked corpse? And he became repentant. [5:31]

فَبَعَثَ ٱللَّهُ غُرَابًا يَبْحَثُ فِى ٱلْأَرْضِ لِيُرِيَهُۥ كَيْفَ يُوَٰرِى سَوْءَةَ أَخِيهِ ۚ قَالَ يَٰوَيْلَتَىٰٓ أَعَجَزْتُ أَنْ أَكُونَ مِثْلَ هَٰذَا ٱلْغُرَابِ فَأُوَٰرِىَ سَوْءَةَ أَخِى ۖ فَأَصْبَحَ مِنَ ٱلنَّٰدِمِينَ ﴿٣١﴾

Cain was overcome with shame and remorse. "Woe unto me!" he exclaimed. "I was unable to do what this raven has done, that is to hide my brother's corpse." This was also the first burial of man.

**Quranic**: Allah, the Merciful, said: And recite to them the story of Adam's two sons, in truth, when they both offered a sacrifice [to Allah], and it was accepted from one of them but was not accepted from the other. Said [the latter], 'I will surely kill you.' Said [the former], 'Indeed, Allah only accepts from the righteous [who fear Him].' (5:27)

۞ وَٱتْلُ عَلَيْهِمْ نَبَأَ ٱبْنَىْ ءَادَمَ بِٱلْحَقِّ إِذْ قَرَّبَا قُرْبَانًا فَتُقُبِّلَ مِنْ أَحَدِهِمَا وَلَمْ يُتَقَبَّلْ مِنَ ٱلْءَاخَرِ قَالَ لَأَقْتُلَنَّكَ ۖ قَالَ إِنَّمَا يَتَقَبَّلُ ٱللَّهُ مِنَ ٱلْمُتَّقِينَ ﴿٢٧﴾

Ibn Al-Jawzi may Allah have mercy upon him said: Hawwa (Eve) gave birth to 40 children, boys and girls, from Prophet Adam (peace be upon him), in twenty pregnancies, and it is said that she was giving birth to twins each time, a boy and a girl. The first of his children were the twins Cain (Qabil) and Qaleemah, and it is also said that her name was Qaythamah, and his last children were twins Abdul-Mugheeth and Amatul-Mutheeth.

## Adam's Successor, Seth

Adam was utterly grief stricken by the loss of his two sons. One was dead, the other was won over by the devil. Adam prayed for his son and turned to mundane matters for he had to toil for his sustenance. At the same time he was a prophet advising his children and grandchildren, telling them about Allah and calling them to believe. Adam told them about Iblis and warned them by recounting his own experience with the devil and of how the devil had tempted Cain to kill his brother. Years and years passed, Adam grew old and his children spread all over the earth.

Muhammad Ibn Ishaq related that when Adam's death drew near, he appointed his son Seth to be his successor and taught him the hours of the day and night along with their appropriate acts of worship. Abu Dhar narrated that the Prophet Muhammad (pbuh) said: "Allah sent down 104 psalms, of which 50 were sent down to Seth."

## Adam's Death

Abdullah Ibn Al Imam Ahmad Ibn Hanbal narrated that Ubai Ibn Kab said: When Adam's death was near, he said to his children: "O my children, indeed I feel an appetite for the fruits of Paradise." So they went away searching for what Adam had requested. They met with the angels, who had with them his shroud and what he was to be embalmed with. They said to them: "O Children of Adam, what are you searching for? What do you want? Where are you going?" They said: "Our father is sick and has an appetite for the fruits of Paradise." The angels said to them: "Go back, for your father is going to meet his end soon."

So they returned (with the angels) and when Eve saw them she recognized them. Eve tried to hide herself behind Adam. He said to her. "Leave me alone. Do not go between me and the angels of my Lord." So they took his soul, embalmed and wrapped him, dug the grave and laid him in it. They prayed on him and put him in his grave, saying: "O Children of Adam, this is your tradition at the time of death." Before his death Adam reassured his children that Allah would not leave man alone on the earth, but would send His prophets to guide them. The prophets would have different names, traits and miracles, but they would be united in one thing; the call to worship Allah alone. This was Adam's bequest to his children.

Adam finished speaking and closed his eyes. Then the angels entered his room and surrounded him. When he recognized the Angel of Death among them, his heart smiled peacefully.

# Prophet Idris (Enoch)

After Adam's death, his son Seth (Shiith) took over the responsibilities of prophethood. When the time of his death came, Seth's son Anoush succeeded him. He in turn, was succeeded by his son Qinan, who was succeeded by Mahlabeel. The Persians claim that Mahlabeel was the King of the Seven Regions, that he was the first one to cut down trees to build cities and large forts and that he built the cities of Babylonia. He reigned for a period of forty years. When he died his duties were taken by his son Yard, who on his death, bequeathed them to his son Khonoukh, who is Idris (pbuh) according to the majority of the scholars. And mention in the Book (the Quran) Idris (Enoch). Verily! He was a man of truth, (and) a Prophet. And (remember) Isma'il (Ishmael), and Idris (Enoch) and Dhul-Kifl (Isaiah), all were from among As-Sabirin (the patient ones, etc.). [21:85]

وَإِسْمَٰعِيلَ وَإِدْرِيسَ وَذَا ٱلْكِفْلِ ۖ كُلٌّ مِّنَ ٱلصَّٰبِرِينَ ۝

Allah praised Prophet Enoch (Idris) (peace be upon him). Allah described him as being truthful and trustworthy: And mention in the Book, Idris. Indeed, he was a man of truth and a prophet. And We raised him to a high station. [19:56]

وَٱذْكُرْ فِى ٱلْكِتَٰبِ إِدْرِيسَ ۚ إِنَّهُۥ كَانَ صِدِّيقًا نَّبِيًّا ۝

And We raised him to a high station. [19:57]

وَرَفَعْنَٰهُ مَكَانًا عَلِيًّا ۝

Who has taught (the writing) by the pen [the first person to write was Prophet Idris (Enoch)]. [96:4]

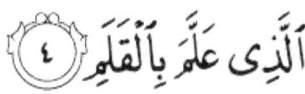

### Birth and Teachings

Idris was born and raised in Babylon following the teachings and religion of Prophet Adam (pbuh) and his son Seth (peace be upon him). Enoch was the 5th generation of the Prophet Adam. He called the people back to his forefathers' religion, but very few listened to him. The majority turned away. Prophet Idris and his followers left Babylon for Egypt. There he carried on his mission, calling people to what is just and fair, teaching them certain prayers and instructing them to fast on certain days and to give a portion of their wealth to the poor.

### The Wise Sayings of Prophet Idris

Idris was the first of the Children of Adam to be given prophethood after Adam and Seth (peace upon them). It is reported that he was the first to invent the basic form of writing. Some of his wise sayings are: "Happy is he who looks at his own deeds and appoints them as pleaders to his Lord." "None can show better gratitude for Allah's favors than he who shares them with others." "Do not envy people for what they have as they will only enjoy it for a short while." "He who indulges in excess will not benefit from it." "The real joy of life is to have wisdom."

# Prophet Nuh (Noah)

Prophet Noah was Ibn Lamik, Ibn Mitoshilkh, Ibn Idris, Ibn yard, Ibn Mahlabeel, Ibn Qinan, Ibn Anoush, Ibn Seth, Ibn Adam the Father of Mankind (pbuh). According to the history of the People of the Torah and the Bible, so called by Allah because they received Revealed Books: the *Taurat*, the *Zabur* and the *Injeel* (*Bible*). These names are translated 'Torah, Psalms, and Gospels' respectively, but these books have been changed over time. Of the Revealed Books, only the Quran remains exactly as it was revealed. Noah (peace be upon him) was born one 146 years after the death of Adam (peace be upon him). Ibn Abbas narrated that the Prophet Muhammad (peace be upon him) said: "The period between Adam and Noah was ten centuries." (Sahih Bukhari) Noah was born 1056 years after Adam's creation. Thus, this hadith does not contradict the previous statement from the People of the Book as it may first appear to do.

## Noah's People - Idolaters

Noah's people worshiped statues and they called gods. They believed that these gods would bring them good, protect them from evil and provide all their needs. They gave their idols names. These idols represented, respectively, manly power; mutability, beauty; brute strength, swiftness, sharp sight, insight, according to the power they thought these gods possessed. Allah revealed: They (idolaters) have said: 'Never leave your gods and never leave Waddan or Suwa or Yaghuth and Ya'uq and Nasr.' [71:23]

وَقَالُوا۟ لَا تَذَرُنَّ ءَالِهَتَكُمْ وَلَا تَذَرُنَّ وَدًّا وَلَا سُوَاعًا وَلَا يَغُوثَ وَيَعُوقَ وَنَسْرًا ۝

Most of these were the names of good people who had lived among them. After their deaths, statues of them were erected to keep their memories alive. After sometime, however, people began to worship these statues. Later generations did not even know why they had been erected; they only knew their parents had prayed to them. That is how idol worshipping began.

## Various Hadith describing the Origin of Idolatry

Following upon the death of those righteous men, Satan inspired their people to erect statues in the places where they used to sit. They did this, but these statues were not worshiped until the coming generations deviated from the right way of life. Then they worshipped them as their idols.

In his version, Ibn Jarir narrated: There were righteous people who lived in the period between Adam and Noah and who had followers who held them as models. After their death, their friends who used to emulate them said: If we make statues of them, it will be more pleasing to us in our worship and will remind us of them. So they built statues of them, and, after they had died and others came after them, Iblis crept into their minds saying: your forefathers used to worship them, and through that worship they got rain. So they worshipped them. Waddan was a righteous man who was loved by his people. When he died, they withdrew to his grave in the land of Babylonia and were overwhelmed by sadness. When Iblis saw their sorrow caused by his death, he disguised himself in the form of a man saying: I have seen your sorrow because of this man's death; can I make a statue like him which could be put in your meeting place to make you remember him?' They said: Yes. So he made the statue like him. They put it in their meeting place in order to be reminded of him. When Iblis saw their interest in remembering him, he said: Can I build a statue of him in the home of each one of you so that he would be in everyone's house and you could remember him? They agreed. Their children learned about and saw what they were doing. They also learned about their remembrance of him instead of Allah.

So the first to be worshipped instead of Allah was Waddan, the idol which they named thus. The essence of this point is that every idol from those earlier mentioned was worshipped by a certain group of people. It was mentioned that people made pictures and as the ages passed they made these pictures into statues, so that their forms could be fully recognized; afterwards they were worshipped instead of Allah.

It was narrated that Umm Salmah and Umm Habibah told Allah's Prophet Muhammad (pbuh) about the church called *Maria* which they had seen in the land of Abyssinia. They described its beauty and the pictures therein. He said: Those are the people who build places of worship on the grave of every dead man who was righteous and then worshiped him. Those are the worst. (Sahih al-Bukhari).

## Commentary - Idolatry

Worshipping anything other than Allah is a tragedy that results not only in the loss of freedom; its serious effect reaches man's mind and destroys it as well. Almighty Allah created man and his mind with its purpose set on achieving knowledge the most important of which is that Allah alone is the Creator and all the rest are worshippers (slaves). Disbelief in Allah results in the loss of freedom, the destruction of the mind, and the absence of a noble target in life. By worshipping anything other than Allah, man becomes enslaved to Satan, who is himself a creature and becomes harnessed to his own baser qualities. Into this environment Allah sent Noah with His message to his people. Noah was the only intellectual not caught in the whirlpool of man's destruction which was caused by polytheism.

## Noah's Reasoning with his People

Allah in His Mercy sent His Messenger Noah (peace be upon him) to guide his people. Noah was an excellent speaker and a very patient man. He pointed out to his people the mysteries of life and the wonders of the universe. He pointed out how the night is regularly followed by the day and that the balance between these opposites were designed by Allah the Almighty for our good. The night gives coolness and rest while the day gives warmth and awakens activity. The sun encourages growth, keeping all plants and animals alive, while the moon and stars assist in the reckoning of time, direction and seasons. He pointed out that the ownership of the heavens and the earth belongs only to the Divine Creator. Therefore, he explained to this people, there cannot have been more than one deity. The people listened to him in silence. His words touched the hearts of the weak, the poor, and the miserable and soothed their wounds with its mercy. As for the rich, the strong, the mighty and the rulers they looked upon the warning with cold distrust. They believed they would be better off if things stayed as they were.

Therefore they started their war of words against Noah. The chiefs of the disbelievers among his people said tp Noah: We see you but a man like ourselves. He, however, had never said anything other than that. He asserted that, indeed, he was only a human being; Allah had sent a human messenger because the earth was inhabited by humans. If it had been inhabited by angels, Allah would have sent an angelic messenger.

The rulers had thought at first that Noah's call would soon fade on its own. When they found that his call attracted the poor, the helpless and common laborers, they started to verbally attack him: You are only followed by the poor, the meek and the worthless. Allah said: And We had certainly sent Noah to his people, [saying], Indeed, I am to you a clear warner. That you not worship except Allah. Indeed, I fear for you the punishment of a painful day. [11:25, 26]

وَلَقَدْ أَرْسَلْنَا نُوحًا إِلَىٰ قَوْمِهِ إِنِّي لَكُمْ نَذِيرٌ مُّبِينٌ ﴿٢٥﴾

أَن لَّا تَعْبُدُوٓاْ إِلَّا ٱللَّهَ إِنِّيٓ أَخَافُ عَلَيْكُمْ عَذَابَ يَوْمٍ أَلِيمٍ ﴿٢٦﴾

So the chiefs among those who disbelieved from his people said: "We do not see you but as a man like ourselves, and we do not see you followed except by those who are the lowest of us [and] at first suggestion. And we do not see in you over us any merit; rather, we think you are liars." (11:27)

فَقَالَ ٱلْمَلَأُ ٱلَّذِينَ كَفَرُواْ مِن قَوْمِهِ مَا نَرَىٰكَ إِلَّا بَشَرًا مِّثْلَنَا وَمَا نَرَىٰكَ ٱتَّبَعَكَ إِلَّا ٱلَّذِينَ هُمْ أَرَاذِلُنَا بَادِىَ ٱلرَّأْيِ وَمَا نَرَىٰ لَكُمْ عَلَيْنَا مِن فَضْلٍ بَلْ نَظُنُّكُمْ كَٰذِبِينَ ﴿٢٧﴾

### The Disbelievers Attempt to Bargain

The disbelievers tried to bargain: "Listen Noah, if you want us to believe in you, then dismiss your believers. They are meek and poor, while we are elite and rich; no faith can include us both." Noah listened to the heathens of his community and realized they were being obstinate. However, he was gentle in his response. He explained to his people that he could not dismiss the believers as they were not his guests but Allah's.

Noah appealed to them: "And O my people, I ask not of you for it any wealth. My reward is not but from Allah. And I am not one to drive away those who have believed. Indeed, they will meet their Lord, but I see that you are a people behaving ignorantly." (11:29)

$$\text{وَيَٰقَوْمِ لَآ أَسْـَٔلُكُمْ عَلَيْهِ مَالًا ۖ إِنْ أَجْرِىَ إِلَّا عَلَى ٱللَّهِ ۚ وَمَآ أَنَا۠ بِطَارِدِ ٱلَّذِينَ ءَامَنُوٓا۟ ۚ إِنَّهُم مُّلَٰقُوا۟ رَبِّهِمْ وَلَٰكِنِّىٓ أَرَىٰكُمْ قَوْمًا تَجْهَلُونَ ۝٢٩}$$

My people! Who will help me against Allah, if I drove them away? Will you not then give a thought? And I do not say to you that with me are the Treasures of Allah nor that I know the unseen, nor do I say I am an angel, and I do not say of those whom your eyes look down upon that Allah will not bestow any good on them. Allah knows what is in their inner selves (regards to Belief). In that case, I should, indeed be one of the Zalimeen (wrongdoers, oppressors etc.)." (Ch 11:29-31 Quran). Noah refuted the arguments of the disbelievers with the noble knowledge of the prophets. It is the logic of intellect that rids itself of personal pride and interests.

## The Disbelievers Remain Ignorant

The rulers were tired of Noah's arguments. Allah the Exalted related their attitude: They said: "O Noah! You have disputed with us and much have you prolonged the dispute with us, now bring upon us what you threaten us with, if you are of the truthful." He said: "Only Allah will bring it (the punishment) on you, if He will, and then you will escape not. And my advice will not profit you, even if I wish to give you counsel, if Allah's Will is to keep you astray. He is your Lord! And to Him you shall return." [11:32-34] The battle continued; the arguments between the disbelievers and Noah became prolonged. When all the refutations of the disbelievers collapsed and they had no more to say, they began to be rude and insulted Allah's prophet: "The leaders of his people said: "Verily, we see you in plain error." [7:60] Noah responded in the manner of the prophets: "O my people! There is no error in me, but I am a Messenger from the Lord of the Alamin (mankind, jinn and all that exists)! I convey unto you the Messages of my Lord and give sincere advice to you. And I know from Allah what you know not." [7:61-62] Noah continued appealing to his people to believe in Allah hour after hour, day after day year after year. He admonished his people and called them to Allah day and night, in secret and openly.

He gave them examples, explained Allah's signs and illustrated Allah's ability in the formation of His creatures. But whenever he called them to Allah, they ran away from him. Whenever he urged them to ask Allah to forgive them, they put their fingers in their ears and became too proud to listen to the truth.

## Noah's Appeal to His People

Allah the Almighty related what Noah faced: "Verily, We sent Noah to his people saying: Warn your people before there comes to them a painful torment." He said: "O my people! Verily, I am a plain Warner to you, that you should worship Allah alone, be dutiful to Him and obey me, He (Allah) will forgive you of your sins and respite you to an appointed term. Verily, the term of Allah when it comes, cannot be delayed, if you but knew." He said: "O my Lord! Verily, I have called my people night and day (secretly and openly to accept the doctrine of Islamic Monotheism), but all my calling added nothing but to their flight from the truth. Verily! Every time I called unto them that You might forgive them, they thrust their fingers into their ears, covered themselves up with their garments, and persisted (in their refusal), and magnified themselves in pride. Then verily, I called to them openly (aloud); then verily, I proclaimed to them in public, and I have appealed to them in private, I said to them: Ask forgiveness from your Lord, Verily, He is Oft Forgiving; He will send rain to you in abundance, and give you increase in wealth and children, and bestow on you gardens and bestow on you rivers. What is the matter with you that you fear not Allah (His Punishment), and you hope not for reward from Allah or you believe not in His Oneness. While He has created you in different stages." [23:13].

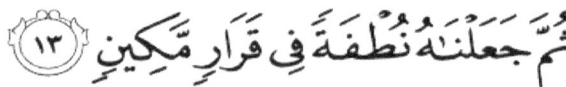

Allah created the seven heavens one above another, and has made the moon a light therein and made the sun a lamp? And Allah has brought you forth from the dust of earth. Afterwards He will return you into it (the earth), and bring you forth (again on the Day of Resurrection) Allah has made for you the earth wide spread (an expanse) that you may go about therein broad roads. Noah said: "My Lord, indeed they have disobeyed me and followed him whose wealth and children will not increase him except in loss. And they conspired an immense conspiracy. And said: 'never leave your gods and never leave Wadd or Suwa or Yaghuth and Ya'uq and Nasr.' [71:21-23] Because of their sins they were drowned and put into the Fire, and they found not for themselves besides Allah [any] helpers." [71:25].

## The Length of Noah's Preaching

Allah the Almighty said: "And We certainly sent Noah to his people, and he remained among them a thousand years minus fifty years, and the flood seized them while they were wrongdoers." [29:14]

وَلَقَدْ أَرْسَلْنَا نُوحًا إِلَىٰ قَوْمِهِ فَلَبِثَ فِيهِمْ أَلْفَ سَنَةٍ إِلَّا خَمْسِينَ عَامًا فَأَخَذَهُمُ ٱلطُّوفَانُ وَهُمْ ظَٰلِمُونَ ﴿١٤﴾

It happened that every passing generation admonished the succeeding one not to believe Noah and to wage war against him. The father used to teach his child about the matter that was between himself and Noah and counsel him to reject his call when he reached adulthood. Their natural disposition rejected believing and following the truth. Noah saw that the number of believers was not increasing, while that of the disbelievers was. He was sad for his people, but he never reached the point of despair.

## Noah Prays for the Disbeliever's End

There came a day when Allah revealed to Noah that no others would believe. Allah inspired him not to grieve for them at which point Noah prayed that the disbelievers be destroyed. And Nuh (Noah) said: "My Lord! Leave not one of the disbelievers on the earth! [71:26]

وَقَالَ نُوحٌ رَّبِّ لَا تَذَرْ عَلَى ٱلْأَرْضِ مِنَ ٱلْكَٰفِرِينَ دَيَّارًا ﴿٢٦﴾

Allah accepted Noah's prayer. The case was closed, and He passed His judgment on the disbelievers in the form of a flood. Allah ordered His worshipper Noah to build an ark with His knowledge and instructions and with the help of angels. Allah commanded: "And construct the ship under Our observation and Our inspiration and do not address Me concerning those who have wronged; indeed, they are [to be] drowned." (11:37).

وَٱصْنَعِ ٱلْفُلْكَ بِأَعْيُنِنَا وَوَحْيِنَا وَلَا تُخَٰطِبْنِي فِي ٱلَّذِينَ ظَلَمُوٓا۟ إِنَّهُم مُّغْرَقُونَ ﴿٣٧﴾

## Noah Builds the Ark

Noah chose a place outside the city, far from the sea. He collected wood and tools and began to day and night to build the ark. The people's mockery continued: "O Noah! Does carpentry appeal to you more than prophet hood? Why are you building an ark so far from the sea? Are you going to drag it to the water or is the wind going to carry it for you?"

Noah replied: "You will come to know who will be put to shame and suffer." Allah narrated: "And he constructed the ship, and whenever an assembly of the eminent of his people passed by him, they ridiculed him. He said, "If you ridicule us, then we will ridicule you just as you ridicule." (11:38)

وَيَصْنَعُ ٱلْفُلْكَ وَكُلَّمَا مَرَّ عَلَيْهِ مَلَأٌ مِّن قَوْمِهِۦ سَخِرُوا۟ مِنْهُ قَالَ إِن تَسْخَرُوا۟ مِنَّا فَإِنَّا نَسْخَرُ مِنكُمْ كَمَا تَسْخَرُونَ ﴿٣٨﴾

## The Flood begins

The ship was constructed, and Noah sat waiting Allah's command. Allah revealed to him that when water miraculously gushed forth from the oven at Noah's house that would be the sign of the start of the flood, and the sign for Noah to act. The terrible day arrived when the oven at Noah's house overflowed. Noah hurried to open the ark and summon the believers. He also took with him a pair, male and female, of every type of animal, bird and insect. Seeing him taking these creatures to the ark, the people laughed loudly: "Noah must have gone out of his head! What is he going to do with the animals?" Almighty Allah narrated: [So it was], until when Our command came and the oven overflowed, We said, "Load upon the ship of each [creature] two mates and your family, except those about whom the word has preceded, and [include] whoever has believed." But none had believed with him, except a few. (11:40).

حَتَّىٰٓ إِذَا جَآءَ أَمْرُنَا وَفَارَ ٱلتَّنُّورُ قُلْنَا ٱحْمِلْ فِيهَا مِن كُلٍّ زَوْجَيْنِ ٱثْنَيْنِ وَأَهْلَكَ إِلَّا مَن سَبَقَ عَلَيْهِ ٱلْقَوْلُ وَمَنْ ءَامَنَ وَمَآ ءَامَنَ مَعَهُۥٓ إِلَّا قَلِيلٌ ﴿٤٠﴾

## The Number of Believers

Noah's wife was not a believer with him so she did not join him; neither did one of Noah's son, who was secretly a disbeliever but had pretended faith in front of Noah. Likewise most of the people were disbelievers and did not go on board. The scholars hold different opinions on the number of those who were with Noah on the ship. Ibn Abbas stated that there were 80 believers while Kaab al Ahbar held that there were 72 believers. Others said that there were only 10 believers.

## Description of the Flood

Water rose from the cracks in the earth; there was not a crack from which water did not rise. Rain poured from the sky in quantities never seen before on earth. Water continued pouring from the sky rising from the cracks; hour after hour the level rose. The seas and waves invaded the land. The interior of the earth moved in a strange way, and the ocean floors lifted suddenly, flooding the dry land. The earth, for the first time was submerged.

## Noah Appeals to his Son

Allah told the story thus: "And [Noah] said, "Embark therein; in the name of Allah is its course and its anchorage. Indeed, my Lord is Forgiving and Merciful."

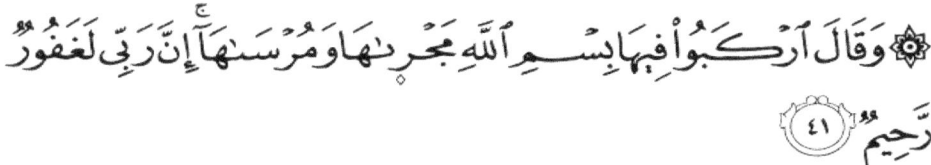

And it sailed with them through waves like mountains, and Noah called to his son who was apart [from them], "O my son, come aboard with us and be not with the disbelievers."

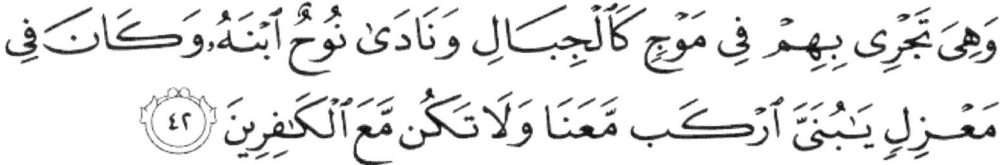

[But] he said, "I will take refuge on a mountain to protect me from the water." [Noah] said, "There is no protector today from the decree of Allah, except for whom He gives mercy." And the waves came between them, and he was among the drowned. (11:41-43)

قَالَ سَـَٔاوِىٓ إِلَىٰ جَبَلٍ يَعْصِمُنِى مِنَ ٱلْمَآءِ ۚ قَالَ لَا عَاصِمَ ٱلْيَوْمَ مِنْ أَمْرِ ٱللَّهِ إِلَّا مَن رَّحِمَ ۚ وَحَالَ بَيْنَهُمَا ٱلْمَوْجُ فَكَانَ مِنَ ٱلْمُغْرَقِينَ ۝٤٣

### The Flood Ends

And it was said, "O earth, swallow your water, and O sky, withhold [your rain]." And the water subsided, and the matter was accomplished, and the ship came to rest on the [mountain of] Judiyy. And it was said, "Away with the wrongdoing people." [11:44]

وَقِيلَ يَـٰٓأَرْضُ ٱبْلَعِى مَآءَكِ وَيَـٰسَمَآءُ أَقْلِعِى وَغِيضَ ٱلْمَآءُ وَقُضِىَ ٱلْأَمْرُ وَٱسْتَوَتْ عَلَى ٱلْجُودِىِّ ۖ وَقِيلَ بُعْدًا لِّلْقَوْمِ ٱلظَّـٰلِمِينَ ۝٤٤

And Noah called to his Lord and said, "My Lord, indeed my son is of my family; and indeed, Your promise is true; and You are the most just of judges!" [11:45-46]

وَنَادَىٰ نُوحٌ رَّبَّهُۥ فَقَالَ رَبِّ إِنَّ ٱبْنِى مِنْ أَهْلِى وَإِنَّ وَعْدَكَ ٱلْحَقُّ وَأَنتَ أَحْكَمُ ٱلْحَـٰكِمِينَ ۝٤٥

He said, "O Noah, indeed he is not of your family; indeed, he is [one whose] work was other than righteous, so ask Me not for that about which you have no knowledge. Indeed, I advise you, lest you be among the ignorant."

قَالَ يَـٰنُوحُ إِنَّهُۥ لَيْسَ مِنْ أَهْلِكَ ۖ إِنَّهُۥ عَمَلٌ غَيْرُ صَـٰلِحٍ ۖ فَلَا تَسْـَٔلْنِ مَا لَيْسَ لَكَ بِهِۦ عِلْمٌ ۖ إِنِّىٓ أَعِظُكَ أَن تَكُونَ مِنَ ٱلْجَـٰهِلِينَ ۝٤٦

### The Believers Disembark and Noah's Death

Noah released the birds, and the animals which scattered over the earth. After that the believers disembarked. Noah put his forehead to the ground in prostration. The survivors kindled a fire and sat around it. None of them had eaten hot food during the entire period of the flood. Following the disembarkation there was a day of fasting in thanks to Allah. The Quran draws the curtain on Noah's story. Prophet Muhammad (pbuh) said: "When the death of the Messenger of Allah Noah approached, he admonished his sons: "Indeed I would give you far reaching advice, commanding you to do two things, and warning you against doing two things as well. I charge you to believe that there is no god but Allah and that if the seven heavens and the seven earths were put on one side of a scale and the words "there is no god but Allah" were put on the other, the latter would outweigh the former. I warn you against associating partners with Allah and against pride." (Sahih al Bukhari) Some traditions said that his grave is in the Scared Mosque in Mecca, while others in Baalabak, a city in Iraq.

# Prophet Hud

And if they deny you, [O Muhammad] - so, before them, did the people of Noah and Aad and Thamud deny [their prophets]. [22:42]

وَإِن يُكَذِّبُوكَ فَقَدْ كَذَّبَتْ قَبْلَهُمْ قَوْمُ نُوحٍ وَعَادٌ وَثَمُودُ ۝

The people of Aad lived for many years in the windswept hills of an area between Oman and Yemen. They were physically well built and renowned for their craftsmanship especially in the construction of tall buildings with lofty towers. They were outstanding among all the nations in power and wealth, which, unfortunately, made them arrogant and boastful.

Their political power was held in the hand of unjust rulers, against whom no one dared to raise a voice. They were not ignorant of the existence of Allah, nor did they refuse to worship Him. What they did refuse was to worship Allah alone. They worshipped other gods, also, including idols. This is one sin Allah does not forgive.

And they were [therefore] followed in this world with a curse and [as well] on the Day of Resurrection. Unquestionably, Aad denied their Lord; then away with Aad, the people of Hud. [11:60]

$$وَأُتْبِعُوا۟ فِى هَٰذِهِ ٱلدُّنْيَا لَعْنَةً وَيَوْمَ ٱلْقِيَٰمَةِ ۗ أَلَآ إِنَّ عَادًا كَفَرُوا۟ رَبَّهُمْ ۗ أَلَا بُعْدًا لِّعَادٍ قَوْمِ هُودٍ ۝٦٠$$

## Hud's Appeal to His People

Allah wanted to guide these people so He sent a prophet from among them. This prophet was Hud (peace be upon him). Priophet Hud was a noble man who handled this task with great resoluteness and tolerance. Ibn Jarir reported that he was Hud Ibn Shalikh, Ibn Arfakhshand, Ibn Sam, and Ibn Noah (pbuh). He also reported that Prophet Hud (peace be upon him) was from a tribe called Ad Ibn Us Ibn Sam Ibn Noah, who were Arabs living in Al Ahqaf in Yemen between Oman and Hadramaut, on a land called Ashar stretching out into the sea. The name of their valley was Mughiith. Some traditions claimed that Hud (pbuh) was the first person who spoke Arabic while others claimed that Noah (pbuh) was the first. It was also said that Adam was the first. Hud (pbuh) condemned idol worship and admonished his people. "My people, what is the benefit of these stones that you carve with your own hands and worship? In reality it is an insult to the intellect. There is only One Deity worthy of worship and that is Allah. Worship of Him and Him alone, is compulsory on you. He created you, He provides for you and He is the One Who will cause you to die. He gave you wonderful physiques and blessed you in many ways. So believe in Him and do not be blind to His favors, or the same fate that destroyed Noah's people will overtake you." With such reasoning Hud hoped to instill faith in them, but they refused. His people asked him: "Do you desire to be our master with your call? What payment do you want?" Hud tried to make them understand that he would receive his payment (reward) from Allah; he did not demand anything from them except that they let the light of truth touch their hearts. Allah the Almighty states: "And to Ad people We sent their brother Hud. He said: "O my people, worship Allah; you have no deity other than Him. Then will you not fear Him?" [7:65]

$$۞ وَإِلَىٰ عَادٍ أَخَاهُمْ هُودًا ۗ قَالَ يَٰقَوْمِ ٱعْبُدُوا۟ ٱللَّهَ مَا لَكُم مِّنْ إِلَٰهٍ غَيْرُهُۥ ۚ أَفَلَا تَتَّقُونَ ۝٦٥$$

[Hud] said, "O my people, there is not foolishness in me, but I am a messenger from the Lord of the worlds." (7:67)

قَالَ يَٰقَوْمِ لَيْسَ بِى سَفَاهَةٌ وَلَٰكِنِّى رَسُولٌ مِّن رَّبِّ ٱلْعَٰلَمِينَ ۝

He said, "O my people, worship Allah; you have no deity other than Him. You are not but inventors [of falsehood]. [11:50-57]

وَإِلَىٰ عَادٍ أَخَاهُمْ هُودًا ۗ قَالَ يَٰقَوْمِ ٱعْبُدُوا۟ ٱللَّهَ مَا لَكُم مِّنْ إِلَٰهٍ غَيْرُهُۥٓ ۖ إِنْ أَنتُمْ إِلَّا مُفْتَرُونَ ۝

I do not ask you for it any reward. My reward is only from the one who created me. Then will you not reason?

يَٰقَوْمِ لَآ أَسْـَٔلُكُمْ عَلَيْهِ أَجْرًا ۖ إِنْ أَجْرِىَ إِلَّا عَلَى ٱلَّذِى فَطَرَنِىٓ ۚ أَفَلَا تَعْقِلُونَ ۝

And O my people, ask forgiveness of your Lord and then repent to Him. He will send [rain from] the sky upon you in showers and increase you in strength [added] to your strength. And do not turn away, [being] criminals."

وَيَٰقَوْمِ ٱسْتَغْفِرُوا۟ رَبَّكُمْ ثُمَّ تُوبُوٓا۟ إِلَيْهِ يُرْسِلِ ٱلسَّمَآءَ عَلَيْكُم مِّدْرَارًا وَيَزِدْكُمْ قُوَّةً إِلَىٰ قُوَّتِكُمْ وَلَا تَتَوَلَّوْا۟ مُجْرِمِينَ ۝

They said, "O Hud, you have not brought us clear evidence, and we are not ones to leave our gods on your say-so. Nor are we believers in you."

قَالُوا۟ يَـٰهُودُ مَا جِئْتَنَا بِبَيِّنَةٍ وَمَا نَحْنُ بِتَارِكِىٓ ءَالِهَتِنَا عَن قَوْلِكَ وَمَا نَحْنُ لَكَ بِمُؤْمِنِينَ ﴿٥٣﴾

"We only say that some of our gods have possessed you with evil." He said, "Indeed, I call Allah to witness, and witness [yourselves] that I am free from whatever you associate with Allah."

إِن نَّقُولُ إِلَّا ٱعْتَرَىٰكَ بَعْضُ ءَالِهَتِنَا بِسُوٓءٍ ۗ قَالَ إِنِّىٓ أُشْهِدُ ٱللَّهَ وَٱشْهَدُوٓا۟ أَنِّى بَرِىٓءٌ مِّمَّا تُشْرِكُونَ ﴿٥٤﴾

Other than Him. So plot against me all together; then do not give me respite.

مِن دُونِهِۦ ۖ فَكِيدُونِى جَمِيعًا ثُمَّ لَا تُنظِرُونِ ﴿٥٥﴾

Indeed, I have relied upon Allah my Lord and your Lord. There is no creature but that He holds its forelock. Indeed, my Lord is on a path [that is] straight."

إِنِّى تَوَكَّلْتُ عَلَى ٱللَّهِ رَبِّى وَرَبِّكُم ۚ مَّا مِن دَآبَّةٍ إِلَّا هُوَ ءَاخِذٌۢ بِنَاصِيَتِهَآ ۚ إِنَّ رَبِّى عَلَىٰ صِرَٰطٍ مُّسْتَقِيمٍ ﴿٥٦﴾

But if they turn away, [say], "I have already conveyed that with which I was sent to you. My Lord will give succession to a people other than you, and you will not harm Him at all. Indeed my Lord is, over all things, Guardian."

فَإِن تَوَلَّوْا۟ فَقَدْ أَبْلَغْتُكُم مَّآ أُرْسِلْتُ بِهِۦٓ إِلَيْكُمْ ۚ وَيَسْتَخْلِفُ رَبِّى قَوْمًا غَيْرَكُمْ وَلَا تَضُرُّونَهُۥ شَيْـًٔا ۚ إِنَّ رَبِّى عَلَىٰ كُلِّ شَىْءٍ حَفِيظٌ ﴿٥٧﴾

## Prophet Hud explains the Day of Judgement

Hud tried to speak to them and to explain about Allah's blessings: how Allah the Almighty had made them Noah's successors, how He had given them strength and power, and how He sent them rain to revive the soil. Hud's people looked about them and found they were the strongest on earth, so they become prouder and more obstinate. Thus they argued a lot with Hud. They asked "O Hud! Do you say that later we die and turn into dust, we will be resurrected?" He replied, "Yes, you will come back on the Day of Judgment and each of you will be asked about what you did." A peal of laughter was heard after the last statement. "How strange Hud's claims are!" The disbelievers muttered among themselves. They believed that when man dies his body decays and turns into dust, which is swept away by the wind. How could that return to its original state? Then what is the significance of the Day of Judgment? Why does the dead return to life? All these questions were patiently received by Hud. He then addressed his people concerning the Day of Judgment. He explained that belief in the Day of Judgment is essential to Allah's justice, teaching them the same thing that every prophet taught about it. Hud explained that justice demands that there be a Day of Judgment because good is not always victorious in life. Sometimes evil overpowers good. Will such crimes go unpunished? If we suppose there is no Day of Judgment, then a great injustice will have prevailed, but Allah has forbidden injustice to be incurred by Himself or His subjects. Therefore, the existence of the Day of Judgment, a day of accounting for our deeds and being rewarded or punished for them, reveals the extent of Allah's justice. Hud spoke to them about all of these things. They listened but disbelieved him.

## The Disbeliever's Attitude

Allah recounts Hud's people's attitude towards the Day of Judgment: The chiefs of his people, whom disbelieved and denied the meeting in the Hereafter, and to who We had given the luxuries and comforts of this life, said: He is no more than a human being like you, he eats of that which you eat, and drinks of what you drink. [23:33]

وَقَالَ ٱلْمَلَأُ مِن قَوْمِهِ ٱلَّذِينَ كَفَرُوا۟ وَكَذَّبُوا۟ بِلِقَآءِ ٱلْآخِرَةِ وَأَتْرَفْنَٰهُمْ فِى ٱلْحَيَوٰةِ ٱلدُّنْيَا مَا هَٰذَآ إِلَّا بَشَرٌ مِّثْلُكُمْ يَأْكُلُ مِمَّا تَأْكُلُونَ مِنْهُ وَيَشْرَبُ مِمَّا تَشْرَبُونَ ﴿٣٣﴾

If you were to obey a human being like yourselves then verily! You indeed would be losers. Does he promise you that when you have died and have become dust and bones, you shall come out alive (resurrected)? Far, very far, is that which you are promised. There is nothing but our life of this world! We die and we live! We are not going to be resurrected! He is only a man who has invented a lie against Allah, but we are not going to believe in him. [23:34-38]

$$\text{إِنْ هُوَ إِلَّا رَجُلٌ افْتَرَىٰ عَلَى اللَّهِ كَذِبًا وَمَا نَحْنُ لَهُ بِمُؤْمِنِينَ ﴿٣٨﴾}$$

The chiefs of Hud's people asked: "Is it not strange that Allah's chooses one of us to reveal His message to?" Hud replied: "What is strange in that? Allah wants to guide you to the right way of life, so He sent me to warn you. Noah's flood and his story are not far away from you, so do not forget what happened. All the disbelievers were destroyed, no matter how strong they were." "Who is going to destroy us Hud?" the chiefs asked. "Allah," replied Hud. The disbelievers among his people answered: "We will be saved by our gods." Prophet Hud clarified to them that the gods they worshipped would be the reason for their destruction, that it is Allah alone Who saves people, and that no other power on earth can benefit or harm anyone. The conflict between Hud and his people continued. The years passed, and they became prouder and more obstinate, and more tyrannical and more defiant of their prophet's message.

## Hud Warns his People

Furthermore, they started to accuse Hud (peace be upon him) of being a crazy lunatic. One day they told him: "We now understand the secret of your madness you insulted our gods and they harmed you; that is why you have become insane." Allah repeated their words in the Quran: "O my Hud! No evidence have you brought us, and we shall not leave our gods for your mere saying! And we are not believers in you. All that we say is that some of our gods (false deities) have seized you with evil (madness)." [11:53-54]

$$\text{قَالُوا يَا هُودُ مَا جِئْتَنَا بِبَيِّنَةٍ وَمَا نَحْنُ بِتَارِكِي آلِهَتِنَا عَن قَوْلِكَ وَمَا نَحْنُ لَكَ بِمُؤْمِنِينَ ﴿٥٣﴾ إِن نَّقُولُ إِلَّا اعْتَرَاكَ بَعْضُ آلِهَتِنَا بِسُوءٍ ۗ قَالَ إِنِّي أُشْهِدُ اللَّهَ وَاشْهَدُوا أَنِّي بَرِيءٌ مِّمَّا تُشْرِكُونَ ﴿٥٤﴾}$$

Hud had to return their challenge. He had no other way but to turn to Allah alone, no other alternative but to give them a threatening ultimatum. He declared to them: "I call Allah to witness and bear you witness that I am free from that which you ascribe as pin worship with Him (Allah). So plot against me, all of you and give me no respite. I put my trust in Allah, my Lord your Lord! There is not a moving (living) creature but He has grasp of its forelock. Verily, my Lord is on the Straight Path (the truth). So if you turn away, still I have conveyed the message with which was sent to you. My Lord will make another people succeed you, and you will not harm Him." [11:56-57]

إِنِّى تَوَكَّلْتُ عَلَى ٱللَّهِ رَبِّى وَرَبِّكُم ۚ مَّا مِن دَآبَّةٍ إِلَّا هُوَ ءَاخِذٌۢ بِنَاصِيَتِهَآ ۚ إِنَّ رَبِّى عَلَىٰ صِرَٰطٍ مُّسْتَقِيمٍ ۝

فَإِن تَوَلَّوْا۟ فَقَدْ أَبْلَغْتُكُم مَّآ أُرْسِلْتُ بِهِۦٓ إِلَيْكُمْ ۚ وَيَسْتَخْلِفُ رَبِّى قَوْمًا غَيْرَكُمْ وَلَا تَضُرُّونَهُۥ شَيْـًٔا ۚ إِنَّ رَبِّى عَلَىٰ كُلِّ شَىْءٍ حَفِيظٌ ۝

## The Punishment

Thus Prophet Hud (peace be upon him) renounced them and their gods and affirmed his dependence on Allah Who had created him. Hud realized that punishment would be incurred on the disbelievers among his people. It is one of the laws of life. Allah punishes the disbelievers, no matter how rich, tyrannical or great they are. Hud and his people waited for Allah's promise. A drought spread throughout the land, for the sky no longer sent its rain. The sun scorched the desert sands, looking like a disk of fire which settled on people's heads. Hud's people hastened to him asking: "What is that drought Hud?" Hud answered: "Allah is angry with you. If you believe in Him, He will accept you and the rain will fall and you will become stronger than you are." They mocked him and became more obstinate, sarcastic and preserve in their unbelief. The drought increased, the trees turned yellow, and plants died. A day came when they found the sky full of clouds. Hud's people were glad as they came out of their tents crying: "A cloud, which will give us rain!" The weather changed suddenly from burning dry and hot to stinging cold with wind that shook everything; trees, plants, tents, men and women. The wind increased day after day and night after night. Hud's people started to flee.

They ran to their tents to hide but the gale became stronger, ripping their tents from their stakes. They hid under cloth covers but the gale became stronger and tore away the covers. It slashed clothing and skin. It penetrated the apertures of the body and destroyed it. It hardly touched anything before it was destroyed or killed, its core sucked out to decompose and rot. The storm raged for 8 days and 7 nights. Almighty Allah recounts: "Then when they saw it as a dense cloud coming towards their valleys, they said: 'This is a cloud bringing us rain!' Nay but it is that torment which you were asking to be hastened! A wind wherein is a painful torment! Destroying everything by the command of its Lord!" [46:24-25].

فَلَمَّا رَأَوْهُ عَارِضًا مُّسْتَقْبِلَ أَوْدِيَتِهِمْ قَالُوا هَٰذَا عَارِضٌ مُّمْطِرُنَا بَلْ هُوَ مَا اسْتَعْجَلْتُم بِهِ ۖ رِيحٌ فِيهَا عَذَابٌ أَلِيمٌ ﴿٢٤﴾

تُدَمِّرُ كُلَّ شَيْءٍ بِأَمْرِ رَبِّهَا فَأَصْبَحُوا لَا يُرَىٰ إِلَّا مَسَاكِنُهُمْ ۚ كَذَٰلِكَ نَجْزِي الْقَوْمَ الْمُجْرِمِينَ ﴿٢٥﴾

Allah the Exalted described it thus: "And as for Aad, they were destroyed by a screaming, violent wind." [69:6-7]

وَأَمَّا عَادٌ فَأُهْلِكُوا بِرِيحٍ صَرْصَرٍ عَاتِيَةٍ ﴿٦﴾

Which Allah imposed upon them for seven nights and eight days in succession, so you would see the people therein fallen as if they were hollow trunks of palm trees.

سَخَّرَهَا عَلَيْهِمْ سَبْعَ لَيَالٍ وَثَمَانِيَةَ أَيَّامٍ حُسُومًا فَتَرَى الْقَوْمَ فِيهَا صَرْعَىٰ كَأَنَّهُمْ أَعْجَازُ نَخْلٍ خَاوِيَةٍ ﴿٧﴾

That violent gale did not stop until the entire region was reduced to ruins and its wicked people destroyed, swallowed by the sands of the desert. Only Hud and his followers remained unharmed. They migrated to Hadramaut and lived there in peace, worshipping Allah, their true Lord.

# Prophet Salih

After the destruction of the people of Ad, the tribe of Thamud succeeded them. However, they too forgot God. They fell to idol-worshipping. As their material wealth increased so, too, did their evil ways while their virtue decreased. Like the people of Ad, they erected huge buildings on the plains and hewed beautiful homes out of the hills. Tyranny and oppression became prevalent as evil men ruled the land. Allah sent unto them His Prophet Salih (pbuh), a good man from among them. His name was Salih Ibn Ubeid, Ibn Maseh, Ibn Ubeid, Ibn Hader, Ibn Thamud, Ibn Ather, Ibn Eram, and Ibn Noah. He called his people to worship Allah alone, and to not associate partners with Him. While some of them believed him, the majority of them disbelieved and harmed him by both words and deeds. Salih directed them: O my people, worship Allah; you have no deity other than Him. He has produced you from the earth and settled you in it, so ask forgiveness of Him and then repent to Him. Indeed, my Lord is near and responsive. [11:61]

وَإِلَىٰ ثَمُودَ أَخَاهُمْ صَٰلِحًا ۚ قَالَ يَٰقَوْمِ ٱعْبُدُوا۟ ٱللَّهَ مَا لَكُم مِّنْ إِلَٰهٍ غَيْرُهُۥ ۖ هُوَ أَنشَأَكُم مِّنَ ٱلْأَرْضِ وَٱسْتَعْمَرَكُمْ فِيهَا فَٱسْتَغْفِرُوهُ ثُمَّ تُوبُوٓا۟ إِلَيْهِ ۚ إِنَّ رَبِّى قَرِيبٌ مُّجِيبٌ ﴿٦١﴾

They said, O Salih, you were among us a man of promise before this. Do you forbid us to worship what our fathers worshipped? And indeed we are, about that to which you invite us, in disquieting doubt. [11:62]

قَالُوا۟ يَٰصَٰلِحُ قَدْ كُنتَ فِينَا مَرْجُوًّا قَبْلَ هَٰذَآ ۖ أَتَنْهَىٰنَآ أَن نَّعْبُدَ مَا يَعْبُدُ ءَابَآؤُنَا وَإِنَّنَا لَفِى شَكٍّ مِّمَّا تَدْعُونَآ إِلَيْهِ مُرِيبٍ ﴿٦٢﴾

## Salih's People Demand a Miracle

The people wanted to worship the same gods as their fathers had, with no reason, no proof, no thought. The proof of Salih's (pbuh) message was evident, but despite this it was obvious that most of his people did not believe him. They doubted his words, thinking he was charmed, and they saw that he would not stop preaching.

Fearing that his followers would increase, they tried to put him off by assigning him an important task; to prove that he was a messenger of Allah by performing a miracle. Let a unique she camel issue from the mountains. Allah granted Salih this miracle and a huge, unique, she camel appeared from the direction of the mountain. The Quranic commentators said that the people of Thamud gathered on a certain day at their meeting place, and the prophet Salih (pbuh) came and addressed them to believe in Allah, reminding them of the favors Allah had granted them. Then pointing at a rock, they demanded: "Ask your Lord to make a she camel, which must be 10 months pregnant, tall and attractive, issue from the rock for us." Salih replied: "Look now! If Allah sends you what you have requested, just as you have described, will you believe in that which I have come to you with and have faith in the message I have been sent with?" They answered: "Yes." So he took a vow from them on this, then prayed to Allah the Almighty to grant their request.

Allah ordered the distant rock to split asunder, to bringing forth a great ten month pregnant she camel. When their eyes set on it, they were amazed. They saw a great thing, a wonderful sight, a dazzling power and clear evidence. Some of Salih's people believed, yet most of them continued in their disbelief, stubbornness, and going astray. Allah said: And nothing has prevented Us from sending signs except that the former peoples denied them. And We gave Thamud the she-camel as a visible sign, but they wronged her. And We send not the signs except as a warning. [17:59]

وَمَا مَنَعَنَا أَن نُّرْسِلَ بِٱلْءَايَٰتِ إِلَّآ أَن كَذَّبَ بِهَا ٱلْأَوَّلُونَ وَءَاتَيْنَا ثَمُودَ ٱلنَّاقَةَ مُبْصِرَةً فَظَلَمُوا۟ بِهَا وَمَا نُرْسِلُ بِٱلْءَايَٰتِ إِلَّا تَخْوِيفًا ﴿٥٩﴾

There are many number of ancient stories of this camel and its miraculous nature. It was said that the she camel was miraculous because a rock in the mountain split open and it came forth from it, followed by its young offspring. Other accounts said that the she camel used to drink all the water in the wells in one day, and no other animals could approach the water. Many people claimed that the she camel gave milk sufficient for all the people to drink, on the same day that it drank all the water, leaving none for them. At first, the people of Thamud were greatly surprised when the she camel issued from the mountain rocks. It was a blessed camel, and its milk sufficient for thousands. If the camel slept in a place that place was abandoned by other animals. Thus it was obvious that is was not an ordinary camel, but one of Allah's signs. It lived among Salih's people, some of whom believed in Allah while the majority continued in their obstinacy and disbelief. Their hatred of Salih turned towards the blessed She camel and became centered on it.

A conspiracy started to be hatched against the camel by the disbelievers, and they secretly plotted against it. Salih feared that they might kill the camel, so he warned them: And O my people, this is the she-camel of Allah - [she is] to you a sign. So let her feed upon Allah's earth and do not touch her with harm, or you will be taken by an impending punishment. (11:64).

وَيَٰقَوْمِ هَٰذِهِۦ نَاقَةُ ٱللَّهِ لَكُمْ ءَايَةً فَذَرُوهَا تَأْكُلْ فِىٓ أَرْضِ ٱللَّهِ وَلَا تَمَسُّوهَا بِسُوٓءٍ فَيَأْخُذَكُمْ عَذَابٌ قَرِيبٌ ۝

For a while, Salih's people let the camel graze and drink freely, but in their hearts they hated it. However, the miraculous appearance of the unique camel caused many to become Salih's followers, and they clung to their belief in Allah. The disbelievers began complaining that this huge she camel with its unusual qualities drank most of the water and frightened their cattle. Therefore, they laid a plot to kill the camel, and sought the help of their women folk to tempt the men to carry out their commands. Saduq bint of Mahya, who was from a rich and noble family, offered herself to a young man named Masrai Ibn Mahraj on condition that he hamstring the camel. Aniza, an old woman, offered one of her daughters to a young man, Qudar Ibn Saluf, in return for killing the camel. Naturally these young men were tempted and set about finding seven others to assist them. They watched the camel closely, observing all its movements. As the she camel came to drink at the well, Masarai shot it in the leg with an arrow. It tried to escape but was hampered by the arrow. Qudar followed the camel and struck it with a sword in the other leg. As it fell to the ground, he pierced it with his sword.

The people who killed the camel were given a hero's welcome, cheered with songs and poetry composed in their praise. In their arrogance they mocked Salih, but he warned them: "Enjoy life for 3 more days then the punishment will descend upon you." Salih was hoping that they would see the folly of their ways and change their attitude before the three days went out. "Why in three days?" they asked. "Let the punishment come as quickly as possible." Prophet Salih pleaded with them: "My people, why do you hasten to evil rather than good? Why do not you ask pardon of Allah so that you may receive mercy?" They replied: "We see your presence and that of your followers as bringing evil on us." Almighty Allah related their story: "And indeed We sent to Thamud their brother Salih, saying "Worship Allah Alone and none else." Then look! They became two parties (believers and disbelievers) quarreling with each other. He said: "O my people! Why do you seek to hasten the evil (torment) before the good (Allah's Mercy)? Why seek you not the Forgiveness of Allah, that you may receive mercy?" They said: We augur till omen from you and those with you." he said: "Your ill omen is with Allah; nay, but you are a people that are being tested."

And there were in the city nine men (from the sons of their chiefs), who made mischief in the land, and would not reform. They said: "Swear to another by Allah that we shall make a secret night attack on him and his household, and afterwards we will surely say to his near relatives: "We witnessed not the destruction of his household, and verily! And they planned a plan, and We planned a plan, while they perceived not. [27:50-53]

$$ \text{وَمَكَرُوا مَكْرًا وَمَكَرْنَا مَكْرًا وَهُمْ لَا يَشْعُرُونَ ۝} $$

Then look how was the outcome of their plan - that We destroyed them and their people, all. And We saved those who believed and used to fear Allah. Three days after Salih's warning, thunderbolts filled the air, followed by severe earthquakes which destroyed the entire tribe and its homeland.

$$ \text{فَتِلْكَ بُيُوتُهُمْ خَاوِيَةً بِمَا ظَلَمُوا إِنَّ فِي ذَٰلِكَ لَآيَةً لِقَوْمٍ يَعْلَمُونَ ۝ وَأَنجَيْنَا الَّذِينَ آمَنُوا وَكَانُوا يَتَّقُونَ ۝} $$

Remember the graces bestowed upon you from Allah, and do not go about making mischief on the earth. The leaders of those who were arrogant among his people said to those who were counted weak to such of them as believed: "Know you that Salih is one sent from his Lord." They said: "We indeed believe in that with which he has been sent." Those who were arrogant said: "Verily, we disbelieve in that which you believe in." While the Prophet Muhammad (pbuh) was passing by Thamud's houses on his way to the battle of Tabuk, he stopped together with the people there. The people fetched water from the wells from which the people of Thamud used to drink. They prepared their dough (for baking) and filled their water skins from it (the water from the wells). The Prophet of Allah (pbuh) ordered them to empty the water skins and give the prepared dough to the camels. Then he went away with them until they stopped at the well from which the she camel (of Salih) used to drink. He warned them against entering upon the people that had been punished, saying "I fear that you may be affected by what afflicted them; so do no enter upon them."

## Prophet Ibrahim (Abraham)

And mention in the Book [the story of] Abraham. Indeed, he was a man of truth and a prophet. [19:41]

$$\text{وَاذْكُرْ فِي ٱلْكِتَٰبِ إِبْرَٰهِيمَ ۚ إِنَّهُۥ كَانَ صِدِّيقًا نَّبِيًّا ﴿٤١﴾}$$

Some of the People of the Bible and Torah stated that his name was Abraham Ibn Tarikh, Ibn Nahur, Ibn Sarough, Ibn Raghu, Ibn Phaligh, Ibn Aher, Ibn Shalih, Ibn Arfghshand, Ibn Sam, and Ibn Noah. They said that when Tarikh was seventy five years old, he had Abraham, Nahor (Nohour) and Haran. Haran had a son named Lot. They also said that Abraham was the middle child and that Haran died in the lifetime of his father in the land where he was born, the land of Babylonia. At that time some people worshipped idols of stone and wood; others worshipped the planets, stars, sun and moon; still others worshipped their kings and rulers. Abraham was born into that atmosphere, into a typical family of that ancient time. The head of the family was not even an ordinary idolater, but was one who totally rejected Allah and who used to make the idols with his own hands. Some traditions claimed that Abraham's father died before his birth and he was raised by an uncle whom Abraham called father. Other traditions said that his father was alive and was named Azer. Into that family Abraham was born. But Abraham stood against all kinds of polytheism. Allah said: And We had certainly given Abraham his sound judgement before, and We were of him well-Knowing.

$$\text{۞ وَلَقَدْ ءَاتَيْنَآ إِبْرَٰهِيمَ رُشْدَهُۥ مِن قَبْلُ وَكُنَّا بِهِۦ عَٰلِمِينَ ﴿٥١﴾}$$

During Abraham's early childhood Abraham saw that his father made strange statues. One day, he asked him about what it, His father said that he made statues of gods. Abraham rejected the idea. He played with such statues sitting on their backs as people sit on the backs of donkeys. One day his father saw him riding the statue of Mardukh, he became furious. Abraham asked: "What is this statue, father? It has big ears, bigger than ours." His father answered: "It is Mardukh, the god of gods! These big ears show his deep knowledge." This made Abraham laugh, he was only seven years old at that time. Years passed and Abraham grew. He noticed that these idols did not eat, drink or talk and could not even turn themselves right side up if someone turned them upside down. How then could people believe that such statues could harm or benefit them? Abraham's people had a big temple full of idols. When he said to his father and his people: "What are these statues to which you are devoted?" [21:52]

$$\text{إِذْ قَالَ لِأَبِيهِ وَقَوْمِهِ مَا هَٰذِهِ ٱلتَّمَاثِيلُ ٱلَّتِىٓ أَنتُمْ لَهَا عَٰكِفُونَ ﴿٥٢﴾}$$

What surprised him was the way his people behaved when they entered the temple; they bowed and started to cry, begging and imploring their gods for help. Such a sight was so funny to Abraham, but later he felt angry. It was astonishing that all those people could be so foolish? Moreover, his father wanted him to be a priest. One night Abraham left to the mountains. He walked alone in the dark until he chose a cave in the mountain where he sat resting his back against its wall. He looked at the sky. He looked at planets and stars which were worshipped by some people on earth. His young heart was filled with tremendous pain. He considered what was beyond the moon, the stars and the planets (i.e. Allah) and was astonished that these celestial bodies were worshipped. Almighty Allah revealed: "And thus did We show Abraham the realm of the heavens and the earth that he would be among the certain [in faith]." [6:75]

$$\text{وَكَذَٰلِكَ نُرِىٓ إِبْرَٰهِيمَ مَلَكُوتَ ٱلسَّمَٰوَٰتِ وَٱلْأَرْضِ وَلِيَكُونَ مِنَ ٱلْمُوقِنِينَ ﴿٧٥﴾}$$

When the night covered him over with darkness he saw a star. He said: "This is my lord." But when it set, he said: "I like not that those who set." When he saw the moon rising up he said: "This is my lord." But when it set he said: "Unless my Lord guides me, I shall surely be among the erring people." When he saw the sun rising up he said: "This is my lord, this is greater." But when it set, he said: "O my people! I am indeed free from all that you join as partners in worship with Allah. His people said, "Have you come to us with truth, or are you of those who jest?" [21:55-56] He said: "[No], rather, your Lord is the Lord of the heavens and the earth who created them, and I, to that, am of those who testify."

قَالُوٓا۟ أَجِئْتَنَا بِٱلْحَقِّ أَمْ أَنتَ مِنَ ٱللَّٰعِبِينَ ﴿٥٥﴾
قَالَ بَل رَّبُّكُمْ رَبُّ ٱلسَّمَٰوَٰتِ وَٱلْأَرْضِ ٱلَّذِى فَطَرَهُنَّ وَأَنَا۠ عَلَىٰ ذَٰلِكُم مِّنَ ٱلشَّٰهِدِينَ ﴿٥٦﴾

He said: "Do you dispute with me concerning Allah while He has guided me and I fear not those whom you associate with Allah in worship. (Nothing can happen to me) except when my Lord (Allah) wills something. And how should I fear those whom you associate in worship with Allah (though they can neither benefit nor harm), while you fear not that you have joined in worship with Allah things for which He has not sent down to you any authority." And that was Our [conclusive] argument which We gave Abraham against his people. We raise by degrees whom We will. Indeed, your Lord is Wise and Knowing. [6:84]

وَتِلْكَ حُجَّتُنَآ ءَاتَيْنَٰهَآ إِبْرَٰهِيمَ عَلَىٰ قَوْمِهِۦ نَرْفَعُ دَرَجَٰتٍ مَّن نَّشَآءُ إِنَّ رَبَّكَ حَكِيمٌ عَلِيمٌ ﴿٨٣﴾

All was finished between Abraham and his people, but the struggle began. The other problem was his father, he not only worshipped idols but sculpted and sold them as well. And [mention, O Muhammad], when Abraham said to his father Azar, "Do you take idols as deities? Indeed, I see you and your people to be in manifest error." [6:74]

۞ وَإِذْ قَالَ إِبْرَٰهِيمُ لِأَبِيهِ ءَازَرَ أَتَتَّخِذُ أَصْنَامًا ءَالِهَةً إِنِّىٓ أَرَىٰكَ وَقَوْمَكَ فِى ضَلَٰلٍ مُّبِينٍ ﴿٧٤﴾

Being a wise son he did not make his father feel foolish, nor did he openly laugh at his conduct. He told him that he loved him, thereby hoping to generate fatherly love. Then he gently asked him why he worshipped lifeless idols who could not hear, see or protect him. Before his father could become angry he hastily added: O my father, indeed there has come to me of knowledge that which has not come to you, so follow me; I will guide you to an even path. [19:43]

يَـٰٓأَبَتِ إِنِّى قَدْ جَآءَنِى مِنَ ٱلْعِلْمِ مَا لَمْ يَأْتِكَ فَٱتَّبِعْنِىٓ أَهْدِكَ صِرَٰطًا سَوِيًّا ﴿٤٣﴾

O my father, do not worship Satan. Indeed Satan has ever been, to the Most Merciful, disobedient. [19:44]

يَـٰٓأَبَتِ لَا تَعْبُدِ ٱلشَّيْطَـٰنَ إِنَّ ٱلشَّيْطَـٰنَ كَانَ لِلرَّحْمَـٰنِ عَصِيًّا ﴿٤٤﴾

O my father, indeed I fear that there will touch you a punishment from the Most Merciful so you would be to Satan a companion [in Hellfire] [19:45]

يَـٰٓأَبَتِ إِنِّىٓ أَخَافُ أَن يَمَسَّكَ عَذَابٌ مِّنَ ٱلرَّحْمَـٰنِ فَتَكُونَ لِلشَّيْطَـٰنِ وَلِيًّا ﴿٤٥﴾

[His father] said, "Have you no desire for my gods, O Abraham? If you do not desist, I will surely stone you, so avoid me a prolonged time. [19:46]

قَالَ أَرَاغِبٌ أَنتَ عَنْ ءَالِهَتِى يَـٰٓإِبْرَٰهِيمُ لَئِن لَّمْ تَنتَهِ لَأَرْجُمَنَّكَ وَٱهْجُرْنِى مَلِيًّا ﴿٤٦﴾

[Abraham] said, "Peace will be upon you. I will ask forgiveness for you of my Lord. Indeed, He is ever gracious to me. [19:47]

قَالَ سَلَـٰمٌ عَلَيْكَ سَأَسْتَغْفِرُ لَكَ رَبِّىٓ إِنَّهُۥ كَانَ بِى حَفِيًّا ﴿٤٧﴾

## Abraham Breaks the Idols

Abraham explained to the people and his father, the beauty of Allah's creation, His power and wisdom. Idol worship is detested by Allah for Allah is the Lord of the universe Who created mankind, guided him and provided him with food and drink and cured him when he was sick and Who will cause him to die and be raised up again. However, they would not give up but clung to idolatry. Abraham left his father's house and abandoned his people and what they worshipped. But he decided to do something about their state of disbelief, but did not reveal it. He knew that there was going to be a great celebration on the other bank of the river which would be attended by all the people. Abraham waited until the city was empty, then he went to the temple. Abraham went to the temple carrying a sharp axe. He looked at the stone and wood statues of the gods and at the food laid in front of them as offerings. He approached one of the statues and asked: "The food is getting cold. Why don't you eat? What is [wrong] with you that you do not speak?" [71:91-98]

Abraham asked all the other statues around him: "Will you not eat of the offering before you? And then he turned upon them a blow with [his] axe. Then the people came toward him, hastening.

فَرَاغَ عَلَيْهِمْ ضَرْبًا بِٱلْيَمِينِ ۝ فَأَقْبَلُوٓا۟ إِلَيْهِ يَزِفُّونَ ۝

They said: "Construct for him a fire and throw him into the burning fire." And they intended for him a plan, but We made them the most debased.

قَالُوا۟ ٱبْنُوا۟ لَهُۥ بُنْيَٰنًا فَأَلْقُوهُ فِى ٱلْجَحِيمِ ۝ فَأَرَادُوا۟ بِهِۦ كَيْدًا فَجَعَلْنَٰهُمُ ٱلْأَسْفَلِينَ ۝

At first they began to guess who had done that to their gods, then Abraham's name came to their minds. Allah the Almighty said: They said, "Who has done this to our gods? Indeed, he is of the wrongdoers." [21:59-63]

قَالُوا۟ مَن فَعَلَ هَٰذَا بِـَٔالِهَتِنَآ إِنَّهُۥ لَمِنَ ٱلظَّٰلِمِينَ ۝

They said: "Are you the one who has done this to our gods, O (Abraham)?"

قَالُوٓا۟ ءَأَنتَ فَعَلْتَ هَٰذَا بِـَٔالِهَتِنَا يَٰٓإِبْرَٰهِيمُ ۝٦٢

He said, "Rather, this - the largest of them - did it, so ask them, if they should [be able to] speak."

قَالَ بَلْ فَعَلَهُۥ كَبِيرُهُمْ هَٰذَا فَسْـَٔلُوهُمْ إِن كَانُوا۟ يَنطِقُونَ ۝٦٣

They said: "You have already known that these do not speak!" [21:65-70]

ثُمَّ نُكِسُوا۟ عَلَىٰ رُءُوسِهِمْ لَقَدْ عَلِمْتَ مَا هَٰٓؤُلَآءِ يَنطِقُونَ ۝٦٥

He said, "Then do you worship instead of Allah that which does not benefit you at all or harm you?

قَالَ أَفَتَعْبُدُونَ مِن دُونِ ٱللَّهِ مَا لَا يَنفَعُكُمْ شَيْـًٔا وَلَا يَضُرُّكُمْ ۝٦٦

They realized the senselessness of their beliefs; however, their arrogance would not allow them to admit their foolishness. All they could do was to use their power of authority as tyrants usually do to punish Abraham. They said, "Burn him and support your gods - if you are to act."

قَالُوا۟ حَرِّقُوهُ وَٱنصُرُوٓا۟ ءَالِهَتَكُمْ إِن كُنتُمْ فَٰعِلِينَ ۝٦٨

Allah said, "O fire, be coolness and safety upon Abraham. And they intended for him harm, but We made them the greatest losers."

قُلْنَا يَٰنَارُ كُونِى بَرْدًا وَسَلَٰمًا عَلَىٰٓ إِبْرَٰهِيمَ ۝٦٩

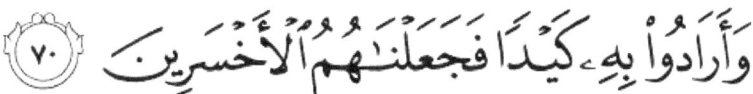

For several days they collected wood for the fire. They dug a big pit, filled it with firewood and ignited it. Abraham was put on the catapult, his hands and feet were tied. The fire was ready with its flame reaching the sky. The priest gave his order to cast Abraham into the fire. The angel Gabriel came near Abraham's head and asked him: "O Abraham do you wish for anything?" Abraham replied: "Nothing from you." The catapult was shot and Abraham was cast into the fire. But his descent into the blaze was as descent on steps in a cool garden. The flames were still there, but they did not burn for Allah the Almighty had issued His command: "O fire! Be you coolness and safety for Abraham." The fire submitted to the will of Allah, becoming cool and safe for Abraham. The fire only burned his bonds, and he sat in the midst of the fire as if he were sitting in a garden. He glorified and praised Allah the Almighty, with a heart that contained only his love for Allah. There was not any vacant space therein for fear, awe, or worry. It was filled with love only. Fear and awe were dead, and the fire was turned into coolness, making the air pleasant. Those who love Allah as Abraham do did not fear. This miracle shamed the tyrants, but it did not cool the flame of anger in their hearts. However after his event many of the people followed Abraham, although some kept their belief a secret for fear of harm or death at the hands of the rulers.

### Abraham challenges those who proclaim themselves as gods, King Namrud

Abraham had established a definite reasoning against idolaters. Nothing was left for him except to reason against the people who proclaimed themselves gods. When the king, Namrud, heard of Abraham's safe exit from the fire he became very angry. He feared that the status of godhead he had proclaimed for himself was not challenged by an ordinary human being. He summoned Abraham to the palace and held a dialogue with him which Allah Almighty recounted: Have you not thought about him who disputed with Abraham about his Lord (Allah) because Allah had given him the kingdom? When Abraham said to him: 'My Lord (Allah) is He Who gives life and causes death. He said: I give life and cause death. Abraham said: Verily, Allah causes the sun to rise from the east; then cause it you to rise from the west. So the disbeliever was utterly defeated. Allah guides not the people who are Zalimeen (wrongdoers etc.). [2:258]

Abraham's fame spread throughout the entire kingdom. People talked about how he had been saved from the blazing fire and how he had debated with the king and left him speechless. In the meantime, Abraham continued calling people to believe in Allah, exerting a great effort to guide his people to the right path. He tried every means to convince them. However in spite of his love and care for his people, they felt angry and deserted him. Only one woman and one man of his people shared his belief in Allah.

The woman's name was Sarah and she became his wife. The man's name was Lot and he became a prophet. When Abraham realized that no one else was going to believe in his call, he decided to emigrate. He left his people and traveled with his wife and Lot to a city called Ur, then another called Haran, and then to Palestine. Allah the Almighty told us: "So Lot believed in him (Abraham's message of Islamic Monotheism). He (Abraham) said: "I will emigrate for the sake of my Lord. Verily, He is the All Mighty, the All Wise." (Ch 29:26). After Palestine, Abraham traveled to Egypt, calling people to believe in Allah wherever he traveled, judging fairly between people, and guiding them to truth and righteousness. Hadith about Abraham, Sarah and Hajar. Abu Hurairah narrated that Abraham (pbuh) did not tell a lie except on three occasions, twice for the sake of Allah (Exalted and Almighty) when he said: "I am sick," (when his people were holding a festival in honor of their gods, Abraham excused himself by saying he was sick. [37:89] and when he said: "(I have not done this but) the big idol has done it." The (third was) that while Abraham and Sarah (his wife) were going (on a journey), they passed by (the territory of) a tyrant. Someone said to the tyrant: "This man (Abraham is accompanied by a very charming lady." So, he sent for Abraham and asked him about Sarah saying "Who is this lady?" Abraham said: "She is my sister." Abraham went to Sarah said "O Sarah! There are no believers on the surface of the earth except you and me. This man asked me about you and I have told him that you are my sister do not contradict my statement." the tyrant then called Sarah, and when she went to him, he tried to take a hold of her with his hand, but his hand got stiff and he was confounded. He asked Sarah: "Pray to Allah for me and I shall not harm you." So Sarah asked Allah to cure him and he got cured.

He tried to take hold of her for the second time, but his hand got as stiff as or stiffer than before and he was more confounded. He again requested Sarah: "Pray to Allah for me, and I will not harm you." Sarah asked Allah to again, and he became all right. He then called one of his guards who had brought her and said: "You have not brought me a human being but have brought me a devil." The tyrant then gave Hajar as a maid servant to Sarah. Abraham, gesturing with his hand, asked: "What has happened?" She replied: "Allah has spoiled the evil plot of the infidel or immoral person and gave me Hajar for service." Abu Hurairah then addressed his listeners saying: "That Hajar was your mother, O Bani Ma is Sama (Arab, the descendants of Ishmael, Hajar's son)."

## Hajar and Sarah

Abraham's wife Sarah was sterile. She had been given an Egyptian woman Hajar, as a servant. Abraham had aged and his hair was gray and after many years spent in calling people to Allah. Sarah thought she and Abraham were lonely because she could not have a child. Therefore, she offered her husband her servant Hajar in marriage. Hajar gave birth to her first son Ishmael (Ismail) when Abraham was an old man.

## Abraham Questions Resurrection

Abraham lived on earth worshipping Allah and calling people to monotheism, but he was journeying to Allah, knowing that his days on earth were limited and that they would be followed by death and finally resurrection. The knowledge of life after death filled Abraham with peace and love and certitude. One day he begged Allah to show him how He brought the dead back to life. Allah commanded Abraham to take four birds, cut them up and mingle their body parts, divide them into four portions and place them on top of four different hills, then call back the birds in Allah's name. Abraham did as he was told. Immediately the mingled parts of the birds separated to join their original bodies in different places and the birds flew back to Abraham. Almighty Allah revealed: "Remember when Abraham said: "My Lord, show me how You give life to the dead." [Allah] said, "Have you not believed?" He said, "Yes, but [I ask] only that my heart may be satisfied." [Allah] said, "Take four birds and commit them to yourself. Then [after slaughtering them] put on each hill a portion of them; then call them - they will come [flying] to you in haste. And know that Allah is Exalted in Might and Wise." [2:260].

وَإِذْ قَالَ إِبْرَاهِيمُ رَبِّ أَرِنِي كَيْفَ تُحْيِ ٱلْمَوْتَىٰ قَالَ أَوَلَمْ تُؤْمِن قَالَ بَلَىٰ وَلَٰكِن لِّيَطْمَئِنَّ قَلْبِي قَالَ فَخُذْ أَرْبَعَةً مِّنَ ٱلطَّيْرِ فَصُرْهُنَّ إِلَيْكَ ثُمَّ ٱجْعَلْ عَلَىٰ كُلِّ جَبَلٍ مِّنْهُنَّ جُزْءًا ثُمَّ ٱدْعُهُنَّ يَأْتِينَكَ سَعْيًا وَٱعْلَمْ أَنَّ ٱللَّهَ عَزِيزٌ حَكِيمٌ ﴿٢٦٠﴾

## Prophet Ismail (Ishmael)

And Ishmael and Elisha and Jonah and Lot - and all [of them] We preferred over the worlds. (6:86)

وَإِسْمَٰعِيلَ وَٱلْيَسَعَ وَيُونُسَ وَلُوطًا وَكُلًّا فَضَّلْنَا عَلَى ٱلْعَٰلَمِينَ ﴿٨٦﴾

One day, Abraham woke up and then he asked his wife Hajar to get her son and prepare for a journey. In a few days Abraham started out with his wife Hajar and their son Ishmael. The child was still nursing and not yet weaned. Abraham walked through cultivated land, desert, and mountains until he reached the desert of the Arabian Peninsula and came to an uncultivated valley having no fruit, no trees, no food, and no water. The valley had no sign of life. After Abraham had helped his wife and child to dismount, he left them with a small amount of food and water which was hardly enough for 2 days. He turned around and walked away. He wife hurried after him asking: "Where are you going Abraham, leaving us in this barren valley?" Abraham did not answer her, but continued walking. She repeated what she had said, but he remained silent. Finally she understood that he was not acting on his own initiative. She realized that Allah had commanded him to do this. She asked him: "Did Allah command you to do so?" He replied: "Yes." Then his great wife said: "We are not going to be lost, since Allah Who has commanded you is with us." Abraham invoked Almighty Allah thus: "O Our Lord! I have made some of my offspring to dwell in a valley with no cultivation, by Your Sacred House (the Ka'ba at Mecca); in order, O our Lord, that they may offer prayers perfectly (Iqamat as salat) so fill some hearts among men with love towards them, and O Allah provide them with fruits so that they may give thanks. O our Lord! Certainly, You know what we conceal and what we reveal. Nothing on the earth or in the heavens is hidden from Allah." [14:37-38]

### Hajar and Ishmael - Narrated by Ibn Abbas

The first woman to use a girdle was the mother of Ishmael. She used a girdle so that she might hide her tracks from Sarah (by dragging it). Abraham brought her and her son Ishmael while she was suckling him to a place near the Kaba under a tree on the spot of ZamZam at the highest place in the mosque. During those days there was nobody in Mecca, nor was there any water so he made them sit over there and placed near them a leather bag containing some dates and a small water skin containing some water and set out homeward.

Ishmael's mother followed him saying: "O Abraham! Where are you going, leaving us in this valley where there is no person whose company we may enjoy, nor is there anything to enjoy?" she repeated that to him many times, but he did not look back at her. Then she asked him: "Has Allah ordered you to do so?" He said: "Yes." She then said: "Then He will not neglect us." She returned while Abraham proceeded onwards. On reaching the Thaniya where they could not see him, he faced the Kabba and raising both hands, invoked Allah saying the following prayers: "My Lord, make this a secure city and provide its people with fruits - whoever of them believes in Allah and the Last Day." [Allah ] said. "And whoever disbelieves - I will grant him enjoyment for a little; then I will force him to the punishment of the Fire, and wretched is the destination." [2:126]

$$\text{وَإِذْ قَالَ إِبْرَاهِيمُ رَبِّ اجْعَلْ هَٰذَا بَلَدًا آمِنًا وَارْزُقْ أَهْلَهُ مِنَ الثَّمَرَاتِ مَنْ آمَنَ مِنْهُم بِاللَّهِ وَالْيَوْمِ الْآخِرِ ۖ قَالَ وَمَن كَفَرَ فَأُمَتِّعُهُ قَلِيلًا ثُمَّ أَضْطَرُّهُ إِلَىٰ عَذَابِ النَّارِ ۖ وَبِئْسَ الْمَصِيرُ ﴿١٢٦﴾}$$

So fill some hearts among men with love towards them, and O Allah provide them with fruits so that they may give thanks." [14:37] Ibn Abbas's narration continued; "Ishmael's mother went on suckling Ishmael and drinking from the water (she had) When the water in the water skin had been used up, she became thirsty and her child also became thirsty, She started looking at him (Ishmael) tossing in agony. She left him, for she could not endure looking at him, and found that the mountain of As-Safa was the nearest mountain to her on that land. She started looking at the valley keenly so that she might see somebody, but she could not see anybody. Then she descended for As-Safa and when she reached the valley, she tucked up her robe and ran in the valley like a person in distress and trouble till she crossed the valley and reached the mountain of Al Marwa. There she stood and started looking expecting to see somebody, but she could not see anybody. She repeated that running between Safa and Marwa seven times."

### Hajar sees Zam-zam - by Prophet Muhammad

The prophet Muhammad (pbuh) said: This is the source of the tradition of the Sa'y (rituals of the hajj, pilgrimage) the going of people between them (As-Safa and Al-Marwa). When she reached Al Marwa (for the last time) she heard a voice and she asked herself to be quiet and listened attentively. She heard the voice again and said: O whoever you maybe! You have made me hear your voice; have you got something to help me? And behold! She saw an angel at the place of Zam-zam, digging the earth with his heel (or his wing) till water flowed from that place.

She started to make something like a basin around it, using her hand in this way, and started filling her water skin with water with her hands and the water was flowing out water she had scooped some of it. The Prophet (pbuh) added: "May Allah bestow mercy on Ishmael's mother! Had she let the Zam-zam flow without trying to control it, or had she not scooped from that water to fill her water skin, Zam-zam would have been a stream flowing on the surface of the earth."

The Prophet (peace be upon him) continued: "Then she drank water and suckled her child. The angel said to her: "Don't be afraid of being neglected, for this is the House of Allah which will be built by this boy and his father, and Allah never neglects His people." The House (Kaba) at that time was on a high place resembling a hillock, and when torrents came, they flowed to its right and left. "She lived in that way till some people from the tribe of Jurhum or a family from Jurhum passed by her and her child as they (the Jurhum people) were coming through the way of Kada. They landed in the lower part of Mecca where they saw a bird that had the habit of flying around water and not leaving it. They said: "This bird must be flying around water, though we know that there is no water in this valley." They sent one or two messengers who discovered the source of water and returned to inform them of the water. So they all came towards the water. Ishmael's mother was sitting near the water. They asked her: "Do you allow us to stay with you?" She replied: "Yes, but you will have no right to possess the water." They agreed to that. Ishmael's mother was pleased with the whole situation, as she used to love to enjoy the company of the people, so they settled there, and later on they sent for their families who came and settled with them so that some families became permanent residents there. The child (Ishmael) grew up and learned Arabic from them and (his virtues) caused them to love and admire him as he grew up and when he reached the age of puberty they made him marry a woman from amongst them."

## Prophet Ishmael's Wives

The Prophet (pbuh) continued: "After Ishmael's mother had died, Abraham came after Ishmael's marriage in order to see his family that he had left before but he did not find Ishmael there. When he asked Ishmael's wife about him, she replied: "He has gone in search of livelihood." Then he asked her about their way of living and their condition, and she replied, "We are living in misery; we are living in hardship and destitution," complaining to him. He said: "When your husband returns, convey my salutations to him and tell him to change the threshold of the gate (of his house)." When Ishmael came, he seemed to have felt something unusual, so he asked his wife: "Has anyone visited you?" she replied, "Yes, an old man of such and such description came and asked me about you and I informed him and he asked about our state of living and I told him that we were living in a hardship and poverty." On that Ishmael said: "Did he advise you anything?"

She said: "Yes he told me to convey his salutation to you and to tell you to change the threshold of your gate." Ishmael said: "It was my father and he has ordered me to divorce you. Go back to your family." So, Ishmael divorced her and married another woman from among them (Jurhum).

## The Kabba is built - by Prophet Muhammad

"Then Abraham stayed away from them for a period as long as Allah wished and called on them again but did not find Ishmael. So he came to Ishmael's wife and asked her about Ishmael. She said: 'he has gone in for our livelihood.' Abraham asked her; 'how are you getting on?' asking her about their sustenance and living. She replied: 'we are prosperous and well off (we have everything in abundance).' then she thanked Allah. Abraham said: 'What kind of food do you eat?' she said: 'meat.' he said: 'what do you drink?' she said: 'water.' he said: 'O Allah! Bless their meat and water." The Prophet (pbuh) added: "At that time they did not have grain, and if they had grain he would have also invoked Allah to bless it. If somebody has only these two things as his sustenance, his health and disposition will be badly affected unless he lives in Mecca." The Prophet (pbuh) continued: "Then Abraham said to Ishmael's wife: 'When your husband comes give my regards to him and tell him that he should keep firm the threshold of his gate.' When Ishmael came back he asked his wife, 'did anyone call no you?' She replied: 'yes, a good looking old man came to me,' so she praised him and added: 'He asked about you and I informed him that we were in a good condition.'

Ishmael asked her: 'Did he give you any piece of advice?' she said: 'yes, he told me to give his regards to you and ordered that you should keep firm the threshold of your gate.' on that Ishmael said: 'It was my father, and you are the threshold of the gate. He has ordered me to keep you with me.' Then Abraham stayed away from them for a period as long as Allah wished and called on them afterwards. He saw Ishmael under a tree near Zam-zam, sharpening his arrows. When he saw Abraham, he rose up to welcome him (and they greeted each other as a father does with his son or a son does with his father). Abraham said: 'O Ishmael! Allah has given me an order.' Ishmael said: 'Do what your Lord has ordered you to do.' Abraham asked: 'will you help me?' Ishmael said: 'I will help you.' Abraham said: 'Allah has ordered me to build a house here,' pointing to a hillock higher than the land surrounding it. "Then they raised the foundations of the House (the Kaba). Ishmael brought the stones while Abraham built and when the walls became high Ishmael brought this stone and put it for Abraham who stood over it and carried on building. While Ishmael was handing him the stones, and both of them were saying: "Our Lord! Accept this service from us, verily, You are the All Hearer, the All Knower." [2:127] The Prophet (pbuh) added: "Then both of them went on building and going round the Kaba saying: "O our Lord! Accept this service from us, verily, You are the All Hearer, the All Knower." (Sahih Bukhari).

## Hajar sees ZamZam - by Ibn Abbas

Ibn Abbas narrated a slightly different version: When Abraham had differences with his wife (because of her jealousy of Hajar, Ishmael's mother), he took Ishmael and his mother and went away. They had a water skin with them containing some water. Ishmael's mother used to drink water from the water skin so that her milk would increase for her child. When Abraham reached Mecca, he made her sit under a tree and afterwards returned home. Ishmael's mother followed him and when they reached Kada, she called him from behind: 'O Abraham! To whom are you leaving us?' He replied: '(I am leaving you) to Allah's care.' she said: 'I am satisfied to be with Allah.' She returned to her place and started drinking water from the water skin and her milk increased for her child. "When the water had all been used up, she said to herself: 'I had better go and look so that I may see somebody.' she ascended As-Safa Mountain and looked hoping to see somebody but in vain. When she came down to the valley, she ran till she reached Al-Marwa Mountain. She ran to and for (between the two mountains) many times. Then she said to herself; 'I had better go and see the state of the child.' she went and found it in a state of one on the point of dying. She could not endure to watch it dying and said to herself: 'If I go and look I may find somebody.' she went and ascended al-Safa Mountain and looked for a long while but could not find anybody. Thus she completed seven rounds of running between As-Safa and Al-Marwa. Again she said to herself: 'I had better go back and see the state of the child.' but suddenly she heard a voice, and she said to that strange voice. 'Help us if you can offer any help.'

It was Gabriel (who had made the voice) Gabriel hit the earth with his heel like this (Ibn Abbas hit the earth with his heel to illustrate it), and so the water gushed out. Ishmael's mother was astonished and started digging. Abu Al Qasim, the Prophet (pbuh) said: "If she had left the water, (flow naturally, without her intervention) it would have been flowing on the surface of the earth."

## Makka is settled - by Ibn Abbas

Ibn Abbas continued narrating: "Ishmael's mother started drinking from the water, and her milk increased for her child. Afterwards some people of the tribe of Hurhum saw some birds while passing through the bottom of the valley and that astonished them. They said: "birds can only be found at a place where there is water." They sent a messenger who searched the place and found the water and returned to inform them about it. Then they all went to her and said: "O Ishmael's mother! Will you allow us to be with you (or dwell with you)?" Then they stayed there.

## Ishmael's Wives - by Ibn Abbas

Later on her boy reached the age of puberty and married a lady from them. Then an idea occurred to Abraham, which he disclosed to his wife (Sarah). 'I want to call on my dependents I left at Mecca.' When he went there he greeted Ishmael's wife and said: 'where is Ishmael?' She replied: 'He has gone out hunting.' Abraham said to her: 'When he comes, tell him to change the threshold of his gate.' When Ishmael came she told him the same and whereupon Ishmael said to her: 'you are the threshold so go to your family (you are divorced).' Again Abraham thought of visiting his dependents whom he had left at Mecca, and told his wife (Sarah) of his intentions. Abraham came to Ishmael's house and asked: 'Where is Ishmael?' Ishmael's wife replied: 'He has gone out hunting,' and added: 'will you stay for some time and have something to eat and drink?' Abraham said: 'what is your food and what is your drink?' she replied: 'our food is meat and our drink is water.' he replied: 'O Allah! Bless their meals and their drink.' Abu Al Qasim (the Prophet) (pbuh) said: "Because of Abraham's invocation there are blessings in Mecca." Ibn Abbas continued: "Once more Abraham thought of visiting his family he had left at Mecca and he told his wife (Sarah) of his decision. He went and found Ishmael behind the Zam-zam well, mending his arrows. He said: 'O Ishmael, your Lord has ordered me to build a house for Him.' Ishmael said: 'Obey the order of your Lord.' Abraham said: 'Allah has also ordered me that you should help me therein.' Ishmael said: 'Then I will do so.' So both of them were saying: "O our Lord! Accept this service of us, verily, You are the All Hearer, the All Knower." [2:127] When the building became high and the old man (Abraham) could no longer lift the stones to such a high position, he stood over the stone of Al Maqam and Ishmael carried on handing him the stones and both of them were saying: "O our Lord! Accept this service of us, verily You are the All Hearer, the All Knower."

## Abraham and Ishmael (pbuh) - The Sacrifice

Allah the Almighty told us of Abraham's affliction with his beloved son: "And he said after his rescue from the fire: 'Verily! I am going to my Lord. He will guide me! My Lord! Grant me (offspring) from the righteous. So We gave him the glad tidings of a forbearing boy. And when he reached with him [the age of] exertion, he said, "O my son, indeed I have seen in a dream that I [must] sacrifice you, so see what you think." He said, "O my father, do as you are commanded. You will find me, if Allah wills, of the steadfast." [37:102]

فَلَمَّا بَلَغَ مَعَهُ ٱلسَّعْىَ قَالَ يَٰبُنَىَّ إِنِّىٓ أَرَىٰ فِى ٱلْمَنَامِ أَنِّىٓ أَذْبَحُكَ فَٱنظُرْ مَاذَا تَرَىٰ ۚ قَالَ يَٰٓأَبَتِ ٱفْعَلْ مَا تُؤْمَرُ ۖ سَتَجِدُنِىٓ إِن شَآءَ ٱللَّهُ مِنَ ٱلصَّٰبِرِينَ ﴿١٠٢﴾

Then when they had both submitted themselves to the Will of Allah and he had laid him prostrate on his forehead (or on the side of his forehead for slaughtering); and We called out to him: O Abraham! You have fulfilled the dream (vision! Verily! Thus do We reward those who perform good deeds, totally for Allah's sake only. Verily, that indeed was a manifest trial and We ransomed him with a great sacrifice (a ram;) and We left for him (a goodly remembrance) among generations (to come) in later times. Salamun (peace) be upon Abraham! Thus indeed do We reward the Muhsineen (good doers). Verily, he was one of Our believing slaves." [37:99-111] Time passed. One day Abraham was sitting outside his tent thinking of his son Ishmael and Allah's sacrifice. His heart was filled with awe and love for Allah for His countless blessings. A big tear dropped from his eyes and reminded him of Ishmael.

## Tidings of Isaac

In the meantime, three angels descended to the earth; Gabriel, Israphael, and Michael. They came in human shapes and saluted Abraham. Abraham arose and welcomed them. He took them inside his tent thinking they were strangers and guests. He seated them and made sure that they were comfortable, then excused himself to go to his people. His wife Sarah arose when he entered. She had become old and white haired. Abraham said to her: "We have three strangers in the house." "Who are they?" she asked. "I do not know any of them," he answered. "What food have we got?" He asked. Half a sheep." She replied, "Half a sheep! Slaughter a fat calf for them; they are strangers and guests." he ordered while leaving. The servants roasted and served a calf. Abraham invited the angels to eat and he started eating so as to encourage them. He continued, but when he glanced at his guests to assure they were eating, he noticed that none of them had touched the food. He said to them: "Are you not going to eat?" He resumed eating, but when he glanced at them again he found that they were still not eating. Their hands did not reach out for the food. He began to fear them. Abraham's fears increased. The angels, however were reading his inner thoughts and one of them said: "Do not fear." Abraham raised his head and replied: "Indeed I am in fear. I have asked you to eat food but you do not stretch out your hands to eat. Do you intend me evil?" One of the angels smiled and said: "We do not eat. We are Allah's angels." One of them then turned towards his wife and conveyed the glad tidings about Isaac. Almighty Allah revealed: "Verily! There came Our Messengers to Abraham with glad tidings." They said: "Salaam (greetings or peace)!" He answered: "Salaam (greetings or peace)!" And he hastened to entertain them with a roasted calf. But, when he saw their hands went not towards it (the meal), he felt some mistrust of them, and conceived a fear of them. They said: "Fear not, we have been sent against the people of Lot." And his wife was standing there and she laughed (either, because the Messengers did not eat their food or for being glad for the destruction of the people of Lot). And We gave him good tidings of Isaac, a prophet from among the righteous. [37:112]

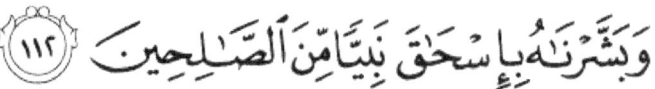

# Prophet (Issac) Ishaq

And We blessed him and Isaac. But among their descendants is the doer of good and the clearly unjust to himself. [37:113]

وَبَارَكْنَا عَلَيْهِ وَعَلَىٰ إِسْحَاقَ وَمِن ذُرِّيَّتِهِمَا مُحْسِنٌ وَظَالِمٌ لِّنَفْسِهِ مُبِينٌ ﴿١١٣﴾

۞ إِنَّا أَوْحَيْنَا إِلَيْكَ كَمَا أَوْحَيْنَا إِلَىٰ نُوحٍ وَالنَّبِيِّينَ مِن بَعْدِهِ ۚ وَأَوْحَيْنَا إِلَىٰ إِبْرَاهِيمَ وَإِسْمَاعِيلَ وَإِسْحَاقَ وَيَعْقُوبَ وَالْأَسْبَاطِ وَعِيسَىٰ وَأَيُّوبَ وَيُونُسَ وَهَارُونَ وَسُلَيْمَانَ ۚ وَآتَيْنَا دَاوُودَ زَبُورًا ﴿١٦٣﴾

Indeed, We have revealed to you, [O Muhammad], as We revealed to Noah and the prophets after him. And we revealed to Abraham, Ishmael, Isaac, Jacob, the Descendants, Jesus, Job, Jonah, Aaron, and Solomon, and to David We gave the book [of Psalms].

The Quran does not give much details of Isaac's life (pbuh), but reliable scholars said that when Abraham felt that his life was drawing to a close, he wished to see Isaac married. He did not want Isaac to marry one of the Canaanites, who were pagans, so he sent a trustworthy servant to Haran in Iraq to choose a bride for Isaac. The servant's choice fell upon Rebekah Bint Bethuel, Ibn Nahor (who was a brother of Abraham). Isaac married her and she gave birth to a set of twins, Esau (Al Eis) and Jacob (Yaqub). Ill feelings developed between the two brothers when they grew into manhood. Esau disliked the fact that Jacob was favored by his father and by Allah with prophet hood. This ill feeling became so serious that Esau threatened to kill his brother. Fearing for his life, Jacob fled the country.

### Isaac's Sons - from the People of the Book

The People of the Bible and the Torah said that when Isaac was forty years old, he married Rebekah Bint Bethuel, during his father's life. They said she was sterile, so Isaac prayed to Allah and then she became pregnant. She gave birth to twin boys. The first one was called Esau whom the Arabs called Al-Eis. He became the father of Rum. The second one was called Jacob, which means Israel, (belonging to the people of Israel).

### Isaac's Death

Jacob came to his father Isaac and settled with him in the village of Hebron which lies in the land of Canaan where Abraham had lived. Then Isaac fell ill and died when he was one hundred eighty years old. His sons Esau and Jacob buried him with his father Abraham Al Khalil in a cave which he had bought. It was said that Abraham died at the age of 175.

# Prophet Yaqub (Jacob)

And We gave to Abraham, Isaac and Jacob - all [of them] We guided. And Noah, We guided before; and among his descendants, David and Solomon and Job and Joseph and Moses and Aaron. Thus do We reward the doers of good. [6:84]

وَوَهَبْنَا لَهُۥٓ إِسْحَٰقَ وَيَعْقُوبَ كُلًّا هَدَيْنَا وَنُوحًا هَدَيْنَا مِن قَبْلُ وَمِن ذُرِّيَّتِهِۦ دَاوُۥدَ وَسُلَيْمَٰنَ وَأَيُّوبَ وَيُوسُفَ وَمُوسَىٰ وَهَٰرُونَ وَكَذَٰلِكَ نَجْزِى ٱلْمُحْسِنِينَ ﴿٨٤﴾

Prophet Isaac married Rebekah Bint Bethuel, Ibn Nahor. She gave birth to twins, Esau (Al-Eis) and Jacob (Yaqub). However, angry feelings developed between the two brothers when they grew into manhood. Esau disliked the fact that Jacob was favored by his father and by Allah with prophet hood. This ill feeling became so serious that Esau threatened to kill his brother. Fearing for his life, Jacob fled the country. The People of the Bible and the Torah said that when Isaac was forty years old, he married Rebekah, Bint Bethuel, during his father's life. They said she was sterile, so Isaac prayed to Allah and then she became pregnant. She gave birth to twin boys. The first one was called Esau whom the Arabs called Al-Eis. He became the father of Rum.

The second one was called Jacob, which means Israel, (belonging to the people of Israel). The People of the Bible and the Torah claimed that when Isaac (pbuh) grew old and his eye sight had weakened, he had a desire for food, so he asked his son Esau to go hunting and bring him some cooked game. Esau asked him to bless the food and pray for him. Esau, a hunter, went out to get his father the meat. Rebekah, overhearing this, ordered her son Jacob to slaughter two goats of his best flock and cook them as his father liked and bring it to him before his brother returned. She dressed Jacob in his brother's clothes and put goat skin on his arms and neck, for Esau was hairy while Jacob was not. When he approached his father with the food, his father asked: 'Who are you?' Jacob answered: 'I am your son.' When his father finished eating, he prayed for his son to be the more blessed brother and to prevail over them and all people, and for Allah to sustain him and his children. When he left his father, his brother Esau, who had carried out his father's command, entered. Isaac asked him: "What is this my son?" He answered: "This is the food you like." Isaac asked: "Did you bring it an hour ago and ask me to pray for you?" Esau said: "No, I swear I did not," and he knew his brother had preceded him in this matter and he was sick at heart.

## Jacob Leaves his Home - from the People of the Book

The People of the Book said Esau threatened to kill his brother when their father was dead. They also said that he asked his father to pray for him that Allah make the earth good for his offspring and multiply his sustenance and fruits. When their mother knew that Esau threatened his brother Jacob, she commanded her son Jacob to go to her brother Laban in the land of Haran and abide with him for a time until his brother's anger had abated, and to marry one of the Laban's daughters. She told her husband Isaac to command him with that advice and pray for him, and he did.

## Jacob's Promise

Jacob (pbuh) left his family, when night came he found a place to rest. He took a stone and put it under his head and slept. He dreamed of a ladder from heaven to earth. Angels were ascending and descending and the Lord addressed him and said to him; "I will bless you and your offspring and make this land for you and for those who come after you." When he awoke he felt joyful from what he had seen in his dream and vowed, for Allah's sake that if he returned to his family safely, he would build here a temple for Allah the Almighty. He also vowed to give one tenth of his property for the sake of Allah. He poured oil on the stone so as to recognize it and called the place "Ayle's House" (Bethel), which means "House of Allah". It was to be the location of Jerusalem later.

The People of the Book also said that when Jacob came to his maternal uncle in the land of Harran, his uncle had two daughters. The elder one was called Leah (Lia) and the younger one was Rachel (Rahil). The latter was the better and lovelier of the two. His uncle agreed to marry his daughter to him on the condition that Jacob pasture his sheep for seven years. After a period of time, his uncle prepared a feast and gathered people for the wedding. He married Leah, his elder daughter, to him at night. She was weak-sighted and ugly. When morning came, Jacob discovered she was Leah and he complained to his uncle. "You deceived me; I was engaged to Rachel and you married me to Leah." His uncle said: "It is not our tradition to marry the younger daughter before the elder daughter. However, if you love her sister, work another seven years and I will marry you to both of them." Jacob worked for seven years and then married Rachel. It was acceptable in their time, as described in the Torah, for a man to marry two sisters. Laban gave a female slave to each daughter. Leah's slave was called Zilpah and Rachel's slave was called Bilha.

### Jacob's Children - from the People of the Book

Almighty Allah compensated Leah's weakness by giving her sons. The first one was named Rueben (Robel), after whom there were Simon (Shamun), Levi (Lawi), and Judah (Yahudh). Rachel felt jealous of Leah's having sons, as she was barren. She gave her slave Bilha to her husband and he had relations with her until she became pregnant. She gave birth to a son and named him Naphtali. Leah was vexed that Rachel's slave had given birth to a son, so she in turn gave her slave Zilpah to Jacob (pbuh), Zilpah gave birth to two sons, Gad and Asher. Then Leah got pregnant and gave birth to her fifth son, Issachar, and later she gave birth to a sixth son Zebulun. After this Leah gave birth to a daughter named Dinah. Thus, Leah had seven sons from Jacob. When Rachel prayed to Allah to give her a son from Jacob. Allah heard her call and responded to her prayer. She gave birth to a son, great, honorable, and beautiful. She named him Joseph (Yusuf). All of this happened when they were in the land of Haran and Jacob (pbuh) was pasturing his uncle's sheep, which he did for a period of twenty years.

### Jacob's Request - from the People of the Book

Jacob then asked his uncle Laban to let him go and visit his family. His uncle said to him: "I have been blessed because of you; ask for whatever money you need." Jacob said: "Give me each spotted and speckled goat born this year and each black lamb." But at Laban's command his sons removed their father's goat that were striped, spotted or speckled, and the black lambs, lest others should be born with those traits. They walked for three days with their father's goats and sheep while Jacob tended the remaining flock. The People of the Book said that Jacob (pbuh) took fresh rods of poplar, almond, and plane.

He peeled streaks in them and cast them into the water through for the goats to look at. The young inside their abdomens were terrified and moved and they were born striped, spotted or speckled. When the sheep were breeding, he set their faces towards the black sheep in Laban's flock and put the rods among them. Their lambs were born black. This was considered an example of supernatural powers, a miracle. Jacob had many goats, sheep, beast and slaves. His uncle and his sons' faces changed as if they the sheep and goats had been stolen from them.

## Jacob Accused of Taking Idols

Allah the Almighty inspired Jacob to return to the country of his father and people, and He promised to stand by him. Jacob told his family that, and they responded and obeyed him. Jacob did not tell Laban of his plans, however, and left without bidding farewell. Upon leaving, Rachel stole her father's idols. After Jacob and his people had fled for his country, Laban and his people followed them. When Laban met with Jacob, he blamed him for leaving him without his knowledge. He would have liked to know so that he could have made them leave with celebration and joy, with drums and songs. Why have they taken his idols with them? Jacob had no knowledge of his idols, so he denied that he had taken them from him. Then Laban entered the tents of his daughters and slaves to search, but he found nothing, for Rachel had put the idols in the camel saddle under her. She did not get up, apologizing that she had her menses. Thus, he could not perceive what they had done. Then they sat on a hill called Galeed and made a covenant there. Jacob would not ill-treat Laban's daughters nor marry others. Neither Laban nor Jacob would pass the hill into the other's country. They cooked food and their people ate with them. Each bade the other farewell as they departed, each returning to his own country.

When Jacob approached the land of Seir, the angels greeted him. He sent a messenger ahead with greetings to his brother Esau, asking forgiveness and humbling himself before him. The messenger returned greetings and told Jacob that Esau was riding towards him with four hundred men. This made Jacob afraid and he entreated and prayed to Allah Almighty. He prostrated in humiliation and asked Him to fulfill His promise which He had made before. He asked Him to stop the evil of his brother Esau. Then Jacob (peace be upon him) prepared a great present for his brother: two hundred female goats and twenty male goats, two hundred ewes and twenty rams, and thirty camels, forty cows and two bulls, twenty female donkeys and ten male donkeys. He commanded his slaves to take the animals, each drove by itself, and pass on ahead of him with a space between the droves. He instructed them: "When you meet my brother Esau he will ask you, 'to whom do you belong? Where are you going?' you shall say, 'they belong to your servant Jacob; they are a present to my master Esau. Moreover, he is behind us." Jacob stayed behind with his two wives, his slaves and his children for two nights, then continued walking by night and resting by day.

## Jacob becomes Israel

When the dawn of the second day came one of the angels appeared in the shape of a man. Jacob began to wrestle with him. They were neck and neck until the angel injured his thigh and Jacob became lame. When the day was breaking, the angel said to him: 'What is your name?' He answered: 'Jacob.' The angel said: "After today you shall not be called anything but Israel." Jacob asked: "Who are you? What is your name?" He vanished. Then Jacob knew that he was one of the angels. Jacob was lame, and for this reason the children of Israel do not eat the thigh muscle on the hip socket.

## Jacob and Esau Meet

Jacob raised his eyes and saw his Brother Esau coming. Jacob prostrated seven times before him for it was their salutation in that time. It was lawful for them just as the angels had prostration in salutation to Adam. When Esau saw him, he ran towards him, embraced and kissed him and wept. When Esau raised his eyes and saw the women and children he asked: "Who are these with you?" Jacob answered: "Those whom Allah has given me, your servant." Leah, Rachel, their slaves, and all the children approached and prostrated before him. Jacob asked Esau to accept his gift and insisted until he did so. Esau returned and went in advance before him. Jacob and his family followed with the flocks and herds and slaves to the mountains (Seir).

## Jacob Builds Ayl

When he came to Succoth (Sahur), he built a house for himself and shades for his beasts. Then he passed by Jerusalem, the village of Shechem, and camped before the village. He bought a farm from Shcehm Ibn Hamor with one hundred goats and built an altar, which he called Ayl, as Allah commanded him. He built the altar where Jerusalem stands today and later Solomon son of David (pbuh) rebuilt it. It is in the place of the stone which he had earlier anointed with oil as was mentioned before.

## Dinah's Story - from the People of the Book

The people of the book tell a story of Dinah, daughter of Jacob and Leah. Shechem Ibn Hamor seized her and lay with her by force. Then he asked her father and brothers to let him marry her. Her brothers said: "Circumcise all of you, and we will give our daughters to you, and we will take your daughters for ourselves; but we do not marry with uncircumcised people." They (the men of the city) agreed to that, and all of them were circumcised. When the third day came, the pain from the circumcision had increased, Jacob's sons approached and killed them till the last one.

They killed Shchem and his father for the evil they had committed against them and for their worship of idols. That is why Jacob's sons killed them and seized their money as spoils.

## Rachel's Death

Then Rachel got pregnant and gave birth to a son, Benjamin, but she had a hard labor and died after delivery. Jacob buried her in Ephrath (afrath). The tomb of Rachel is there till the present day.

## The Sons of Jacob

Jacob's sons were twelve men. From Leah there were Rueben (Robil), Simon (Shamun), Levi (Lawi), Judah (Yahudh), Issachar (Isakher), and Zebulun (Zablun). From Rachel there were Joseph (Yusuf) (pbuh) and Benjamin. From Rachel's slave there were Dan and Naphtali (Neftali), and from Leah's slave there were Gad and Asher.

## Isaac's Death

Jacob came to his father Isaac and settled with him in the village of Hebron which lies in the land of Canaan where Abraham had lived. Then Isaac fell ill and died when he was one hundred eighty years old. His sons Esau and Jacob buried him with his father Abraham Al Khalil in a cave which he had bought. It was said that Abraham died at the age of one hundred seventy five.

## The Prophet's last Wish

Allah the Almighty declared in the Glorious Quran: "And who turns away from the religion of Abraham (Islamic Monotheism) except him who befools himself? Truly, We chose him in this world and verily, in the Hereafter he will be among the righteous. When his Lord said to him: "Submit (be a Muslim)!" He said: "I have submitted myself (as a Muslim) to the Lord of the Alamin (mankind, jinn and all that exists)."

And this (submission to Allah, Islam) was enjoined by Abraham upon his sons and by Jacob, (saying): "O my sons! Allah has chosen for you the true religion, then die not except in the Faith of Islam (as Muslims -- Islamic Monotheism)." Or were you witnesses when death approached Jacob? When he said unto his sons: "What will you worship after me?" They said: "We shall worship you (Ilah (God - Allah) the Ilah (God) of your fathers, Abraham, Ishmael, Isaac, One Ilah (God), and to Him we submit (in Islam)." That was a nation who had passed away. They shall receive the reward of what they earned and you of what you earn. And you will not be asked of what they used to do.

## Quran's Way of Confronting People of the Book

They say: "Be Jews or Christians, and then you will be guided." Say (to them O Muhammad): "Nay (we follow) only the religion of Abraham, Hanifan (to worship none but Allah Alone, and he was not of the Al Mushrikeen (those who worshipped others along with Allah)." Say (O Muslims): "We believe in Allah and that which has been sent down to us and that which had been sent down to Abraham, Ishmael, Isaac, Jacob and to Al-Asbat (the twelve sons of Jacob), and that which has been given to Moses and Jesus and that which has been given to the Prophets from their Lord. We make no distinction between any of them, and to Him we have submitted (in Islam)."

So if they believe in the like of that which you believe, then they are rightly guided, but if they turn away, then they are only in opposition. So, Allah, will suffice you against them. He is the All Hearer, the All Knower.

Say (O Muhammad, to the Jews and Christians): "Dispute you with us about Allah while He is our Lord and your Lord? And we are to be rewarded for our deeds and you for your deeds. We are sincere to Him in worship and obedience (i.e., we worship Him Alone and none else, and we obey His Orders)." Or say you that Abraham, Ishmael, Isaac, Jacob, and Al-Asbat (the twelve sons of Jacob) were Jews or Christians? Say: "Do you know better or does Allah know better....that they all were Muslims? And who is more unjust than he who conceals the testimony (to believe in the Prophet Muhammad, when he comes written in their books) he has from Allah? Allah is not unaware of what you do." [2:130-140] In another surah Almighty Allah declared: "O People of the Scripture (Jews and Christians)! Why do you dispute about Abraham, while the Torah and the Gospel were not revealed till after him? Have you then no sense? Verily, you are those who have disputed about that of which you have no knowledge. Why do then dispute concerning that which you have no knowledge? It is Allah Who knows, and you know not.

Abraham was neither a Jew nor a Christian, but he was a true Muslim Hanifan (Islamic Monotheism), to worship none but Allah Alone and he was not of the polytheists (he joined none in worship with Allah). Verily, among mankind who have the best claim to Abraham are those who followed him, and this Prophet (Muhammad) and those who have believed (Muslims). And Allah is the Wali (Protector and Helper) of the believers. [3:65]

$$\text{يَٰٓأَهْلَ ٱلْكِتَٰبِ لِمَ تُحَآجُّونَ فِىٓ إِبْرَٰهِيمَ وَمَآ أُنزِلَتِ ٱلتَّوْرَىٰةُ وَٱلْإِنجِيلُ إِلَّا مِنۢ بَعْدِهِۦٓ ۚ أَفَلَا تَعْقِلُونَ ۝٦٥}$$

Allah the Exalted also affirmed: "Then verily! Your Lord for those who do evil (commit sins and are disobedient to Allah) in ignorance and afterward repent and do righteous deeds, verily, your Lord thereafter to such is Forgiving, Most Merciful. Verily, Abraham was an Ummah (a leader having all the good righteous qualities or a nation), obedient to Allah, Hanifan (to worship none but Allah), and he was not one of those who were Al Mushrikeen (polytheists, idolaters, disbelievers in the Oneness of Allah and those who joined partners with Allah). He was thankful for His (Allah's) Graces. He (Allah) chose him (as an intimate friend) and guided him to a Straight Path (Islamic Monotheism, neither Judaism nor Christianity). We gave him good in this world and in the Hereafter he shall be of the righteous. Then, We have inspired you (O Muhammad saying): "Follow the religion of Abraham Hanifan (Islamic Monotheism to worship none but Allah) and he was not of the Mushrikeen." [16:119-123]

When death approached Jacob, when he said to his sons, "What will you worship after me?" They said, "We will worship your God and the God of your fathers, Abraham and Ishmael and Isaac - one God. And we are Muslims [in submission] to Him." [2:133]

$$\text{أَمْ كُنتُمْ شُهَدَآءَ إِذْ حَضَرَ يَعْقُوبَ ٱلْمَوْتُ إِذْ قَالَ لِبَنِيهِ مَا تَعْبُدُونَ مِنۢ بَعْدِى قَالُوا۟ نَعْبُدُ إِلَٰهَكَ وَإِلَٰهَ ءَابَآئِكَ إِبْرَٰهِۦمَ وَإِسْمَٰعِيلَ وَإِسْحَٰقَ إِلَٰهًا وَٰحِدًا وَنَحْنُ لَهُۥ مُسْلِمُونَ ۝١٣٣}$$

# Prophet Lot (Lut)

And Isma'il (Ishmael) and Al-Yas'a (Elisha), and Yunus (Jonah) and Lut (Lot), and each one of them We preferred above the 'Alamin (mankind and jinns) (of their times) [6:86]

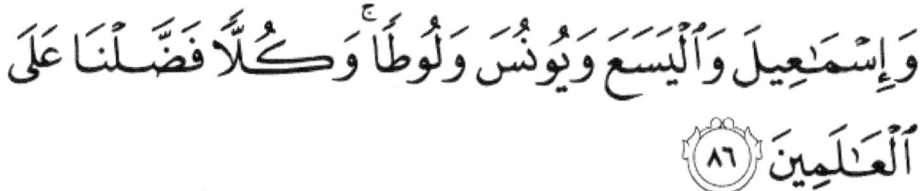

Prophet Abraham (pbuh) left Egypt with his nephew Lut (pbuh), who then went to the city of Sodom (Sadum), which was on the western shore of the Dead Sea. This city was filled with evil. Its residents waylaid, robbed and killed travelers.

Another common evil among them was that men had sex with men instead of with women. This unnatural act later became known as sodomy (after the city of Sodom). It was practiced openly and unashamedly.

Lut's Message

It was at the height of these crimes and sins that Allah revealed to Prophet Lut (pbuh) that he should summon his people to give up their indecent behavior, but they were so deeply sunk in their immoral habits that they were deaf to Lot's preaching. Swamped in their unnatural desires, they refused to listen, even when Lot warned them of Allah's punishment. Instead, they threatened to drive him out of the city if he kept on preaching. Allah the Almighty revealed: "The people of Lot (those dwelt in the towns of Sodom in Palestine) belied the Messengers when their brother Lot said to them: "Will you not fear Allah and obey Him? Verily! I am a trustworthy Messenger to you. SO fear Allah, keep your duty to Him, and obey me. No reward do I ask of you for it (my Message of Islamic Monotheism) my reward is only from the Lord of the Alamin (mankind, jinn and all that exists). Go you in unto the males of the Alamin (mankind), and leave those whom Allah has created for you to be your wives? Nay, you are a trespassing people!" They said: "If you cease not, O Lot! Verily, you will be one of those who are driven out!" He said: "I am indeed, of those who disapprove with severe anger and this evil action (of sodomy). My Lord! Save me and my family from what they do." So saved him and his family, all except an old woman (this wife) among those who remained behind. [26:160-171]

## Lut's Wife

Allah presents an example of those who disbelieved: the wife of Noah and the wife of Lut. They were under two of Our righteous servants but betrayed them, so those prophets did not avail them from Allah at all, and it was said, "Enter the Fire with those who enter." [66:10]

ضَرَبَ ٱللَّهُ مَثَلًا لِّلَّذِينَ كَفَرُوا۟ ٱمْرَأَتَ نُوحٍ وَٱمْرَأَتَ لُوطٍ ۖ كَانَتَا تَحْتَ عَبْدَيْنِ مِنْ عِبَادِنَا صَٰلِحَيْنِ فَخَانَتَاهُمَا فَلَمْ يُغْنِيَا عَنْهُمَا مِنَ ٱللَّهِ شَيْـًٔا وَقِيلَ ٱدْخُلَا ٱلنَّارَ مَعَ ٱلدَّٰخِلِينَ ﴿١٠﴾

The doings of Lut's people saddened his heart. Their unwholesome reputation spread throughout the land, while he struggled against them. As the years passed, he persisted in his mission but to no avail. No one responded to his call and believed except for the members of his family, and even in his household, not all the members believed. Lot's wife, like Noah's wife, a disbeliever. Allah the Almighty declared: "Allah set forth an example for those who disbelieve, the wife of Noah and the wife of Lut. They were under two of Our righteous slaves, but they both betrayed their (husbands, by rejecting their doctrines) so they (Noah & Lut) benefited them (their respective wives) not, against Allah, and it was said: "Enter the Fire along with those who enter!" [66:10]

## Angels Come to Meet Lut

If home is the place of comfort and rest, then Lut found none, for he was tormented both inside and outside his home. His life was continuous torture and he suffered greatly, but he remained patient and steadfast with his people. The years rolled by, and still not one believed in him. Instead, they belittled his message and mockingly challenged him: "Bring Allah's Torment upon us if you are one of the truthful!" [29:29] Overwhelmed with despair, Lot prayed to Allah to grant him victory and destroy the corrupt. Therefore, the angels left Abraham (pbuh) and headed for Sodom the town of Lut (pbuh). They reached the walls of the town in the afternoon. The first person who caught sight of them was Lot's daughter, who was sitting beside the river, filling her jug with water. When she lifted her face and saw them, she was stunned that there could be men of such magnificent beauty on earth. One of the tree men (angels) asked her: "O maiden, is there a place to rest?"

Remembering the character of her people she replied, "Stay here and do not enter until I inform my father and return." Leaving her jug by the river, she swiftly ran home. "O father!" she cried. "You are wanted by young men at the town gate and I have never before seen the like of their faces!" Lot felt distressed as he quickly ran to his guests. He asked them where they came from and where they were going. They did not answer his questions. Instead they asked if he could host them. He started talking with them and impressed upon them the subject of his people's nature. Lot was filled with turmoil; he wanted to convince his guests without offending them, not to spend the night there, yet at the same time he wanted to extend to them the expected hospitality normally accorded to guests. In vain he tried to make them understand the perilous situation. He requested them to wait until the night fell, for then no one would see them.

## The Mob at Lot's House

When darkness fell on the town, Lot escorted his guest to his home. No one was aware of their presence. However, as soon as Lot's wife saw them, she slipped out of the house quietly so that no one noticed her. Quickly, she ran to her people with the news and it spread to all the inhabitants like wildfire.

The people rushed towards Lot quickly and excitedly. Lot was surprised by their discovery of his guests. And he wondered who could have informed them. The matter became clear, however, when he could not find his wife, anywhere, thus adding grief to his sorrow. When Lot saw the mob approaching his house, he shut the door, but they kept on banging on it. He pleaded with them to leave the visitors alone and fear Allah's punishment. He urged them to seek sexual fulfillment with their wives, for that is what Allah had made lawful. Lot's people waited until he had finished his short sermon, and then they roared with laughter. Blinded by passion, they broke down the door. Lut became very angry, but he stood powerless before these violent people. He was unable to prevent the abuse of his guests, but he firmly stood his ground and continued to plead with the mob.

## The Punishment

At that terrible moment, he wished he had the power to push them away from his guests. Seeing him in a state of helplessness, and grief the guests said: "Do not be anxious or frightened, Lut for we are angels, and these people will not harm you." On hearing this, the mob was terrified and fled from Lot's house, hurling threats at him as they left. The angels warned Prophet Lut (peace be upon him) to leave his house before sunrise, taking with him all his family except his wife. Allah had decreed that the city of Sodom should perish. An earthquake rocked the town. It was as if a mighty power had lifted the entire city and flung it down in one jolt. A storm of stones rained on the city. Everyone and everything was destroyed, including Lut's wife.

## The Angels Meet Abraham

Allah the Almighty recounted this story: "And tell them about the guests (angels) of Abraham. When they entered unto him, and said: "Salaam on (peace)!" Abraham said: "Indeed! We are afraid of you." They (the angels) said: "Do not be afraid! We give you glad tidings of a boy (son) possessing much knowledge and wisdom." (Abraham) said: "Do you give me glad tidings (of a son) when old age has overtaken me? Of what then is your news?" They (the angels) said: "We give you glad tidings in truth. So be not of the despairing." Abraham said: "And who despairs of the Mercy of his Lord except those who are astray?" (Abraham again) said: "What then is the business on which you have come, O Messengers?" They (the angels) said: "We have been sent to a people who are Mujrimeen (criminals, disbelievers, polytheists, sinners). (All) but the family of Lut. Them all we are surely going to save (from destruction)." Except his wife, of whom We have decreed that she shall be of those who remain behind (she will be destroyed). Then when the Messengers (the angels) came unto the family of Lot, he said: "Verily! You are people unknown to me." They said: "Nay! We have come to you with that (torment) which they have been doubting.

And we have brought to you the truth (the news of the destruction of your nation) and certainly, we tell the truth. Then travel in a part of the night with your family, and you go behind them in the rear, and let no one amongst you look back, but go on to where you are ordered." And We made known this decree to him that the root of those (sinners) was to be cut off in the early morning. The inhabitants of the city came rejoicing (at the news of the young men's arrival). Lot said: "Verily! These are my guests, so shame me not. And fear Allah and disgrace me not."

They (people of the city) said: "Did we not forbid you to entertain (or protect) any of the Alamin (people, foreigner, strangers etc.) from us?" Lut said: "These (the girls of the nation) are my daughters to marry lawfully) if you must act so." Verily, by your life (O Muhammad), in their wild intoxication they were wandering blindly. So As Saliha (torment, awful cry etc.) overtook them at the time of sunrise; and We turned (the towns of Sodom in Palestine) upside down and rained down on them stones of baked clay. Surely! In this are signs for those who see (or understand or learn the lessons from the Signs of Allah). And verily! They (the cities) are right on the highroad (from Mecca to Syria, i.e. the place where the Dead Sea is now). Surely! Therein is indeed a sign for the believers." [15:51-77]

Allah the Exalted also declared: "So we saved him and his family, all, except an old woman (his wife) among those who remained behind. Then afterward We destroyed the others. We rained on them a rain of torment. How evil was the rain of those who had been warned. Verily, in this is indeed a sign yet most of them are not believers. Verily! Your Lord, He is indeed the All Mighty, the Most Merciful." [26:170-175]

## Lut's Life after Sodom

The book was closed on the people of Lut (peace be upon him). Their towns and names have been erased from the face of the earth. Gone are they from memory. One book was closed of the books of corruption. Lut proceeded towards Abraham (peace be upon him). He visited him, and when he recounted the story of his people, he was surprised to learn that Abraham already knew. So Lut continued to invite people to Allah, as did Abraham (pbuh), the patient one who turned to Allah repentantly, and the two held firm to their mission. And We delivered him and Lot to the land which We had blessed for the worlds. [21:71]

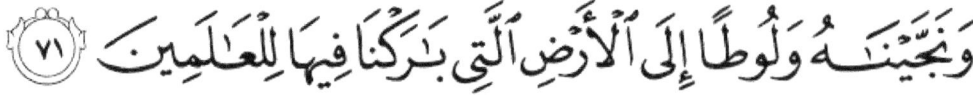

# Prophet Shu'aib

Allah the Almighty revealed the story of Shu'aib (pbuh): "And to [the people of] Madyan [We sent] their brother Shu'ayb. He said, "O my people, worship Allah; you have no deity other than Him. There has come to you clear evidence from your Lord. So fulfill the measure and weight and do not deprive people of their due and cause not corruption upon the earth after its reformation. That is better for you, if you are believers." [7:85]

وَإِلَىٰ مَدْيَنَ أَخَاهُمْ شُعَيْبًا ۗ قَالَ يَٰقَوْمِ ٱعْبُدُوا۟ ٱللَّهَ مَا لَكُم مِّنْ إِلَٰهٍ غَيْرُهُ ۖ قَدْ جَآءَتْكُم بَيِّنَةٌ مِّن رَّبِّكُمْ ۖ فَأَوْفُوا۟ ٱلْكَيْلَ وَٱلْمِيزَانَ وَلَا تَبْخَسُوا۟ ٱلنَّاسَ أَشْيَآءَهُمْ وَلَا تُفْسِدُوا۟ فِى ٱلْأَرْضِ بَعْدَ إِصْلَٰحِهَا ۚ ذَٰلِكُمْ خَيْرٌ لَّكُمْ إِن كُنتُم مُّؤْمِنِينَ ﴿٨٥﴾

The chiefs of those who were arrogant among his people said: "We shall certainly drive you out, O Shu'aib, and those who have believed with you from our town, or else you (all) shall return to our religion." He said: "Even though we hate it! [7:88]

﴿ قَالَ ٱلْمَلَأُ ٱلَّذِينَ ٱسْتَكْبَرُوا۟ مِن قَوْمِهِۦ لَنُخْرِجَنَّكَ يَٰشُعَيْبُ وَٱلَّذِينَ ءَامَنُوا۟ مَعَكَ مِن قَرْيَتِنَآ أَوْ لَتَعُودُنَّ فِى مِلَّتِنَا ۚ قَالَ أَوَلَوْ كُنَّا كَٰرِهِينَ ﴿٨٨﴾

The chiefs of those who disbelieved among his people said (to their people): "If you follow Shu'aib, be sure then you will be the losers!" [7:90]

$$وَقَالَ ٱلْمَلَأُ ٱلَّذِينَ كَفَرُوا۟ مِن قَوْمِهِۦ لَئِنِ ٱتَّبَعْتُمْ شُعَيْبًا إِنَّكُمْ إِذًا لَّخَـٰسِرُونَ ۝٩٠$$

The people of Madyan were Arabs who lived in the country of Maan, part of which today is Syria. They were a greedy people who did not believe that Allah existed and who led a very wicked live. They gave short measure, praised their goods beyond their worth, and hid their defects. They lied to their customers, thereby cheating them. Allah sent His Prophet Shu'aib (pbuh) armed with many miracles. Shu'aib preached to them, begging them to be mindful of Allah's favors and warning them of the consequences of their evil ways, but they only mocked him. Shu'aib remained calm as he reminded them of his kinship to them and that what he was doing was not for his personal gain. They seized the belongings of Shu'aib and his followers, then drove them out of the city. The Messenger turned to his Lord for help, and his plea was answered. Allah sent down on them scorching heat and they suffered terribly. On seeing a cloud gathering in the sky, they thought it would bring cool, refreshing rain, and rushed outside in the hope of enjoying the rainfall. Instead the cloud burst, hurling thunderbolts and fire. They heard a thunderous sound from above which caused the earth under their feet to tremble. The evil doers perished in this state of horror. "So each We seized for his sin; and among them were those upon whom We sent a storm of stones, and among them were those who were seized by the blast [from the sky], and among them were those whom We caused the earth to swallow, and among them were those whom We drowned. And Allah would not have wronged them, but it was they who were wronging themselves." [29:40]

$$فَكُلًّا أَخَذْنَا بِذَنۢبِهِۦ ۖ فَمِنْهُم مَّنْ أَرْسَلْنَا عَلَيْهِ حَاصِبًا وَمِنْهُم مَّنْ أَخَذَتْهُ ٱلصَّيْحَةُ وَمِنْهُم مَّنْ خَسَفْنَا بِهِ ٱلْأَرْضَ وَمِنْهُم مَّنْ أَغْرَقْنَا ۚ وَمَا كَانَ ٱللَّهُ لِيَظْلِمَهُمْ وَلَـٰكِن كَانُوٓا۟ أَنفُسَهُمْ يَظْلِمُونَ ۝٤٠$$

## The Disbeliever's Ignorance

Allah the Exalted stated: The dwellers of Al Aiyka (near Midian, or Madyan) belied the Messengers. When Shu'aib said to them: "Will you not fear Allah and obey Him? I am a trustworthy Messenger to you. So fear Allah, keep your duty to Him, and obey me. No reward do I ask of you for it (my message of Islamic Monotheism), my reward is only from the Lord of the Alamin (mankind, jinn and all that exists). Give full measure, and cause no loss to others. And weigh with the true and straight balance. Defraud not people by reducing their things nor do evil making corruption and mischief in the land. Fear Him Who created you and the generations of the men of old."

They said: "You are only one of those bewitched! You are but a human being like us and verily, we think that you are one of the liars! So cause a piece of heaven to fall on us, if you are of the truthful!" [26:185-189]

قَالُوٓا۟ إِنَّمَآ أَنتَ مِنَ ٱلْمُسَحَّرِينَ ﴿١٨٥﴾

وَمَآ أَنتَ إِلَّا بَشَرٌ مِّثْلُنَا وَإِن نَّظُنُّكَ لَمِنَ ٱلْكَٰذِبِينَ ﴿١٨٦﴾

فَأَسْقِطْ عَلَيْنَا كِسَفًا مِّنَ ٱلسَّمَآءِ إِن كُنتَ مِنَ ٱلصَّٰدِقِينَ ﴿١٨٧﴾

He said, "My Lord is most knowing of what you do."

قَالَ رَبِّىٓ أَعْلَمُ بِمَا تَعْمَلُونَ ﴿١٨٨﴾

And they denied him, so the punishment of the day of the black cloud seized them. Indeed, it was the punishment of a terrible day.

فَكَذَّبُوهُ فَأَخَذَهُمْ عَذَابُ يَوْمِ ٱلظُّلَّةِ ۚ إِنَّهُۥ كَانَ عَذَابَ يَوْمٍ عَظِيمٍ ﴿١٨٩﴾

# Prophet Yusuf (Joseph)

And We gave to Abraham, Isaac and Jacob - all [of them] We guided. And Noah, We guided before; and among his descendants, David and Solomon and Job and Joseph and Moses and Aaron. Thus do We reward the doers of good. [6:84]

وَوَهَبْنَا لَهُ إِسْحَٰقَ وَيَعْقُوبَ كُلًّا هَدَيْنَا وَنُوحًا هَدَيْنَا مِن قَبْلُ وَمِن ذُرِّيَّتِهِۦ دَاوُۥدَ وَسُلَيْمَٰنَ وَأَيُّوبَ وَيُوسُفَ وَمُوسَىٰ وَهَٰرُونَ وَكَذَٰلِكَ نَجْزِى ٱلْمُحْسِنِينَ ۝

Prophet Yusuf's story is the most detailed and fascinating story in the Quran, involving both human weaknesses such as jealousy, hatred, pride, passion, deception, intrigue, cruelty, and terror as well as noble qualities such as patience, loyalty, bravery, nobility, and compassion. It is related that among the reasons for its revelation is that the Jews asked the Prophet Muhammad (pbuh) to tell them about Joseph (pbuh) who was one of their old prophets. His story had been distorted in parts and marred in others with interpolation and exclusions. Therefore it was revealed in the Book of Allah (Quran), complete in its minute and careful details. Allah the Almighty declared: "We relate to you, [O Muhammad], the best of stories in what We have revealed to you of this Qur'an although you were, before it, among the unaware." [12:3]

نَحْنُ نَقُصُّ عَلَيْكَ أَحْسَنَ ٱلْقَصَصِ بِمَا أَوْحَيْنَا إِلَيْكَ هَٰذَا ٱلْقُرْءَانَ وَإِن كُنتَ مِن قَبْلِهِۦ لَمِنَ ٱلْغَٰفِلِينَ ۝

The story of Joseph (pbuh) moves in a stream from beginning to end; its substance and form are equally coherent. It inspires you with a feeling for the depth of Allah's power and supremacy and the execution of His rulings despite the challenge of human intervention. We established Joseph in the land that We might teach him the interpretation of events. And Allah is predominant over His affair, but most of the people do not know. [12:21]

## Summary of Joseph's Story

Joseph lived all his life confronting schemes made by the people closest to him. His brothers plotted to kill him, but they amended it to exiling him. This happened to him while he was a boy. He was sold into the slave market in Egypt, where he was bought for a nominal sum. Then he fell victim to the attempted seduction by a great man's wife who, when her wish was foiled, sent him to prison, where he remained for some time. In spite of all of this, he at length approached close to the Egyptian throne and became the king's chief minister. He then began his call to Allah from the position of the ruling authority. Allah's plans were carried out, and the matter ended. The story is presented in a sequence of episodes. It gives you scene after scene and the transition is inspiring, informative, and stirring to the imagination. There are also artistic loopholes, which leave it to the imagination of the reader to complete the sense, as well as the depth of the picture, the like of which no human artist can bring forth.

## Joseph's Childhood

The story begins with a dream and ends with its interpretation. As the sun appeared over the horizon, bathing the earth in its morning glory, Joseph (pbuh), son of the Prophet Jacob (pbuh) awoke from his sleep, delighted by a pleasant dream he had had. Filled with excitement he ran to his father and related it. "O my father, indeed I have seen [in a dream] eleven stars and the sun and the moon; I saw them prostrating to me." [12:4]

إِذْ قَالَ يُوسُفُ لِأَبِيهِ يَٰٓأَبَتِ إِنِّى رَأَيْتُ أَحَدَ عَشَرَ كَوْكَبًا وَٱلشَّمْسَ وَٱلْقَمَرَ رَأَيْتُهُمْ لِى سَٰجِدِينَ ۝

His father's face lit up. He foresaw that Joseph would be one through whom the prophecy of his grandfather, Prophet Abraham (pbuh), would be fulfilled, in that his offspring would keep the light of Abraham's house alive and spread Allah's message to mankind. Jacob said, "O my son, do not relate your vision to your brothers or they will contrive against you a plan. Indeed Satan, to man, is a manifest enemy." [12:5]

قَالَ يَٰبُنَىَّ لَا تَقْصُصْ رُءْيَاكَ عَلَىٰٓ إِخْوَتِكَ فَيَكِيدُوا۟ لَكَ كَيْدًا إِنَّ ٱلشَّيْطَٰنَ لِلْإِنسَٰنِ عَدُوٌّ مُّبِينٌ ۝

Joseph heeded his father's warning. He did not tell his brothers what he had seen. It is well known that they hated him so much that it was difficult for him to feel secure telling them what was in his heart and in his dreams. "Certainly were there in Joseph and his brothers signs for those who ask." [12:7]

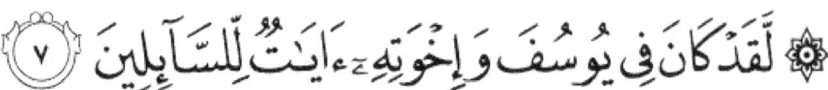

### Description of Joseph

Joseph was eighteen years old, very handsome and robust, with a gentle temperament. He was respectful, kind and considerate. His brother Benjamin was equally pleasant. Both were from one mother, Rachel. Because of their refined qualities, the father loved the two more than his other children, and would not let them out of his sight. To protect them, he kept them busy with work in the house garden.

### The Evil Plot of Joseph's Brothers

The scene of Jacob and his son closes. Another opens on Joseph's brothers plotting against him. "Truly, Joseph and his brother (Benjamin) are loved more by our father than we, but we are Usbah (a strong group). Really our father is in a plain error. Kill Joseph or cast him out to some other land, so that the favor of your father may be given to you alone, and after that you will be righteous folk (by intending repentance before committing the sin)." Said a speaker among them, "Do not kill Joseph but throw him into the bottom of the well; some travelers will pick him up - if you would do [something]." (12:8-10)

إِذْ قَالُواْ لَيُوسُفُ وَأَخُوهُ أَحَبُّ إِلَىٰ أَبِينَا مِنَّا وَنَحْنُ عُصْبَةٌ إِنَّ أَبَانَا لَفِى ضَلَٰلٍ مُّبِينٍ ۝

ٱقْتُلُواْ يُوسُفَ أَوِ ٱطْرَحُوهُ أَرْضًا يَخْلُ لَكُمْ وَجْهُ أَبِيكُمْ وَتَكُونُواْ مِنۢ بَعْدِهِۦ قَوْمًا صَٰلِحِينَ ۝

$$\text{قَالَ قَآئِلٌ مِّنْهُمْ لَا تَقْتُلُوا۟ يُوسُفَ وَأَلْقُوهُ فِى غَيَـٰبَتِ ٱلْجُبِّ يَلْتَقِطْهُ بَعْضُ ٱلسَّيَّارَةِ إِن كُنتُمْ فَـٰعِلِينَ ۝١٠}$$

The pages of the Old Testament say that Joseph told them his dream, whereas the Quran does not say that happened. Had it been so, the brothers would have said so themselves. The Old Testament claims they had lost their own rights by him, and so they would kill him. Indeed Joseph kept his father's order and did not tell his brothers about his vision. The brothers sat down to conspire against him. One of them asked: "Why does our father love Joseph more than us?" Another answered: "Perhaps because of his beauty." A third said: "Joseph and his brother occupied our father's heart." The first complained: "Our father has gone all astray." One of them suggested a solution to the matter; kill Joseph. "Where should we kill him?" "We should banish him away from these grounds." "We will send him to a distant land." "Why should we not kill him and have rest so that the favor of your father may be given to you alone?" However, Judah (Yahudh), the eldest and most intelligent among them, said: "There is no need to kill him when all you want is to get rid of him. Look here, let us throw him into a well and he will be picked up by a passing caravan. They will take him with them to a distant land. He will disappear from your father's sight and our purpose will be served with his exile. Then after that we shall repent for our crime and become good people once again."

The discussion continued on the idea of dropping Joseph into a well, as it was seen as the safest solution. The plan to kill him was defeated; kidnap into a distant land was approved.

## The Brothers Approach Jacob

Their next movement opened the scene between them and their father Jacob (pbuh). They said, "O our father, why do you not entrust us with Joseph while indeed, we are to him sincere counselors. Send him with us tomorrow that he may eat well and play. And indeed, we will be his guardians." [12:11-12]

$$\text{قَالُوا۟ يَـٰٓأَبَانَا مَا لَكَ لَا تَأْمَنَّا عَلَىٰ يُوسُفَ وَإِنَّا لَهُۥ لَنَـٰصِحُونَ ۝١١}$$

$$\text{أَرْسِلْهُ مَعَنَا غَدًا يَرْتَعْ وَيَلْعَبْ وَإِنَّا لَهُۥ لَحَـٰفِظُونَ ۝١٢}$$

[Jacob] said, "Indeed, it saddens me that you should take him, and I fear that a wolf would eat him while you are of him unaware." [12:13]

$$\قَالَ إِنِّي لَيَحْزُنُنِي أَن تَذْهَبُوا۟ بِهِ وَأَخَافُ أَن يَأْكُلَهُ ٱلذِّئْبُ وَأَنتُمْ عَنْهُ غَافِلُونَ ﴿١٣﴾$$

They said, "If a wolf should eat him while we are a [strong] clan, indeed, we would then be losers." [12:14]

$$\قَالُوا۟ لَئِنْ أَكَلَهُ ٱلذِّئْبُ وَنَحْنُ عُصْبَةٌ إِنَّا إِذًا لَّخَٰسِرُونَ ﴿١٤﴾$$

Jacob suggested a point, which had not occurred to them in their discussion: he feared that desert wolves would eat him! The wolves within them, or did he mean the wild wolves? No one but Allah knows. They coaxed their father to send Joseph with them; he agreed under their pressure.

### Joseph Thrown into the Well

They were excited that they could now get rid of Joseph for after this they could stand a better chance of receiving their father's affection. On leaving home, they went directly to the well, as they had planned, on the pretext of drinking water. One of them put his arms around Joseph and held him tightly. Startled by this unusual behavior, Joseph struggled to free himself. More brothers rushed to hold him. One of them removed his shirt. Some more joined in to lift Joseph up and cast him into the deep well. Joseph's piteous pleas made no difference to their cruel hearts. Then Allah revealed to Joseph that he was safe and should not fear, for he would meet them again someday to remind them of what they had done. There was water in the well, which buoyed Joseph's body, so he was not harmed. He sat lonely in the water, then clung to a rock ledge overheard and climbed on top of it. His brothers left him in this desolate place. Then they killed a sheep and soaked Joseph's shirt in its blood. One brother said that they should swear to keep their deed a close secret. All of them took the oath. And they came to their father at night, weeping. The scene here is dark night, broken by the crying of ten men. The father is sitting in his house when the sons enter, the darkness of night covering the darkness of their hearts and the darkness of their lies struggling to come out. Jacob wondered aloud: "Why this weeping? Has anything happened to our flock?"

They answered crying: They said, "O our father, indeed we went racing each other and left Joseph with our possessions, and a wolf ate him. But you would not believe us, even if we were truthful." [12:17]

$$\text{قَالُوا۟ يَـٰٓأَبَانَآ إِنَّا ذَهَبْنَا نَسْتَبِقُ وَتَرَكْنَا يُوسُفَ عِندَ مَتَـٰعِنَا فَأَكَلَهُ ٱلذِّئْبُ ۖ وَمَآ أَنتَ بِمُؤْمِنٍ لَّنَا وَلَوْ كُنَّا صَـٰدِقِينَ ﴿١٧﴾}$$

And they brought upon his shirt false blood. [Jacob] said, "Rather, your souls have enticed you to something, so patience is most fitting. And Allah is the one sought for help against that which you describe." [12:18]

$$\text{وَجَآءُو عَلَىٰ قَمِيصِهِۦ بِدَمٍ كَذِبٍ ۚ قَالَ بَلْ سَوَّلَتْ لَكُمْ أَنفُسُكُمْ أَمْرًا ۖ فَصَبْرٌ جَمِيلٌ ۖ وَٱللَّهُ ٱلْمُسْتَعَانُ عَلَىٰ مَا تَصِفُونَ ﴿١٨﴾}$$

Deep down in the heart Jacob knew that his beloved son was still alive and that his other sons were lying. He held the blood stained shirt in his hands, spread it out and remarked: "What a merciful wolf! He ate up my beloved son without tearing his shirt!" Their faces turned red when he demanded more information, but each swore by Allah that he was telling the truth. The father acted wisely by praying for mighty patience, which is free of doubt, and by trusting in Allah for help against what they had plotted against him and his son. This scene dims, and the scene opens in the well with which Joseph had been thrown.

## Joseph Finds Comfort in Allah

In the dark well Joseph managed to find a stone ledge to hold onto. Around him was total darkness and an eerie silence. Fearful thoughts entered his mind: what would happen to him? Where would he find food? Why had his own brothers turned against him? Would his father know of his plight? His father's smile flashed before him recalling the love and affection he had always shown him. Joseph began to pray earnestly, pleading to Allah for salvation. Gradually his fear began to subside. His Creator was testing the young man with a great misfortune in order to infuse in him a spirit of patience and courage. Joseph, surrendered himself to the will of his Lord.

## Joseph from the Well to Slavery

The next scene shows the wide desert. At the horizon is a long line of camels, horses, and men; a caravan on its way to Egypt. The caravan of merchants halted at this famous well for water. A man lowered in his bucket. Joseph was startled by the bucket hurtling down and grabbed hold of it before it could land in the water. As the man began to haul he felt the load unusually heavy, so he peeped into the well. What he saw shocked him; a boy was clinging to the rope! He held the rope tightly and shouted to his friends: "Better give me a hand fellows! Looks like I found real treasure in the well!" His companions rushed to the well and helped him to pull out the stranger holding onto the rope. Standing before them was a healthy, handsome youth, beaming with an angelic smile. They saw in him a handsome prize, for money was all that mattered to them. Immediately, they clapped iron shackles on his feet and took him along to Egypt, far away from his beloved homeland of Canaan. All over the Egyptian city the news spread that an unusually handsome, robust young slave was on sale. People gathered by the hundreds at the slave market. Some were spectators, others were bidders the elite and the rich, each one craning his neck to view the handsome specimen. The auctioneer had a field day as the bidding went wild, each buyer trying to outbid the other. Eventually, the Aziz, the chief minister of Egypt, outbid all the others and took Joseph to his mansion. "And they sold him for a reduced price - a few dirhams - and they were, concerning him, of those content with little." [12:20]

وَشَرَوْهُ بِثَمَنٍ بَخْسٍ دَرَاهِمَ مَعْدُودَةٍ وَكَانُواْ فِيهِ مِنَ ٱلزَّٰهِدِينَ ﴿٢٠﴾

"And the one from Egypt who bought him said to his wife, "Make his residence comfortable. Perhaps he will benefit us, or we will adopt him as a son." And thus, We established Joseph in the land that We might teach him the interpretation of events. And Allah is predominant over His affair, but most of the people do not know." [12:21]

وَقَالَ ٱلَّذِى ٱشْتَرَىٰهُ مِن مِّصْرَ لِٱمْرَأَتِهِۦٓ أَكْرِمِى مَثْوَىٰهُ عَسَىٰٓ أَن يَنفَعَنَآ أَوْ نَتَّخِذَهُۥ وَلَدًا وَكَذَٰلِكَ مَكَّنَّا لِيُوسُفَ فِى ٱلْأَرْضِ وَلِنُعَلِّمَهُۥ مِن تَأْوِيلِ ٱلْأَحَادِيثِ وَٱللَّهُ غَالِبٌ عَلَىٰٓ أَمْرِهِۦ وَلَٰكِنَّ أَكْثَرَ ٱلنَّاسِ لَا يَعْلَمُونَ ﴿٢١﴾

## Joseph's Master

What we see as hazards and slander is the first step of the ladder on Joseph's way to greatness. Allah is decisive in His action. His plan is carried out despite the plans of others and while theirs are still being made. So He spoils their plan, and Allah's promise is realized. Allah has promise Joseph (peace be upon him) prophethood. Love for Joseph was thrust into the heart of the man who bought him, and he was a man of no mean position. He was an important personage, one of the ruling class of Egypt. Therefore, Joseph was pleasantly surprised when the chief minister of Egypt ordered his men to remove the heavy shackles from his swollen feet. He was also surprised when he told Joseph not to betray his trust; he would not be ill- treated if he behaved himself. Joseph smiled at his benefactor, thanked him, and promised to be loyal.

Joseph felt at ease, for at last he was sheltered and would be well cared for. He thanked Allah. Over and over and wondered at the mysterious of life. Not so long ago he had been cast into a deep, dark well with no hope of ever coming out alive. Next he was rescued, then enslaved in iron shackles, and now he was moving freely in a luxurious mansion with enough food to enjoy. However, his heart ached with longing for his parents and Brother Benjamin, and he shed tears daily. Joseph was made the personal attendant of the chief minister's wife. He was obedient and ever-obliging. With his pleasant manners and charming behavior, he won everybody's heart. Joseph's handsomeness became the talk of the town. People referred to him as the most attractive man they had ever seen and wrote poetry about him. His face carried immaculate beauty. The purity of his inner soul and his heart showed in his face, increasing his beauty. People from afar came to the city to have a glimpse of him. The prettiest of maidens and the richest of ladies came to see him, but not once did he show haughtiness or conceit. He was always humble and polite.

## Joseph's Qualities

The days passed and Joseph grew. Almighty Allah said: "And when Joseph reached maturity, We gave him judgment and knowledge. And thus We reward the doers of good." [12:22]

وَلَمَّا بَلَغَ أَشُدَّهُ ءَاتَيْنَهُ حُكْمًا وَعِلْمًا وَكَذَلِكَ نَجْزِي ٱلْمُحْسِنِينَ ﴿٢٢﴾

He was given wisdom in affairs and knowledge of life and its conditions. He has given the art of conversation, captivating those who heard him. He was given nobility and self-restraint, which made him an irresistible personality. His master soon knew that Allah had graced him with Joseph.

He understood that Joseph was the most honest, straightforward and noble person he had met in his life. Therefore, he put Joseph in charge of his household, honored him, and treated him as a son.

## Zulaikha's Feelings for Joseph

The wife of the chief minister, Zulaikha, watched Joseph from day to day. She ate with him, talked with him, listened to him, and her love for Joseph increased. Joseph was soon confronted (with his second trial). Zulaikha could not resist the handsome Joseph, and her obsession with him caused her sleepless nights. She loved him very much, and it was very painful for her to be so close to Joseph, yet be unable to hold him. Yet, she was not a wayward woman, for in her position she could get any man she desired. By all accounts, she must have been a very pretty and intelligent lady, or why would the chief minister have chosen her of all the pretty women in the kingdom? Although she bore him no child, he would not take another wife, as he loved her passionately. The Quran raises the curtain on the scene of this fierce and devouring love on the part of the lady.

Allah the Almighty told us: And she, in whose house he was, sought to seduce him. She closed the doors and said, 'Come, you.' He said, '[I seek] the refuge of Allah. Indeed, he is my master, who has made good my residence. Indeed, wrongdoers will not succeed.' [12:23]

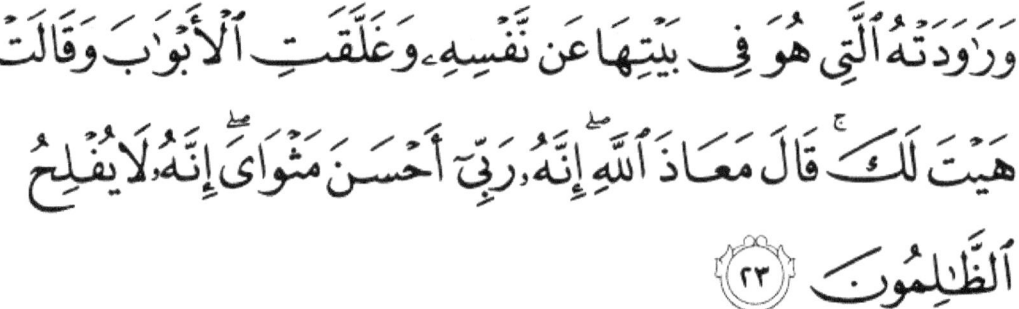

## Joseph's Feelings for Zulaikha

Commentators are unanimous about her intention of disobedience but disagree about his own intention. There are those who say that she tempted him and he tempted her to sin, although he did not follow through with his intent. Others say that she merely wanted him to kiss her, and he attempted to strike her. Yet others say that this anxiety had been there before this incident. There was a psychological disturbance in Joseph when he reached adolescence, which Almighty Allah rid him of.

The safest commentary for us is that there is temptation and resistance in the verse, for He Most High stated: "And she certainly determined [to seduce] him, and he would have inclined to her had he not seen the proof of his Lord. And thus [it was] that We should avert from him evil and immorality. Indeed, he was of Our chosen servants." [12:24]

$$\text{وَلَقَدْ هَمَّتْ بِهِ ۖ وَهَمَّ بِهَا لَوْلَا أَن رَّءَا بُرْهَٰنَ رَبِّهِ ۚ كَذَٰلِكَ لِنَصْرِفَ عَنْهُ ٱلسُّوٓءَ وَٱلْفَحْشَآءَ ۚ إِنَّهُۥ مِنْ عِبَادِنَا ٱلْمُخْلَصِينَ ﴿٢٤﴾}$$

Abu Ubaidah said that this is a temptation and resistance meaning that she had tried to seduce him; had he not seen the proof of Allah, he would have been seduced. This is in keeping with the infallibility of prophets, as it suits the words, which immediately follow: "Thus it was that We might turn away from forbidden sex. He was one of Our chosen, guided slaves." [12:24] This verse proves that Joseph was an upright worshipper of Allah; it also testifies to his rescue from the authority of Satan. The Almighty said to the devil (Iblis) on the Day of Creation: "Certainly, you shall no authority over My slaves, except those who follow you of the Ghawin (Mushrikeen, and those who go astray, criminals, polytheists, and evildoers, etc)" [15:42]

$$\text{إِنَّ عِبَادِى لَيْسَ لَكَ عَلَيْهِمْ سُلْطَٰنٌ إِلَّا مَنِ ٱتَّبَعَكَ مِنَ ٱلْغَاوِينَ ﴿٤٢﴾}$$

## Zulaikha's False Accusation

Joseph's refusal only heightened her passion. As he moved to the door to escape, she ran after him and caught hold of his shirt, like a drowning person clinging to the boat. In her tugging she tore his shirt and held the torn piece in her hand. They reached the door together. It opened suddenly, there stood her husband and a relative of hers. Almighty Allah said: And they both raced to the door, and she tore his shirt from the back, and they found her husband at the door. She said, "What is the recompense of one who intended evil for your wife but that he be imprisoned or a painful punishment?"

وَٱسْتَبَقَا ٱلْبَابَ وَقَدَّتْ قَمِيصَهُۥ مِن دُبُرٍ وَأَلْفَيَا سَيِّدَهَا لَدَا ٱلْبَابِ ۚ قَالَتْ مَا جَزَآءُ مَنْ أَرَادَ بِأَهْلِكَ سُوٓءًا إِلَّآ أَن يُسْجَنَ أَوْ عَذَابٌ أَلِيمٌ ﴿٢٥﴾

The sly woman immediately changed her tone to anger. She was now accusing Joseph of molesting her, to give the impression that she was innocent and a victim of Joseph's sexual desire. Though bewildered Joseph denied it: [Joseph] said, "It was she who sought to seduce me." And a witness from her family testified: "If his shirt is torn from the front, then she has told the truth, and he is of the liars. But if his shirt is torn from the back, then she has lied, and he is of the truthful."

قَالَ هِيَ رَٰوَدَتْنِي عَن نَّفْسِي ۚ وَشَهِدَ شَاهِدٌ مِّنْ أَهْلِهَآ إِن كَانَ قَمِيصُهُۥ قُدَّ مِن قُبُلٍ فَصَدَقَتْ وَهُوَ مِنَ ٱلْكَٰذِبِينَ ﴿٢٦﴾

The shirt was passed from hand to hand, while she watched. The witness (her cousin) looked at it and found that it was torn at the back. The evidence showed that she was guilty. The disappointed husband remarked to his wife: So when her husband saw his shirt torn from the back, he said, "Indeed, it is of the women's plan. Indeed, your plan is great." [12:28]

وَإِن كَانَ قَمِيصُهُۥ قُدَّ مِن دُبُرٍ فَكَذَبَتْ وَهُوَ مِنَ ٱلصَّٰدِقِينَ ﴿٢٧﴾

فَلَمَّا رَءَا قَمِيصَهُۥ قُدَّ مِن دُبُرٍ قَالَ إِنَّهُۥ مِن كَيْدِكُنَّ ۖ إِنَّ كَيْدَكُنَّ عَظِيمٌ ﴿٢٨﴾

The wise and just Aziz apologized to Joseph for his wife's indecency. He also instructed her to beg Joseph's forgiveness for accusing him falsely. "Joseph, ignore this. And, [my wife], ask forgiveness for your sin. Indeed, you were of the sinful."

$$\text{يُوسُفُ أَعْرِضْ عَنْ هَٰذَا ۚ وَاسْتَغْفِرِي لِذَنبِكِ ۖ إِنَّكِ كُنتِ مِنَ الْخَاطِئِينَ ﴿٢٩﴾}$$

### Zulaikha is ridiculed by the People

An incident like this cannot remain a secret in a house filled with servants, and the story spread. Women began to see her behavior as scandalous. They remarked: "The wife of Al-Aziz is seeking to seduce her (slave) young man, indeed she loves him violently; verily, we see her in plain error." [12:30]

$$\text{وَقَالَ نِسْوَةٌ فِي الْمَدِينَةِ امْرَأَتُ الْعَزِيزِ تُرَاوِدُ فَتَاهَا عَن نَّفْسِهِ ۖ قَدْ شَغَفَهَا حُبًّا ۖ إِنَّا لَنَرَاهَا فِي ضَلَالٍ مُّبِينٍ ﴿٣٠﴾}$$

Naturally their gossip distressed Zulaikha. She honestly believed that it was not easy for any women to resist a man as handsome as Joseph. To prove her helplessness, she planned to subject the women to the same temptation she faced. She invited them to a lavish banquet. No one so invited would want to miss the honor of dining with the chief minister's wife; besides, they secretly harbored the desire to meet the handsome Joseph face to face. Some of her close friends jokingly said they would come only if she introduced them to Joseph. The invitation was restricted to ladies. The banquet began, laughter and mirth abounded. Etiquette dictated that the ladies not mention the topic of Joseph. They were shocked, therefore, when Zulaikha opened the topic. "I have heard of those who say I have fallen in love with the young Hebrew man, Joseph." Silence fell upon the banquet. At once all the guests hands stopped, and all eyes fell on the chief minister's wife. She said, while giving orders for the fruit to be served: "I admit that he is charming fellow. I do not deny that I love him. I have loved him for a long time." The confession of the chief minister's wife removed the tension among the ladies. After finishing their dinner, the guests began cutting their fruit. At that very moment she summoned Joseph to make his appearance. He entered the hall gracefully, his gaze lowered. Zulaikha called him by his name and he raised his head. The guests were astonished and dumbfounded. His face was shining and full of man angelic beauty. It reflected complete innocence, so much so that one could feel the peace of mind in the depth of his soul. They exclaimed in astonishment while continuing to cut the fruit.

All their eyes were on Joseph. So it was that the women began to cut their palms without feeling that they had cut them. One of the ladies gasped: "Good gracious!" Another whispered: "This is not a mortal being!" Another stammered, patting her hair: "This is but a noble angel." Then the chief minister's wife stood up and announced: "This is the one for whom I have been blamed. I do not deny that I tempted him. You have been enchanted by Joseph, and see what has happened to your hands. I have tempted him, and if he does not do what I want of him he shall be imprisoned."

## The Women's Reaction - Quranic

Almighty Allah related the scene of the banquet in His words: So when she heard of their scheming, she sent for them and prepared for them a banquet and gave each one of them a knife and said [to Joseph], 'Come out before them.' And when they saw him, they greatly admired him and cut their hands and said, 'Perfect is Allah! This is not a man; this is none but a noble angel.' [12:31]

فَلَمَّا سَمِعَتْ بِمَكْرِهِنَّ أَرْسَلَتْ إِلَيْهِنَّ وَأَعْتَدَتْ لَهُنَّ مُتَّكَأً وَءَاتَتْ كُلَّ وَاحِدَةٍ مِنْهُنَّ سِكِّينًا وَقَالَتِ ٱخْرُجْ عَلَيْهِنَّ فَلَمَّا رَأَيْنَهُۥ أَكْبَرْنَهُۥ وَقَطَّعْنَ أَيْدِيَهُنَّ وَقُلْنَ حَٰشَ لِلَّهِ مَا هَٰذَا بَشَرًا إِنْ هَٰذَآ إِلَّا مَلَكٌ كَرِيمٌ ﴿٣١﴾

She said, "That is the one about whom you blamed me. And I certainly sought to seduce him, but he firmly refused; and if he will not do what I order him, he will surely be imprisoned and will be of those debased."

قَالَتْ فَذَٰلِكُنَّ ٱلَّذِى لُمْتُنَّنِى فِيهِ وَلَقَدْ رَٰوَدتُّهُۥ عَن نَّفْسِهِۦ فَٱسْتَعْصَمَ وَلَئِن لَّمْ يَفْعَلْ مَآ ءَامُرُهُۥ لَيُسْجَنَنَّ وَلَيَكُونًا مِّنَ ٱلصَّٰغِرِينَ ﴿٣٢﴾

She said, "This is he (the young man) about whom you did blame me (for his love) and I did seek to seduce him, but he refused. And now if he refuses to obey my order, he shall certainly be cast into prison, and will be one of those who are disgraced." He said: "O my Lord! Prison is more to my liking than that to which they invite me. Unless You turn away their plot from me, I will feel inclined towards them and be one of those who commit sin and deserve blame or those who do deeds of the ignorant."

So his Lord answered his prayer and turned away from him their plot. Verily he is the All Hearer, the All Knower." [12:31-34] That evening, Zulaikha convinced her husband that the only way to save her honor was to put Joseph in prison; otherwise she would not be able to control herself or to safeguard his prestige. The chief minister knew Joseph was absolutely innocent, that he was a young man of honor, a loyal servant, and he loved him for these reasons. It was not an easy decision for him to put an innocent man behind bars. However, he was left with no choice. He reasoned that Joseph's honor would also be safeguarded if he was kept out of Zulaikha's sight. That night, with a heavy heart, the minister sent Joseph to prison.

## Joseph's Time in Prison

Prison was Joseph's third test. During this period Allah blessed him with an extraordinary gift; the ability to interpret dreams. At about the same time two other men landed in the prison. One was the cupbearer of the king; the other was the king's cook. The two men sensed that Joseph was not a common criminal, for an aura of piety glowed on his face. Both men had vivid dreams, and they were anxious to have them explained. The king's cook dreamed that he stood in a place with bread on his head, and two birds were eating the bread. The cupbearer dreamed that he was serving the king wine. The two went to Joseph and told him their dreams, asking him to give them their meaning. First, Joseph called them to Allah. Then he said that the cook would be crucified until he died and that the cupbearer would return to the service of the king. Joseph told the cupbearer to remember him to the king and to say that there was a wronged soul called Joseph in prison. What Joseph predicted did happen; the cook was crucified and the cupbearer returned to the palace. After the cupbearer returned to service, Satan made him forget to mention Joseph's name to the king. Therefore, Joseph remained in prison for a few years, but he made patience his own, praying to Allah. Almighty Allah narrated: And there entered the prison with him two young men. One of them said, "Indeed, I have seen myself [in a dream] pressing wine." The other said, "Indeed, I have seen myself carrying upon my head [some] bread, from which the birds were eating. Inform us of its interpretation; indeed, we see you to be of those who do good." [12:37]

قَالَ لَا يَأْتِيكُمَا طَعَامٌ تُرْزَقَانِهِ إِلَّا نَبَّأْتُكُمَا بِتَأْوِيلِهِ قَبْلَ أَن يَأْتِيَكُمَا ذَٰلِكُمَا مِمَّا عَلَّمَنِي رَبِّي إِنِّي تَرَكْتُ مِلَّةَ قَوْمٍ لَّا يُؤْمِنُونَ بِاللَّهِ وَهُم بِالْآخِرَةِ هُمْ كَافِرُونَ ۝٣٧

He said, "You will not receive food that is provided to you except that I will inform you of its interpretation before it comes to you. That is from what my Lord has taught me. Indeed, I have left the religion of a people who do not believe in Allah, and they, in the Hereafter, are disbelievers." [12:38]

$$\text{وَاتَّبَعْتُ مِلَّةَ ءَابَآءِىٓ إِبْرَٰهِيمَ وَإِسْحَٰقَ وَيَعْقُوبَ ۚ مَا كَانَ لَنَآ أَن نُّشْرِكَ بِٱللَّهِ مِن شَىْءٍ ۚ ذَٰلِكَ مِن فَضْلِ ٱللَّهِ عَلَيْنَا وَعَلَى ٱلنَّاسِ وَلَٰكِنَّ أَكْثَرَ ٱلنَّاسِ لَا يَشْكُرُونَ ۝}$$

### The King's Dream

The scene in the prison closes; a new scene opens in the bedchamber of the king. The king is asleep. He sees himself on the banks of the Nile River. The water is receding before him, becoming mere mud. The fish begin to skip and jump in the mud. Seven fat cows come out of the river followed by seven lean cows. The seven lean ones devour the seven fat ones. The king is terrified. The seven ears of green grain grow on the riverbanks and disappear in the mud. One the same spot grow seven dray ears of grain. The king awoke frightened, shocked, and depressed, not knowing what all this meant. He sent for the sorcerers, priests and ministers, and told them his dream. The sorcerers said: "This is a mixed up dream. How can any of that be? It is a nightmare." The priests said: "Perhaps his majesty had a heavy supper." The chief minister said: "Could it be that his majesty was exposed and did not draw the blanket up at night?" The king's jester said, jokingly: "His majesty is beginning to grow old, and so his dreams are confused." They reached a unanimous conclusion that it was only a nightmare. The news reached the cupbearer. He recollected the dream he had in prison and compared it to the king's dream, and, therefore Joseph came to mind. He ran to the king to tell him about Joseph, who was the only one capable to interpreting the dream. The cupbearer said: "He had asked me to remember him to you, but I forgot." The king sent the cupbearer to ask Joseph about the dream.

### Joseph's Interpretation of the Dream

Joseph interpreted it to him: "There will be seven years of abundance. If the land is properly cultivated, there will be an excess of good harvest, more than the people will need. This should be stored. Thereafter, seven years of famine will follow, during which time the excess grain could be used." He also advised that during the famine they should save some grain to be used for seed for the next harvest. Joseph then added; "After seven years of drought, there will be a year during which water will be plentiful.

If the water is properly used, grapevines and olive trees will grow in abundance, providing plenty of grapes and olive oil." The cupbearer hurried back with the good news. The king was fascinated by Joseph's interpretation. The king was greatly astonished. Who could this person be? He commanded that Joseph be set free from prison and presented to him at once. The king's envoy went to fetch him immediately, but Joseph refused to leave the prison unless his innocence was proven. Perhaps they accused him of cutting the ladies hands, or trying to rape them. Perhaps any other false accusation was made. We do not know exactly what was said to the people to justify Joseph's sentence to prison. The envoy returned to the king. The king asked him: "Where is Joseph? Did I not command you to fetch him?" The envoy replied: "He refused to leave until his innocence is established regarding the ladies who cut their hands." The king ordered: "Bring the wives of the ministers and the wife of the chief minister at once." The king felt that Joseph had been harmed unfairly but he did not know exactly how. The wife of the chief minister came with the other ministers' wives. The king asked: "What is the story of Joseph? What do you know about him? Is it true that…?" One of the ladies interrupted the king exclaiming: "Allah forbid!" A second said "We know of no evil he has done." A third said: "He enjoys the innocence of angels." The eyes of everyone turned to the wife of the chief minister. She now wore a wrinkled face and had lost weight. She had been overwhelmed by sorrow over Joseph while he was in prison. She boldly confessed that she had lied and he had told the truth. "I tempted him; but he refused.: She confirmed what she said, not out of fear of the king or the other ladies, but for Joseph to know that she had never betrayed him during his absence, for he was still in her mind and soul. Of all creation he was the only one she cared for, so she confirmed his innocence before all. Almighty Allah narrated this incident thus: And the king of Egypt said, "Indeed, I have seen [in a dream] seven fat cows being eaten by seven [that were] lean, and seven green spikes [of grain] and others [that were] dry. O eminent ones, explain to me my vision, if you should interpret visions." [12:43]

وَقَالَ ٱلْمَلِكُ إِنِّىٓ أَرَىٰ سَبْعَ بَقَرَٰتٍ سِمَانٍ يَأْكُلُهُنَّ سَبْعٌ عِجَافٌ وَسَبْعَ سُنۢبُلَٰتٍ خُضْرٍ وَأُخَرَ يَابِسَٰتٍ ۖ يَٰٓأَيُّهَا ٱلْمَلَأُ أَفْتُونِى فِى رُءْيَٰىَ إِن كُنتُمْ لِلرُّءْيَا تَعْبُرُونَ ۝٤٣

[He said], "Joseph, O man of truth, explain to us about seven fat cows eaten by seven [that were] lean, and seven green spikes [of grain] and others [that were] dry - that I may return to the people; perhaps they will know [about you]." [12:46]

$$\text{يُوسُفُ أَيُّهَا الصِّدِّيقُ أَفْتِنَا فِي سَبْعِ بَقَرَاتٍ سِمَانٍ يَأْكُلُهُنَّ سَبْعٌ عِجَافٌ وَسَبْعِ سُنبُلَاتٍ خُضْرٍ وَأُخَرَ يَابِسَاتٍ لَّعَلِّي أَرْجِعُ إِلَى النَّاسِ لَعَلَّهُمْ يَعْلَمُونَ ۝}$$

[Joseph] said, "You will plant for seven years consecutively; and what you harvest leave in its spikes, except a little from which you will eat. Then will come after that seven difficult [years] which will consume what you saved for them, except a little from which you will store. Then will come after that a year in which the people will be given rain and in which they will press [olives and grapes]." [12-47-49]

### Zulaikha's Life Afterwards

Reflecting on these verses suggests that she had turned to Joseph's religion, monotheism. His imprisonment was a great turning point in her life. After this, the Quranic style neglects the story of the chief minister's wife completely. We do not know what happened to her after she gave her clear evidence. Yet still, there are legends about her. It has been said that after her husband died she married Joseph, and, behold she was a virgin. She confessed that her husband had been old and had never touched women. Other legends said that she lost her sight, weeping for Joseph. She abandoned her palace and wandered in the streets of the city. However, the lady disappeared from the Quranic narrative at the suitable stage, at the climax of her trouble. Perhaps she lingers in memory longer than if we had known the ending.

### Joseph's High Position

The king informed Joseph that his innocence was established and ordered him to come to the palace for an interview. The king recognized his noble qualities. When Joseph came, the king spoke to him in his tongue. Joseph's replies astonished the king with his cultural refinement and wide knowledge. Then the conversation turned to the dream. Joseph advised the king to start planning for years of famine ahead. He informed him that the famine would affect not only Egypt but the neighboring countries as well. The king offered him a high position. Joseph asked to be made controller of the granaries, so that he could guard the nation's harvest and thereby safeguard it during the anticipated drought. By this Joseph did not mean to seize an opportunity or personal gain; he merely wanted to rescue hungry nations for a personal gain; he merely wanted to rescue hungry nations for a period of seven years. It was a sheer nobleness on his part in that he wanted to ensure that many people would not die as a result.

## Joseph's High Position - Quranic

Almighty Allah said: And the king said, "Bring him to me; I will appoint him exclusively for myself." And when he spoke to him, he said, "Indeed, you are today established [in position] and trusted." [12:54]

وَقَالَ ٱلْمَلِكُ ٱئْتُونِى بِهِۦٓ أَسْتَخْلِصْهُ لِنَفْسِى ۖ فَلَمَّا كَلَّمَهُۥ قَالَ إِنَّكَ ٱلْيَوْمَ لَدَيْنَا مَكِينٌ أَمِينٌ ﴿٥٤﴾

[Joseph] said, "Appoint me over the storehouses of the land. Indeed, I will be a knowing guardian." [12:55]

قَالَ ٱجْعَلْنِى عَلَىٰ خَزَآئِنِ ٱلْأَرْضِ ۖ إِنِّى حَفِيظٌ عَلِيمٌ ﴿٥٥﴾

(As a minister of finance in Egypt, in place of Al-Aziz who was dead at that time). And thus We established Joseph in the land to settle therein wherever he willed. We touch with Our mercy whom We will, and We do not allow to be lost the reward of those who do good. [12:56]

## Joseph Meets His Brothers

The wheels of time turned. During the seven good years, Joseph had full control over the cultivation, harvesting, and storage of crops. During the following seven years, drought followed and famine spread throughout the region, including Canaan, the homeland of Joseph. Joseph advised the king that as his kingdom was blessed with reserved grain, he should sell his grain to the needy nations at a fair price. The king agreed, and the good news spread all over the region. Jacob sent ten of his sons, all except Benjamin, to Egypt to purchase provisions. Joseph heard of the ten brothers who had come from afar and who could not speak the language of the Egyptians. When they called on him to purchase their needs, Joseph immediately recognized his brothers, but they did not know him. How could they? To them Joseph no longer existed; he had been thrown into the deep, dark well many years ago! Joseph received them warmly. After supplying them with provisions, he asked where they had come from. They explained: "We are eleven brothers, the children of a noble prophet. The youngest is at home tending to the needs of our aging father." On hearing this, Joseph's eyes filled with tears; his longing for home swelled up in his heart, as well as his longing for his beloved parents and his loving brother Benjamin. "Are you truthful people?" Joseph asked them. Perturbed they replied, "What reason should we have to state an untruth?" "If what you say is true then bring your brother as proof and I will reward you with double rations. But if you do not bring him to me, it would be better if you do not return," Joseph warned them.

They assured him that they would gladly fulfill his command but that they would have to get their father's permission. As an inducement to return with their brother, Joseph ordered his servant to secretly place the purse, with the money they had paid, into one of their grain sacks.

## Joseph Meets His Brothers - Quranic

Allah the Almighty said: "And the brothers of Joseph came [seeking food], and they entered upon him; and he recognized them, but he was to them unknown." [12:58]

وَجَاءَ إِخْوَةُ يُوسُفَ فَدَخَلُوا عَلَيْهِ فَعَرَفَهُمْ وَهُمْ لَهُ مُنكِرُونَ ۝

And when he had furnished them with their supplies, he said, "Bring me a brother of yours from your father. Do not you see that I give full measure and that I am the best of accommodators? But if you do not bring him to me, no measure will there be [hereafter] for you from me, nor will you approach me." They said, "We will attempt to dissuade his father from [keeping] him, and indeed, we will do [it]." And [Joseph] said to his servants, "Put their merchandise into their saddlebags so they might recognize it when they have gone back to their people that perhaps they will [again] return." [12:59-62]

## The Brothers Return to Canaan

The scene dims in Egypt and lights in Canaan. The brothers returned to their father. Before they could unload the camels, they greeted him, then reproved him: "We were denied some supplies because you did not let your son go with us. They would not give us food for absentees. Why would you not entrust him with us? Please, send him with us, and we shall take care of him." Jacob became sad and told them: "I will not permit Benjamin to travel with you. I will not part with him, for I entrusted Joseph to you and you failed me." Later, when they opened their grain sacks, they were surprised to find the money purse returned intact. They rushed to their father; "Look, father! The noble official has returned our money; this is surely proof that he would not harm our brother and it can only benefit us." But Jacob refused to send Benjamin with them. After some time, when they had no more grain, Jacob asked them to travel to Egypt for more. They reminded him of the warning the Egyptian official had given them. They could not return without Benjamin. Jacob agreed, but not before he extracted a pledge from them. "I will not send him with you unless you give me a pledge in Allah's name that you shall bring him back to me as safely as you take him." They gave their solemn pledge. He reminded them: "Allah is witness to your pledge." He advised them to enter the city through several different gates.

### The Brothers Return to Canaan - Quranic

So when they returned to their father, they said, "O our father, [further] measure has been denied to us, so send with us our brother [that] we will be given measure. And indeed, we will be his guardians." [12:63-67]

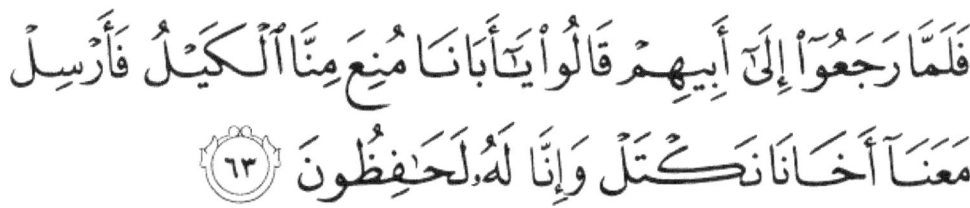

He said, "Should I entrust you with him except [under coercion] as I entrusted you with his brother before? But Allah is the best guardian, and He is the most merciful of the merciful." And when they opened our father, what [more] could we desire? This is our merchandise returned to us. And we will obtain their baggage, they found their merchandise returned to them. They said, "O supplies for our family and protect our brother and obtain an increase of a camel's load; that is an easy measurement." [Jacob] said, "Never will I send him with you until you give me a promise by Allah that you will bring him [back] to me, unless you should be surrounded by enemies." And when they had given their promise, he said, "Allah, over what we say, is Witness." And he said, "O my sons, do not enter from one gate but enter from different gates; and I cannot avail you against [the decree of] Allah at all. The decision is only for Allah; upon Him I have relied, and upon Him let those who would rely [indeed] rely."

### Joseph and Benjamin Meet

Joseph welcomed them heartily, although, with difficulty, he suppressed the desire to embrace Benjamin that arose within him. He prepared a feast for them and seated them in pairs. Joseph arranged to sit next to his beloved brother Benjamin, who began to weep. Joseph asked him why he was crying. He replied: "If my brother Joseph had been here, I would have sat next to him." That night, when Joseph and Benjamin were alone in a room, Joseph asked whether he would have him for a brother. Benjamin respectfully answered that he regarded his host as a wonderful person, but he could never take the place of his brother. Joseph broke down, and amidst flowing tears said; "My loving brother, I am the brother who was lost and whose name you are constantly repeating. Fate has brought us together after many years of separation. This is Allah's favor. But let it be a secret between us for the time being." Benjamin hugged Joseph and both brothers shed tears of joy. The next day, while their bags were being filled with grains to load onto the camels, Joseph ordered one of his attendants to place the king's gold cup which was used for measuring the grain into Benjamin's saddlebag.

When the brothers were ready to set out, the gates were locked, and the court crier shouted: "O you travelers, you are thieves!" The accusation was most unusual, and the people gathered around Joseph's brothers. "What have you lost?" his brothers inquired. A soldier said: "The king's golden cup. Whoever can trace it we will give a beast load of grain." Joseph's brothers said with all innocence: "We have not come here to corrupt the land and steal." Joseph's officers said (as he had instructed them): What punishment should you choose for the thief?" The brothers answered: "According to our law, whoever steals becomes a slave to the owner of the property."

The officers agreed: "We shall apply your law instead of the Egyptian law, which provides for imprisonment." The chief officer ordered his soldiers to start searching the caravan. Joseph was watching the incident from high upon his throne. He had given instructions for Benjamin's bag to be the last to be searched. When they did not find the cup in the bags of the ten older brothers, the brothers sighed in relief.

## Benjamin is accused

There remained only the bag of their youngest brother. Joseph said, intervening for the first time, that there was no need to search his saddle as he did not look like a thief. His brothers affirmed: "We will not move an inch unless his saddle is searched as well. We are the sons of a noble man, not thieves." The soldiers reached in their hands and pulled out the king's cup. The brothers exclaimed: "If he steals now, a brother of his has stolen before." They strayed from the present issue in order to blame a particular group of the children of Jacob. Joseph heard their resentment with his own ears and was filled with regret. Yet, he swallowed his own resentment, keeping it within. He said to himself, "you went further and fared worse; it shall go bad with you and worse hereafter, and Allah knows your intention." Silence fell upon them after these remarks by the brothers. Then they forgot their secret satisfaction and thought of Jacob; they had taken an oath with him that they would not betray his son.

They began to beg Joseph for mercy. "Joseph, O minister! Take one of us instead. He is the son of a good man, and you are a good man." Joseph answered calmly: "How can you want to set free the man who has stolen the king's cup? It would be sinful." The brothers went on pleading for mercy. However, the guards said that the king had spoken and his word was law. Judah, the eldest, was much worried and told the others: "We promised our father in the name of Allah not to fail him. I will, therefore, stay behind and will only return if my father permits me to do so."

## Joseph Meets Benjamin and the Accusation - Quranic

So when he had furnished them with their supplies, he put the [gold measuring] bowl into the bag of his brother. Then an announcer called out, "O caravan, indeed you are thieves." They said while approaching them, "What is it you are missing?" [12:70-71]

فَلَمَّا جَهَّزَهُم بِجَهَازِهِمْ جَعَلَ ٱلسِّقَايَةَ فِى رَحْلِ أَخِيهِ ثُمَّ أَذَّنَ مُؤَذِّنٌ أَيَّتُهَا ٱلْعِيرُ إِنَّكُمْ لَسَٰرِقُونَ ﴿٧٠﴾ قَالُوا۟ وَأَقْبَلُوا۟ عَلَيْهِم مَّاذَا تَفْقِدُونَ ﴿٧١﴾

They said, "We are missing the measure of the king. And for he who produces it is [the reward of] a camel's load, and I am responsible for it." [12:72]

قَالُوا۟ نَفْقِدُ صُوَاعَ ٱلْمَلِكِ وَلِمَن جَآءَ بِهِۦ حِمْلُ بَعِيرٍ وَأَنَا۠ بِهِۦ زَعِيمٌ ﴿٧٢﴾

They said, "By Allah, you have certainly known that we did not come to cause corruption in the land, and we have not been thieves." The accusers said, "Then what would be its recompense if you should be liars?" [The brothers] said, "Its recompense is that he in whose bag it is found - he [himself] will be its recompense. Thus do we recompense the wrongdoers." So he began [the search] with their bags before the bag of his brother; then he extracted it from the bag of his brother. Thus did We plan for Joseph. He could not have taken his brother within the religion of the king except that Allah willed. We raise in degrees whom We will, but over every possessor of knowledge is one [more] knowing. They said, "If he steals - a brother of his has stolen before." But Joseph kept it within himself and did not reveal it to them. He said, "You are worse in position, and Allah is most knowing of what you describe." They said, "O 'Azeez, indeed he has a father [who is] an old man, so take one of us in place of him. Indeed, we see you as a doer of good." He said, "[I seek] the refuge of Allah [to prevent] that we take except him with whom we found our possession. Indeed, we would then be unjust." [12:72-79]

So when they had despaired of him, they secluded themselves in private consultation. The eldest of them said, "Do you not know that your father has taken upon you an oath by Allah and [that] before you failed in [your duty to] Joseph? So I will never leave [this] land until my father permits me or Allah decides for me, and He is the best of judges."

Return to your father and say, "O our father, indeed your son has stolen, and we did not testify except to what we knew. And we were not witnesses of the unseen." [12:80-81]

$$\text{ٱرْجِعُوٓا۟ إِلَىٰٓ أَبِيكُمْ فَقُولُوا۟ يَـٰٓأَبَانَآ إِنَّ ٱبْنَكَ سَرَقَ وَمَا شَهِدْنَآ إِلَّا بِمَا عَلِمْنَا وَمَا كُنَّا لِلْغَيْبِ حَـٰفِظِينَ ۝٨١}$$

$$\text{ٱرْجِعُوٓا۟ إِلَىٰٓ أَبِيكُمْ فَقُولُوا۟ يَـٰٓأَبَانَآ إِنَّ ٱبْنَكَ سَرَقَ وَمَا شَهِدْنَآ إِلَّا بِمَا عَلِمْنَا وَمَا كُنَّا لِلْغَيْبِ حَـٰفِظِينَ ۝٨١}$$

### Joseph's Plan

The brothers left enough provisions behind for Judah, who stayed at a tavern awaiting the fate of Benjamin. In the meantime, Joseph kept Benjamin in his house as his personal guest and told him how he had devised the plot to put the king's cup in his bag, in order to keep him behind, so as to protect him. He was also glad that Judah had stayed behind, as he was a good hearted brother. Joseph secretly arranged to watch over Judah's well-being. Joseph's plan in sending the others back was to test their sincerity, to see if they would come back for the two brothers they had left behind.

### The Brothers Confront Jacob

When they arrived home, they entered upon their father calling: "O our father! Your son has stolen!" He was puzzled, scarcely believing the news. He was overwhelmed with sorrow and his eyes wept tears. [Jacob] said, "Rather, your souls have enticed you to something, so patience is most fitting. Perhaps Allah will bring them to me all together. Indeed it is He who is the Knowing, the Wise." [12:83]

$$\text{قَالَ بَلْ سَوَّلَتْ لَكُمْ أَنفُسُكُمْ أَمْرًا ۖ فَصَبْرٌ جَمِيلٌ ۖ عَسَى ٱللَّهُ أَن يَأْتِيَنِى بِهِمْ جَمِيعًا ۚ إِنَّهُۥ هُوَ ٱلْعَلِيمُ ٱلْحَكِيمُ ۝٨٣}$$

## Jacob's Request to Find Joseph

The father was deeply hurt. Only prayer could comfort him and strengthen his faith and patience. Weeping all those years for his beloved son Joseph - and now one more of his best sons had been snatched from him - Jacob almost lost his sight. The other sons pleaded with him: "O father, you are a noble prophet and a great messenger of Allah. Unto you descended revelation and people received guidance and faith from you. Why are you destroying yourself in this way?" Jacob replied: "Rebuking me will not lessen my grief. Only the return of my sons will comfort me. My sons, go in search of Joseph and his brother; do not despair of Allah's mercy."

## Jacob's Request to Find Joseph - Quranic

Allah, the Almighty told us: "Jacob turned away from them and said, "Oh, my sorrow over Joseph," and his eyes became white from grief, for he was [of that] a suppressor." [12:84]

وَتَوَلَّىٰ عَنْهُمْ وَقَالَ يَٰأَسَفَىٰ عَلَىٰ يُوسُفَ وَٱبْيَضَّتْ عَيْنَاهُ مِنَ ٱلْحُزْنِ فَهُوَ كَظِيمٌ ﴿٨٤﴾

They said, "By Allah, you will not cease remembering Joseph until you become fatally ill or become of those who perish." [12:85]

قَالُوا۟ تَٱللَّهِ تَفْتَؤُا۟ تَذْكُرُ يُوسُفَ حَتَّىٰ تَكُونَ حَرَضًا أَوْ تَكُونَ مِنَ ٱلْهَٰلِكِينَ ﴿٨٥﴾

He said, "I only complain of my suffering and my grief to Allah, and I know from Allah that which you do not know. O my sons, go and find out about Joseph and his brother and despair not of relief from Allah. Indeed, no one despairs of relief from Allah except the disbelieving people." [12:86-87]

قَالَ إِنَّمَآ أَشْكُوا۟ بَثِّى وَحُزْنِىٓ إِلَى ٱللَّهِ وَأَعْلَمُ مِنَ ٱللَّهِ مَا لَا تَعْلَمُونَ ﴿٨٦﴾

يَـٰبَنِىَّ اذْهَبُوا۟ فَتَحَسَّسُوا۟ مِن يُوسُفَ وَأَخِيهِ وَلَا تَا۟يْـَٔسُوا۟ مِن رَّوْحِ ٱللَّهِ ۖ إِنَّهُۥ لَا يَا۟يْـَٔسُ مِن رَّوْحِ ٱللَّهِ إِلَّا ٱلْقَوْمُ ٱلْكَـٰفِرُونَ ۝

## Joseph Reveals Himself

The caravan set out for Egypt. The brothers - on their way to see the chief minister (Joseph) - were poor and depressed. On reaching Egypt they collected Judah and called on Joseph, to whom they pleaded: "O ruler of the land! A hard time has hit us and our family, and we have brought but poor capital, so pay us full measure and be charitable to us. Truly, Allah does reward the charitable." [12:88] At the end, they begged Joseph. They asked alms of him, appealing to his heart, reminding him that Allah rewards alms givers. At this moment, in the midst of their plight, Joseph spoke to them in their native tongue saying: "Do you know what you did with Joseph and his brother when you were ignorant?" They said: "Are you indeed Joseph?" He said: "I am Joseph, and his is my brother (Benjamin). Allah has indeed been Gracious to us. Verily, he who fears Allah with obedience to Him (by abstaining from sins and evil deeds, and by performing righteous good deeds), and is patient, then surely, Allah makes not the reward of the good doers to be lost." They said: "By Allah! Indeed Allah has preferred you above us, and we certainly have been sinners." [12:89- 91] The brothers began to tremble with fear, but Joseph comforted them: "No reproach on you this day, may Allah forgive you, and He is the Most Merciful of those who show mercy!" [12:92]

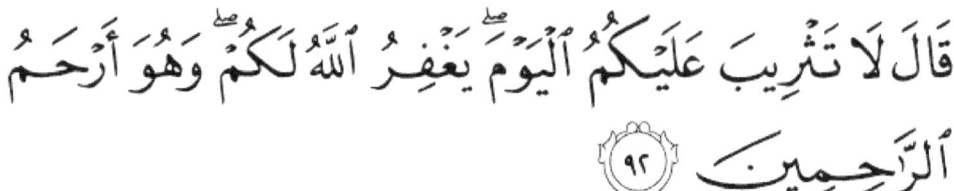

## Jacob Learns About Joseph

Joseph embraced them, and together they wept with joy. It was not possible for Joseph to leave his responsible office without proper replacement, so he advised his brothers: "Go with this shirt of mine, and cast it over the face of my father, he will become clear-sighted, and bring to me all your family." [12:93] And so the caravan headed back for Palestine. We leave the scene in Egypt and return to Palestine and the house of Jacob. The old man is sitting in his room; tears have been flowing down his cheeks. He stands up all of a sudden, dresses and goes out to his son's wives. Then he lifts up his face to Heaven and sniffs the air. The wife of the eldest son remarked: "Jacob has come out of his room today." The women inquired about what was amiss.

There was a hint of a smile on his face. The others asked him: "How do you feel today?" Jacob answered: "I can smell Joseph in the air." The wives left him alone, saying to one another that there was no hope for the old man. "He will die of weeping over Joseph. Did he talk about Joseph's shirt?" "I do not know. He said he could smell him; perhaps he has gone mad." That day the old man wanted a cup of milk to break his fast, for he had been fasting. At night he changed his clothes. The caravan was traveling in the desert with Joseph's shirt hidden among the grain. It neared the old man's estate. He gesticulated in his room, and then he prayed a long time, lifting his hands to heaven and sniffing the air. He was weeping as the shirt was nearing him. And when the caravan departed, their father said: "I do indeed feel the smell of Joseph, if only you think me not a dotard (a person who has weakness of mind because of old age)." They said: "By Allah! Certainly, you are in your old error." Then, when the bearer of the glad tidings arrived, he cast the shirt over his face, and he became clear sighted. He said: "Did I not say to you, I know from Allah that which you know not." They said: "O our father! Ask Forgiveness from Allah for our sins, indeed we have been sinners." He said, "I will ask forgiveness for you from my Lord. Indeed, it is He who is the Forgiving, the Merciful." [12:94-97]

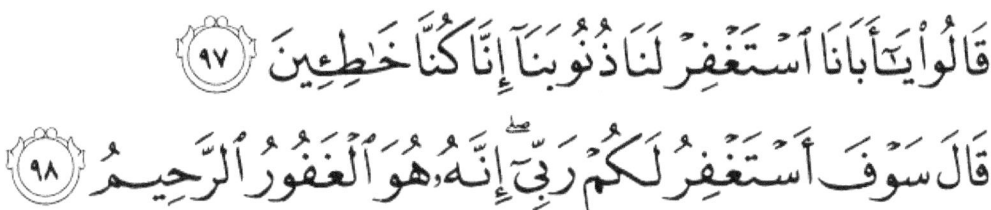

## Jacob and Joseph (peace be upon them) Meet

The story began with a dream and it ends with the interpretation of the dream. And when they entered upon Joseph, he took his parents to himself and said, "Enter Egypt, Allah willing, safe [and secure]." And he raised his parents upon the throne, and they bowed to him in prostration. [12:99] Joseph said, "O my father, this is the explanation of my vision of before. My Lord has made it reality. And He was certainly good to me when He took me out of prison and brought you [here] from bedouin life after Satan had induced [estrangement] between me and my brothers. Indeed, my Lord is subtle in what He wills. Indeed, it is He who is the Knowing, the Wise." [12:100].

وَرَفَعَ أَبَوَيْهِ عَلَى ٱلْعَرْشِ وَخَرُّواْ لَهُۥ سُجَّدًا ۖ وَقَالَ يَٰٓأَبَتِ هَٰذَا تَأْوِيلُ رُءْيَٰىَ مِن قَبْلُ قَدْ جَعَلَهَا رَبِّى حَقًّا ۖ وَقَدْ أَحْسَنَ بِىٓ إِذْ أَخْرَجَنِى مِنَ ٱلسِّجْنِ وَجَآءَ بِكُم مِّنَ ٱلْبَدْوِ مِنۢ بَعْدِ أَن نَّزَغَ ٱلشَّيْطَٰنُ بَيْنِى وَبَيْنَ إِخْوَتِىٓ ۚ إِنَّ رَبِّى لَطِيفٌ لِّمَا يَشَآءُ ۚ إِنَّهُۥ هُوَ ٱلْعَلِيمُ ٱلْحَكِيمُ ۝١٠٠

### Epilogue

Consider his feelings now that his dream has come true. He prays to Allah: "My Lord, You have given me [something] of sovereignty and taught me of the interpretation of dreams. Creator of the heavens and earth, You are my protector in this world and in the Hereafter. Cause me to die a Muslim and join me with the righteous." [12:101].

رَبِّ قَدْ ءَاتَيْتَنِى مِنَ ٱلْمُلْكِ وَعَلَّمْتَنِى مِن تَأْوِيلِ ٱلْأَحَادِيثِ ۚ فَاطِرَ ٱلسَّمَٰوَٰتِ وَٱلْأَرْضِ أَنتَ وَلِىِّۦ فِى ٱلدُّنْيَا وَٱلْءَاخِرَةِ ۖ تَوَفَّنِى مُسْلِمًا وَأَلْحِقْنِى بِٱلصَّٰلِحِينَ ۝١٠١

Joseph arranged an audience with the king for himself and his family, to ask the king's permission for them to settle in Egypt. Joseph was an asset to the kingdom, and the king was happy to have him remain with his household. Joseph prostrated to Allah in gratitude. Never was the Qur'an a narration invented, but a confirmation of what was before it and a detailed explanation of all things and guidance and mercy for a people who believe. [12:111]

$$\text{لَقَدْ كَانَ فِي قَصَصِهِمْ عِبْرَةٌ لِأُولِي الْأَلْبَابِ مَا كَانَ حَدِيثًا يُفْتَرَىٰ وَلَٰكِن تَصْدِيقَ الَّذِي بَيْنَ يَدَيْهِ وَتَفْصِيلَ كُلِّ شَيْءٍ وَهُدًى وَرَحْمَةً لِّقَوْمٍ يُؤْمِنُونَ ﴿١١١﴾}$$

### The Death of Jacob and Joseph (peace be upon them)

Before he died, Jacob (pbuh) advised his children to adhere to the teachings of Islam, the religion of all of Allah's prophets. Allah the Almighty revealed: "Or were you witnesses when death approached Jacob? Jacob said to his sons, "What will you worship after me?" They said, "We will worship your God and the God of your fathers, Abraham and Ishmael and Isaac - one God, Allah. And we are Muslims [in submission] to Him." [2:133]. Joseph (pbuh), at the moment of his death, asked his brothers to bury him beside his forefathers if they were to leave Egypt. So when Joseph (pbuh) passed away, he was mummified and placed in a coffin until such a time as he could be taken out of Egypt and buried beside his forefathers, as he had requested. It was said that he died at the age of one hundred ten.

$$\text{أَمْ كُنتُمْ شُهَدَاءَ إِذْ حَضَرَ يَعْقُوبَ الْمَوْتُ إِذْ قَالَ لِبَنِيهِ مَا تَعْبُدُونَ مِن بَعْدِي قَالُوا نَعْبُدُ إِلَٰهَكَ وَإِلَٰهَ آبَائِكَ إِبْرَاهِيمَ وَإِسْمَاعِيلَ وَإِسْحَاقَ إِلَٰهًا وَاحِدًا وَنَحْنُ لَهُ مُسْلِمُونَ ﴿١٣٣﴾}$$

# Prophet Job (Ayoub)

And remember Our servant Job, when he called to his Lord, "Indeed, Satan has touched me with hardship and torment." [38:41]

وَٱذْكُرْ عَبْدَنَآ أَيُّوبَ إِذْ نَادَىٰ رَبَّهُۥٓ أَنِّى مَسَّنِىَ ٱلشَّيْطَـٰنُ بِنُصْبٍ وَعَذَابٍ ﴿٤١﴾

Prophet Job's mother was a daughter of Lot (pbuh). It was said that his father was one who believed in Abraham (pbuh) when he was cast into the fire. The first opinion is the most plausible, because he was a descendant of Abraham's offspring. Allah Almighty declared: "That was Our proof which We gave Abraham against his people. We raise whom We will in degrees. Certainly your Lord is All-Wise, All Knowing. And We bestowed upon him Isaac and Jacob, each of them We guided and before him, We guided Noah, and among his progeny David, Solomon, Job, Joseph, Moses, and Aaron. Thus do We reward the good doers." [6:83-84]

وَتِلْكَ حُجَّتُنَآ ءَاتَيْنَـٰهَآ إِبْرَٰهِيمَ عَلَىٰ قَوْمِهِۦ نَرْفَعُ دَرَجَـٰتٍ مَّن نَّشَآءُ إِنَّ رَبَّكَ حَكِيمٌ عَلِيمٌ ﴿٨٣﴾ وَوَهَبْنَا لَهُۥٓ إِسْحَـٰقَ وَيَعْقُوبَ كُلًّا هَدَيْنَا وَنُوحًا هَدَيْنَا مِن قَبْلُ وَمِن ذُرِّيَّتِهِۦ دَاوُۥدَ وَسُلَيْمَـٰنَ وَأَيُّوبَ وَيُوسُفَ وَمُوسَىٰ وَهَـٰرُونَ وَكَذَٰلِكَ نَجْزِى ٱلْمُحْسِنِينَ ﴿٨٤﴾

## Allah's Praises of Job

Allah the Almighty praised His worshipper Job in His Glorious Quran: [We said], "And take in your hand a bunch [of grass] and strike with it and do not break your oath." Indeed, We found him patient, an excellent servant. Indeed, he was one repeatedly turning back [to Allah]." [38:44]

Prophet Job (pbuh) was repentant, remembering Allah with thankfulness, patience, and steadfastness. This was the cause of his rescue and the secret of Allah's praising him. A group of angels were discussing Allah's other human creatures, how those who were humble earned Allah's pleasure, while those who were arrogant incurred His displeasure. One of the angels remarked: "The best creature on earth today is Job, a man of noble character who displays great patience and always remembers his Generous Lord. He is an excellent model for the worshippers of Allah. In return, his Lord has blessed him with a long life and plenty of servants, as well as the needy and the poor to share in his good fortune; he feeds and clothes the poor and buys slaves to set them free. He makes those who receive his charity feel as if they are favoring him so kind and gentle is he." Iblis (Satan) overhearing all of this, became annoyed. He planned to tempt Job to corruption and disbelief, so he hastened to him. He tried to distract Job from his prayers by whispering to him about the good things in life but Job was a true believer and would not let evil thoughts tempt him. This disturbed Iblis, so he began to hate Job even more.

## Iblis (Satan) Destroys Job's Wealth

Iblis complained to Allah about Job. He said that although he was continuously glorifying Allah he was not doing so out of his sincerity but to satisfy Allah so that his wealth should not be taken away. It was all a show, all out of greed. "If You remove his wealth then You will find that his tongue will no longer mention Your name and his praying will stop." Allah told Iblis that Job was one of His most sincere devotees.

He did not worship Him because of the favors; his worship stemmed from his heart and had nothing to do with material things. But to prove to Iblis the depth of Job's sincerity and patience, Allah allowed him to do whatever he and his helpers wished with Job's wealth. Iblis was very happy. He gathered his helpers and set about destroying Job's cattle, servants and farms until he was left with no possessions.

Rubbing his hands in glee, Iblis appeared before Job in the guise of a wise old man and said to him: "All your wealth is lost, some people say that it is because you gave too much charity and that you are wasting your time with your continuous prayers to Allah. Others say that Allah has brought this upon you in order to please your enemies. If Allah had the capacity to prevent harm, then He would have protected your wealth." True to his belief, Job replied: "What Allah has taken away from me belongs to Him. I was only its trustee for a while. He gives to whom He wills and withholds from whom He wills." With these words, Job again prostrated to his Lord.

### Iblis Destroys Job's Children

When Iblis saw this, he felt frustrated, so he again addressed Allah: "I have stripped Job of all his possessions, but he still remains grateful to You. However he is only hiding his disappointment, for he places great store by his many children. The real test of a parent is through his children. You will see how Job will reject You." Allah granted Iblis authority but warned him that it would not reduce Job' faith in His Lord nor his patience. Iblis again gathered his helpers and set about his evil deeds.

He shook the house in which Job's children were living and sent the building crashing, killing all of them. Then he went to Job disguised as a man who had come to sympathize with him. In a comforting tone he said to Job: "The circumstances under which your children died were sad. Surely, your Lord is not rewarding you properly for all your prayers." Having said this, Iblis waited anxiously hoping Job was now ready to reject Allah. But again Job disappointed him by replying: "Allah sometimes gives and sometimes takes. He is sometimes pleased and sometimes displeased with our deeds. Whether a thing is beneficial or harmful to me, I will remain firm in my belief and remain thankful to my Creator." Job prostrated to his Lord. At this Iblis was extremely vexed.

### Iblis Destroys Job's Health

Iblis called on Allah. "O my Lord, Job's wealth is gone, his children are dead, and he is still healthy in body, and as long as he enjoys good health he will continue to worship You in the hope of regaining his wealth and producing more children. Grant me authority over his body so that I may weaken it. He will surely neglect worshipping You and will thus become disobedient." Allah wanted to teach Iblis a lesson that Job was a devoted servant of his Lord so He granted Iblis his third request but placed a condition: "I give you authority over his body but not over his soul, intellect or heart, for in these places reside the knowledge of Me and My religion." Armed with this new authority, Iblis began to take revenge on Job's body and filled it with disease until it was reduced to mere skin and bone and he suffered severe pain. But through all the suffering Job remained strong in his faith, patiently bearing all the hardships without complaining. Allah's righteous servant did not despair or turn to others for help but remained hopeful of Allah's mercy.

Even close relatives and friends deserted him. Only his kind, loving wife stayed with him. In his hour of need, she showered her kindness on him and cared for him. She remained his sole companion and comforter through the many years of suffering.

## Job's Life - Summary

Ibn Asaker narrated: "Job was a man having much wealth of all kinds; beats, slaves, sheep, vast lands of Haran and many children. All those favors were taken from him and he was physically afflicted as well. Never a single organ was sound except his heart and tongue, with both of which he glorified Allah, the Almighty all the time day and night. His disease lasted for a long time until his visitors felt disgusted with him. His friends kept away from him and people abstained from visiting him. No one felt sympathy for him except his wife. She took good care of him, knowing his former charity and pity for her."

## Job's Prayer for Mercy

Therefore Iblis became desperate. He consulted his helpers, but they could not advise him. They asked: "How is it that your cleverness cannot work against Job, yet you succeeded in misleading Adam the father of man, out of Paradise?" Iblis went to Job's wife in the form of a man. "Where is your husband?" He asked her. She pointed to an almost lifeless form crumbled on the bed and said: "There he is, suspended between life and death." Iblis reminded her of the days, when Job had good health, wealth and children. Suddenly, the painful memory of years of hardship overcame her, and she burst into tears. She said to Job: "How long are you going to bear this torture from our Lord? Are we to remain without wealth, children or friends forever? Why don't you call upon Allah to remove this suffering?" Job sighed, and in a soft voice replied, "blis must have whispered to you and made you dissatisfied. Tell me how long did I enjoy good health and riches?" She replied: "80 years." Then Job replied: "How long am I suffering like this?" She said: "7 years."

Job then told her: "In that case I am ashamed to call on my Lord to remove the hardship, for I have not suffered longer than the years of good health and plenty. It seems your faith has weakened and you are dissatisfied with the fate of Allah. If I ever regain health, I swear I will punish you with a hundred strokes! From this day onward, I forbid myself to eat or drink anything by your hand. Leave me alone and let my Lord do with me as He pleases."

## Job's health is restored

Crying bitterly and with a heavy heart, she had no choice but to leave him and seek shelter elsewhere. In this helpless state, Job turned to Allah, not to complain but to seek His mercy: "Verily! distress has seized me and You are the Most Merciful of all those who show mercy." "So We answered his call, and we removed the distress that was on him, and We restored his family to him (that he had lost), and the like thereof along with them as a mercy from Ourselves and a Reminder for all who worship Us." [21:83- 84].

$$\text{﴿ وَأَيُّوبَ إِذْ نَادَىٰ رَبَّهُۥٓ أَنِّى مَسَّنِىَ ٱلضُّرُّ وَأَنتَ أَرْحَمُ ٱلرَّٰحِمِينَ ۝}$$

$$\text{فَٱسْتَجَبْنَا لَهُۥ فَكَشَفْنَا مَا بِهِۦ مِن ضُرٍّ ۖ وَءَاتَيْنَٰهُ أَهْلَهُۥ وَمِثْلَهُم مَّعَهُمْ رَحْمَةً مِّنْ عِندِنَا وَذِكْرَىٰ لِلْعَٰبِدِينَ ۝}$$

And remember Our servant Job, when he called to his Lord, "Indeed, Satan has touched me with hardship and torment." [So he was told], "Strike [the ground] with your foot; this is a [spring for] a cool bath and drink." And We granted him his family and a like [number] with them as mercy from Us and a reminder for those of understanding. [38:41-43]

$$\text{وَٱذْكُرْ عَبْدَنَآ أَيُّوبَ إِذْ نَادَىٰ رَبَّهُۥٓ أَنِّى مَسَّنِىَ ٱلشَّيْطَٰنُ بِنُصْبٍ وَعَذَابٍ ۝}$$

$$\text{ٱرْكُضْ بِرِجْلِكَ ۖ هَٰذَا مُغْتَسَلٌۢ بَارِدٌ وَشَرَابٌ ۝}$$

$$\text{وَوَهَبْنَا لَهُۥٓ أَهْلَهُۥ وَمِثْلَهُم مَّعَهُمْ رَحْمَةً مِّنَّا وَذِكْرَىٰ لِأُو۟لِى ٱلْأَلْبَٰبِ ۝}$$

Job obeyed and almost immediately his good health was restored. Meanwhile, his faithful wife could no longer bear to be parted from her husband and returned to him to beg his forgiveness, desiring to serve him. On entering her house, she was amazed at the sudden change: Job was again healthy! She embraced him and thanked Allah for His mercy. Job was not worried, for he had taken an oath to punish her with a hundred strokes if he had regained health but he had no desire to hurt her. He knew if he did not fulfill the oath, he would be guilty of breaking a promise to Allah.

Therefore in His wisdom and mercy, Allah came to the assistance of His faithful servant and advised him: [We said], "And take in your hand a bunch [of grass] and strike with it and do not break your oath." Indeed, We found him patient, an excellent servant. Indeed, he was one repeatedly turning back [to Allah ]." [38:44]

$$\text{وَخُذْ بِيَدِكَ ضِغْثًا فَاضْرِب بِّهِ وَلَا تَحْنَثْ ۗ إِنَّا وَجَدْنَاهُ صَابِرًا ۚ نِّعْمَ ٱلْعَبْدُ إِنَّهُۥ أَوَّابٌ ﴿٤٤﴾}$$

Abu Hurairah (may Allah be pleased with him) narrated that the Prophet Muhammad (pbuh) said: "While Job was naked, taking a bath, a swarm of gold locusts fell on him, and he started collecting them in his garment. Allah called him: "O Job! Have I not made you too rich to need what you see?" He said: "Yes, My Lord! But I cannot shun Your Blessings." (Al Bukhari)

## Prophet Dhul – Kifl (Isaiah)

Allah the Almighty declared: "And (remember) Isma'il (Ishmael), and Idris (Enoch) and Dhul-Kifl (Isaiah), all were from among As-Sabirin (the patient ones, etc.)." [21:85]

$$\text{وَإِسْمَاعِيلَ وَإِدْرِيسَ وَذَا ٱلْكِفْلِ ۖ كُلٌّ مِّنَ ٱلصَّابِرِينَ ﴿٨٥﴾}$$

"And We admitted them into Our mercy. Indeed, they were of the righteous." [21:86]

$$\text{وَأَدْخَلْنَاهُمْ فِي رَحْمَتِنَا ۖ إِنَّهُم مِّنَ ٱلصَّالِحِينَ ﴿٨٦﴾}$$

Almighty Allah also said: "Remember Our slaves, Abraham, Isaac, and Jacob (all) owners of strength (in worshipping Us) and also of religious understanding." [38:45]

$$\text{وَٱذْكُرْ عِبَادَنَا إِبْرَاهِيمَ وَإِسْحَاقَ وَيَعْقُوبَ أُو۟لِى ٱلْأَيْدِى وَٱلْأَبْصَارِ ﴿٤٥﴾}$$

"Verily, We did choose them by granting them (a good thing) the remembrance of the home (in the Hereafter and they used to make the people remember it and also they used to invite the people to obey Allah and to do good deeds for the Hereafter). And they are in Our Sight, verily of the chosen and the best! Indeed, We chose them for an exclusive quality: remembrance of the home [of the Hereafter]." [38:46]

إِنَّا أَخْلَصْنَٰهُم بِخَالِصَةٍ ذِكْرَى ٱلدَّارِ ﴿٤٦﴾

"And indeed they are, to Us, among the chosen and outstanding." [38:47]

وَإِنَّهُمْ عِندَنَا لَمِنَ ٱلْمُصْطَفَيْنَ ٱلْأَخْيَارِ ﴿٤٧﴾

"And remember Ishmael, Elisha, Dhul-Kifl, and all are among the outstanding." [38:48]

وَٱذْكُرْ إِسْمَٰعِيلَ وَٱلْيَسَعَ وَذَا ٱلْكِفْلِ وَكُلٌّ مِّنَ ٱلْأَخْيَارِ ﴿٤٨﴾

It is obvious from his being mentioned and praised in the Glorious Quran along with those other prophets that Dhul - Kifl was also a great prophet. However, some of the Quranic commentators assumed that he was not a prophet but that he was righteous and strictly just.

### The meaning of Dhul Kifl

Ibn Jarir narrated that he was not a prophet but he was a righteous man. He supported his people to suffice their needs and administered justice among them. That is why he was called Dhul - Kifl. (Dhul - Kifl literally means "possessor of, or giving, a double requital or portion".)

# Prophet Yunus (Jonah) (Dhan-Nun)

Prophet Jonah (Yunus) (pbuh) also known by Dhan-Nun. About his people Almighty Allah said: "Was there any town (community) that believed (after se Dhan-Nun eing the punishment), and its Faith (at that moment) saved it ... of Yunus (Jonah); when they believed, We removed from them the?" [10:98]

$$\text{فَلَوْلَا كَانَتْ قَرْيَةٌ ءَامَنَتْ فَنَفَعَهَا إِيمَانُهَا إِلَّا قَوْمَ يُونُسَ لَمَّا ءَامَنُوا۟ كَشَفْنَا عَنْهُمْ عَذَابَ ٱلْخِزْىِ فِى ٱلْحَيَوٰةِ ٱلدُّنْيَا وَمَتَّعْنَٰهُمْ إِلَىٰ حِينٍ ۝٩٨}$$

(The answer is none)--except the people of Jonah; when they believed, We removed from them the torment of disgrace in the life of the present world, and permitted them to enjoy for a while. "And had your Lord willed, those on earth would have believed - all of them entirely." [10:99]

$$\text{وَلَوْ شَآءَ رَبُّكَ لَءَامَنَ مَن فِى ٱلْأَرْضِ كُلُّهُمْ جَمِيعًا أَفَأَنتَ تُكْرِهُ ٱلنَّاسَ حَتَّىٰ يَكُونُوا۟ مُؤْمِنِينَ ۝٩٩}$$

The inhabitants of the town of Nineveh were idolaters who lived a shameless life. Prophet Jonah (pbuh) was sent to teach them the worship of Allah. The people disliked his interference in their way of worship, so they argued: "We and our forefathers have worshipped these gods for many years and no harm has come to us."

## Jonah Leaves His People

Jonah (pbuh) tried to convince them of the foolishness of idolatry and of the goodness of Allah's laws, but they ignored him. He warned them that if they kept on with their foolishness, Allah's punishment would soon follow. Instead of fearing Allah, they told Jonah that they were not afraid of his threats. "Let it happen," they told him. Jonah was disheartened. Jonah told them then in that case, I will leave you to your misery! He left Nineveh, fearing that Allah's anger would soon follow. "And (remember) Dhan-Nun (Jonah), when he went off in anger, and imagined that We shall not punish him (i.e. the calamites which had befallen him)! But he cried through the darkness (saying):

La ilaha illa Anta [none has the right to be worshipped but You (O Allah)], Glorified (and Exalted) are You [above all that (evil) they associate with You]. Truly, I have been of the wrong-doers." [21:87]

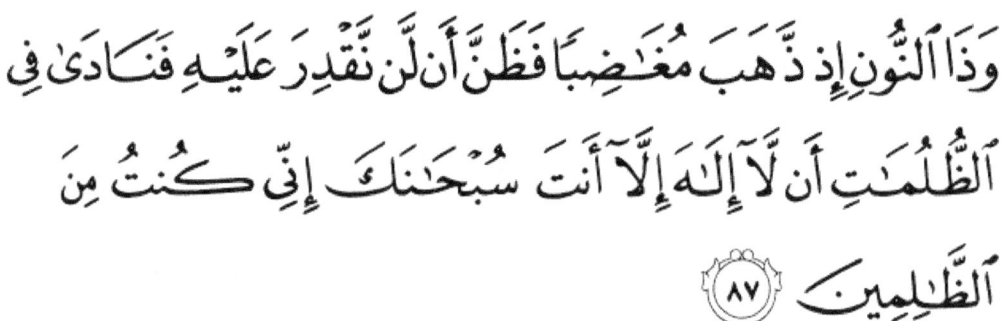

### The People are forgiven

Hardly had he left the city when the skies began to change color and looked as if they were on fire. The people were filled with fear by this sight. They recalled the destruction of the people of 'Ad, Thamud and Noah. Was theirs to be a similar fate? Slowly faith penetrated their hearts. They all gathered on the mountain and started to beseech Allah for His mercy and forgiveness. The mountains echoed with their cries. It was a momentous hour, filled with sincere repentance. Allah removed His wrath and showered His blessings upon them once again. When the threatening storm was lifted, they prayed for the return of Jonah so that he could guide them.

### The Storm at Sea

Meanwhile, Jonah had boarded a small ship in the company of other passengers. It sailed all day in calm waters with a good wind blowing at the sails. When night came, the sea suddenly changed. A horrible storm blew as if it were going to split the ship into pieces. The waves looked wild. They rose up as high as mountains then plunged down like valleys, tossing the ship and sweeping over the deck. Behind the ship, a large whale was splitting the water and opening its mouth. A command had been issued from Almighty Allah to one of the greatest whales of the sea to surface. It obeyed. The whale hurried to the surface of the sea and followed the ship as it had been commanded. The tempest continued and the chief crewman asked the crew to lighten the ship's heavy load. They threw their baggage overboard, but this was not enough. Their safety lay in reducing the weight further, so they decided among themselves to lighten their load by removing at least one person.

## Jonah Jumps into the Sea

The captain directed: "We will make lots with all of the travelers' names. The one whose name is drawn will be thrown into the sea." Jonah knew this was one of the seamen's traditions when facing a tempest. It was a strange polytheistic tradition, but it was practiced at that time. Jonah's affliction and crisis began. Here was the prophet, subjected to polytheistic rules that considered the sea and the wind to have gods that riot. The captain had to please these gods. Jonah reluctantly participated in the lot, and his name was added to the other travelers' names. The lot was drawn and "Jonah" appeared. Since they knew him to be the most honorable among them, they did not wish to throw him into the angry sea. Therefore, they decided to draw a second lot. Again Jonah's name was drawn. They gave him a final chance and drew a third lot. Unfortunately for Jonah, his name came up again. Jonah realized that Allah's hand was in all this, for he had abandoned his mission without Allah's consent. The matter was over, and it was decided that Jonah should throw himself into the water. Jonah stood at the edge of the ship looking at the furious sea. It was night and there was no moon. The stars were hidden behind a black fog. But before he could be thrown overboard, Jonah kept mentioning Allah's name as he jumped into the raging sea and disappeared beneath the huge waves.

## The Whale Swallows Jonah

The whale found Jonah floating on the waves before it. It swallowed Jonah into its furious stomach and shut its ivory teeth on him as if they were white bolts locking the door of his prison. The whale dived to the bottom of the sea, the sea that runs in the abyss of darkness. Three layers of darkness enveloped him, one above the other; the darkness of the whale's stomach, the darkness of the bottom of the sea, the darkness of the night. Jonah imaged himself to be dead, but his senses became alert when he found he could move. He knew that he was alive and imprisoned in the midst of three layers of darkness. His heart was moved by remembering Allah. "And (remember) Dhan-Nun (Jonah), when he went off in anger, and imagined that We shall not punish him (i.e. the calamites which had befallen him)! But he cried through the darkness (saying): La ilaha illa Anta [none has the right to be worshipped but You (O Allah)], Glorified (and Exalted) are You [above all that (evil) they associate with You]. Truly, I have been of the wrong-doers." [21:97]

وَذَا ٱلنُّونِ إِذ ذَّهَبَ مُغَٰضِبًا فَظَنَّ أَن لَّن نَّقْدِرَ عَلَيْهِ فَنَادَىٰ فِى ٱلظُّلُمَٰتِ أَن لَّآ إِلَٰهَ إِلَّآ أَنتَ سُبْحَٰنَكَ إِنِّى كُنتُ مِنَ ٱلظَّٰلِمِينَ ﴿٨٧﴾

Jonah continued praying to Allah, repeating this invocation. Fishes, whales, seaweeds, and all the creatures that lived in the sea heard the voice of Jonah praying, heard the celebration of Allah's praises issuing from the whale's stomach. All these creatures gathered around the whale and began to celebrate the praises of Allah in their turn, each in its own way and in its own language. The whale also participated in celebrating the praises of Allah and understood that it had swallowed a prophet. Therefore it felt afraid; however, it said to itself; "Why should I be afraid? Allah commanded me to swallow him."

### Allah Forgives Jonah

Allah Almighty saw the sincere repentance of Jonah and heard his invocation in the whale's stomach. Allah commanded the whale to surface and eject Jonah onto an island. The whale obeyed and swam to the farthest side of the ocean. Allah commanded it to rise towards the warm, refreshing sun and the pleasant earth.

The whale ejected Jonah onto a remote island. His body was inflamed because of the acids inside the whale's stomach. He was ill, and when the sun rose, its ray burned his inflamed body so that he was on the verge of screaming for the pain. However, he endured the pain and continued to repeat his invocation to Allah. Almighty Allah caused a vine to grow to considerable length over him for protection. Then Allah Exalted caused Jonah to recover and forgave him. Allah told Jonah that if it had not been for his praying to Him, he would have stayed in the whale's stomach till the Day of Judgment.

### Summary of Jonah's Story

Almighty Allah recounted: "And, verily, Yunus (Jonah) was one of the Messengers." [37:139-148]

"[Mention] when he ran away to the laden ship."

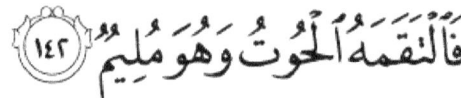

"And he drew lots and was among the losers."

فَسَاهَمَ فَكَانَ مِنَ ٱلْمُدْحَضِينَ ﴿١٤١﴾

"Then a (big) fish swallowed him and he had done an act worthy of blame."

فَٱلْتَقَمَهُ ٱلْحُوتُ وَهُوَ مُلِيمٌ ﴿١٤٢﴾

"And had he not been of those who exalt Allah,"

فَلَوْلَآ أَنَّهُۥ كَانَ مِنَ ٱلْمُسَبِّحِينَ ﴿١٤٣﴾

"He would have remained inside its belly until the Day they are resurrected."

لَلَبِثَ فِى بَطْنِهِۦٓ إِلَىٰ يَوْمِ يُبْعَثُونَ ﴿١٤٤﴾

"But We threw him onto the open shore while he was ill."

فَنَبَذْنَٰهُ بِٱلْعَرَآءِ وَهُوَ سَقِيمٌ ﴿١٤٥﴾

"And We caused to grow over him a gourd vine."

وَأَنۢبَتْنَا عَلَيْهِ شَجَرَةً مِّن يَقْطِينٍ ﴿١٤٦﴾

"And We sent him to a hundred thousand (people) or even more."

وَأَرْسَلْنَٰهُ إِلَىٰ مِا۟ئَةِ أَلْفٍ أَوْ يَزِيدُونَ ﴿١٤٧﴾

"And they believed; so We gave them enjoyment for a while."

فَـَٔامَنُوا۟ فَمَتَّعْنَٰهُمْ إِلَىٰ حِينٍ ﴿١٤٨﴾

### Jonah's People - Changed

Gradually he regained his strength and found his way to his hometown, Nineveh. He was pleasantly surprised to notice the change that had taken place there. The entire population turned out to welcome him. They informed him that they had turned to believe in Allah. Together they led a prayer of thanksgiving to their Merciful Lord.

### Prophet Muhammad's Saying about Jonah (pbut)

Ibn Abbas narrated: "The Prophet Muhammad (peace be upon him) said: 'One should not say I am better than Jonah Ibn Matta.'" (Sahih Bukhari).

# Prophet Musa (Moses) and Harun (Aaron)

And, Indeed We gave Our Grace to Musa (Moses) and (Harun) Aaron. [37:114] We gave Moses the Scripture and appointed with him his brother Aaron as an assistant. [25:35] Peace be upon Moses and Aaron. [37:20]

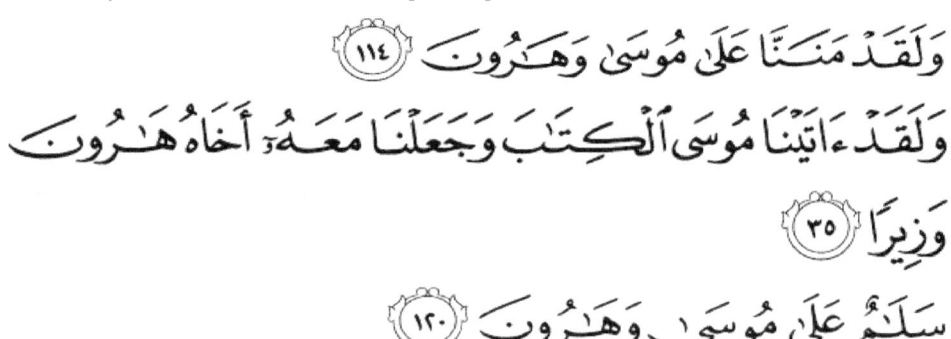

The pharaoh who ruled Egypt was a tyrant. He oppressed the descendants of Jacob (pbuh), known as the children of Israel (Bani Israel). He used every means to demean and disgrace them. They were kept in bondage and forced to work for him for small wages or nothing. Under this system the people obeyed and worshipped the pharaoh, and the ruling class carried out his orders, thereby authorizing his tyranny and crazy whims. The pharaoh wanted the people to obey him only, and to believe in the gods of his invention. Perhaps, during that time, there were many classes of people who did not believe in or practice polytheism; however, they kept this to themselves and outwardly did as they were expected to do, without revolting or revealing themselves to anyone. Thus, successive dynasties came to Egypt and assumed that they were gods or their representative or spokesmen.

## Visions of Dethroning the Pharaoh

One night the Pharaoh saw in his vision a fire, which came from Jerusalem and burned the houses of the Egyptians, but did not do harm the children of Israel. When he woke up, he was horrified. He then gathered his priests and magicians and asked them about this vision. They said: "this means a boy will be born of them and the Egyptian people will perish at his hands." The Pharaoh then issued a decree to slay any male child that would be born to the children of Israel.

## The Birth of Aaron and Moses (peace be upon them)

The killing of the children of Israel was carried out until a wise man said to Pharaoh: "The aged of the children of Israel die and the young are slaughtered. This will lead to their annihilation. As a result, Pharaoh will lose the manpower of those who work for him, those whom he enslaves, and their women whom he exploits. It is better to regulate this procedure by initiating the following policy: males should be slaughtered in one year but spared to live the next year." Pharaoh found that solution to be safer economically. Moses' mother was pregnant with Aaron (pbuh) in a year that boys were spared; thus she gave birth to the child publicly and safely. During a year in which boys were to be slain, she gave birth to Moses (pbuh); thus his birth caused her much terror. She was afraid he would be slain, so she nursed him secretly.

## Description of the Pharaoh and Birth of Moses - Quranic

Allah the Almighty revealed: "These are Verses of the manifest Book (that makes clear truth from falsehood, good from evil, etc.). We recite to you from the news of Moses and Pharaoh in truth for a people who believe." [28-2-7]

نَتْلُواْ عَلَيْكَ مِن نَّبَإِ مُوسَىٰ وَفِرْعَوْنَ بِٱلْحَقِّ لِقَوْمٍ يُؤْمِنُونَ ﴿٣﴾

"Indeed, Pharaoh exalted himself in the land and made its people into factions, oppressing a sector among them, slaughtering their [newborn] sons and keeping their females alive. Indeed, he was of the corrupters."

إِنَّ فِرْعَوْنَ عَلَا فِى ٱلْأَرْضِ وَجَعَلَ أَهْلَهَا شِيَعًا يَسْتَضْعِفُ طَآئِفَةً مِّنْهُمْ يُذَبِّحُ أَبْنَآءَهُمْ وَيَسْتَحْىِۦ نِسَآءَهُمْ إِنَّهُۥ كَانَ مِنَ ٱلْمُفْسِدِينَ ﴿٤﴾

"And We wanted to confer favor upon those who were oppressed in the land and make them leaders and make them inheritors."

وَنُرِيدُ أَن نَّمُنَّ عَلَى ٱلَّذِينَ ٱسْتُضْعِفُوا۟ فِى ٱلْأَرْضِ وَنَجْعَلَهُمْ أَئِمَّةً وَنَجْعَلَهُمُ ٱلْوَٰرِثِينَ ﴿٥﴾

"And establish them in the land and show Pharaoh and [his minister] Haman and their soldiers through them that which they had feared." [28:6]

وَنُمَكِّنَ لَهُمْ فِى ٱلْأَرْضِ وَنُرِىَ فِرْعَوْنَ وَهَٰمَٰنَ وَجُنُودَهُمَا مِنْهُم مَّا كَانُوا۟ يَحْذَرُونَ ﴿٦﴾

And We inspired to the mother of Moses, "Suckle him; but when you fear for him, cast him into the river and do not fear and do not grieve. Indeed, We will return him to you and will make him [one] of the messengers."

وَأَوْحَيْنَا إِلَىٰٓ أُمِّ مُوسَىٰٓ أَنْ أَرْضِعِيهِ ۖ فَإِذَا خِفْتِ عَلَيْهِ فَأَلْقِيهِ فِى ٱلْيَمِّ وَلَا تَخَافِى وَلَا تَحْزَنِىٓ ۖ إِنَّا رَآدُّوهُ إِلَيْكِ وَجَاعِلُوهُ مِنَ ٱلْمُرْسَلِينَ ﴿٧﴾

### Moses Thrown into the Nile

No sooner had the divine revelation finished that she obeyed the sacred and merciful call. She was commanded to make a basket for Moses. She nursed him, put him into the basket, then went to the shore of the Nile and threw it into the water. Her mother's heart, the most merciful one in the world, grieved as she threw her son into the Nile. However, she was aware that Allah was much more merciful to Moses than to her, that He loved him more than her. Allah was his Lord and the Lord of the Nile. Hardly had the basket touched the water of the Nile than Allah issued His command to the waves to be calm and gentle while carrying the child would one day be a prophet. She instructed her daughter to follow the course of the basket and to report back to her. As the daughter followed the floating basket along the riverbank, she found herself right in the palace grounds and saw what was unfolding before her eyes. The basket came to rest at the riverbank, which skirted the king's palace. The palace servants found the basket with the baby and took it to the Pharaoh and his queen. When the queen beheld the lovely infant, Allah instilled in her a strong love for this baby.

The Pharaoh's wife was very different from Pharaoh. He was a disbeliever; she was a believer. He was cruel; she was merciful. He was a tyrant; she was delicate and goodhearted. She was sad because she was infertile and had hoped to have a son. Hardly had she held the baby than she kissed him. Pharaoh was much amazed when he saw his wife hugging this baby to her breast. He was much astonished because his wife was weeping with joy, something he had never seen her do before. She requested her husband: "Let me keep the baby and let him be a son to us."

## Moses Finds a Home – Quranic

Almighty Allah said: "Then the household of Pharaoh picked him up, that he might become for them an enemy and a cause of grief. Verily! Pharaoh, Haman, and their hosts were sinners. And the wife of Pharaoh said; "A comfort of the eye for me and for you. Kill him not, perhaps he maybe of a benefit to us, or we may adopt him as a son." And they perceived not (the result of that). [28:9]

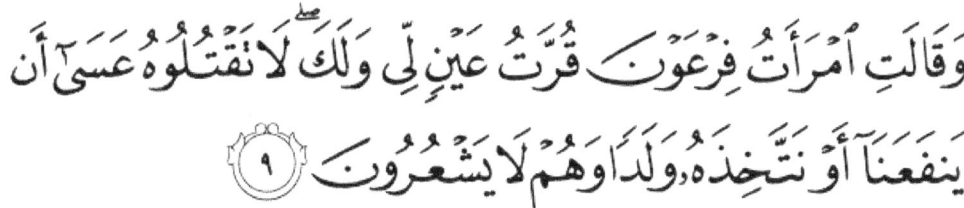

## Moses and His Mother Reunited

The queen summoned a few wet nurses to suckle the baby Moses, but he would not take any of their breasts. The queen was distressed and sent for more wet nurses. Moses' sister was also worried, as her baby brother was without milk for a long time. Seeing the queen's anxiety, she blurted that she knew a mother who would suckle the child affectionately. They asked her why she was following the floating basket. She said she did so out of curiosity. Her excuse sounded reasonable, so they believed her. They ordered her to rush and fetch the woman she was talking about. Her mother also was waiting with a heavy heart, worried about the fate of her baby. Just then her daughter rushed in with the good news. Her heart lifted and she lost no time in reaching the palace. As the child was put to her breast, he immediately started suckling. Pharaoh was astonished and asked: "Who are you? This child has refused to take any other breast but yours." Had she told the truth, Pharaoh would have known that the child was an Israelite and would have killed Moses instantly. However, Allah gave her inner strength and she replied: "I am a woman of sweet milk and sweet smell, and no child refuses me." This answer satisfied Pharaoh. From that day onward, she was appointed as Moses's wet nurse. She continued to breast-feed him for a long time. When he was bigger and was weaned, she was allowed the privilege of visiting him. Moses was raised in the palace as a prince.

## Moses and His Mother Reunited - Quranic

"And the heart of the mother of Mûsa (Moses) became empty [from every thought, except the thought of Mûsa (Moses)]. She was very near to disclose his (case, i.e. the child is her son), had We not strengthened her heart (with Faith), so that she might remain as one of the believers. And she said to his [Musa's (Moses)] sister: "Follow him." So she (his sister) watched him from a far place secretly, while they perceived not. And We had already forbidden (other) foster suckling mothers for him, until she (his sister came up and) said: "Shall I direct you to a household who will rear him for you, and sincerely they will look after him in a good manner?" So did We restore him to his mother, that she might be delighted, and that she might not grieve, and that she might know that the Promise of Allah is true. But most of them know not." [28:10-13]. And when he attained his full strength, and was perfect (in manhood), We bestowed on him Hukman (Prophethood, right judgment of the affairs) and religious knowledge (of the religion of his forefathers, Islamic Monotheism). And thus do We reward the Muhsineen (good-doers)." [28:14]

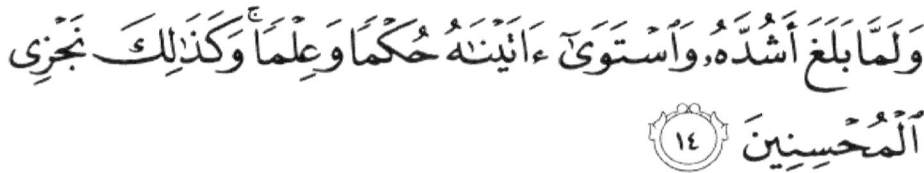

## Moses Kills an Egyptian

Allah had granted Moses (pbuh) good health, strength, knowledge, and wisdom. The weak and oppressed turned to him for protection and justice. One day in the main city, he saw two men fighting. One was an Israelite, who was being beaten by the other, an Egyptian. On seeing Moses, the Israelite begged him for help. Moses became involved in the dispute and, in a state of anger, struck a heavy blow on the Egyptian, who died on the spot. Upon realizing that he had killed a human being, Moses's heart was filled with deep sorrow, and immediately he begged Allah for forgiveness. He had not intended to kill the man. He pleaded with Almighty Allah to forgive him, and he felt a sense of peace filling his whole being. Thereafter Moses began to show more patience and sympathy towards people.

Days later Moses saw the same Israelite involved in another fight. Moses went to him and said: "You seem to be a quarrelsome fellow. You have a new quarrel with one person or another each day." Fearing that Moses might strike him, the Israelite warned Moses: "Would you kill me as you killed the wretch yesterday?" The Egyptian with whom the Israelite was fighting overheard this remark and reported Moses to the authorities. Soon thereafter, as Moses was passing through the city, a man approached and alerted him: "O Moses, the chiefs have taken counsel against you. You are to be tried and killed. I would advise you to escape."

## Moses Kills an Egyptian - Quranic

Moses knew that the penalty for killing an Egyptian was death. Allah the Exalted recounted: "And he entered the city at a time of unawareness of its people, and he found there two men fighting, one of his party (his religion, from the children of Israel), and the other of his foes. The man of his own party asked him for help against his foe, so Moses struck him with his fist and killed him. He said, "This is of Satan's doing, verily, he is a plain misleading enemy." He said: "My Lord! Verily, I have wronged myself, so forgive me." Then He forgave him. Verily, He is the Oft- Forgiving, the Most Merciful. He said: "My Lord! For that with which You have favored me, I will never more be a helper for the Mujrimeen (criminals, disobedient to Allah, polytheists, sinners, etc.)!" So he became afraid, looking about in the city (waiting as to what will be the result of his crime of killing), when behold, the man who had sought his help the day before, called for his help again. Moses said to him: "Verily, you are a plain misleader!" Then when he decided to seize the man who was an enemy to both of them, the man said: "O Moses! Is it your intention to kill me as you killed a man yesterday? Your aim is nothing but to become a tyrant in the land, and not to be one of those who do right." And there came a man running, from the farthest end of the city. He said: "O Moses! Verily, the chiefs are taking counsel together about you, to kill you, so escape. Truly, I am to you of those who give sincere advice." So he escaped from there, looking about in a state of fear. He said: "My Lord! Save me from the people who are Zalimeen (polytheists, and wrong-doers)!" [28:15-21].

## Moses Leaves Egypt

Moses left Egypt in a hurry without going to Pharaoh's palace. He was not prepared for traveling. He did not have a beast of burden upon which to ride, and he was not in a caravan. Instead, he left as soon as the believer came and warned him of Pharaoh's plans. He traveled in the direction of the country of Midian, which was the nearest inhabited land between Syria and Egypt. His only companion in this hot desert was Allah, and his only provision was piety. There was not a single root to pick to lessen his hunger. The hot sand burned the soles of his feet. However, fearing pursuit by Pharaoh's men, he forced himself to continue on.

## Moses Helps Women Shepherds

He traveled for eight nights, hiding during the day. After crossing the main desert, he reached a watering hole outside Midian where shepherds were watering their flocks. No sooner had Moses reached the Midian than he threw himself under a tree to rest. He suffered from hunger and fatigue. The soles of his feet felt as if they were worn out from hard walking on sand and rocks and from the dust. He did not have any money to buy a new pair of sandals, nor to buy food or drink.

Moses noticed a band of shepherds watering their sheep. He went to the spring, where he saw two young women preventing their sheep from mixing with the others. Moses sensed that the women were in need of help. Forgetting his thirst, he drew nearer to them and asked if he could help them in any way. The older sister said: "We are waiting until the shepherds finish watering their sheep, then we will water ours." Moses asked again: "Why are you waiting?" The younger one: "We cannot push men." Moses was surprised that women were shepherding, as only men were supposed to do it. It is hard and tiresome work, and one needs to be on the alert. Moses asked: "Why are you shepherding?" The younger sister said: "Our father is an old man; his health is too poor for him to go outdoors for pasturing sheep." Moses (pbuh) said: "I will water the sheep for you." When Moses approached the water, he saw that the shepherds had put over the mouth of the spring an immense rock that could only be moved by ten men. Moses embraced the rock and lifted it out of the spring's mouth, the veins of his neck and hands standing out as he did so. Moses was certainly strong. He watered their sheep and put the rock back in its place. He returned to sit in the shade of the tree. At this moment he realized that he had forgotten to drink. His stomach was sunken because of hunger.

## Moses Helps Women Shepherds - Quranic

Almighty Allah described this event: "And when he arrived at the water of Midian (Midyan) he found there a group of men watering their flocks, and besides them he found two women who were keeping back their flocks. He said: "What is the matter with you?" They said: "We cannot water (our flocks) until the shepherds take their flocks. And our father is a very old man." So he watered their flocks for them, then he turned back to shade, and said: "My Lord! Truly, I am in need of whatever good that You bestow on me!" [28:22-24]

## Moses Finds a Home among Shepherds

The young ladies returned home earlier than usual, which surprised their father. They related the incident at the spring which was the reason that they were back early. Their father sent one of his daughters to invite the stranger to his home. Bashfully, the woman approached Moses and delivered the message. "My father is grateful for what you have done for us. He invites you to our home so that he may thank you personally." Moses welcomed this invitation and accompanied the maiden to her father.

Moses could see that they lived comfortably as a happy and peaceful household. He introduced himself and told the old man about the misfortune that he had befallen him and had compelled him to flee from Egypt. The old man comforted him: "Fear not, you have escaped from the wrong-doers." Moses's gentle behavior was noticed by the father and his daughters. The kind man invited him to stay with them. Moses felt at home with this happy household, for they were friendly and feared Allah.

## Moses Becomes a Shepherd

One of the daughters suggested to her father that he employ Moses, as he was strong and trustworthy. They needed someone like him, especially at the water hole, which was visited by ruffians. The father asked her how she could be sure of his trustworthiness in such a short time. She replied: "When I bade him to follow me to our home, he insisted that I walk behind him so he would not observe my form (to avoid sexual attraction)." The old man was pleased to hear this. He approached Moses and said: "I wish to marry you to one of my daughters on condition that you agree to work for me for a period of eight years." This offer suited Moses well, for being a stranger, he would soon have to search for shelter, and work. Moses married the Midianite's daughter and looked after the old man's animals for ten long years.

## Moses Becomes a Shepherd - Quranic

Almighty Allah recounted: "Then there came to him one of the two women, walking shyly. She said: "Verily, my father calls you that he may reward you for having watered our flocks for us." So when he came to him and narrated the story, he said; "Fear you not. You have escaped from the people who are Zalimeen (polytheists, disbelievers, and wrong- doers)." And said one of them (the two women): "O my father! Hire him! He is strong and trustworthy." He said: "I intend to wed one of these two daughters of mine to you, on condition that you serve me for eight years, but if you complete ten years, it will be a favor from you. But I intend not to place you under a difficulty. If Allah wills, you will find me one of the righteous." He (Moses) said: "That is settled between me and you whichever of the two terms I fulfill, there will be no injustice to me, and Allah is Surety over what we say." [28:25-28]

## The Ten Years of Preparation

Time passed, and he lived in seclusion far from his family and his people. This period of ten years was of importance in his life. It was a period of major preparation. Certainly Moses's mind was absorbed in the stars every night. He followed the sunrise and the sunset every day. He pondered on the plant and how it splits and soil and appears thereafter. He contemplated water and how the earth is revived by it and flourishes after its death. Of course, he was immersed in the Glorious Book of Allah, open to the insight and heart. He was immersed in the existence of Allah. All these became latent within him. The religion of Moses (pbuh) was the same as that of Jacob (pbuh), which was Islamic monotheism. His forefather was Jacob (pbuh) the grandson of Abraham (pbuh). Moses (pbuh), therefore, was one of the descendants of Abraham (pbuh) and every prophet who came after Abraham was one of Abraham's successors. In addition to physical preparation, there was a similar spiritual preparation. It was made in complete seclusion, in the middle of the desert, and in the places of pasture.

Silence was his way of life, and seclusion was his vehicle. Allah the Almighty prepared for His prophet the tools he would need later on to righteously bear the commands of Allah the Exalted.

## Moses Decides to Return to Egypt

One day after the end of this period, a vague homesickness arose in Moses's heart. He wanted to return to Egypt. He was fast and firm in making his decision, telling his wife: "Tomorrow we shall leave for Egypt." His wife said to herself. "There are a thousand dangers in departing that have not yet been revealed." However, she obeyed her husband. Moses himself did not know the secret of the quick and sudden decision to return to Egypt. After all, he had fled from their ten years ago with a price on his head. Why should he go back now? Did he look forward to seeing his mother and brother? Did he think of visiting Pharaoh's wife who had raised him and who loved him as if she were his mother? No one knows what went through Moses's mind when he returned to Egypt. All we know is that a mute obedience to Allah's destinies impelled him to make a decision and he did. These supreme destinies steered his steps towards a matter of great importance.

## Moses Begins His Prophethood

Moses left Midian with his family and traveled through the desert until he reached Mount Sinai. There Moses discovered that he had lost his way. He sought Allah's direction and was shown the right course. At nightfall they reached Mount Tur. Moses noticed a fire in the distance. "I shall fetch a firebrand to warm us." As he neared the fire, he heard a sonorous voice calling him: "O Moses, I am Allah, the Lord of the Universe." Moses was bewildered and looked around. He again heard the strange voice. "And what is in you right hand, O Moses?" Shivering, Moses answered: "This is my staff on which I lean, and with which I beat down branches for my sheep, and for which I find other uses." (This question was asked so that Moses' attention would focus on the staff and to prepare him for the miracle which was to happen. This was the beginning of Moses's mission as a prophet (pbuh). The same voice commanded him: "Throw down your staff!" He did so, and at once the staff became a wriggling snake. Moses turned to run, but the voice again addressed him: "Fear not and grasp it; We shall return it to its former state." The snake changed back into his staff. Moses's fear subsided and was replaced by peace, for he realized that he was witnessing the Truth. Next, Allah commanded him to thrust his hand into his robe at the armpit. When he pulled it out, the hand had a brilliant shine.

Allah then commanded Moses: "You have two signs from Your Lord; go to Pharaoh and his chiefs, for they are an evil gang and have transgressed all bounds." However, Moses feared that he would be arrested by Pharaoh, so he turned to Allah saying: "My Lord! I have killed a man among them and I fear that they will kill me."

Allah assured him of his safety and set his heart at rest. Almighty Allah narrated this event: "And has there come to you the story of Moses? When he saw a fire, he said to his family: "Wait! Verily, I have seen a fire, perhaps I can bring you some burning brand therefrom, or find some guidance at the fire." And when he came to it the fire, he was called by name: "O Moses! Verily! I am your Lord! So take off your shoes, you are in the sacred valley, Tuwa. And I have chosen you. So listen to that which is inspired to you. Verily! I am Allah! La ilaha illa Ana (none has the right to be worshipped but I), so worship Me, and offer prayers perfectly, for My Remembrance. Verily, the Hour is coming - and My Will is to keep it hidden - that every person may be rewarded for that which he strives. Therefore, let the one who believes not therein (in the Day of Resurrection, Reckoning, Paradise and Hell etc.) but follows his own lusts, divert your therefrom lest you perish. And what is that in your right hand, O Moses?" He said: "This is my stick, whereon I lean, and wherewith I beat down branches for my sheep and wherein I find other uses." Allah said: "Cast it down, O Moses!" He cast it down, and behold! It was a snake, moving quickly. Allah said: "Grasp it, and fear not, We shall return it to its former state, and press your right hand to your left side, it will come forth white and shining, and without any disease as another sign, that We may show you some of Our Greater Signs. "Go To Pharaoh! Verily! He has transgressed (all bounds in disbelief & disobedience, and has behaved as an arrogant, and as a tyrant)." [20:9-24].

## Moses and Aaron (peace be upon them) Given Their Duties - Quranic

Moses said: "O my Lord! Open for me my chest (grant me self-confidence, contentment, and boldness). And ease my task for me; and make loose the knot (the defect) from my tongue, (remove the incorrectness of my speech) that they understand my speech, and appoint for me a helper from my family, Aaron, my brother; increase my strength with him, and let him share my task (of conveying Allah's Message and Prophet hood), and we may glorify You much, and remember You much, Verily! You are of us Ever a Well-Seer." Allah said: "You are granted your request, O Moses! And indeed We conferred a favor on you another time before. When We inspired your mother with that which We inspired, saying: "put him (the child) into the Tabut (a box or a case or a chest) and put him into the river (Nile), and then the river shall cast it up on the bank, and there, an enemy of Mine and an enemy of his shall take him.' And I endured you with love from Me, in order that you may be brought up under My Eye, when your sister went and said; "shall I show you one who will nurse him?' So We restored you to your mother that she might cool her eyes and she should not grieve. Then you did kill a man, but We saved you from a great distress and tried you with a heavy trial. Then you stayed a number of years with the people of Midian.

Then you came here according to the term which I ordained (for you), O Moses! "And I have Istana'tuka (chosen you for My Inspiration and My Message) for Myself. Go you and your brother with My Ayat (proofs, lessons, verses, evidences, signs, revelations, etc.), and do not, you both, slacken and become weak in My Remembrance.

"Go, both of you, to Pharaoh, verily, he has transgressed all bounds in disbelief and disobedience and behaved as an arrogant and as a tyrant. And speak to him mildly, perhaps he may accept admonition or fear Allah." They said: "Our Lord! Verily! We fear lest he should hasten to punish us or lest he should transgress all bounds against us." He (Allah) said: "Fear not, Verily! I am with you both, Hearing and Seeing. So go you both to him, and say: "Verily, we are Messengers of your Lord, so let the children of Israel go with us, and torment them not; indeed, we have come with a sign from your Lord! And peace will be upon him who follows the guidance! Truly, it has been revealed to us that the torment will be for him who denies (believes not in the Oneness of Allah, and in His Messengers, etc.), and turns away' (from the truth, and obedience of Allah)." [20:9-48]

## Moses and Aaron (pbut) Talk to the Pharaoh

Moses (pbuh) and Aaron (pbuh) went together to Pharaoh and delivered their message. Moses spoke to him about Allah, His mercy and His Paradise and about the obligations of monotheism and His worship. Pharaoh listened to Moses' speech with disdain. He thought that Moses was crazy because he dared to question his supreme position. Then he raised his hand and asked: "What do you want?" Moses answered: "I want you to send the children of Israel with us." Pharaoh asked: "Why should I send them, as they are my slaves?" Moses replied: "They are the slaves of Allah, Lord of the Worlds." Pharaoh then inquired sarcastically if his name was Moses. Moses said "Yes." "Are you not the Moses whom we picked up from the Nile as a helpless baby? Are you not the Moses whom we reared in this palace, who ate and drank from our provisions and whom our wealth showered with charity? Are you not the Moses who is a fugitive, the killer of an Egyptian man, if my memory does not betray me? It is said that killing is an act of disbelief. Therefore, you were a disbeliever when you killed. You are a fugitive from justice and you come to speak to me! What were you talking about Moses, I forgot?" Moses knew that Pharaoh's mentioning his past, his upbringing, and his receiving Pharaoh's charity was Pharaoh's way of threatening him.

Moses ignored his sarcasm and explained that he was not a disbeliever when he killed the Egyptian, he only went astray and Allah the Almighty had not yet given him the revelation at that time. He made Pharaoh understand that he fled from Egypt because he was afraid of their revenge upon him, even though the killing was an accident. He informed him that Allah had granted him forgiveness and made him one of the messengers.

## Moses and Aaron (pbut) Talk to the Pharaoh - Quranic

Allah the Almighty revealed to us part of the dialogue between Moses (pbuh) and Pharaoh: Allah said: "Nay! Go you both with Our Signs, Verily! We shall be with you, listening. And when you both come to Pharaoh, say: We are the Messengers of the Lord of the Alamin (mankind, jinn and all that exists), and so allow the children of Israel to go with us." Pharaoh said to Moses: "Did we not bring you up among us as a child? And you did dwell many years of your life with us. And you did your deed which you did (the crime of killing a man) and you are one of the ingrates." Moses said: "I did it then, when I was an ignorant (as regards my Lord and His Message). So I fled from you when I feared you. But my Lord has granted me Hukman (religious knowledge, right judgments of the affairs and Prophet Hood), and appointed me as one of the Messengers. And this is the past favor with which you reproach me, and that you have enslaved the children of Israel." Pharaoh said: "And what is the Lord of the Alamin (mankind, jinn and all that exists)?" Moses replied: "Lord of the heavens, and the earth, and all that is between them, if you seek to be convinced with certainty."

Pharaoh said to those around: "Do you not hear what he says?" Moses said: "Your Lord and the Lord of your ancient fathers!" Pharaoh said: "Verily, your Messenger who has been sent to you is a madman!" Moses said: "Lord of the east, and the west, and all that is between them, if you did but understand!" Pharaoh said: "If you choose a god other than me, I will certainly put you among the prisoners." Moses said: "Even if I bring you something manifest (and convincing)." Pharaoh said: "Bring it forth then, if you are of the truthful!" [26:16-31]

فَأْتِيَا فِرْعَوْنَ فَقُولَا إِنَّا رَسُولُ رَبِّ ٱلْعَٰلَمِينَ ﴿١٦﴾

أَنْ أَرْسِلْ مَعَنَا بَنِىٓ إِسْرَٰٓءِيلَ ﴿١٧﴾

وَفَعَلْتَ فَعْلَتَكَ ٱلَّتِى فَعَلْتَ وَأَنتَ مِنَ ٱلْكَٰفِرِينَ ﴿١٩﴾

قَالَ فَعَلْتُهَآ إِذًا وَأَنَا۠ مِنَ ٱلضَّآلِّينَ ﴿٢٠﴾

$$\text{فَفَرَرْتُ مِنكُمْ لَمَّا خِفْتُكُمْ فَوَهَبَ لِي رَبِّي حُكْمًا وَجَعَلَنِي مِنَ الْمُرْسَلِينَ ﴿٢١﴾}$$

### Moses Proves Himself Right

The degree of the conflict expressed in this dialogue reached its apex; thus, the tone of dialogue changed. Moses used a convincing intellectual argument against Pharaoh. However, Pharaoh escaped from the circle of dialogue based on the logic and began a dialogue of another type, a type which Moses could not bear to follow; a dialogue of menacing and threatening. Pharaoh deliberately adopted the style of the absolute ruler. He asked Moses how he dared to worship Allah! Did he not know that Pharaoh was a god? After declaring his divinity, Pharaoh asked Moses how he dared to worship another god. The punishment for this crime was imprisonment. It was not permitted for anyone to worship anyone other than the Pharaoh. Moses understood that the intellectual arguments did not succeed. The calm dialogue was converted from sarcasm to mentioning charity, then to scorn, then to the threat of imprisonment. Moses said: "Even if I bring you something manifest and convincing." The Pharaoh said: "Bring it forth, then, if you are of the truthful!" So Moses threw his stick, and behold, it was a serpent, manifest. And he drew out his hand, and behold, it was white to all beholders! [26:30-33].

### Moses Defeats the Magicians

Pharaoh's amazement turned to terror. Fearing that his rule was in danger, he addressed his advisors: "These are two wizards who will strip you of your best traditions and drive you of the country with their magic. What do you advice?" they counseled Pharaoh to detain Moses and his brother while they summoned the cleverest magicians in the country. Then they too, could show their skills of magic and change sticks into serpents. In this way they sought to reduce the influence of Moses's miracles on the masses. Pharaoh detained Moses and Aaron. He dispatched couriers all over the land to enlist the best magicians. He offered each successful magician a big reward, including appointment as a royal courtier. On the customary festival day, which attracted citizens from all over the Egyptian empire, Pharaoh arranged for a public contest between Moses and the magicians. The people came in droves as near before when they heard of the greatest contest ever between Pharaoh's many magicians and a single man who claimed to be a prophet. They had also heard of a baby who had once floated down the river Nile in a basket, landed on Pharaoh's palace grounds, been reared as a prince, and who later had fled for killing an Egyptian with a single blow.

Everyone was eager and excited to watch this great contest. Before it began, Moses arose. There was a hush in the huge crowd. Moses addressed the magicians. "Woe unto you, if you invent a lie against Allah by calling His miracles magic and by not being honest with the Pharaoh. Woe unto you, if you do not know the difference between the truth and falsehood. Allah will destroy you with His punishment, for he who lies against Allah fails miserably." Moses had spoken sincerely and made the magicians think. But they were overwhelmed by their greed for money and glory. They hoped to impress the people with their magic and to expose Moses as a fraud and a cheat. Moses asked the magicians to perform first. They threw their magical objects down on the ground. Their staffs and ropes took the forms of wriggling serpents while the crowd watched in amazement. Pharaoh and his men applauded loudly. Then Moses threw his staff. It began to wriggle and became an enormous serpent. The people stood up, craning their necks for a better view. Pharaoh and his men sat silently as, one by one, Moses's huge serpent swallowed all the snakes. Moses bent to pick it up, and it became a staff in his hand. The crowd rose like a great wave, shouting and screaming with excitement. A wonder like this had never been seen before! On witnessing the power of Moses, the magicians prostrated themselves to Allah, declaring: "We believe in the Lord of Moses and Aaron." Pharaoh was angry and began plotting his next move. He charged that the demonstration had been arranged secretly between Moses and the magicians. He demanded that the magicians confess to their scheme, threatening them with death. They refused to denounce Allah and stuck to their sincerity of their belief. No longer hiding his cruel nature, Pharaoh threatened to cut off their hands and feet and to crucify them on the trunks of palm trees as an example to his subjects.

## Moses Defeats the Magicians - Quranic

Almighty Allah recounted this event: "He (Pharaoh) said: "Have you come to drive us out of our land with your magic, O Moses? Then verily, we can produce magic the like thereof; so appoint a meeting between us and you, which neither we, nor you shall fail to keep, in an open wide place where both shall have a just and equal chance (and beholders could witness the competition)."  Moses said: "your appointed meeting is the day of the festival, and let the people assemble when the sun has risen (forenoon)." The Pharaoh withdrew, devised his plot and then came back. Moses said to them: "Woe unto you! Invent not a lie against Allah, lest He should destroy you completely by a torment. And surely, he who invents a lie (against Allah) will fail miserably." Then they debated with one another what they must do, and they kept their talk secret. They said: "Verily! There are two magicians. Their object is to drive you out from your land with magic and overcome your chiefs and nobles. So devise your plot, and then assemble in line. And whoever overcomes this day will be indeed successful." They said: "O Moses! Either you throw first or we be the first to throw?" Moses said: "nay, throw you (first)!" Then behold, their ropes and their sticks, by their magic, appeared to him as though they moved fast. So Moses conceived a fear in himself. We (Allah) said: "Fear not! Surely, you will have the upper hand. Throw that which is in your right hand! It will swallow up that which they have made.

That which they have made is only a magician's trick, and the magician will never be successful, no matter whatever amount of skill he may attain." So the magicians fell down prostrate. They said: "We believe in the Lord of Aaron and Moses." Pharaoh said: "Believe you in him (Moses) before I give you permission? Verily! He is your chief who taught you magic. So I will surely cut off your hands and feet on opposite sides, and I will surely crucify you on the trunks of palm trees, and you shall surely know which of us (I Pharaoh,) or the Lord of (Moses) (Allah), can give the severe and more lasting torment." They said: "We prefer you not over the clear signs that have come to us, and to Him (Allah) Who created us. So decree (regarding) this life of the world. Verily! We have believed in our Lord, that He may forgive us our faults, and the magic to which you did compel us. And Allah is better as regards reward in comparison to your (Pharaoh's) reward, and more lasting (as regards punishment in comparison to you punishment)."

## Allah's Description of Believers and Non-Believers - Quranic

Verily! Whoever comes to his Lord as a Mujrim (criminal, polytheist, disbeliever, in the Oneness of Allah and His Messengers, sinner, etc.), then surely, for him is Hell, therein he will neither die nor live. But whoever comes to Him (Allah) as a believer (in the Oneness of Allah, etc.), and has done righteous good deeds, for such are the high ranks (in the Hereafter), - Everlasting Gardens (And Paradise), under which rivers flow, wherein they will abide forever; such is the reward of those who purify themselves (by abstaining from all kinds of sins and evil deeds which Allah has forbidden and by doing all that which Allah has ordained). [20:58-76]

## The People's Non-Reaction to the defeat of the magicians

The magicians represented the elite of the Egyptian society. They were its scholars. They prostrated before righteousness, but the people abandoned them and left them to their fate. The path of righteousness was plain, but in spite of this, the people did nothing but stand by and watch. If every one of the Egyptians had stopped to pick up a piece of brick and had thrown it at Pharaoh, he would have fallen dead and the history of Egypt would have been changed. This obviously did not happen. None of the people moved. Each one stood motionless in his place. The people did nothing but watch, and they paid the price of this inactivity: they were drowned later as the price for the cowardice of one day.

## The Pharaoh's Reaction to Moses Victory

Moses and Aaron left, and Pharaoh returned to his palace. Pharaoh entered to his palace. Pharaoh was completely stupefied when he faced the two miracles. When Moses went out of his presence, his emotions changed from amazement and fear to violent rage. He quarreled with his ministers and men, reviled them bitterly for no reason, and commanded them to get out of his presence. When he was left alone, he tried to think more calmly. He drank several cups of wine, but his anger did not abate. Then he summoned all the ministers, leaders, and responsible men for a serious meeting. Pharaoh entered the meeting with a rigid face.

It was obvious that he would never surrender easily. He had established a kingdom on the basis of his being a god worshipped by the Egyptian people. Now Moses came to destroy what he had built. Moses said that there was no Lord other than Allah in existence. This meant that Pharaoh was a liar. Pharaoh opened the session by throwing a sudden question at Haman: "Am I a liar, O Haman?" Haman fell to his knees in amazement and asked: "Who dared to accuse Pharaoh of lying?" Pharaoh said: "Has he (Moses) not said that there is a Lord in the heaven?" Haman answered: "Moses is lying." Turning his face to the other side, Pharaoh asserted impatiently: "I know he is a liar." Then he looked towards Haman (and cried): "O Haman! Build me a tower that I may arrive at the ways, - the ways of the heavens, and I may look upon the Ilah (God) of Moses but verily, I think him to be a liar." Thus it was made fair seeming, in Pharaoh's eyes, the evil of his deeds, and he was hindered from the Right Path, and the plot of Pharaoh led to nothing but loss and destruction for him. [40:36-37]. The Pharaoh issued his royal command to erect a lofty tower, its height to reach the heavens. Pharaoh's command depended fundamentally upon Egyptian civilization and its fondness for building what Pharaoh wanted. However, he ignored the rules of engineering. In spite of this, Haman assented (hypocritically), knowing that it was impossible to erect such a tower. He said that he would issue a command to build it immediately. "However, your majesty, let me object to Pharaoh for the first time. You will never find anyone in the heavens. There is no god but you." Pharaoh listened to a settled fact. Then he declared in the famous meeting his historic line: "O chiefs! I know not a god other than me." [28:38].

وَقَالَ فِرْعَوْنُ يَٰٓأَيُّهَا ٱلْمَلَأُ مَا عَلِمْتُ لَكُم مِّنْ إِلَٰهٍ غَيْرِى فَأَوْقِدْ لِى يَٰهَٰمَٰنُ عَلَى ٱلطِّينِ فَٱجْعَل لِّى صَرْحًا لَّعَلِّىٓ أَطَّلِعُ إِلَىٰٓ إِلَٰهِ مُوسَىٰ وَإِنِّى لَأَظُنُّهُۥ مِنَ ٱلْكَٰذِبِينَ ﴿٣٨﴾

## Pharaoh's Men Spread Rumors

Pharaoh was absorbed in his new problem. A series of serious meetings began in his palace. He summoned those responsible for the army, the police and, what we call today his director of intelligence. He also summoned the ministers, princes, and priests. He called whoever had a powerful effect on the direction of events. Pharaoh asked his director of intelligence: "What do people say?" He said: "My men have spread among them that Moses won the contest because of a plot and that a major magician had joined with him in this plan. The plot had been disclosed, and we believe an unknown authority financed it." Pharaoh asked his director of police: "What about the magicians' corpses?" He said: "My men hung them in public squares and markets to terrify the people. We will spread a rumor that Pharaoh will kill whoever had anything to do with the plot."

Then Pharaoh asked the commander of the army: "What does the army say?" He said: "The army hopes that commands will be issued to move in whatever direction Pharaoh desires." Pharaoh said: "The role of the army has not come yet. Its role will come."

## Pharaoh's Men Harm the Believers

Pharaoh fell silent. Haman, the Prime Minister, moved and raised his hand to speak. Pharaoh permitted him and Haman asked: "Will we leave Moses and his people to corrupt the rest of the people on the earth so that they leave your worship?" Pharaoh said: "You read my thoughts, O Haman. We will kill their sons, rape their women, and conquer them." He issued commands, and Pharaoh's men rushed to slay the sons, rape the women, and imprison whomever objected to these acts. Moses stood watching what was happening. He could not interfere, nor did he have the power to forbid these acts. All he could do was to advise his people to be patient. He ordered them to ask Allah the Almighty for a calamity on the Egyptians. He pointed out to them the model of the Egyptian magicians who endured for Allah's sake without complaint. He helped them to understand that Pharaoh's soldiers behaved on earth as if they were its private owners. Pharaoh's terrorism infused the children of Israel with a spirit of defeat. They complained to Moses: "We (children of Israel) had suffered troubles before you came to us, and since you have come to us." He said: "It may be that your Lord will destroy your enemy and make you successors on the earth, so that He may see how you act." [7:129].

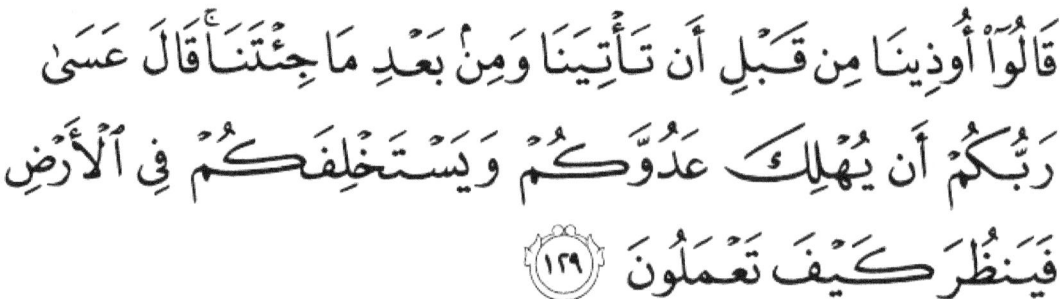

## Korah - His Actions and Destruction

Moses began to face a difficult situation. He had to confront Pharaoh's anger and his plots, while at the same time he had to deal with the mutiny of his people. In the midst of all this, Korah moved. Korah was one of Moses' people. He was very rich and lived in a magnificent mansion. He wore only the most expensive clothes. Numerous slaves waited on him and he indulged in every known luxury. His enormous wealth made him arrogant. Korah treated the poor with contempt and told them that their poverty was due to their lack of intelligence. He believed that what he owned was due to his own cleverness and business ability. Moses reminded Korah to pay alms (zakat) on his wealth, a portion of which was rightfully due to the poor. Alms are compulsory upon all the believers.

Korah was annoyed by this advice and told Moses that his being wealthy was proof that he was favored by Allah, Who approved of his life-style and increased his wealth daily. Moses argued with him and warned him of the result of his wicked thoughts. When Korah calculated the alms due on his wealth, he was shocked at the large amount he had to part with. He not only refused to give alms, but spread a rumor that Moses had invented the law of zakat for his own gain. He even bribed the people to oppose Moses and to spread wicked rumors about him. Allah warned Moses of Korah's plot. Moses appealed to Allah to punish him for his stinginess and for defying His laws. Allah's anger fell on Korah. The earth opened up and swallowed him, his mansion and all his wealth, as if he had never existed.

## Korah - His Actions and Destruction - Quranic

Almighty Allah revealed: "Verily, Korah was of Moses's people, but he behaved arrogantly towards them. And We gave him treasures that of which the keys would have been a burden to a body of strong men. When his people said to him: "Do not be glad with ungratefulness to Allah's Favors). Verily! Allah likes not those who are glad (with wealth) which Allah has bestowed on you, the home of the Hereafter, and forget nor your portion of legal enjoyment in this world, and do good as Allah has been good to you, and seek not mischief in the land. Verily, Allah likes not the Mufsideen (those who commit great crimes and sins, oppressors, tyrants)." He said: "This has been given to me only because of my knowledge." Did he not know that Allah had destroyed before him generations, men who were stronger than him in might and greater in the amount of wealth but the Murimun (criminals, disbelievers, polytheists, sinners, etc.) will not be questioned of their sins (because Allah knows them well, so they will be punished without account). So he went forth before his people in his pomp. Those who were desirous of the life of the world said: "Ah, would that we had the like of what Korah has been given! Verily! He is the owner of a great fortune." But those who had been given religious knowledge said: "Woe to you! The Reward of Allah (in the Hereafter) is better for those who believe and do righteous good deeds, and this none shall attain except those who are patient (in following the truth)." So We caused the earth to swallow him and his dwelling place. Then he had no group or party to help him against Allah, nor was he one of those who could save themselves. And those who had desired (for a position like) his position, the day before, began to say; "Know you not that it is Allah Who enlarges the provision or restricts it to whomsoever He please of His slaves? Had it not been that Allah was Gracious to us, He could have caused the earth to swallow us up also!" Know you not that the disbelievers will never be successful? [28:76-82].

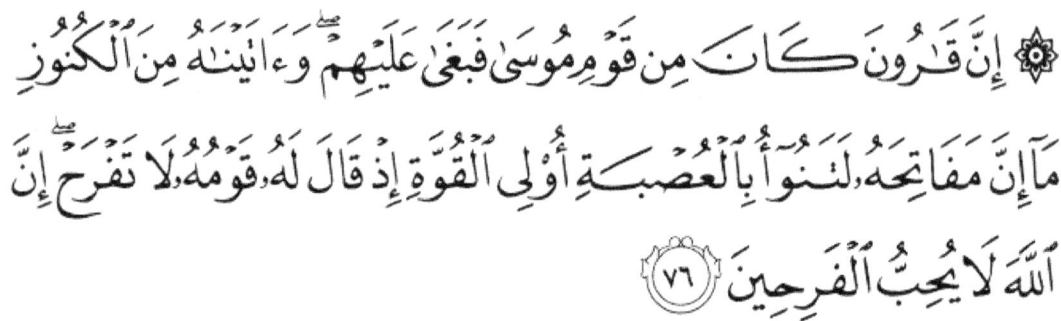

### The Pharaohs Relative Defends Moses

When the Egyptians and children of Israel examined the miracle, the conflict between Moses and Pharaoh again reached a crisis because Pharaoh believed that Moses was threatening his kingdom. Pharaoh was afraid that the people would be misled by Moses. He suggested to his ministers and notable men that Moses be killed. We believe that Haman supported the idea along with a front of disbelievers. It was on the verge of approval, except for the vote of one of the notable men of the state, whose name is not mentioned in the Quran. The Quran says only that this man was a believer. This believer spoke in the assembly where the idea of killing Moses had been introduced. He proved that it was not a good idea: "Moses did not say more than that Allah is his Lord. Later, he came with clear evidence that he is a messenger. There are two possibilities; either Moses is righteous or a liar. If he lies, he will be responsible for his lie. If he is righteous and we slay him, where is the guarantee that we will be rescued from the torment of Allah? Neither way, he neither says nor does anything that merits our killing him." This angered Pharaoh and his counselors and they threatened to harm the man, but he refused to budge from his stance. Then they tried to woo him back, but he still warned them that they were inviting their doom. This angered Pharaoh more, and he now threatened to kill the man. However, Allah protected His believer.

The Pharaoh's Relative Defends Moses - Quranic Almighty Allah revealed their dialogue: Pharaoh said: "Leave me to kill Moses, and let him call his Lord (to stop me from killing him)! I fear that he may change your religion, or that he may cause mischief to appear in the land!" Moses said: "Verily, I seek refuge in my Lord and your Lord from every arrogant who believes not in the Day of Reckoning!" And a believing man of Pharaoh's family, who hid his faith said: "Would you kill a man because he says: My Lord is Allah, and he has come to you with clear signs (proofs) from your Lord? And if he is a liar, upon him will be (the sin of) his lie; but if he is telling the truth, then some of that calamity wherewith he threatens you will befall on you.

Verily, Allah guides not one who is a Musrif (a polytheist, or a murderer who shed blood without a right, or those who commit great sins, oppressor, transgressor, a liar! O my people! Yours is the kingdom this day, you are uppermost in the land. But, who will save us from the Torment of Allah, should it befall us?" Pharaoh said: "I show you only that which I see correct and I guide you only to the path of right policy!" And he who believed said: "O my people! Verily, I fear for you a fate like that day of disaster of the confederate of old! Like the fate of the people of Noah, and 'Ad, and Thamud, and those who came after them. And Allah wills no injustice for His slaves. And, O my people! Verily! I fear for you the Day when there will be mutual calling between the people of Hell and of Paradise."

A Day when you will turn your backs and flee having no protector from Allah, and whomsoever Allah sends astray, for him there is no guide. And indeed Joseph did come to you, in times gone by, with clear signs, but you ceased not to doubt in that which he did bring to you, till when he died you said: "No Messenger will Allah send after him." Thus Allah leaves astray him who is a Musrif (a polytheist, oppressor, a criminal, sinner who commits great sins) and a Murtab (one who doubts Allah's warning and His Oneness). Those who dispute about the Ayat (proofs, evidences, verses, lessons, revelations and signs, etc.) of Allah, without any authority that has come to them, it is greatly hateful in the Sight of Allah and in the sigh of those who believe. Thus does Allah seal up the heart of every arrogant, tyrant. (So they cannot guide themselves to the Right Path). And Pharaoh said: "O Haman! Build me a tower that I may arrive at the ways, - the ways of the heavens, and I may look upon the Ilah (God) of Moses but verily, I think him to be a liar."

Thus it was made fair seeming, in Pharaoh's eyes, the evil of his deeds, and he was hindered from the Right Path, and the plot of Pharaoh led to nothing but loss and destruction for him. And the man who believed said: "O my people! Follow me, I will guide you to the way of right conduct (guide you to Allah's Religion of Islamic Monotheism with which Moses has been sent). O my people! Truly, this life of the world is nothing but a (quick passing) enjoyment, and verily, the Hereafter that is the home that will remain forever. Whosoever does an evil deed, will not be requited except the like thereof, and whosoever does a righteous deed, whether male or female, and is a true believer (in the Oneness of Allah), such will enter Paradise, where they will be provided therein (with all things in abundance) without limit." "And O my people! How is it that I call you to salvation while you call me to the Fire! You invite me to disbelieve in Allah (and in His Oneness), and to join partners in worship with Him, of which I have no knowledge, and I invite you to the All-Mighty, the Oft-Forgiving! No doubt you call me to worship one who cannot grant me my request or respond to my invocation in this world or in the Hereafter. And our return will be to Allah, and Al-Musrifeen (polytheists, and arrogant, those who commit great sins, the transgressors of Allah's set limits)! They shall be the dwellers of the Fire! And you will remember what I am telling you, and my affair I leave it to Allah." So Allah saved him from the evils that they plotted (against him), while an evil torment encompassed Pharaoh's people. [40:26-45]

## The Plagues of Egypt

Moses repeated his demand that Pharaoh release the children of Israel from slavery. In response, Pharaoh called his subjects, including the children of Israel, to a huge gathering where he reminded them that he was their lord and provided all their needs. Moses, he said, had no gold amulets nor angels following him; he was just a poor man. Being a people who had been oppressed for a very long time, they lacked vision. Their judgment were limited to what they could see in the material world. They regarded their ruler to be wealthy and able to provide all their worldly needs. In ignorance, they obeyed Pharaoh and ignored Moses's call.

## Egypt Suffers a Drought and a Flood, Crops are destroyed by Locusts

Allah commanded Moses to warn Pharaoh of a punishment in this world for his faithlessness and his persecution of the children of Israel. As a portent of the punishment which Allah would meet out, the Nile did not flood its banks to soak the dry land as it normally did. As a result, crops failed, leading to famine. However Pharaoh remained arrogant, so Allah caused a huge flood, which devastated the land. As often as they were troubled grievously, they appealed to Moses thus: "O Moses! Invoke your Lord for us because of His Promise to you. IF you will remove the punishment from us, we indeed shall believe in you, and we shall let the children of Israel go with you." [7:134]

وَلَمَّا وَقَعَ عَلَيْهِمُ ٱلرِّجْزُ قَالُوا۟ يَٰمُوسَى ٱدْعُ لَنَا رَبَّكَ بِمَا عَهِدَ عِندَكَ لَئِن كَشَفْتَ عَنَّا ٱلرِّجْزَ لَنُؤْمِنَنَّ لَكَ وَلَنُرْسِلَنَّ مَعَكَ بَنِىٓ إِسْرَٰٓءِيلَ ﴿١٣٤﴾

Moses prayed to his Lord and He relived the suffering caused by the flood. The surging water ceased and withdrew from the land, and it became cultivatable. But when Moses bade them to fulfill their promise to release the children of Israel, they did not respond. Then Allah sent swarms of locusts which ate whatever corps they had grown. The people hurried to Moses, asking him to invoke Allah to remove this affliction and promising they would send the children of Israel with him this time. The locusts departed, but they did not fulfill their promise.

## Egypt Becomes Infested with Lice and Frogs

Then another sign came, the sign of lice, which spread amongst the Egyptians, carrying diseases. Their refuge to Moses and their promise to him was repeated. His prayer to Allah was repeated and so, too, their breach of promise, as usual. A sign of frogs was revealed. The land suddenly filled with frogs. They jumped on the food of the Egyptians, shared their houses, and distressed them greatly. The Egyptians went to Moses again, promising him to release the children of Israel. He prayed to his Lord, and Allah relieved them of the problem of the frogs, but they again broke their promise.

## Nile's water was changed to Blood

Then the last sign was revealed, the sign of blood. The Nile water was changed into blood. When Moses and his people drank the water, it was, for them, ordinary water. However, if any Egyptian filled his cup with the water, he discovered his cup full of blood. They hurried to Moses as usual, but as soon as everything returned to normal, they turned their backs on Allah.

## Allah's Punishments on the Disbelievers - Quranic

Almighty Allah said: "And indeed We punished the people of Pharaoh with years of drought, and shortness of fruits (crops, etc.), that they might remember (take heed). But whenever good came to them, they said: "Ours is this." And if evil came to them, they ascribed it to evil omens connected with Moses and those with him. Be informed! Verily, their evil omens are with Allah but most of them know not. They said to Moses: "Whatever Ayat (proofs, evidences, verses, lessons, signs, revelations, etc.) you may bring to us, to work there with your sorcery on us, we shall never believe in you." So We sent on them: the flood, the locusts, the lice, the frogs, and the blood: (as a succession of) manifest signs, yet they remained arrogant, and they were of those people who were Mujrimeen (criminals, polytheists, sinners, etc.) [7:130-133]. Almighty Allah also said: "But when We removed the punishment from them to a fixed term, which they had to reach, behold! They broke their word! [7:135].

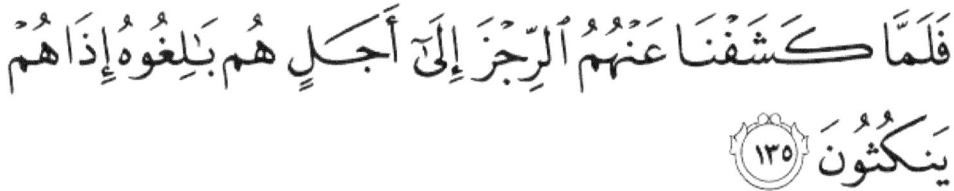

## Moses' Story - Condensed and Quranic

Pharaoh became ruder and more arrogant. He proclaimed to his people. "Pharaoh is the only god. Has he not the kingdom of Egypt and rivers flowing under it?" He declared that Moses was a liar, a magician, and a poor man who did not wear even one bracelet of gold. Almighty Allah declared: "And indeed We did sent Moses with Our Ayat (proofs, evidences, verses, lessons, signs, revelations, etc.) to Pharaoh and his chiefs (inviting them to Allah's Religion of Islam). He said: "Verily! I am a Messenger of the Lord of the Alamin (mankind, jinn and all that exists). But when he came to them with our Ayat (proofs, evidences, verses, lessons, signs, revelations, etc.) behold! They laughed at them. And not an Ayah (sign, etc.) We showed them but it was greater than its fellow, and We seized them with torment in order that they might turn from their polytheism to Allah's Religion (Islamic Monotheism). And they said to Moses: "O you sorcerer! Invoke your Lord for us according to what He has covenanted with you. Verily, we shall guide ourselves." But when We removed the torment from them, behold! They broke their covenant (that they will believe if We remove the torment for them). And Pharaoh proclaimed among his people, saying "O my people! Is not mine the dominion of Egypt, and the rivers flowing underneath me. See you not then? Am I not better than this one (Moses), and who is Mahin (has no honor nor any respect, and is weak, and despicable) and can scarcely express himself clearly? Why then are not golden bracelets bestowed on him, or angels sent along with him?" Thus he (Pharaoh) befooled and misled his people, and they obeyed him. Verily, they were Fasiqeen (rebellious, disobedient to Allah). So when they angered Us, We punished them, and drowned them all. And We made them a precedent (as a lesson for those coming after them), and an example to later generations. [43:46-56]

## Pharaoh and his Army Perish - Moses Allowed to Leave Egypt

It appeared that Pharaoh would never believe in Moses' message, nor would he stop the torture of the children of Israel. Therefore, Moses prayed to his Lord thus: "Our Lord! You have indeed bestowed on Pharaoh and his chief's splendor and wealth in the life of this world, our Lord! That they may lead men astray from Your Path. Our Lord! Destroy their wealth, and harden their hearts, so that they will not believe until they see the painful torment." Allah said: "Verily, the invocation of you both is accepted. So you both keep to the Straight Way (keep on doing good deeds, and preaching Allah's Message with patience), and follow not the path of those who know not (the truth, to believe in the Oneness of Allah, and also to believe in the Reward of Allah: Paradise etc.)." (Ch 10:88-89 Quran). Allah inspired Moses to conduct his people of Egypt, but only a few of his people believed in his message. Allah revealed: "But none believed in Moses except the offspring of his people, because of the fear of Pharaoh and his chiefs lest they should persecute them; and verily, Pharaoh was an arrogant tyrant on the earth, he was indeed one of the Musrifeen (polytheists, sinners, and transgressors, those who give up the truth and follow the evil, and commit all kinds of great sins).

And Moses said: "O my people! If you have believed in Allah, then put your trust in Him if you are Muslims (those who submit to Allah's Will)." They said: "In Allah we put our trust. Our Lord! Make us not a trial for the folk who are Zalimeen (polytheists, and wrong-doing) (do not make them overpower us). And save us by Your Mercy from the disbelieving folk." [10:83-86]

فَمَآ ءَامَنَ لِمُوسَىٰٓ إِلَّا ذُرِّيَّةٌ مِّن قَوْمِهِۦ عَلَىٰ خَوْفٍ مِّن فِرْعَوْنَ وَمَلَإِيْهِمْ أَن يَفْتِنَهُمْ ۚ وَإِنَّ فِرْعَوْنَ لَعَالٍ فِى ٱلْأَرْضِ وَإِنَّهُۥ لَمِنَ ٱلْمُسْرِفِينَ ﴿٨٣﴾

وَقَالَ مُوسَىٰ يَٰقَوْمِ إِن كُنتُمْ ءَامَنتُم بِٱللَّهِ فَعَلَيْهِ تَوَكَّلُوٓاْ إِن كُنتُم مُّسْلِمِينَ ﴿٨٤﴾

فَقَالُواْ عَلَى ٱللَّهِ تَوَكَّلْنَا رَبَّنَا لَا تَجْعَلْنَا فِتْنَةً لِّلْقَوْمِ ٱلظَّٰلِمِينَ ﴿٨٥﴾

وَنَجِّنَا بِرَحْمَتِكَ مِنَ ٱلْقَوْمِ ٱلْكَٰفِرِينَ ﴿٨٦﴾

Almighty Allah decided to put an end to Pharaoh's crimes after He had given him several chances. Allah commanded Moses to depart, and the children of Israel received reluctant permission from the Pharaoh to go out of the city for the feast. They prepared themselves to leave Egypt. This later became known as Exodus. They carried with them their jewels and borrowed a lot of jewels from the Egyptians.

The Pharaoh Learns of the Believer's Escape

In the darkness of night, Moses led his people towards the Red Sea, and in the morning they reached the beach. By then Pharaoh was aware of their departure, so he mobilized a huge army to pursue them.

## The Parting of the Red Sea

The impatient children of Israel soon became agitated and Joshua (Yusha), Ibn Nun, exclaimed: "In front of us is this impassable barrier, the sea, and behind us the enemy; surely death cannot be avoided!" Moses replied that he would wait for further guidance from Allah. These words filled them with some hope, but man is always impatient for results: they were willing to surrender themselves back into slavery. At that moment Allah revealed to Moses: "Smite the sea with your staff!" Moses did as he was commanded. A fierce wind blew, the sun shone brightly, and in a flash the sea parted, the crests of the waves standing like mountains on each side. Moses led his people across. This miracle proved Moses's oft-repeated claim. "Verily! My Lord is with me!" As they looked back, they saw Pharaoh and his army approaching, about to take the very path which had been opened for them. In great fear and panic, they pleaded with Moses to ask Allah to close the sea. However, Allah commanded Moses not to smite the sea with his staff again, for Allah's decree was already in action.

## The Death of the Pharaoh

Pharaoh and his army had seen the miracle, how the sea had parted, but being the pretender that he was, Pharaoh turned to his men and proclaimed: "Look! The sea has opened at my command so that I may follow those rebels and arrest them!" They rushed across the parted waters, and when they were midway, Allah commanded the sea to return to its former state. Terror-stricken Pharaoh, realizing his end had come, declared out of fear: "I believe that there is no god worthy of worship except Allah in Whom the children of Israel believe, and I am of those who surrender to Him." But Allah did not accept this declaration from the tyrant, and the waters closed over him, drowning him and his entire army. Almighty Allah narrated: "And We inspired Moses, saying: "Take away My slaves by night, verily, you will be pursued." Then Pharaoh sent callers to all the cities. Saying: "Verily! These indeed are but a small band. And verily, they have done what has enraged us; but we are host all assembled, amply fore-warned." So, We expelled them from gardens and springs, treasures, and every kind of honorable place. Thus (We turned them Pharaoh's people) out, and We caused the children of Israel to inherit them. So they pursued them at sunrise. And when the two hosts saw each other, the people of Moses said: "We are sure to be overtaken." Moses said: "Nay, verily! With me is my Lord, He will guide me." Then We inspired Moses saying: "Strike the sea with your stick." And it parted, and each separate (part of that sea water) became like the huge, firm mass of a mountain. Then We brought near the others (Pharaoh's party) to that place. And We saved Moses and all those with him. Then We drowned the others. Verily! In this is indeed a sign (or a proof), yet most of them are not believers. And verily, your Lord! He is truly the All-Mighty, the Most Merciful." [26:52-68]

## Moses' People Escape and Pharaoh's Death - Quranic

In another surah Almighty Allah narrated: "And We took the children of Israel across the sea, and Pharaoh with his hosts followed them in oppression and enmity, till when drowning overtook him, he said: "I believe that La ilaha illa huwa (none has the right to be worshipped but) He, in whom the children of Israel believe, and I am one of the Muslims (those who submit to Allah's Will)." Now (you believe) while you refused to believe before and you were one of the mufsideen (evildoers, corrupts, etc.).

So this day We shall deliver your dead body out from the sea that you may be a sign to those who come after you! And verily, many among mankind are heedless or our Ayah (proofs, evidences, verses, lessons, signs, revelations, etc.). [10:90-92]

﴿ وَجَاوَزْنَا بِبَنِى إِسْرَٰٓءِيلَ ٱلْبَحْرَ فَأَتْبَعَهُمْ فِرْعَوْنُ وَجُنُودُهُۥ بَغْيًا وَعَدْوًا ۖ حَتَّىٰٓ إِذَآ أَدْرَكَهُ ٱلْغَرَقُ قَالَ ءَامَنتُ أَنَّهُۥ لَآ إِلَٰهَ إِلَّا ٱلَّذِىٓ ءَامَنَتْ بِهِۦ بَنُوٓاْ إِسْرَٰٓءِيلَ وَأَنَا۠ مِنَ ٱلْمُسْلِمِينَ ﴿٩٠﴾ ءَآلْـَٰٔنَ وَقَدْ عَصَيْتَ قَبْلُ وَكُنتَ مِنَ ٱلْمُفْسِدِينَ ﴿٩١﴾ فَٱلْيَوْمَ نُنَجِّيكَ بِبَدَنِكَ لِتَكُونَ لِمَنْ خَلْفَكَ ءَايَةً ۚ وَإِنَّ كَثِيرًا مِّنَ ٱلنَّاسِ عَنْ ءَايَٰتِنَا لَغَٰفِلُونَ ﴿٩٢﴾

The curtain fell on Pharaoh's tyranny, and the waves threw his corpse up to the western seashore. The Egyptians saw him and knew that their god whom they worshipped and obeyed were mere slaves who could not keep death away from their own necks.

## The Moses' People Desire an Idol

In spite of Pharaoh's death, he left a bad influence on the souls of the children of Israel. It was difficult for the years of oppression and intense humility to pass easily. He had made them accustomed to humbling themselves and submitting to someone other than Allah. He had so suppressed their souls and spoiled their nature that they began to torture Moses out of ignorance and obstinacy.

The miracle of the parting of the sea was still fresh in their minds, damp sea sands were still stuck on their soles, when they passed by a people worshipping idols. Instead of manifesting their indignation at the idolaters' oppression of the intellect by celebrating the praises of Allah for His guidance, they looked to Moses for him to specify a god for them to worship as those other people did. They were jealous of the other people and their idols, and they desired the same. They missed the ancient idolatry which they had lived with during the reign of Pharaoh.

## Moses' People Desire an Idol - Quranic

Allah the Exalted revealed: "And We brought the Children of Israel (with safety) across the sea, and they came upon a people devoted to some of their idols (in worship). They said: "O Mûsa (Moses)! Make for us an ilâhan (a god) as they have âliha (gods)."

He said: "Verily, you are a people who know not (the Majesty and Greatness of Allâh and what is obligatory upon you, i.e. to worship none but Allah Alone, the One and the Only God of all that exists)." [Mûsa (Moses) added:] "Verily, these people will be destroyed for that which they are engaged in (idols-worship). And all that they are doing is in vain." He said: "Shall I seek for you an Ilâhan (a God) other than Allah, while He has given you superiority over the 'Alamîn (mankind and jinns of your time)." And (remember) when We rescued you from Fir'aun's (Pharaoh) people, who were afflicting you with the worst torment, killing your sons and letting your women live. And in that was a great trial from your Lord." [7:138]

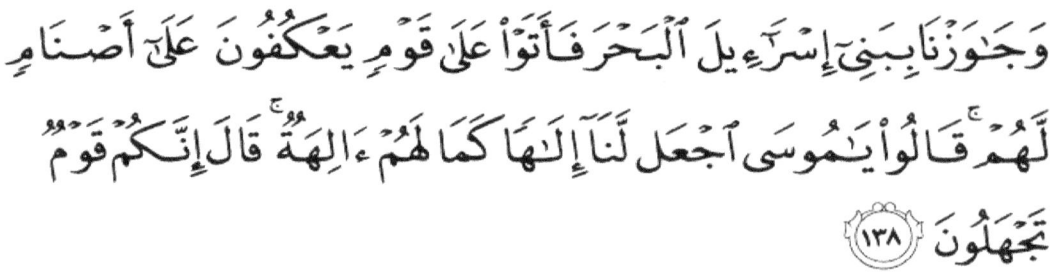

## The Favors of Allah on Moses' People

The children of Israel were favored with Allah's grace and bounty. They were saved from oppression and had witnessed the drowning of their cruel ruler Pharaoh. When they needed water in the dry land, Allah commanded Moses to strike a rock, which parted and sent forth twelve springs of water for the twelve different tribes so that they need not dispute over a shortage of water. Allah also kept the skies cloudy to protect them from the scorching sun. To relieve their hunger, manna (the dried exudate of certain plants) and quail were provided for them. In spite of Allah's generosity, the mean spirited ones began to stir Moses' people to object that they were disgusted with this food; they desires onions, garlic, beans, and lentils, which were traditional Egyptian foods. That is why the children of Israel asked Prophet Moses to pray to Allah to make the earth produce these foods.

Moses again admonished them for oppressing themselves and for their desire to return to a life of humiliation in Egypt. He also pointed out that they were ungrateful for the best and most abundant food. They wanted the worst instead of the best. Allah the Exalted said: "Remember when Moses asked for water for his people, We said: "Strike the stone with your stick." Then gushed forth therefrom twelve springs. Each group of people knew its own place for water. "Eat and drink of what which Allah had provided and do not act corruptly, making mischief on the earth." And remember when you said: "O Moses! We cannot endure one kind of food. So invoke your Lord for us to b ring forth for us of what the earth grows, its herbs, its cucumbers, its Fum (wheat, or garlic), its lentils and its onions." He said: "Would you exchange that which is better for that which is lower? Go you down to any town and you shall find what you want!" [2:60]

﴿ وَإِذِ ٱسْتَسْقَىٰ مُوسَىٰ لِقَوْمِهِۦ فَقُلْنَا ٱضْرِب بِّعَصَاكَ ٱلْحَجَرَۖ فَٱنفَجَرَتْ مِنْهُ ٱثْنَتَا عَشْرَةَ عَيْنًاۖ قَدْ عَلِمَ كُلُّ أُنَاسٍ مَّشْرَبَهُمْۖ كُلُوا۟ وَٱشْرَبُوا۟ مِن رِّزْقِ ٱللَّهِ وَلَا تَعْثَوْا۟ فِى ٱلْأَرْضِ مُفْسِدِينَ ﴾ ﴿٦٠﴾

## The Cowardice of Moses' People

Allah had also directed Moses to lead them to the Promised Land (Palestine) which had been promised to Abraham as a land in which the pious and Allah-fearing of his offspring would live and uphold Allah's law. The children of Israel were an ungrateful people. In spite of all of Allah's favors, they could not stay away from evil and continued to reject Allah's Laws. When Moses ordered them to conquer the town of the Canaanites the Hittites (their enemies who had hounded them), the children of Israel were cowardly and made excuses: "O Moses, a great people dwell therein, We will not go in unless they leave." Ancient books tell that they were six hundred thousand men. Moses did not find among them but two men who were ready to fight. These two said to the people: "Once we enter through the door, Allah will make us victorious." However, all the children of Israel were an incarnation of cowardice and quivered from within, so they were denied Palestine.

## Allah Keeps Moses' People Wandering

Moses knew that his people were fit for nothing. Pharaoh was dead, but his effect upon their souls still remained. Their recovery needed a long period of time. Moses returned to his Lord, telling Him that he was responsible only for the actions of himself and his brother. He prayed to his Lord to judge between his people and himself.

Allah the Exalted issued His judgment against this generation whose nature was corrupted by the Egyptians: they must wander restlessly in the wilderness until this generation had died and had created another generation, a generation which had not been defeated from within and which could fight and score victory.

## The Cowardice of Moses' People - Quranic

Almighty Allah revealed: "And remember when Moses said to his people: "O my people! Remember the Favor of Allah to you, when He made Prophets among you, made you kings, and gave you what He had not given to any other among the Alamin (mankind and jinn), in the past. O my people! Enter the holy land (Palestine) which Allah has assigned to you and turn not back in flight for then you will be returned as losers." They said: "O Moses! In it (this holy land) are a people of great strength, and we shall never enter it, till they leave it; when they leave, then we will enter." Two men of those who feared Allah and in whom Allah had His Grace said: "Assault them through the gate, for when you are in, victory will be yours, and put your trust in Allah if you are believers indeed." They said: "O Moses! We shall never enter it as long as they are there. So go you, and your Lord and fight you two, we are sitting right here." [5: 20-24] He (Moses) said: "O my Lord! I have power only over myself and my brother, so separate us from the people who are the Fasiqeen (rebellious and disobedient to Allah)!" Allah said: "Therefore it (this holy land) is forbidden to them, and so they will wander through the land. So be not sorrowful over the people who are the Fasiqeen (disobedient to Allah)." [5:20-26]

## Moses Fasts for Forty Days

The days of restless wandering began. Each day ended where it began and began where it ended. They started walking to no destination, day and night, morning and evening. They entered Sinai. Moses came to the same place where he had spoken to Allah for the first time. He appealed to Allah for guidance in judging over his people. Allah instructed him to purify himself by fasting for thirty days, after which he was to go to Mount Sinai, where he would be given the law by which he would govern his people. The ancients said that after Moses fasted 30 days, he hated to speak to his Lord because of the odor of his mouth. He ate a plant of the earth and then his Lord said to him: "Why did you break your fast?" Moses said: "O my Lord, I disliked to speak to You with my mouth not having a pleasant smell."  Allah said: "Do you not know, Moses, the odor of the faster's mouth is more fragrant to Me than the rose. Go back and fast ten days; then come back to Me." Moses did what Allah commanded.

## Moses Speaks to Allah - Quranic

Almighty Allah declared: "And We appointed for Moses thirty nights and added to the period ten more, and he completed them term, appointed by his Lord, of forty nights. And Moses said to his brother Aaron: "Replace me among my people, act in the Right Way (by ordering the people to obey Allah and to worship Him Alone) and follow not the way of the Mufsideen (mischief makers)."

And when Moses came the time and place appointed by Us, and his Lord spoke to him, he said: "O my Lord! Show me (yourself), that I may look upon You." Allah said: "You cannot see Me, but look upon the mountain if it stands still in its place then you shall see Me." So when his Lord appeared to the mountain, He made it collapse to dust, and Moses fell down unconscious. Then when he recovered his senses he said: "Glory be to You, I turn to You in repentance and I am the first of the believers." Allah said: "O Moses, I have chosen you above men by My Messages, and by My speaking to you. So hold that which I have given you and be of the grateful." And We wrote for him on the Tablets the lesson to be drawn from all things and the explanation of all things (and said): "hold unto these with firmness, and enjoin your people to take the better therein, I shall show you the home of Al Fasiqeen (the rebellious, disobedient to Allah). I shall turn away from My Ayat (verses from the Quran), those who behave arrogantly on the earth, in a wrongful manner, and even if they see all the Ayat (proofs, evidences, verses, lessons, signs, revelations, etc.) they will not believe in them. And if they see the way of righteousness (monotheism, piety, and good deeds), they will not adopt it as the Way, but if they see the way of error (polytheism, crimes, and evil deeds), they will adopt that way, that is because they have rejected Our Ayat (proofs, evidences, verses, lessons, signs, revelations, etc.) and were heedless to learn a lesson from them. Those who deny Our Ayat (proofs, evidences, verses, lessons, signs, revelations, etc.) and the Meeting in the Hereafter (Day of Resurrection), vain are their deeds. Do they expect to be rewarded with anything except what they used to do?" [7:142-147]

## The Ten Commandments

The Earlier scholars said that The Ten Commandments of the Torah are included in two verses of the Quran. "Say: "Come, I will recite what your Lord has prohibited you from: Join not anything in worship with Him; be good and dutiful to your parents; kill not your children because of poverty- We provide sustenance for you and for them; come not near to shameful sins (illegal sexual intercourse, etc.) whether committed openly or secretly; and kill not anyone whom Allah has forbidden, except for a just cause (according to Islamic law). This He has commanded you that you may understand. And come not near to the orphan's property, except to improve it, until he or she attains the age of full strength; and give full measure and full weight with justice. We burden not any person but that which he can bear. And whenever you give your word (judge between men or give evidences, etc.), say the truth even if a near relative is concerned, and fulfill the Covenant of Allah. This He commands you that you may remember." [6:151-152]

## The Story of Golden Calf - Moses' People Turn to Idolatry

Moses (pbuh) had been gone for forty days and his people were becoming restless, for they did not know that Allah had extended his time by a further ten days. Samiri, a man who was inclined towards evil, suggested that they find themselves another guide, as Moses had broken his promise. He said to them: "In order to find true guidance, you need a god, and I shall provide one for you." So he collected all their gold jewelry, dug a hole in which he placed the lot, and lit a huge fire to melt it down.

During the casting, he threw a handful of dust, making actions like a magician's to impress the ignorant. From the molten metal he fashioned a golden calf. It was hollow, and the wind passing through it produced a sound. Since superstition was imbedded in their past, they quickly linked the strange sound to something supernatural, as if it were a living god. Some of them accept the golden calf as their god.

## Aaron Tries to Reason with the Idolaters

Moses's brother Aaron (pbuh), who acted as their leader in Moses' absence, was grieved and spoke up: "O my people! You have been deceived. Your Lord is the Most Beneficent. Follow and obey me." They replied: "We shall stop worshipping this god only if Moses returns." Those who had remained steadfast in belief separated themselves from the pagans.

## Moses Sees the Idolaters

On his return Moses saw his people singing and dancing around the calf statue. Furious at their paganistic ritual, he flung down the Tablet of the Law he was carrying for them. He tugged Aaron's beard and his hair, crying: "What held you back when you saw them going astray? Why did you not fight this corruption?" Aaron replied: "O son of my mother, let go of my beard! The fold considered me weak and were about to kill me. So make not the enemies rejoice over me, nor put me among the people who are wrong-doers." Moses' anger began to subside when he understood Aaron's helplessness, and he began to handle the situation calmly and wisely. Almighty Allah narrated: "They said: "We broke not the promise to you, of our own will, but we were made to carry the weight of the ornaments of the Pharaoh's people, then we cast them into the fire, and that was what As-Samiri suggested." Then he took out of the fire, for them a statue of a calf which seemed to low. They said: "This is your ilah (god), and the ilah (god) of Moses, but Moses has forgotten (his god)." Did they not see that it could not return them a word (for answer), and that it had no power either to harm them or to do them good? And Aaron indeed had said to them beforehand: "O my people! You are being tried in this, and verily, your Lord is Allah the Most Beneficent, so follow me and obey my order." They said: "We will not stop worshipping it (the calf) until Moses returns to us." [20:87-91].

قَالُوا۟ مَآ أَخْلَفْنَا مَوْعِدَكَ بِمَلْكِنَا وَلَٰكِنَّا حُمِّلْنَآ أَوْزَارًا مِّن زِينَةِ ٱلْقَوْمِ فَقَذَفْنَٰهَا فَكَذَٰلِكَ أَلْقَى ٱلسَّامِرِىُّ ۝

فَأَخْرَجَ لَهُمْ عِجْلًا جَسَدًا لَّهُۥ خُوَارٌ فَقَالُوا۟ هَٰذَآ إِلَٰهُكُمْ وَإِلَٰهُ مُوسَىٰ فَنَسِىَ ۝

## The Conversation between Allah and Moses - Quranic

Allah the Exalted revealed some of the dialogue that took place between Him and Moses on Mount Sinai: "And what made you hasten from your people, O Moses?" He said: "They are close on my footsteps, and I hastened to You, O my Lord! That you might be pleased." Allah said: "Verily! We have tried your people in your absence, and As-Samiri has led them astray." Then Moses returned to his people in a state of anger and sorrow. He said: "O my people! Did not your Lord promise you a fair promise? Did then the promise seem to you long in coming? Or did you desire the Wrath should descend from your Lord on you, so you broke your promise to me (disbelieving in Allah and worshipping the calf)?" (Ch 20: 83-86 Quran). Allah the Exalted revealed what happened further on Moses's return: "Moses said: "O Aaron! What stopped you when you saw them going astray, that you followed me not (according to my advice to you)? Have you then disobeyed my order?" He (Aaron) said; "O my son of my mother! Seize me not by my beard, nor by my head! Verily, I feared lest you should say: 'You have caused a division among the children of Israel, and you have not respected my word!'" (Moses) said: "And what is the matter with you, O Samiri? (Why did you do so?)" Samiri said: "I saw what you saw not, so I took a handful of dust from the hoof print of the Messenger (Gabriel's horse) and threw it (into the fire in which were put the ornaments of the Pharaoh's people, or into the calf). Thus my inner-self suggested to me." Moses said: "Then go away! And verily, your punishment in this life will be that you will say: 'Touch me not' (you will live alone exiled away from mankind); and verily (for a future torment), you have a promise that will not fail. And look at your ilah (god), to which you have been devoted. We will certainly burn it, and scatter its particles in the sea." [20:83-98]

## The Idolaters' Punishment

However, the punishment which was imposed upon the calf worshippers was severe, death. "Remember when Moses said to his people: "O my people! Verily, you have wronged yourselves by worshipping the calf. So turn in repentance to your Creator and kill yourselves (the innocent kill the wrong doers among you), that will be better for you in the Sight of your Creator." Then He accepted your repentance. Truly, He is the One Who accepts repentance, the Most Merciful. Therefore, the crime of worshipping the calf did not pass unpunished. Moses commanded the elite of the children of Israel to pray to Allah for forgiveness and demonstrate their repentance. He chose seventy en out of them and ordered them: "Rush towards Allah and repent for what you did and ask His forgiveness for what you left."

## Moses' People Demand to See Allah

Moses returned to Mount Sinai with the seventy elders and there he communicated with Allah. The elders heard Moses speaking with his Lord. (Allah spoke to Moses directly.) This was, perhaps, the last miracle that they would see, and it was hoped that it would be sufficient enough to convey the religion to their hearts forever.

However, the seventy elite who heard the miracles were dissatisfied. They said to Moses: "O Moses! We shall never believe in you till we see Allah plainly." [2:55]

$$\text{وَإِذْ قُلْتُمْ يَٰمُوسَىٰ لَن نُّؤْمِنَ لَكَ حَتَّىٰ نَرَى ٱللَّهَ جَهْرَةً فَأَخَذَتْكُمُ ٱلصَّٰعِقَةُ وَأَنتُمْ تَنظُرُونَ ۝}$$

This was a tragedy that amazes one. It was a tragedy that indicated those who were hard-hearted and who continued to hold onto sensual and material concerns. Their stubborn demand was rewarded with punishing lightning bolts and a violent quaking that stupefied their souls and bodies at once, leaving them dead. Moses knew what had happened to the seventy elite and was filled with sorrow. He prayed to his Lord, entreating Him to forgive them, for they were fools. Foolishness is only expiated by death. Allah forgave the elders and revived them after their death. Allah the Exalted declared: "Moses chose out of his people seventy of the best men for Our appointed time and place of meeting, and when they were seized with a violent earthquake, he said: "O my Lord, if it had been Your Will, You could have destroyed them and me before; would You destroy us for the deeds of the foolish ones among us? It is only Your Trial by which You lead astray whom You will, and keep guided whom You will. You are our Wali (Protector), so forgive us and have Mercy on us, for You are the Best of Those who forgive. And ordain for us good in this world, and in the Hereafter. Certainly we have turned unto You." He said (as to) My Punishment I afflict therewith whom I will and My Mercy embraces all things. That (Mercy) I shall ordain for those who are the Muttaqun and give Zakat; and those who believe in our Ayat (proofs, evidences, verses, lessons, signs, revelations, etc.);

Those who follow the Messenger, the Prophet who can neither read nor write (Muhammad) whom they find written with them in the Torah and the Gospel, he commands them for Al Ma'ruf (Islamic Monotheism and all that Islam has ordained); and forbids them from Al Munkar (disbelief, polytheism, of all kinds, and all that Islam has forbidden); he allows them as lawful At Tayyibat (all good and lawful) as regards things, deeds beliefs, persons, food, etc. and prohibits them as unlawful Al Khabaith (all evil and unlawful as regards things, deeds, beliefs, persons, food, etc.), he releases them from their heavy burdens (of Allah's Covenant), and from the fetters (bindings) that were upon them. So those who believe in Muhammad and follow the light (the Quran), will be successful. [7:155-157].

## The Story of Israelites and the Cow - The Pious Man and His Son

Moses (pbuh) stayed among his people calling them to Allah. It seems their souls were uneasy in a way that the observant eye could not mistake. Their obstinacy and chattering about what has become known as "The Story of the Cow" was unwarranted. This topic did not need so many negotiations between Moses and the people, nor did it need all their bias. It was said that among the children of Israel there lived a pious man. He was poor but very careful about how he earned the living; it had to be honestly earned. Everything that he did was done for the sake of Allah, never for selfish gain. On his deathbed his last words were: "O Allah, I place my wife, my little son, and my only possession, a calf, in Your care." Strangely, he asked his wife to lead the calf to the forest and leave it there. He did this because he did not trust the children of Israel, for they were a selfish and greedy folk. After a few years when the boy had grown up, his mother told him: "Your father has left you a calf in the trust of Allah. It must have grown into a cow by now." The son was surprised. He did not know of any calf all these years and asked his mother where it was. She replied: "Be like your father and say: 'I trust in Allah,' then go look for it." With a rope in his hand, he went to the forest and prostrated himself before Allah: "O Allah, Lord of Abraham and Jacob and Job, return to me my father's trust." As he raised his head, he saw a cow coming towards him. It stopped submissively beside him. He tied the rope around its neck and led it to his house. The cow would not allow anyone else come near it except the young man. The youth was as pious as his father. He earned his living by cutting wood. Whatever he earned he divided into three equal portions; one he gave to his mother, one he used for his needs, and the last he gave as charity. His nights, too, were divided into three parts; during the early part of the night he helped his mother, the middle part he devoted to the worship of Allah, and during the last part he rested.

## The People Ask Questions about a Cow

About this a wealthy man died, leaving behind an only son, who inherited his father's wealth. His cousins envied his good fortune, and secretly killed him so that they could inherit it. The dead boy's other relatives came to the Prophet Moses (pbuh) and asked his help in tracing the boy's murderer. Moses instructed them to slaughter a cow, remove its tongue and place it on the corpse. This would reveal the murderer, he told them. They accused Moses of joking. He replied: "Allah forbid that I be foolish!" They questioned him about the type of cow they should slaughter, and he said: "This cow is neither young nor mature, but in between the two conditions, so do as you have been commanded." Instead of following his direction, they asked him more questions. "What color must it be?" He replied: "Verily, it is yellow in color." They still were not satisfied with his answer and asked for more details. Moses replied: "It is an unyoked cow; it does not plow the soil nor water the tilth, and is entirely without marks."

They went out in search of such a cow. The only one that matched the description was the one owned by the orphaned youth. They met him on the way and asked the price for which he would sell his cow. He told them he would have to consult his mother first, so they accompanied him to his house and offered her three gold coins. She refused their offer, saying that the cow was worth much more. They were on increasing their offer and the mother kept on refusing. Finally the urged the son to speak to his mother to be reasonable. He told them: "I will not sell the cow without my mother's approval, even if you offered me its skin filled with gold!" On hearing this, his mother smiled and said: "Let that be the price: its skin filled with gold." They realized that no other cow would do; they had to have it at any price. They agreed to buy the cow and paid with its skin filled with gold.

### The People are asked to Slaughter a Cow - Quranic

Allah the Almighty narrated: "And remember when Moses said to his people: "Verily, Allah commands you that you slaughter a cow." They said: "Do you make fun of us?" He said: "I take Allah's Refuge from being among Al Jahileen (the ignorant or the foolish)." They said: "Call upon your Lord for us that He may make plain to us what it is!" He said: "He says, 'Verily, it is a cow neither too old nor too young, but it is between the two conditions, so do what you are commanded." They said; "Call upon your Lord for us to make plain to us its color." He said: "He says, 'It is a yellow cow bright in its color, pleasing to the beholders.'" They said: "Call upon your Lord for us to make plain to us what it is. Verily to us all cows are alike, and surely, if Allah wills, we will be guided." He (Moses) said: "He says, 'It is a cow neither trained to till the soil nor water the fields, sound, having no other color except bright yellow.'" They said: "Now you have brought the truth." So they slaughtered it though they were near to not doing it. And remember when you killed a man and fell into dispute among yourselves to the crime. But Allah brought forth that which you were hiding. So We said: "Strike him (the dead man) with a piece of it (the cow)." Thus Allah brings the dead to life and shows you His Ayat (proofs, evidences, verses, lessons, signs, revelations, etc.) so that you may understand. Then after that your hearts were hardened and became as stone or even worse in hardness. And indeed, there are stones out of which rivers gush forth, and indeed, there are of them stones which fall down for fear of Allah. And Allah is not unaware of what you do. [2:67-74]

وَإِذْ قَالَ مُوسَىٰ لِقَوْمِهِ إِنَّ ٱللَّهَ يَأْمُرُكُمْ أَن تَذْبَحُوا۟ بَقَرَةً قَالُوٓا۟ أَتَتَّخِذُنَا هُزُوًا۟ قَالَ أَعُوذُ بِٱللَّهِ أَنْ أَكُونَ مِنَ ٱلْجَٰهِلِينَ ۝٦٧

## The Story of Moses and Al-Khidr - Moses Informed of a Wise Man

One day Moses (pbuh) delivered such an impressive sermon that all who heard it was deeply moved. Someone in the congregation asked: "O Messenger of Allah, is there another man on earth more learned than you?" Moses replied: "No!" believing so, as Allah had given him the power of miracles and honored him with the Torah. However, Allah revealed to Moses that no man could know all there is to know, nor would one messenger alone be the custodian of all knowledge. There would always be another who knew what others did not. Moses asked Allah: "O Allah, where is this man? I would like to meet him and learn from him." He also asked for a sign to this person's identity. Allah instructed him to take a live fish in a water filled vessel. When the fish disappeared, he would find the man he sought. Moses set out on his journey, accompanied by a young man who carried the vessel with the fish. They reached a place where two rivers met and decided to rest there. Instantly, Moses fell asleep.

## Moses Finds Al-Khidr

While he was asleep, his companion saw the fish wriggle out of the vessel into the river and swim away. However, he forgot to relate the incident to Moses. When he awoke, they continued their journey until they were exhausted and hungry. Moses asked for his morning meal. Only then did his companion recall that the fish they had brought with them had gotten away. Hearing this, Moses exclaimed: "This is exactly what we are seeking!" They hurriedly retraced their steps to the place where the rivers met and where the fish had jumped out. There they found a man, his face partly covered with a hood. His bearing showed he was a saintly man. He was Al-Khidr, the guide. Allah the Almighty narrated: "And remember when Moses said to his boy servant: "I will not give up (traveling) until I reach the junction of the two seas or until I spend years and years in traveling." But when they reached the junction of the two seas, they forgot their fish, and it took its way through the sea as in a tunnel. So when they had passed further on (beyond that fixed place), Moses said to his boy servant: "Bring us our morning meal; truly, we have suffered much fatigue in this, our journey." He said: "Do you remember when we betook ourselves to the dock? I indeed forgot the fish, none but Satan made me forget to remember it. It took its course into the sea in a strange way!" Moses said: "That is what we have been seeking." So they went back retracing their footsteps. Then they found one of Our slaves, unto whom We had bestowed mercy from Us, and whom We had taught knowledge from Us. [18:60-65].

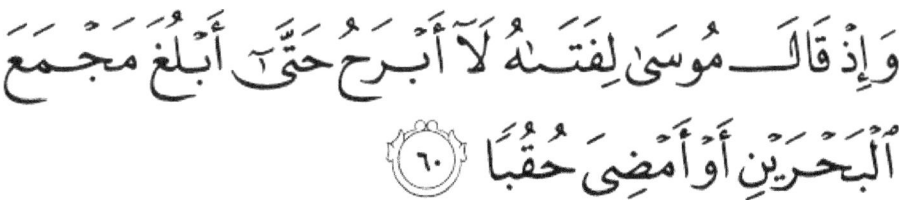

## Moses Speaks to Al-Khidr

Moses said to him (Khidr) "May I follow you so that you teach me something of that knowledge (guidance, and true path) which you have been taught by Allah?" He (Khidr) said: "Verily! You will not be able to have patience with me! And how can you have patience about a thing which you know not?" Moses said; "If Allah will, you will find me patience, and I will not disobey you in aught." He (Khidr) said: "Then, if you follow me, ask me not about anything till I myself mention it to you." So they both proceeded, till, when they were in the ship, he (Khidr) scuttled it. Moses said: "Have you scuttled it in order to drown its people? Verily, you have done Munkar (evil, bad, dreadful) thing." He (Khidr) said: "Did I not tell you, that you would not be able to have patience with me?" Moses said: "Cal me not to account for what I forgot, and be not hard upon me for my affair with you." Then they both proceeded, till they met a boy, he (Khidr) killed him. Moses said: "Have you killed an innocent person who had killed none? Verily, you have done Nukra a great Munkar (prohibited, evil dreadful) thing!" Khidr said: "Did I not tell you that you can have no patience with me?"

Moses said: "If I ask you anything after this, keep me not in your company, you have received an excuse from me." Then they both proceeded, till, when they came to the people of a town, they asked them for food, but they refused to entertain them. Then they found therein a wall about to collapse and he (Khidr) set it up straight. Moses said: "If you had wished, surely you could have taken wages for it!" Khidr said: "This is the parting between me and you, I will tell you the interpretation of those things over which you were unable to hold patience. "As for the ship, it belonged to poor people working in the sea. So I wished to make a defective damage in it, as there was a king after them, who seized every ship by force. And as for the boy, his parents were believers, and we feared lest he should oppress them by rebellion and disbelief. So we intended that their Lord should change him for them for one better in righteousness and near to mercy."

"And as for the wall, it belonged to two orphan boys in the town; and there was under it a treasure belonging to them; and their father was a righteous man, and your Lord intended that they should attain their age of full strength and take out their treasure as a mercy from your Lord. And I did it not of my own accord. That is the interpretation of those (things) over which could not hold patience." [18:66-82].

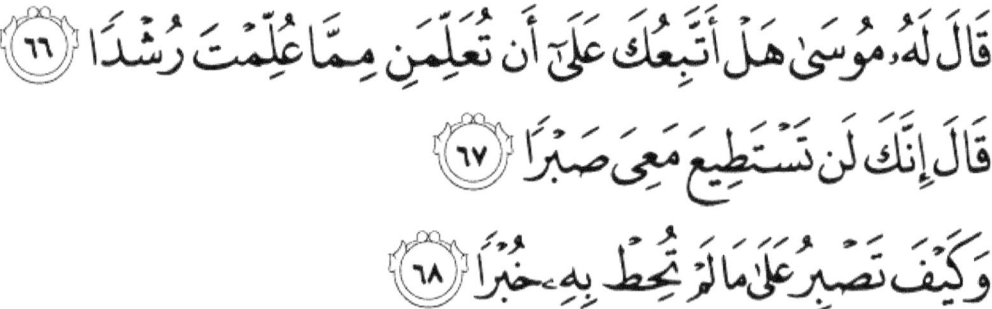

## Moses Seeks Al-Khidr - Hadith

The story of Moses and Al-Khidr is also told in a hadith. Said Ibn Jubair said: "I said to Ibn' Abbas, Nauf Al Bukah claims that Moses, the companion of Al Khidr, was not Moses (the Prophet) of the children of Israel, but some other Moses.' Ibn Abbas said: 'Allah's enemy (Nauf) has told a lie. Ubai Ibn Kab told us that the Prophet (pbuh) said: "Once Moses stood up and addressed Bani Israel. He was asked who was the most learned man amongst the people. He said: "I." Allah admonished him as he did not attribute absolute knowledge to Him (Allah). So, Allah said to him: "Yes, at the junction of the two seas there is a slave of Mine who is more learned than you." Moses said; "O my Lord! How can I meet him?" Allah said: "Take a fish and put it in a large basket and you will find him at the place where you will lose the fish." Moses took a fish and put it in a basket and proceeded along with his servant boy, Joshua (Yusha Ibn Nun), till they reached the rock where they laid their heads (lay down). Moses slept, and the fish, moving out of the basket, fell into the sea. It took its way into the sea straight as in a tunnel. Allah stopped the flow of water over the fish and it became like an arch (the Prophet pointed out this arch with his hands). They traveled the rest of the night, and the next day Moses said to his boy servant: "Give us our food, for indeed, we have suffered much fatigue in this journey of ours."

Moses did not feel tired till he crossed that place which Allah had ordered him to seek after. His boy said to him: "Do you know that when we were sitting near that rock, I forgot the fish, and none but Satan caused me to forget to tell you about it, and it took its course into the sea in an amazing way?" So there was a path for the fish and that astonished them. Moses said: "That was what we were seeking after." So both of them retraced their footsteps till they reached the rock. There they saw a man lying covering with a garment.

## Moses Talks to Al-Khidr - Hadith

Moses greeted him, and he replied saying: "How do people greet each other in your land?" Moses said: "I am Moses." The man asked: "Moses of Bani Israel?" Moses said: "yes, I have come to you so that you may teach me from those things which Allah has taught you." He said: "O Moses! I have some of the knowledge of Allah which Allah has taught me and which you do not know, you have some of the knowledge of Allah which Allah has taught you and which I do not know." Moses asked: "May I follow you?" He said: "But you will not be able to remain patient with me, for how can you be patient about things which you will not be able to understand?" Moses said: "You will find me, if Allah so will, truly patient, and I will not disobey you in aught." So both of them set out walking along the seashore. A boat passed by them, and they asked the crew of the boat to take them on board. The crew recognized Al-Khidr, so they took them on board without fare. When they were on board the boat, a sparrow came and stood on the edge of the boat and dipped its beak once or twice into the sea. Al Khidr said to Moses: "O Moses! My knowledge and your knowledge have not decreased Allah's knowledge except as much as this sparrow has decreased the water of the sea with its beak."

Then suddenly Al Khidr pulled up a plank. Moses said to him: "What have you done? They took us on board charging us nothing; yet you have intentionally made a hole in their boat as to drown its passengers. Verily, you have done a dreadful thing." Al Khidr replied: "Did I not tell you that you would not be able to remain patient with me?" Moses replied: "Do not blame me for what I have forgotten, and do not be hard upon me for my fault." So the first excuse of Moses was that he had forgotten. When they had left the sea, they passed by a boy playing with other boys. Al Khidr took a hold of the boy's head and plucked it with his fingertips as if he were plucking some fruit. Moses said to him: "Have you killed an innocent person who has not killed any person? You have really done a horrible thing." Al Khidr said: "Did I not tell you that you could not remain patient with me?" Moses said: "If I ask you about anything again, do not accompany me." Then both of them went on till they came to some people of a village, and they asked its inhabitants for food but they refused to entertain them as guests. Then they saw therein a wall which was just going to collapse and Al Khidr repaired it just by touching it with his hands. (Sufyan, the sub-narrator, gestured with his hands, illustrating how Al Khidr passed his hands over the wall upwards.) Moses said: "These are the people whom we have called on, but they neither gave us food, nor entertained us as guests, yet you repaired their wall. If you had wished, you could have taken wages for it." Al Khidr said: "This is the parting between you and me, and I shall tell you the explanation of those things on which you could not remain patient." The Prophet (pbuh) added: "We wish that Moses could have remained patient by virtue of which Allah might have told us more about their story." (Sufyan, the sub-narrator, said that the Prophet (pbuh) said: "May Allah bestow His Mercy on Moses! If he had remained patient, we would have been told further about their case." (Sahih Al-Bukhari).

## The Death of Moses - Moses' Suffering

Moses (pbuh) suffered terribly from his people and endured much for the sake of Allah. Abdullah Ibn Omar narrated: "Once the Prophet Muhammad (pbuh) distributed something (among his companions). A man said: "This distribution has not been done (with justice) seeking Allah's Countenance.' I went to the Prophet (pbuh) and told him of that. He became so angry that I saw the signs of anger on his face. Then he said: 'May Allah bestow His Mercy on Moses, for he was harmed more (in a worse manner) than this; yet he endured patiently.'" (Sahih Al-Bukhari) The children of Israel mistreated Moses (pbuh) a lot. His agony was not limited to mutiny, stupidity, chattering, ignorance, and idolatry; it exceeded this and went as far as inflicting personal harm on him. Almighty Allah said: "O you who have believed, be not like those who abused Moses; then Allah cleared him of what they said. And he, in the sight of Allah, was distinguished. [33:69]

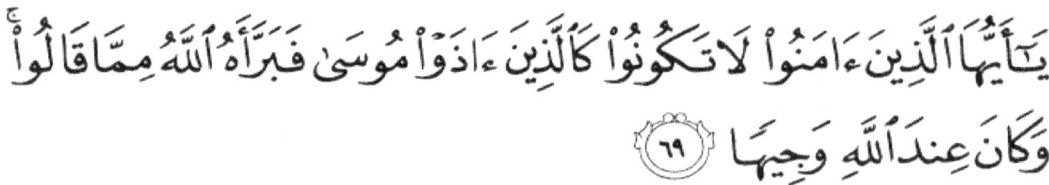

## Allah Clears Moses of False Rumors

Abu Hurairah narrated that Allah's Messenger Muhammad (pbuh) said: "Prophet Moses was a shy person and used to cover his body completely because of his extensive shyness. One of the children of Israel hurt him by saying: 'He covers his body in this way only because of some defect in his skin, either leprosy or scrotal hernia, or he has some other defect.' Allah wished to clear Moses of what they said about him, so one day while Moses was in seclusion, he took his clothes and put them on a stone and started taking a bath. When he had finished the bath, he moved towards his clothes so as to take them, but the stone took his clothes and fled. Moses picked up his stick and ran after the stone saying: 'O stone! Give me my garment!' Until he reached a group of children of Israel who saw him naked then, and found him in the best shape of what Allah had created, and Allah cleared him of what they had accused him of. The stone stopped there, and Moses took and put on his garment and started hitting the stone with his stick. By Allah, the stone still has some traces of the hitting, three, four, or five marks. This was what Allah the Almighty refers to in His saying: "O you who believe! Be not like those who annoyed Moses, but Allah cleared him of that which they alleged, and he was honorable in Allah's sight!" [33:69] (Sahih Al-Bukhari).

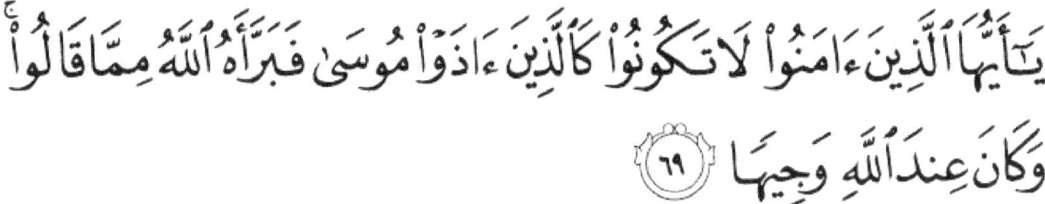

## The Death of Aaron

Aaron (peace be upon him) died shortly before Moses (peace be upon him). His people were still wandering in the wilderness when he died.

## The Death of Moses

Abu Hurairah narrated: "The Angel of Death was sent to Moses (pbuh). When he came to Moses, Moses slapped him on the eye. The Angel returned to his Lord and said: 'You have sent me to a slave who does not want to die.' Allah said: 'Return to him and tell him to put his hand on the back of an ox and for every hair that will come under it, he will be granted one year of life.' Moses said: 'O Lord! What will happen after that?' Allah replied: 'then death.' Moses said: 'Let it come now!' Moses then requested Allah to let him die close to the Holy Land so that he would be at a distance of a stone's throw from it." Abu Hurairah added: "Allah's Messenger (pbuh) said: 'If I were there, I would show you his grave below the red sand hill on the side of the road.'" (Sahih Al Bukhari). Moses (pbuh), Prophet of Allah and the one to whom Allah spoke to directly, met his death with a contented soul and a faithful heart that looked forward to righteousness and made haste to meet with Him Who bore tidings of peace.

# Prophet Hizqeel (Ezekiel)

Allah Resurrects the Dead. Allah said: "Have you not considered those who left their homes in many thousands, fearing death? Allah said to them, "Die"; then He restored them to life. And Allah is full of bounty to the people, but most of the people do not show gratitude." [2:243]

ﷺ أَلَمْ تَرَ إِلَى ٱلَّذِينَ خَرَجُواْ مِن دِيَـٰرِهِمْ وَهُمْ أُلُوفٌ حَذَرَ ٱلْمَوْتِ فَقَالَ لَهُمُ ٱللَّهُ مُوتُواْ ثُمَّ أَحْيَـٰهُمْ ۚ إِنَّ ٱللَّهَ لَذُو فَضْلٍ عَلَى ٱلنَّاسِ وَلَـٰكِنَّ أَكْثَرَ ٱلنَّاسِ لَا يَشْكُرُونَ ﴿٢٤٣﴾

When Allah took Kalih Ibn Yofra (Jephtha) after Joshua, Ezekiel Ibn Buzi succeeded him as the prophet to the Israelites. The people had fled from Palestine for fear of the plague and settled on a plateau. Allah said to them: "Die you all," and they all perished. A few centuries passed, and then Ezekiel, passing by, stopped over them, wondering. There came a voice: "Do you want Allah to resurrect them while you watch?" He said: "Yes." Then he was commanded to call those bones to join one to the other and to be covered with flesh. So he called them by the power of Allah, and the people arose and glorified Allah in the voice of one man.

## Allah Resurrects the Dead through Ezekiel

According to Ibn Abbas, this place was called "Damardan." Its people were ill with the plague, so they fled, while a group of them who remained in the village perished. The Angel of Death called to the survivors: "Die you all," and they perished. After a long time a prophet called Ezekiel passed by them and stood wondering over them, twisting his jaws and fingers. Allah revealed to him: "Do you want Me to show you how I bring them back to life? He said: "Yes." His idea was to marvel at the power of Allah over them. A voice said to him: "Call: 'O you bones, Allah commands you to gather up.'" The bones began to fly one to the other until they became skeletons. Then Allah revealed to him to say; "Call: 'O you bones, Allah commands you to put on flesh and blood and the clothes in which they had died.'" And a voice said: "Allah commands you to call the bodies to rise." And they rose. When they returned to life they said: "Blessed are You, O Lord, and all praises is Yours." Ibn Abbas reported that the dead who were resurrected were four thousand, while Ibn Salih said they were nine thousand.

### Hadith about the Plagues

Regarding plague, Abu Ubaidah Ibn Al-Jarrah related that Omar Ibn Al-Khattab was on his way to Syria and had reached Sarg when the leader of the Muslim army, Abu Ubaidah Ibn Al-Jarrah, and his companions met him and told him of a pestilence that had broken out in Syria. Omar remember the Prophet's (pbuh) saying: "If it (plague) be in a country where you are staying, do not go out fleeing it, and if you hear it is in a country, do not enter it." Omar praised Allah and then went off. Muhammad Ibn Ishaaq stated that we do not know how long Ezekiel (pbuh) stayed among the Israelites before Allah took him away. After him, the Israelites deviated from the right way of life, as they usually did, and deserted Allah's covenant with them. They worshipped many idols, among them Ba'al, so Allah sent to them the Prophet Elijah (peace be upon him).

# Prophet Elisha (Elyas)

"And remember Our servants, Abraham, Isaac and Jacob - those of strength and [religious] vision. Indeed, We chose them for an exclusive quality: remembrance of the home [of the Hereafter]. And indeed they are, to Us, among the chosen and outstanding. And remember Ishmael, Elisha and Dhul-Kifl, and all are among the outstanding." [38:45-48]

وَاذْكُرْ عِبَٰدَنَآ إِبْرَٰهِيمَ وَإِسْحَٰقَ وَيَعْقُوبَ أُو۟لِى ٱلْأَيْدِى وَٱلْأَبْصَٰرِ ﴿٤٥﴾

إِنَّآ أَخْلَصْنَٰهُم بِخَالِصَةٍ ذِكْرَى ٱلدَّارِ ﴿٤٦﴾

وَإِنَّهُمْ عِندَنَا لَمِنَ ٱلْمُصْطَفَيْنَ ٱلْأَخْيَارِ ﴿٤٧﴾

وَاذْكُرْ إِسْمَٰعِيلَ وَٱلْيَسَعَ وَذَا ٱلْكِفْلِ وَكُلٌّ مِّنَ ٱلْأَخْيَارِ ﴿٤٨﴾

Ibn Ishaaq said that Elisha (pbuh) was sent to the children after Elijah (pbuh). He lived among his people, calling them to Allah and abiding by the message and laws of Elijah until he passed away. Then dissension rose among them, and events took momentum. The sins increased everywhere, and tyrants killed the prophets.

### The Family History of Elisha

According to Al-Hafiz Abu Al-Qasim Ibn Asaker, Elisha was Ibn Adi, Ibn Shultam, Ibn Aphraem, Ibn Joseph, Ibn Isaac, and Ibn Abraham. It was said that he was the cousin of Elijah. Other sources said also that he had been hiding with Elijah in a cave in Mount Qasium to escape from the King of Ba'alabak, and when Elijah died, he Elisha succeeded him as a prophet among his people.

# Prophet Shammil (Samuel)

Ibn Jarir reported that the Israelites life deteriorated. They committed many sins and killed whom they wished of the prophets. Consequently Allah sent them tyrannous king who ill-treated them and spilled their blood, and set their enemies from outside against them as well. They used to go war, taking with them The Ark of the Covenant. They did this so that they would be victorious by its blessings, and it became a symbol of calm and a relic left behind by Moses's people. When they went to war with the people of Gaza and Askalon, they were defeated because the Ark of the Covenant was captured from them. When the king of the Israelites heard of this he died on the spot. The children of Israel remained like sheep without a shepherd until Almighty Allah sent them a prophet named Samuel (Shammil) (pbuh). They asked him to appoint a king over them to lead in a war against their enemies.

### The Ark of the Covenant

According to Ibn 'Asaker, the Israelites believed their Ark of the Covenant to be very holy and an important symbol of their history. The carried the Ark even in battle and believed that, because of it, Allah would protect them from their enemies. This belief gave them peace of mind and great courage, and their enemies were terrified by it. Their enemies also believed that it was given special power by Allah. Gradually the Israelites started to ignore Allah's law; evil habits became part of their lives. Allah sent upon them an enemy, the Philistines, who defeated the Israelites, captured their Ark, drove them out of their homes, and took away their children to use or sell as slaves. Their power was broken. They separated from one another and were very disheartened.

### Samuel Comes to the Israelites

Then came Prophet Samuel (pbuh) among them to bring some relief. They asked the prophet's help in appointing a strong leader, a king under whose banner they could unite and fight the Philistines. Prophet Samuel (pbuh), knowing their weakness, told them: "I fear that when the time comes to fight you may refuse."

But they assured him that they had suffered enough insults and were now ready to fight in the way of Allah, even if they lost their lives. Prophet Samuel prayed to Allah for guidance. Allah revealed to him that He had chosen one, Saul (Talut), to be their king. The prophet wanted to know how to recognize the future king. He was told that Saul would come to him by himself and that they must hand over the control of kingdom to him, for he would lead them in battle against the Philistines.

## Saul is Appointed King

Saul was tall and sturdy, pious, and very intelligent. He lived and worked with his father on their farm. One day, several of their donkeys were lost. Accompanied by his servant, Saul went in search of them. They traveled for many days and were very tired. Saul said to his servant: "Let us rather go back, for I am sure that my father will be worried by now, and the other animals must also be cared for." His servant suggested that as they were already in the land of Samuel the prophet, they should go to him to inquire about the lost donkeys. Saul agreed, and they carried on. On their way, they asked directions from some maidens carrying water. They were told to go in the direction of the mountain. Here, a vast crowd was waiting for the Prophet Samuel. When Saul set eyes on him, he instantly recognized him as a prophet by his holy men. Samuel also recognized Saul as the king that Allah had chosen for them. Saul greeted the prophet respectfully. When he asked about his missing donkeys, Samuel told him not to worry, his donkeys were already on their way to his fat's farm. He then told Saul that Allah had chosen him as the king of the children of Israel. His duty would be to take charge of their affairs, to unite them under one banner, and to protect them from their enemies. If he carried out Allah's commands, he would be given victory. Saul was surprised by this sudden honor offered to him. It was also a heavy responsibility. He protested to the prophet. He said that he did not know anything of leadership or kingship and had no wealth. Samuel told him that it was the will of Allah that he should be the king, that he should thank Allah for His favor and be strong in faith.

## Saul is Appointed King - Quranic

Taking Saul by the hand, Samuel led him to the children of Israel, but they insisted on a direct sign from Allah. Prophet Samuel told them to go outside the city to see the sign, which they did. Almighty Allah revealed: Have you not considered the assembly of the Children of Israel after [the time of] Moses when they said to a prophet of theirs, "Send to us a king, and we will fight in the way of Allah "? He said, "Would you perhaps refrain from fighting if fighting was prescribed for you?" They said, "And why should we not fight in the cause of Allah when we have been driven out from our homes and from our children?" But when fighting was prescribed for them, they turned away, except for a few of them. And Allah is Knowing of the wrongdoers. [2:246-250]

أَلَمْ تَرَ إِلَى ٱلْمَلَإِ مِنۢ بَنِىٓ إِسْرَٰٓءِيلَ مِنۢ بَعْدِ مُوسَىٰٓ إِذْ قَالُوا۟ لِنَبِىٍّ لَّهُمُ ٱبْعَثْ لَنَا مَلِكًۭا نُّقَٰتِلْ فِى سَبِيلِ ٱللَّهِ ۖ قَالَ هَلْ عَسَيْتُمْ إِن كُتِبَ عَلَيْكُمُ ٱلْقِتَالُ أَلَّا تُقَٰتِلُوا۟ ۖ قَالُوا۟ وَمَا لَنَآ أَلَّا نُقَٰتِلَ فِى سَبِيلِ ٱللَّهِ وَقَدْ أُخْرِجْنَا مِن دِيَٰرِنَا وَأَبْنَآئِنَا ۖ فَلَمَّا كُتِبَ عَلَيْهِمُ ٱلْقِتَالُ تَوَلَّوْا۟ إِلَّا قَلِيلًۭا مِّنْهُمْ ۗ وَٱللَّهُ عَلِيمٌۢ بِٱلظَّٰلِمِينَ ﴿٢٤٦﴾

And their prophet said to them, "Indeed, Allah has sent to you Saul as a king." They said, "How can he have kingship over us while we are more worthy of kingship than him and he has not been given any measure of wealth?" He said, "Indeed, Allah has chosen him over you and has increased him abundantly in knowledge and stature. And Allah gives His sovereignty to whom He wills. And Allah is all-Encompassing [in favor] and Knowing."

وَقَالَ لَهُمْ نَبِيُّهُمْ إِنَّ ٱللَّهَ قَدْ بَعَثَ لَكُمْ طَالُوتَ مَلِكًۭا ۚ قَالُوٓا۟ أَنَّىٰ يَكُونُ لَهُ ٱلْمُلْكُ عَلَيْنَا وَنَحْنُ أَحَقُّ بِٱلْمُلْكِ مِنْهُ وَلَمْ يُؤْتَ سَعَةًۭ مِّنَ ٱلْمَالِ ۚ قَالَ إِنَّ ٱللَّهَ ٱصْطَفَىٰهُ عَلَيْكُمْ وَزَادَهُۥ بَسْطَةًۭ فِى ٱلْعِلْمِ وَٱلْجِسْمِ ۖ وَٱللَّهُ يُؤْتِى مُلْكَهُۥ مَن يَشَآءُ ۚ وَٱللَّهُ وَٰسِعٌ عَلِيمٌۭ ﴿٢٤٧﴾

And their prophet said to them, "Indeed, a sign of his kingship is that the chest will come to you in which is assurance from your Lord and a remnant of what the family of Moses and the family of Aaron had left, carried by the angels. Indeed in that is a sign for you, if you are believers."

وَقَالَ لَهُمْ نَبِيُّهُمْ إِنَّ ءَايَةَ مُلْكِهِۦ أَن يَأْتِيَكُمُ ٱلتَّابُوتُ فِيهِ سَكِينَةٌ مِّن رَّبِّكُمْ وَبَقِيَّةٌ مِّمَّا تَرَكَ ءَالُ مُوسَىٰ وَءَالُ هَـٰرُونَ تَحْمِلُهُ ٱلْمَلَـٰٓئِكَةُۚ إِنَّ فِى ذَٰلِكَ لَـَٔايَةً لَّكُمْ إِن كُنتُم مُّؤْمِنِينَ ﴿٢٤٨﴾

**Saul Leads an Army - Quranic**

Then when Saul set out with the army, he said: "Verily! Allah will try you by a river. So whoever drinks thereof, he is not of me, and whoever tastes it not, he is of me, except him who takes thereof in the hollow of his hand." Yet, they drank thereof, all, but a few of them. So when he had crossed it (the river), he and those who believed with him, they said: "We have no power on this day against Goliath and his hosts." But those who knew with certainty that they were to meet their Lord, said: "How often a small group overcame a mighty host by Allah's Leave?" And Allah is with the patient. And when they advanced to meet Goliath and his forces, they invoked: "Then when Talut (Saul) set out with the army, he said: "Verily! Allah will try you by a river. So whoever drinks thereof, he is not of me, and whoever tastes it not, he is of me, except him who takes (thereof) in the hollow of his hand." Yet, they drank thereof, all, but a few of them. So when he had crossed it (the river), he and those who believed with him, they said: "We have no power this day against Jalut (Goliath) and his hosts." But those who knew with certainty that they were to meet their Lord, said: "How often a small group overcame a mighty host by Allah's Leave?" And Allah is with As-Sabreen (the patient ones, etc.). And when they advanced to meet Jalut (Goliath) and his forces, they invoked: "Our Lord! Pour forth on us patience and make us victorious over the disbelieving people." Saul set about organizing his army with strong faith and wisdom. He ordered that only men free from responsibilities should join. Those engaged in building homes, men who were about to be married and those occupied with business should not join. After establishing a well-trained army, he decided to put them to the test. He told them that along the route they would pass a river where they should drink enough water to quench their thirst but not more than that.

To his disappointment, he discovered the majority of them drank more water than they should have. He discharged them for disobedience and kept only the few who had obeyed him, as they were the ones who proved their sincerity. This resulted in a split in the army, but he was not bothered. He believed in quality and not numbers; better a small band of true believers he could rely on than a huge army of unreliable men.

### Saul's Army Sees the Enemy

Saul's men sighted the enemy on the other side of the river. Their opponents appeared physically strong and were armed with better weapons. They were led by the mighty warrior Goliath (Galut), known for his huge build and brute strength. A great number of Saul's men ran away on seeing this strong force. The small band that remained was willing to fight, whatever the outcome, for they had heard that there had been many incidents in the past in which Allah had caused a small force to defeat a larger one.

# Prophet Dawud (David)

Goliath challenged any soldier from King Saul's army to combat, as was the custom of battle in those days. However, Goliath also wanted to show off his strength. The men were terrorized, and no one had enough courage to volunteer. The king offered the hand of his pretty daughter in marriage to the man who would fight Goliath, but even this tempting offer did not change the deadly silence among his soldiers. Then, to everyone's surprise, a youth stepped forward. A roar of laughter echoed from the enemy's side, and even Saul's men shook their heads. The young man was David (Dawud), from the city of Bethlehem. His elderly father had chosen three of his sons to join Saul's army. He had instructed the youngest one, David, not to take part in the fighting but to help the army in other ways and to report to his father daily on what was happening on the war front. Saul was very impressed by the youth's courage, but he said: "I admire your courage, but you are no match for that mighty warrior. Let the strong men come forward." David, however, had already decided and was willing to meet the challenge. Proudly, he told the king that only the day before he had killed a lion which had threatened his father's sheep, and on another occasion he had killed a bear. He asked Saul not to judge him by his appearance, for he feared no man or wild beast. Saul, surprised by young David's brave stance, agreed: "My brave soldier, if you are willing, then may Allah guard you and grant you strength!" The king dressed David in battle armor and handed him a sword, but David was not used to wearing battle dress. He felt uncomfortable in it, and it obstructed his movements. He removed the armor, then collected a few pebbles and filled his leather pouch with them. He slung it over his shoulder next to his sling. With his wooden staff in hand, he began to walk towards the enemy. Saul was worried and asked him how on earth, with a sling and a couple of stones was he going to defend himself against the giant?

David replied: "Allah Who protected me from the claws of the bear and the fangs of the lion will certainly protect me from this brute! When Goliath set eyes on the lean young man who looked like a boy, he laughed loudly and roared: "Are you out to play war with one of your playmates, or are you tired of your life? I will cut off your head with a swipe of my sword!" David shouted back: "You may have armor, shield, and sword, but I face you in the name of Allah, the Lord of the Israelites, Whose laws you have mocked. Today you will see that it is not the sword that kills but the will and power of Allah!" So saying, he took his sling and placed in it a pebble from his pouch. He swung and aimed it at Goliath. The pebble shot from the whirling sling with the speed of an arrow and hit Goliath's head with great force. Blood gushed out, and Goliath thumped to the ground, lifeless, before he had a chance to draw his sword. When the rest of his men saw their mighty hero slain, they took to their heels. The Israelites followed in hot pursuit, taking revenge for their years of suffering at the hands of their enemy, killing every soldier they could lay hands on. In this battle the Israelites regained the glory and honor that had been lost for a long time. David became a hero overnight. Saul kept his word and married his daughter Michal (Miqel) to the young warrior and took him under his wing as one of his chief advisors.

## Allah Gives David the Kingdom

Almighty Allah declared: "So they routed them by Allah's Leave and David killed Goliath, and Allah gave him (David) the kingdom (after the death of Saul and Samuel) and wisdom, and taught him of that which He willed. And if Allah did not check one set of people by means of another, the earth would indeed be full of mischief. But Allah is full of Bounty to the Alamin (mankind, jinns and all that exist). (Ch 2:251 Quran). David became the most famous man among the Israelites. However, he was not inveigled by this; he was not a prisoner of fame or leadership but a prisoner of Allah's love. Therefore, after killing Goliath he went out into the desert in the company of nature, glorifying Almighty Allah and contemplating His favors. "Verily, We made the mountains to glorify Our Praises with him (David) in the Ashi (after the mid-day till sunset) and Ishraq (after the sunrise till mid-day). And (so did) the birds assembled: all with him (David) did turn (to Allah, glorified His Praises). We made his kingdom strong and gave him wisdom and sound judgment in speech and decision. [38:18-20]

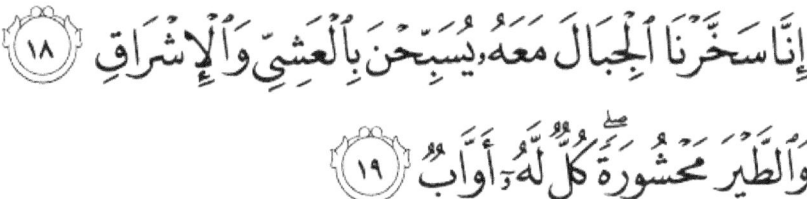

$$\text{لَٰكِنِ ٱلَّذِينَ ٱتَّقَوْا۟ رَبَّهُمْ لَهُمْ غُرَفٌ مِّن فَوْقِهَا غُرَفٌ مَّبْنِيَّةٌ تَجْرِى مِن تَحْتِهَا ٱلْأَنْهَٰرُ ۖ وَعْدَ ٱللَّهِ ۖ لَا يُخْلِفُ ٱللَّهُ ٱلْمِيعَادَ ﴿٢٠﴾}$$

Creatures such as the plants, birds, beasts, and even the mountains responded to his voice glorifying Allah. Allah had chosen David to be a prophet and revealed the Psalms to him. As He the Almighty said: "And to David We gave the Psalms." [17:55]

$$\text{وَرَبُّكَ أَعْلَمُ بِمَن فِى ٱلسَّمَٰوَٰتِ وَٱلْأَرْضِ ۗ وَلَقَدْ فَضَّلْنَا بَعْضَ ٱلنَّبِيِّـۧنَ عَلَىٰ بَعْضٍ ۖ وَءَاتَيْنَا دَاوُۥدَ زَبُورًا ﴿٥٥﴾}$$

### David is granted the Language of Animals

David recited his scripture and glorified Allah while the mountains joined him praise and the birds rallied around him. Almighty Allah directed: Be patient (O Muhammad) of what they say, and remember Our slave David, endured with power. Verily, he was ever oft-returning in all matters and in repentance toward Allah. (Ch 38:17 Quran). David's sincerity was not the only factor responsible for the birds and beasts joining with him in glorifying Allah, nor was the sweetness of his voice. It was a miracle from Allah. This was not his only miracle, for Allah also endowed him with the faculty of understanding the languages of birds and animals.

### David's Fasting and Praying

David (pbuh) fasted every other day. Abdullah Ibn Amr Ibn Al-As narrated: Allah's Apostle (pbuh) said to me: "The most beloved fasting to Allah was the fasting of the Prophet David, who used to fast alternate days. And the most beloved prayer to Allah was the prayer of David, who used to sleep the first half of the night, and pray for one third of it and again sleep for a sixth of it.'" (Sahih Al-Bukhari). Abdullah Ibn Amr Ibn Al-As also narrated: "The Prophet (pbuh) said to me: 'I have been informed that you pray all the nights and observe fast all the days; is this true?' I replied: 'Yes.' He said: 'If you do so, your eyes will be weak and you will get bored. So fast three days a month, for this will be the fasting of a whole year. (Or equal to the fasting of a whole year).' I said: 'I find myself able to fast more.' He said: 'Then fast like the fasting of (the Prophet) David (pbuh) who used to fast on alternate days and would not flee on facing the enemy.'" (Sahih Al-Bukhari).

## Iron Becomes Flexible for David

Allah granted David great influence. His people had a great number of wars in their time, but they had a problem in that the iron armor was too heavy for the fighter to move and fight as he wished. It is said that David was sitting one day, contemplating this problem while toying with a piece of iron. Suddenly, he found his hand sinking in the iron. Almighty Allah had made it flexible for him: "And We made the iron soft for him." (Ch 34:10 Quran). The people praised and loved David. However, the hearts of men are fickle and their memories short. Even great men can feel insecure and become petty-minded. One day David found Saul in a worried state. He sensed something strange in Saul's attitude towards him. That night, when he shared his feeling with his wife, she started to weep bitterly and said: "O David, I will never keep any secrets from you." She told him that her father had become jealous of his popularity and feared that he would lose his kingdom to him. She advised him to be on his guard. This information shocked David very much. He prayed and hoped that Saul's good nature would overcome the darker side of his character. The following day, Saul summoned David to inform him that Canaan had gathered its forces and would march on the kingdom. He ordered David to advance on them with the army and not to return unless victory was gained. David sensed that this was an excuse to get rid of him; either the enemy would kill him, or in the thick of battle, Saul's henchmen might stab him in the back. Yet he hastened with his troops to meet the army of Canaan. They fought the Canaanites, without thinking of their own safety. Allah granted them victory, and David lived to return to Saul.

## Saul Plots to Kill David but David Forgives Saul

Unfortunately, this only increased Saul's fear, so he plotted to kill David. Such is jealousy that not even a daughter's well-being mattered. Michal learned of her father's plan and hurried to warn her husband. David gathered some food and things, mounted his camel and fled. He found a cave in which he remained hidden for many days. After a time, David's brothers and some citizens joined forces with him. Saul's position became very weak, for he began to rule with a heavy hand. He ill-treated the learned, tortured the reciters of the Talmud, and terrorized his soldiers. This worsened his position, and his subjects began to turn against him. He decided to go war against David. Hearing this news, David marched to confront Saul's army. The king's army had traveled a great distance and was overcome by fatigue, so they decided to rest in a valley, where they fell asleep. Quietly, David crept up to the sleeping Saul, removed his spear, and cut off a piece of his garment with the sword. David then awakened the king and told him: "Oh king, you come out seeking me, but I do not hate you, and I do not want to kill you. If I did, I would have killed you when you were asleep. Here is a piece of your garment. I could have hacked your neck instead, but I did not. My mission is that of love, not malice." The king realized his mistake and begged for forgiveness.

## David Becomes King

Time passed and Saul was killed in a battle in which David did not take part. David succeeded Saul, for the people remembered what he had done for them and elected him king. So it was that David the Prophet was also a king. Allah strengthened the dominion of David and made him victorious. His kingdom was strong and great; his enemies feared him without engaging in war with him.

## David's Son Solomon (peace be upon him)

David had a son named Solomon (Sulaiman), who was intelligent and wise from childhood. When the following story took place, Solomon was eleven years old. One day David, was sitting, as usual, solving the problems of his people when two men, one of whom had a field, came to him. The owner of the field said: "O dear Prophet! This man's sheep came to my field at night and ate up the grapes and I have come to ask for compensation." David asked the owner of the sheep: "Is this true?" He said: "Yes, sir." David said: "I have decided that you give him your sheep in exchange for the field." Solomon, to whom Allah had given wisdom in addition to what he had inherited from his father, spoke up: "I have another opinion. The owner of the sheep should take the field to cultivate until the grapes grow, while the other man should take the sheep and make use of their wool and milk until his field is repaired. If the grapes grow, and the field returns to its former state, then the field owner should take his field and give back the sheep to their owner." David responded: "This is a sound judgment. Praise be to Allah for gifting you with wisdom. You are truly Solomon the Wise." Prophet David was a just and righteous ruler who brought peace and prosperity to his people, and whom Allah honored as a messenger. He delivered Allah's message to the people through the precious gift of his melodious voice. When he recited the Psalms (Zaboor), it was as if the rest of creation chanted with him; people listened as if in a trance. The messages David delivered are famous and well-remembered. They are known in the Bible as the Psalms or Songs of David. David divided his working day into four parts: one to earn a living and to rest, one to pray to his Lord, one to listen to the complaints of his people, and the last part to deliver his sermons.

He also appointed deputies to listen to his subjects' complaints so that in his absence people's problems might not be neglected. Although a king, he did not live on the income of his kingdom. Being well-experienced in the craft of weapon-making, he made and sold weapons and lived on that income. One day, as David was praying in his prayer niche, he ordered his guards not to allow anyone to interrupt him, but two men managed to enter and disturb him. "Who are you?" he asked. One of the men said: "Do not be frightened. We have a dispute and have come for your judgment." David said: "What is it?" The first man said: "This is my brother, has ninety nine sheep, and I have one.

He gave it to me but took it back." David, without hearing from the other party said: "He did you wrong by taking the sheep back, and many partners oppress one another, except for those who are believers." The two men vanished like a cloud, and David realized that they were two angels sent to him to teach him a lesson. He should not have passed a judgment without hearing from the opposing party. Almighty Allah told us of this incident: "And has the news of the litigants reached you? When they climbed over the wall into (his) Mihrab (a praying place or a private room).

When they entered in upon David, he was terrified of them, they said: Fear not! (We are) two litigants, one of whom has wronged the other; therefore judge between us with truth, and treat us not with injustice, and guide us to the Right Way. Verily, this is my brother (in religion) has ninety nine ewes, while I have only one ewe, and he says: 'Hand it over to me,' and he overpowered me in speech." David said immediately without listening to the opponent: "He has wronged you in demanding your ewe in addition to his ewes. And, verily, many partners oppress one another, except those who believe and do righteous good deeds, and they are few." And David guessed that We have tried him and he sought Forgiveness of his Lord, and he fell down prostrate and turned to Allah in repentance. So We forgave him that, and verily, for him is a near access to Us, and as good place of final return Paradise. O David! Verily! We have placed you as a successor on earth, so judge you between men in truth and justice. And follow not your desire for it will mislead you from the Path of Allah. Verily! Those who wander astray from the Path of Allah shall have a severe torment, because they forgot the Day of Reckoning. [38:21-22]

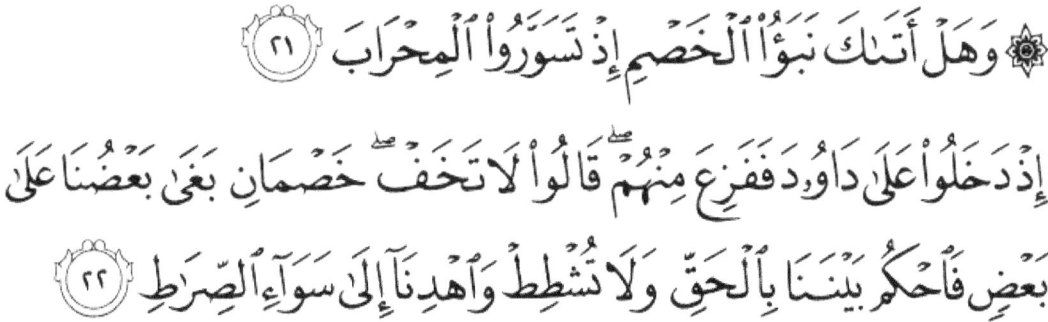

### The Death of Prophet David

David worshipped Allah, glorified Him and sang His praise until he died. According to traditions, David died suddenly and was mourned by four thousand priests as well as thousands of people. It was so hot that people suffered from the intensity of the sun. Solomon called the birds to protect David and the people from the sun, and they did so until he was buried. This was the first sign of his dominion to be witnessed by the people.

# Prophet Sulaiman (Solomon)

Prophet Solomon inherited David's prophethood and dominion. This was not a material inheritance. Prophets do not bequeath their property. It is given away to the poor, not to their relatives. Prophet Muhammad (pbuh) said: "The prophets' property will not be inherited, and whatever we leave is to be used for charity." (Sahih Al-Bukhari). "And indeed We gave knowledge to David and Solomon, and they both said: "All the praises and thanks be to Allah, Who has preferred us above many of His believing slaves!" And Solomon inherited (the knowledge of) David. He said: "O mankind! We have been taught the language of birds, and on us have been bestowed all things. This, verily, is an evident grace (from Allah)." And there were gathered before Solomon his hosts of jinns and men, and birds, and they were all set in battle order (marching forwards). [27:15-17]

وَلَقَدْ ءَاتَيْنَا دَاوُۥدَ وَسُلَيْمَٰنَ عِلْمًا ۖ وَقَالَا ٱلْحَمْدُ لِلَّهِ ٱلَّذِى فَضَّلَنَا عَلَىٰ كَثِيرٍ مِّنْ عِبَادِهِ ٱلْمُؤْمِنِينَ ﴿١٥﴾

وَوَرِثَ سُلَيْمَٰنُ دَاوُۥدَ ۖ وَقَالَ يَٰٓأَيُّهَا ٱلنَّاسُ عُلِّمْنَا مَنطِقَ ٱلطَّيْرِ وَأُوتِينَا مِن كُلِّ شَىْءٍ ۖ إِنَّ هَٰذَا لَهُوَ ٱلْفَضْلُ ٱلْمُبِينُ ﴿١٦﴾

وَحُشِرَ لِسُلَيْمَٰنَ جُنُودُهُۥ مِنَ ٱلْجِنِّ وَٱلْإِنسِ وَٱلطَّيْرِ فَهُمْ يُوزَعُونَ ﴿١٧﴾

### Solomon Becomes King

After his father's death, Solomon became king. He begged Allah for a kingdom such as none after him would have, and Allah granted his wish. Besides wisdom, Allah had blessed Solomon with many abilities. He could command the winds and understand and talk to birds and animals. Allah directed him to teach both men and jinns to mine the earth and extract its minerals to make tools and weapons. He also favored him with a mine of copper, which was a rare metal in those days.

## Solomon's Admiration of Horses

During his time horses were the common mode of transportation. They were very essential for defense, to carry soldiers and cart provisions and weapons of war. The animals were well cared for and well trained. One day Solomon was reviewing a parade of his stable. The fitness, beauty and posture of the horses fascinated him so much that he kept on stroking and admiring them. The sun was nearly setting, and the time for the middle prayer was passing by. When he realized this, he exclaimed: "I surely love the finer things of life than the service of my Lord! Return them to me." Almighty Allah revealed: "And to David We gave Solomon. How excellent a slave! Verily, he was ever oft returning in repentance (to Us)! When there were displayed before him, in the afternoon, well-trained horses of the highest breed (for jihad in Allah's cause). And he said: "Alas! I did love the good (these horses) instead of remembering my Lord (in my 'Asr prayer)" till the time was over, and the sun had hidden in the veil of the night. Then he said: "Bring them (horses) back to me." Then he began to pass his hand over their legs and their necks.

And indeed We did try Solomon and We placed on his throne Jasadan (a devil, so he lost his kingdom for a while) but he did return (to his throne and kingdom by the Grace of Allah and he did return) to Allah with obedience and in repentance. He said: "My Lord! Forgive me, and bestow upon me a kingdom such as shall not belong to any other after me. Verily, You are the Bestower." So, We subjected to him the wind, it blew gently to his order whithersoever he willed, and also the devils from the jinns including every kind of builder and diver, and also other bound in fetters. (Saying of Allah to Solomon): "This is Our gift, so spend you or withhold, no account will be asked." And verily, he enjoyed a near access to Us, and a good final return Paradise. [38:30-40]

## Solomon Hears the Ant's Warning

One day Solomon gathered his army, which had different battalions of men, jinns, birds, and animals. He marched them to the country of Askalon. While they were passing through a valley, an ant saw the approaching army and cried out to warn the other ants: "Run to your homes! Otherwise, unaware, Solomon and his army might crush you!" Solomon, hearing the cry of the ant, smiled. He was glad that the ant knew him to be a prophet who would not intentionally harm Allah's creation. He thanked Allah for saving the ants' lives. Allah the Almighty narrated: And there were gathered before Solomon his hosts of jinns and men, and birds, and they all were set in battle order (marching forwards). Till, when they came to a valley of the ants, one of the ants said: "O ants! Enter your dwellings, lest Solomon and his hosts crush you, while they perceive not."

So he (Solomon) smiled, amused at her speech and said: "My Lord! Inspire and bestow upon me the power and ability that I may be grateful for Your Favors which You have bestowed on me and on my parents, and that I may do righteous good deeds that will please You, and admit me by Your Mercy among Your righteous slaves." (Ch 27:17-19 Quran). In Jerusalem, on a huge rock, Solomon built a beautiful temple to draw the people to worship Allah. Today this building is known as "The Dome of the Rock." From there, a large band of followers joined Solomon on pilgrimage to the Holy Mosque in Mecca. After they had completed their hajj, they traveled to Yemen and arrived in the city of San'a. Solomon was impressed by their clever method of channeling water all over their cities. He was keen to build similar water systems in his own country but did not have enough springs.

## The Hoopoe Brings Information to Solomon

The Hoopoe is a colorful bird found across Afro-Eurasia, notable for its distinctive "crown" of feathers. Solomon set out to find the hoopoe bird, which could detect water under the ground. He sent signals all over the hoopoe to call on him, but it was nowhere to be found. In anger, he declared that unless the bird had a good reason for its absence, he would punish it severely. The hoopoe eventually came to Solomon and explained the reason for its delay.

"I have discovered something of which you are not aware. I have come from Sheba (Sab'a) with important news." Solomon became curious, and his anger subsided. The bird continued: "Sab'a is ruled by a queen named Bilkis (Bilqis), who has plenty of everything, including a splendid throne. But in spite of all this wealth, Satan has entered her heart and the hearts of her people. She rules their minds completely. They worship the sun instead of Allah the Almighty." To check the hoopoe's information, Solomon sent a letter to the queen with the bird. He instructed the bird to remain hidden and to watch everything.

## The Queen of Sheba Sends Gifts

The hoopoe dropped the letter in front of the queen and flew away to hide. She excitedly opened and read it: "Verily! It is from Solomon, and verily! It reads: 'In the Name of Allah, the Most Beneficent, and Most Merciful; be you not exalted against me, but come to me as Muslims (true believers who submit with full submission).'" [27:30-3] The queen was very disturbed and hurriedly summoned her advisors. They reacted as to a challenge, for they felt that there was someone challenging them, hinting at war and defeat, and asking them to submit to his conditions. They told her that they could only offer advice, but it was her right to command action. She sensed that they wanted to meet Solomon's invasion threat with a battle.

She told them: "Peace and friendship are better and wiser; war only brings humiliation, enslaves people and destroys the good things. I have decided to send gifts to Solomon, selected from our most precious treasure. The courtiers who will deliver the gifts will also have an opportunity to learn about Solomon and his military mighty."

## Solomon's Rejects the Queen's Gifts

Solomon's reconnaissance team brought him the news of the arrival of Bilkis' messengers with a gift. He immediately realized that the queen had sent her men on a probing mission thus, he gave orders to rally the army. The envoys of Bilqis, entering amidst the well-equipped army, realized that their wealth was nothing in comparison to that of the kingdom of Solomon's palace floors, which were made of sandalwood and inlaid with gold. They noticed Solomon surveying his army, and they were surprised at the number and variety of soldiers, which included lions, tigers, and birds. The messengers stood in amazement, realizing that they were in front of an irresistible army. The envoys marveled at the splendor surrounding them. They eagerly presented their queen's precious gifts and told Solomon that the queen wished that he would accept them as an act of friendship. They were shocked by his reaction: he did not even ask to open the covers of the containers! He told them: "Allah gave me plenty of wealth, a large kingdom, and prophet hood. I am, therefore, beyond bribery. My only objective is to spread the belief in Tawheed, the Oneness of Allah." He also directed them to take back the gifts to the queen and to tell her that if she did not stop her kind of worship he would uproot her kingdom and drive its people out of the land.

## The Queen Decides to Visit Solomon

The queen's envoys returned with the gifts and delivered the message. They also told her of the wonderful things they had seen. Instead of taking offense, she decided to visit Solomon. Accompanied by her royal officials and servants, she left Sheba, sending a messenger ahead to inform Solomon that she was on her way to meet him. Solomon asked the Jinns in his employ whether anyone among them could bring her throne to the palace before she arrived. One of them said; "I will bring it to you before this sitting is over." Solomon did not react to this offer; it appeared that he was waiting for a faster means. The Jinns competed with each other to please Solomon. One of them named Ifrit said: "I will fetch it for you in the twinkling of an eye!" No sooner had this one - who had the knowledge of the Book - finished his phrase than the throne stood before Solomon. The mission had, indeed, been completed in the blinking of an eye. Solomon's seat was in Palestine, and the throne of Bilqis had been in Yemen, two thousand miles away. This was a great miracle performed by one of those sitting with Solomon.

## The Queen's Visit with Solomon

When Bilqis arrived at Solomon's palace, she was welcomed with pomp and ceremony. Then, pointing to the altered throne, Solomon asked her whether her throne looked like that one. She looked at it again and again. In her mind she was convinced that her throne could not possibly be the one she was looking at, as hers was in her palace; et, she detected a striking similarity and replied: "It is as if it were the very one, and resembles mine in every respect." Solomon judged that she was intelligent and diplomatic. He then invited her into the great hall, the floor of which was laid in glass and shimmering. Thinking it was water, as she stepped on the floor, she lifted her skirt slightly above her heels, for fear of wetting it. Solomon pointed out to her that it was made of solid glass. She was amazed. She had never seen such things before. Bilqis realized that she was in the company of a very knowledgeable person who was not only a ruler of a great kingdom but a messenger of Allah, as well. She repented, gave up sun worship, accepted the faith of Allah, and asked her people to do the same. It was finished; Bilqis saw her people's creed fall apart before Solomon. She realized that the sun which her people worshipped was nothing but one of Allah's creatures. The sun eclipsed within her for the first time, and her heart was lit by a never fading light, the light of Islam.

## Solomon is informed about the Queen of Sheba - Quranic

Almighty Allah told us this story in the Quran: " He inspected the birds, and said: "What is the matter that I see not a hoopoe? Or is he among the absentees? I will surely punish him with a severe torment, or slaughter him, unless he brings me a clear reason." But the hoopoe stayed not long, he came up and said: "I have grasped (the knowledge of a thing) which you have not grasped and I have come to you from Sheba with true news. I found a woman ruling over them, and she has been given all things that could be possessed by any ruler of the earth, and she has a great throne. I found her and her people worshipping the sun instead of Allah, and Satan has made their deeds fair seeming to them, and has barred them from Allah's Way, so they have no guidance." Al-La (this word has two interpretations) [As Satan has barred them from Allah's Way} so that they do not worship (prostrate before) Allah, or so that they may worship (prostrate before) Allah, Who brings light to what is hidden in the heavens and the earth, and knows what you conceal and what you reveal. Allah, La ilaha illa Huwa (none has the right to be worshipped but He), the Lord of the Supreme Throne! (Solomon) said: "We shall see whether you speak the truth or you are one of the liars. Go with this letter of mine, and deliver it to them, then draw back from them, and see what answer they return." She said: "O chiefs! Verily! Here is a delivered to me a noble letter. Verily! It is from Solomon and verily! It (reads): 'In the Name of Allah, the Most Beneficent, the Most Merciful; Be you not exalted against me, but come to me as Muslims (true believers who submit to Allah with full submission)." She said: "O chiefs! Advise me in this case of mine. I decide no case till you are present with me." They said: "We have great strength, and great ability for war, but it is for you to command; so think over what you will command."

She said: "Verily! Kings, when they enter a town (country), they despoil it, and make the most honorable amongst its people low. And thus they do. But verily! I am going to send him a present, and see with what answer the messengers return." So when (the messengers with the present) came to Solomon, he said: "Will you help me in wealth? What Allah has given me is better than that which He has given you! Nay, you rejoice in your gift!" Then Solomon said to the chief of her messengers who brought the present: "Go back to them. We verily shall come to them with hosts that they cannot resist, and we shall drive them out from there is disgrace, and they will be abased." He said: "O chiefs! Which of you can bring me her throne before they come to me surrendering themselves in obedience?" An Ifrit (strong) from the Jinns said: "I will bring it to you before you rise from your place (council). And verily, I am indeed strong, and trustworthy for such work."

One with whom was knowledge of the Scripture said: "I will bring it to you within the twinkling of an eye!" then when Solomon saw it placed before him, he said: "This is by the Grace of my Lord, to test me whether I am grateful or ungrateful! And whoever is grateful, truly, his gratitude is for the good of his own self, and whoever is ungrateful, he is ungrateful only for the loss of his own self. Certainly! My Lord is Rich (Free of all wants), Bountiful!" He said: "Disguise her throne for her that we may see whether she will be guided (to recognize her throne), or she will be one of those not guided." So when she came, it was said to her: "Is your throne like this?" She said: "It is as though it was the very same." And Solomon said: "Knowledge was bestowed on us before her, and we were submitted to Allah (in Islam as Muslims before her)." And that which she used to worship besides Allah has prevented her from Islam, for she was of a disbelieving people. It was said to her: "Enter As-Sarh" (a glass surface with water underneath it) or a palace, but when she saw it, she thought it was a pool, and she tucked up her clothes, uncovering her legs. Solomon said: "Verily, it is Sarh paved smooth with slab of glass." She said: "My Lord! Verily, I have wronged myself, and I submit (in Islam), together with Solomon, to Allah, the Lord of the Alamin (mankind, jinns, and all that exists)." (Ch 27:20-44 Quran)

## The Jinn and Solomon's Death

Solomon's public work was largely carried out by the Jinns. This was a punishment for their sins of making people believe that they were all-powerful, knew the unseen, and could foresee the future. As a prophet, it was Solomon's duty to remove such false beliefs from his followers. Solomon lived amidst glory, and all creatures were subjected to him. Then Allah the Exalted ordained for him to die. His life and death were full of wonders and miracles; thus, his death harmonized with his life and glory. His death, like his life, was unique. The people had to learn that the future is known neither by the Jinns, nor by the prophets, but by Allah alone.

Solomon's effort in this direction did not end with his life, for even his death became an example. He was sitting holding his staff, overseeing the Jinns at work in a mine. He died sitting in this position. For a long time no one was aware of his death, for he was seen sitting erect. The Jinns continued with their sand toil, thinking that Solomon was watching over them. Many days later, a hungry ant began nibbling Solomon's staff. It continued to do so, eating the lower part of the staff, until it fell out of Solomon's hand, and his great body fell to the ground. People hurried to him, realizing that he had died a long time ago and that the Jinns did not perceive the unseen, for had the Jinns known the unseen, they would not have kept working thinking that Solomon was still alive.

### Solomon's Death - Quranic

Allah the Exalted revealed: "And We caused a fount of molten brass to flow for him, and there were Jinns that worked in front of him by the Leave of his Lord, and whosoever of them turned aside from Our Command, We shall cause him to taste of the torment of the blazing Fire. They worked for him what he desired, (making) high rooms, images, basins as large as reservoirs, and (making) cauldrons fixed (in their places).

"Work you, O family of David, with thanks!" But few of My slaves are grateful. Then when we decreed death for him (Solomon), nothing informed them (Jinns) of his death except a little worm of the earth, which kept slowly gnawing away at his stick, so when he fell down, the Jinns saw clearly that if they had known the unseen, they would not have stayed in the humiliating torment. [34:12-14]

# Prophet Shia (Isaiah)

Among the prophets between Prophet David (pbuh) and Prophet Zakariah (pbuh) is Isaiah (pbuh), Ibn Amoz (Amisiah). According to Muhammad Ibn Ishaaq, Isaiah (pbuh) appeared before Zakariah (pbuh) and Yahya (John the Baptist) (pbuh). He is among those who prophesied about Isa (Jesus) (pbuh) and Muhammad (pbuh). The king during his time was called Hezekiah (Hazkia). He listened and was obedient to Isaiah in what he advised him to do and prohibit for the good of the state. Affairs took momentum among the Israelites. The king became sick with an infected foot. While he was sick, King Sennacherib (Sinharib) of Babylon advanced towards Jerusalem with sixty thousand men.

## Allah Grants More Life to Hezekiah

The people were greatly terrified. The King asked Isaiah: "What did Allah reveal to you regarding Sennacherib and his army?" He replied: "He has not yet revealed anything." Then the revelation came down for King Hezekiah to appoint a successor, as he wished, because his end was at hand. When Isaiah told him this, the king turned to the qibla (the direction faced in prayer); he prayed, glorified Allah, invoked Him, and wept. Weeping and invoking Allah the All- Powerful and majestic with a sincere heart, trust and patience, he said: "O Lord of lords, and God of gods! O, Benevolent and Merciful One Whom neither sleep nor nodding can overpower, remember me for my deeds and my just judgment over the children of Israel; and all that was from You, and You know it better than I do, my open acts and my secrets are with You." Allah answered his prayers had compassion on him. He revealed to Isaiah to tell him the glad tidings that He had compassion for his weeping and would extend his life for a further fifteen years and save him from the enemy, Sennacherib. When Isaiah told this to Hezekiah, his disease was healed. Evil and sadness departed, and he fell prostrate, saying: "O Lord, it is You Who grants kingship to whomsoever You wish and dethrones whomsoever You wish and elevates whomsoever You wish and degrades whomsoever You wish, Knower of the unseen and the evident. And lo! You are the First and the Last; the Manifest and the Perceived; You grant mercy and answer the prayers of the troubled ones." When he raised his head, Allah revealed to Isaiah to command the king to extract the water of the fig and apply it to his sore, and he would be whole and cured. He did so and was cured.

## Allah Destroys Hezekiah's Enemies

Then Allah sent death upon the army of Sennacherib. In the morning they were all corpses, except Sennacherib and five of his companions, among them Nebuchadnezzar (Bukhtanasar). The king of Israel immediately sent for them, put them in shackles and displayed them in the land for seventy days to spite and insult them. Every day each of them was fed a loaf of barley bread; after seventy days he confined them in prison. Allah then revealed to Isaiah that the king should send them back to their country so that they might warn their people what would happen to them. When they returned, Sennacherib gathered his people and told them what had happened to them. The priests and magicians said to him: "We told you about their Lord and their prophets, but you did not listen to us. It is a nation which, with their God, nobody can overcome." Sennacherib was afraid of Allah. He died seven years later.

## Israel after Hezekiah's Death and Isaiah's Death

Ibn Ishaaq also reported that when King Hezekiah of Israel died, the Israelites' condition deteriorated; there was political confusion, and their wickedness increased. Isaiah preached to them what Allah revealed to him, directing them to righteousness and warning them of Allah's severe punishment.

His preaching made him their enemy and they decided to kill him, so he escaped from them. Ibn Ishaaq also reported that when Isaiah was passing by a tree, it opened, and he entered therein; but Satan saw him and held onto the loop of his garment so that it stuck out. When the people saw it, they brought a saw and sawed the tree, and him with it. Indeed, from Allah we come and to him we return.

## Prophet Aramaya (Jeremiah)

Prophet Jeremiah (pbuh) Ibn Hilkiah was from the House of Levi Ibn Jacob (pbuh). It has been claimed that he was Al-Khidr. This was related by Al-Dahak from Ibn Abbas but it is not true.

And We conveyed to the Children of Israel in the Scripture that, "You will surely cause corruption on the earth twice, and you will surely reach [a degree of] great haughtiness. [17:4]

$$\text{وَقَضَيْنَا إِلَىٰ بَنِي إِسْرَٰٓءِيلَ فِي ٱلْكِتَٰبِ لَتُفْسِدُنَّ فِي ٱلْأَرْضِ مَرَّتَيْنِ وَلَتَعْلُنَّ عُلُوًّا كَبِيرًا ﴿٤﴾}$$

So when the [time of] promise came for the first of them, We sent against you servants of Ours - those of great military might, and they probed [even] into the homes, and it was a promise fulfilled. [17:5]

$$\text{فَإِذَا جَآءَ وَعْدُ أُولَىٰهُمَا بَعَثْنَا عَلَيْكُمْ عِبَادًا لَّنَآ أُوْلِى بَأْسٍ شَدِيدٍ فَجَاسُوا۟ خِلَٰلَ ٱلدِّيَارِ ۚ وَكَانَ وَعْدًا مَّفْعُولًا ﴿٥﴾}$$

Then We gave back to you a return victory over them. And We reinforced you with wealth and sons and made you more numerous in manpower. [17:6]

$$\text{ثُمَّ رَدَدْنَا لَكُمُ ٱلْكَرَّةَ عَلَيْهِمْ وَأَمْدَدْنَٰكُم بِأَمْوَٰلٍ وَبَنِينَ وَجَعَلْنَٰكُمْ أَكْثَرَ نَفِيرًا ۝}$$

[And said], "If you do good, you do good for yourselves; and if you do evil, [you do it] to yourselves." Then when the final promise came, [We sent your enemies] to sadden your faces and to enter the temple in Jerusalem, as they entered it the first time, and to destroy what they had taken over with [total] destruction. [17:7]

$$\text{إِنْ أَحْسَنتُمْ أَحْسَنتُمْ لِأَنفُسِكُمْ ۖ وَإِنْ أَسَأْتُمْ فَلَهَا ۚ فَإِذَا جَآءَ وَعْدُ ٱلْءَاخِرَةِ لِيَسُٰٓـُٔوا۟ وُجُوهَكُمْ وَلِيَدْخُلُوا۟ ٱلْمَسْجِدَ كَمَا دَخَلُوهُ أَوَّلَ مَرَّةٍ وَلِيُتَبِّرُوا۟ مَا عَلَوْا۟ تَتْبِيرًا ۝}$$

## Traditions about Jeremiah

Ibn Asakir reported that it is written in some scrolls that Jeremiah stood upon the blood of John Ibn Zechariah while it was flowing and he said: "O blood! You have enlightened the people, so take a rest." So it stopped and condensed until it disappeared. There is a tradition that Jeremiah asked Allah: "O Lord! Which of Your slaves is more lovable to You?" He answered: "Those who remember Me most away from their remembrance of My creatures; those who are not thinking of death, nor speak of eternal living; those who, when they are allured by the riches of this world, despise them, and when they lose them are happy; those have My love, indeed, and I shall reward them more than they desired."

## Allah's Warning to the Children of Israel

Almighty Allah declared: "And We gave Moses the Scripture and made it a guidance for the children of Israel (saying): "Take not other than me as your Wakil (Protector, Lord, or Disposer of your affairs, etc). O offspring of those whom We carried in the ship with Noah! Verily, he was a grateful slave." And We decreed for the children of Israel in the Scripture, that indeed you would do mischief of the earth twice and you will become tyrants and extremely arrogant! So, when the promise came for the first of the two, We sent against you slaves of Yours given to terrible warfare.

They entered the very innermost parts of your homes. And it was a promise completely fulfilled. Then We gave you once again, a return of victory over them. And We helped you with wealth and children and made you more numerous in manpower. And We said: "If you do good, you do good for yourselves, and if you do evil (you do it) against yourselves." Then, when the second promise came to pass, (We permitted your enemies) to make your faces sorrowful and to enter the mosque (of Jerusalem) as they had entered it before, and to destroy with utter destruction that fell in their hands. (And We said in the Torah): "It may be that your Lord may show mercy unto you, but if you return to sins, We shall return to Our Punishment. And We have made Hell a prison for the disbelievers." (Ch 17:2-8 Quran).

## Allah's Message to the Children of Israel

Wahb Ibn Munbah reported that when sin increased, Allah revealed to an Israelite prophet called Amos (Mamia) (pbuh) that he should stand before his people and admonish them that they are hard-headed, blind, and deaf and tell them: "I (Allah) remember their forefathers, and that makes Me merciful with them. And ask them about My bounty: can any of them benefit from disobeying Me? And does any suffer who obeys Me?

The beasts remember their countries and return to them, but those people have forgotten why I have favored them for the sake of their forefathers, and have misused their generosity. Your cries have forgotten My tenets and your reciters worship other than Me, and your women have not learned a useful lesson and their rulers have lied against me and My messengers. Their hearts and mouths are full of lies. And I swear by My majesty and power that I will send upon them people with strange tongues, and strange faces, merciless in the face of their tears; and I shall send them a tyrannous cruel king, with an army like clouds, and followers like storms, and their flags like the wings of eagles, and the paces of their hoses like the decades of a journey. They will return buildings to dust, and leave the villages a wilderness. Woe betide it and its inhabitants if they shout and invoke! I will not look at their faces."

## Allah's Warning to the Children of Israel - Variation

Ibn Asaker has related the same in these words: Ishaaq Ibn Bishr said that Idris told them that Wahb Ibn Munbah said that Allah the Exalted sent Jeremiah to the children of Israel when the situation had become worse among them - in disobedience, killing of prophets and covetousness. Allah was determined to revenge Himself upon them vindictively; and so He revealed to Jeremiah: "I am going to destroy Jerusalem (the children of Israel).

Go to the Dome of the Rock. I will give you My commands and revelations." Jeremiah stood up and rent his clothes, and applied ashes to his face and fell prostrate and said: "O Lord! Would that my mother had not borne me, when You made me the last prophet of Israel, and Jerusalem be destroyed in my time." Allah said: "Raise your head." He raised his head, wept, and said: "O my Lord! Whom will You set against them?" He said: "The worshippers of fire who do not fear My punishment, nor expect My reward. Stand up Jeremiah, and hear the news about Israel. Before I chose you, I had made you, favored you, and honored you. Go with the king, guide, and protect him." (He was with the king while he was receiving revelation from Allah, and they forgot how Allah saved them.) "Go and tell them what I have told you." "O Allah! I am weak and if You do not strengthen me." "Do you not know that all affairs are controlled by Me? I am Allah without semblance, or any like Me. I spoke to the oceans so; I am with you, and nothing shall harm you.

Go to your people and tell them: Allah has remembered you, with His remembrance of our forefathers' good deeds. The animals remember their countries and return to them. But those people of yours are drenched in destruction and damnation, for they have forgotten the purpose of My generosity to their forefathers and have misplaced My favors. The scholars and priests have gone astray and have worshipped another god besides Me. "As for their kings and princes, they have been lavished with My bounty and though themselves safe from My fate. They abandon My Book and kill My prophets. Is it possible for Me to have a partner? Is it possible for Me to make a creature to be worshipped and to be obeyed besides Me? As for their reciters and jurists, they teach and learn what they like. As for the children of the prophets, they are oppressed and seduced and go with the crowd. They want the positions of their fathers without the discipline, patience, piety, and kindness of their fathers.

"By my power, I swear, that I shall send woe upon them that no wise man can understand. I shall replace their luxury with ordeal, chains, and fetters and after dwelling in palaces, they will dwell in dust. I will disgrace and degrade their womenfolk. I create My creatures and slaves with mercy and bounty. If they accept and recognize it, I complete My favors and mercy. When I change My mind, I change My mind; and if I change, I am angry; and if I am angry, I punish, and nothing prospers with My anger."

## Jeremiah Pleads on Behalf of His People

According to Ka'b, Jeremiah said: "By your grace I have come to learn before You; how is it possible when I am weak and powerless, to speak before You? But by Your mercy You have spared me to this day. None fears this punishment more than I do, because I have been among them while they disobeyed You, yet without it changing me.

If You punish me, I deserve it, and if You spare me, I expect it of Your kindness. O Lord, You are Overlord! Are you going to destroy their country when it is the place of Your prophets the place of Your revelations? O Lord the Exalted and Blessed by Your Name! For You to destroy this mosque and all pertaining to it, and those houses which landed Your praise! O Lord, for You to kill these people and punish them, when they are the issue of Abraham Your faithful friend and David Your chosen one! O lord, which village will escape Your punishment then? Which worshipper will escape Your vengeance after the children of Your faithful friend Abraham?" He on High said: "He who disobeys Me will not detest My punishment. I had honored them because they obeyed Me. If they disobeyed me I will place them among the disobedient, until I rescue them out of My Mercy." Jeremiah said: "O Lord, You made friends with Abraham and for his sake You preserved us; and Moses You did save; He asked You to save us, not abandon us, nor throw us to the enemy."

And so Allah revealed to him: "O Jeremiah, I made you honored in your mother's womb and have chosen you to this day. If your people had protected the orphans, the widows, the helpless, and the stranded, I would have been their Sustainer. They would have been like a blissful garden to Me; but I complain of the children of Israel to you. I have been the kind shepherd to them; but I honor only those who honor and despise those who despise My command. Those before them feared Me, but these people displayed their obedience of Me in the temple, market place, hill and mountain tops, and under the shade of trees until the heavens wondered at them before Me, and the earth and the mountains, including the beasts, wondered and wailed. All that had no effect on them; nor was the Book useful to them." Ka'b said that when Jeremiah delivered the message of his Lord, and the people heard the threats and warnings in it, they said: "You are lying, if you are saying that Allah shall destroy the land, His temple, His Book, His worship, and monotheism." They captured Jeremiah, tied him up and imprisoned him. At this, Allah sent Nabuchadnezzar upon them. He entered the country with his troops and surrounded the city. When the siege was prolonged they surrendered to his rule. They opened the gates and Nabuchadnezzar's troops streamed in.

Nebuchadnezzar ruled them savagely and punished them cruelly. He killed a third of them, captured a third, and spared the lame and the old; then h trampled upon them with the horses, demolished their houses, drew the youth along, and stood the women in the market places as guards. He intimidated the troops and destroyed the castles and temples. He burned the Torah. He asked about Daniel, the prophet who had written to him, but he was dead. His family took out the letter which he had written to him. Among the family members were Daniel the youngest son of Ezekiel, Azariah, and Mishael. He left that letter for them. The younger Daniel succeeded the elder Daniel. Nabuchadnezzar entered Jerusalem with his troops, then marched to Syria. He killed the children of Israel until he almost exterminated them. He returned to Babylon with booty in the form of treasure and men, among them young princes and children of priests numbering seventy thousand.

## Nebuchadnezzar and Jeremiah Meet

After Nabuchadnezzar had destroyed Jerusalem, he was told that the Israelites had a man who used to predict what had befallen them, describing the king and his actions, foretelling that he would slay their warriors, capture their children, destroy the temple, and burn their Torah. They had said he was lying, and so they had tied him and kept him in prison. Nabuchadnezzar ordered that he be brought out from prison. Jeremiah was released and the king said to him: "Did you warn those people against what has happened to them?" Jeremiah affirmed it and the king said: "I knew that." Jeremiah stated: "Allah sent me to them and they accused me of lying." He asked: "Did they beat you and imprison you?" He replied: "Yes."

The king said: "What a wicked race, to deny their prophet and their Lord's message! So would you like to join me, for me to honor you and make you free? And if you want to remain in your country, I grant you that." Jeremiah replied: "I am still in the security of Allah when I did not go away from the country at all. If the Israelites did not go out of it, they would not fear you, nor any other, nor would you have authority over them." When Nabuchadnezzar heard this, he let him alone, and so Jeremiah went to live in his place in Elia (Elat).

## Nebuchadnezzar and Jeremiah Meet - Variation

According to Hisham Ibn al-Kalbi, Nabuchadnezzar marched on Jerusalem, its king who was a descendant of David, who had built Jerusalem for the Israelites - made peace with him. Nabuchadnezzar took hostages and departed. When he had gone as far as Thahria, he learned that the Israelites had risen against their king and killed him because he had made peace with him. So, Nabuchadnezzar beheaded all the hostages that were with him. He returned to the Israelites and invaded the city, killing the warriors and capturing their families. When he had found Jeremiah in prison and released him, Jeremiah told him his story and his warnings concerning him. Nabuchadnezzar said: "What a wicked people that disobey the prophet of Allah!" He set him free and honored him. Jeremiah gathered around him the remaining weak souls of Israel.

## The Children of Israel Do Not Repent

He said to them: "Woe to us! We have disobeyed Allah. We must repent to Allah, Great and Majestic, for what we have done, and I shall pray to Allah to accept our repentance." He prayed so, and Allah revealed to him that He would not accept it: "If they are sincere, they must stay with you in this country (or town)." He told them what Allah had revealed. They said: "How can we stay in this town when it has been devastated and Allah is angry with its people?" So they refused to stay. Ibn al-Kalbi said that since that time, the children of Israel were dispersed the world over. Some of them went to the Hijaz, Taif and Medina, and others settled in Wadi al Qura. Some went to Egypt, and Nabuchadnezzar wrote to its king, demanding those who had escaped thither, but he refused. So Nabuchadnezzar mounted his army and fought him. He defeated him and captured their children.

Then he marched to Morocco. He returned from Morocco, Egypt, Jerusalem, Palestine, and Jordan with many captives, and among them was Daniel. Ibn al-Kalbi said that it appears that it was Daniel, the youngest son of Ezekiel, and not the elder Daniel, according to Ibn Munbah. Allah knows best.

### Jeremiah Sleeps for 100 Years, Jerusalem is Rebuilt

Hashim ibn Al-Kalbi reported that Allah the Exalted revealed to Jeremiah: "I am going to reconstruct Jerusalem, so go there." He went and found it devastated. He said to himself: "Exalted be Allah! Allah told me to come to this city and that He was reconstructing it. When will Allah rebuild it? And when will He bring it back to life?" Then he slept, and his donkey with him, for seventy years until Nebuchadnezzar and the king over him - Laharasab, who had ruled one hundred twenty years - had perished. Laharasab was succeeded by his son Bashtaasib (According to the Bible, Ezra 1, this would be King Cyrus of Persia). News of the death of Nebuchadnezzar had reached Bashtaasib through Sham (Syria), which was in utter ruin. The wild beats had multiplied in Palestine, for it had become empty of men. Bashtaasib therefore called to the children of Israel in Babylon: "Whoever wants to return to Sham (Syria/Palestine) may do so." It was ruled by one from the House of David, who was ordered by Bashtaasib to rebuild Jerusalem and its temple, so they returned and rebuilt it. Then Jeremiah opened his eyes, blinked from the seventy year sleep, and saw how the city was being reconstructed. He remained in that sleep of his until he had completed 100 years. When Allah awoke him, he thought that he had slept no more than an hour. He had known the city as a devastated land; when he saw it rebuilt, he said: "He grants wisdom to whom He pleases, and he, to whom wisdom is granted, is indeed granted abundant good. But none remember (will receive admonition) except men of understanding." [2:269]

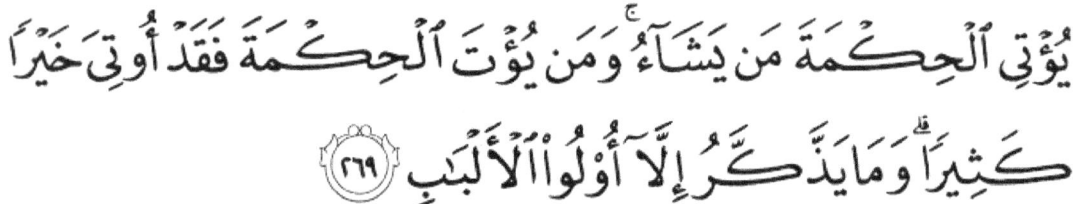

### The History of Israel after its Rebuilding

Ibn Al-Kalbi said that the Israelites settled it, and Allah rebuilt their glory. It remained so until Rome vanquished them in the era of the tribal kings; then they lost their community and their authority after the appearance of Christianity. This is how Ibn Jarir tells their story in his History of Jerusalem. He said that Laharasab was a just king and diplomatic. The people, chiefs, and kings obeyed him, and he was gifted in the construction of cities, canals and institutions. When he grew too weak to rule, after more than one hundred, his son Bashtaasib ascended to the throne. During his reign the religion of Zoroastrianism (al-Majusia) appeared. A man named (Zoroaster) (Zordahst) had been a companion of Jeremiah and had angered him, so Jeremiah cursed him. Zoroaster became a leper.

He went to the land of Azerbaijan, joined Bashtaasib forced people to embrace it and killed many people who disobeyed him. After Bashtaasib, his son Barman ruled. They were among the famous and heroic kings of Persia, and Nebuchadnezzar had been deputy to all three of them. He lived a long time, may Allah torment him! The essence of what has been written by Ibn Jarir is that the person or wayfarer passing through this village was Jeremia. Others say that it was Hosea (Ozir), and this is the consensus of the ancients and those after them, but Allah knows best.

# Prophet Daniel

Scholars narrated that based on a chain of citations. Nabuchadnezzar captured the two lions and threw them into a pit. He then brought Daniel and threw him at them; yet they did not pounce at him; rather, he remained as Allah wished. When then he desired food and drink, Allah revealed to Jeremiah, who was in Sham (Palestine/Syria): "Prepare food and drink for Daniel." He said: "O Lord I am in Jerusalem while Daniel is in Babylon (Iraq)." Allah revealed to him: "Do what I have commanded you to do, and I shall send you one who will carry you and what you have prepared." Jeremiah did so and Allah sent him something that would carry him until he arrived at the brink of the pit. Then Daniel asked: "Who is this?" He answered: "I am Jeremiah." He asked: "What brought you?" He answered: "Your Lord sent me to you." He said: "And so my Lord has remembered me?" He said: "Yes." Daniel said: "Praise be to Allah Who never forgets those who appeal to Him! And Praise be to Him Who compensates good with good, rewards patience with safety, dispels harm after distress, assures us when we are overwhelmed, and is our hope when skill fails us."

## Daniel after Death

Yunus Ibn Bakeer reported that Muhammad Ibn Ishaaq reported that Abu Khalid Ibn Dinar reported that Abul Aa'lia said: "When Tastar was invaded, we found, in the treasure house of Al-Harmazan, a bed on which lay a dead man, with a holy script at his bedside. We took the scripture to Omar Ibn Al Khattab. He called Ka'b and he translated it into Arabic, and I was the first Arab to read it. I read it as I read the Qur'an." Here, I (Khalid Ibn Dinar) said to Abul Aa'lia: "What was in it?" He said: "Life history, annals, songs, speech, and what is to come." I asked: "And what did you do with the man?" He said: "We dug in the river bank 13 separate graves. At nightfall we buried him and leveled all the graves in order to mislead people for they would tamper with him." I asked: "And what did they want from him?" He said: "When the sky was cloudless for them, they went out with his bed, and it rained." I asked: "Who did you think the man was?" He said; "A man called Daniel." I asked: "And for how long had he been dead when you found him?"

He said: "Three hundred years." I asked: "Did not anything change on him?" He said: "No, except for the hairs of his face (beard, and mustache); the skin of the prophets is not harmed by the earth, nor devoured by hyenas." The chain of citation from Abul Aa'lia is good, but if the date of the dead man's death was really three hundred years, then he was not a prophet but a saintly an, because there was no prophet between Isa (Jesus) (pbuh), and the Prophet Muhammad (pbuh), according to the hadith in Bukhari. The span between them (the dead man and Muhammad (pbuh)) was variously reported as four hundred, six hundred, and six hundred twenty years. It could be that he had died eight hundred years earlier, which would be near to Daniel's time, if his being Daniel is correct. However, he could still have been somebody else, either a prophet or a saint. Yet the truth is more likely he was Daniel, because he had been taken by the King of Persia and remained imprisoned as already mentioned. It was narrated with a correct citation that his nose as one span (nine inches) long. Anas Ibn Malik, with a good citation, said that his nose was an arm's stretch long (two feet), on which basis he is thought to be an ancient prophet from before this period. Almighty Allah knows best.

## Daniel's Death - Hadith

Ibn Abu Dunya reported from Abu Bilal that Abu Musa found with Daniel a holy script and a container in which were dirhams, his ring and ointment. He wrote to Omar, who replied: "Send the scripture to us, send some of the ointment, tell the Muslims who are with you to use it, share the dirhams among them, and leave the ring for you. Abu Bakr Ibn Abu Dunya related without citation that when Abu Musa was told that he was Daniel, he stayed with him, embraced him, and kissed him. Then he wrote to Omar that he found with him nearly ten thousand Dhirhams. It used to be that people came to borrow from it, and if they did not return it, they became sick. Omar ordered his burial in a grave to be kept secret and the money to be sent to the treasury, with the box and the ring a gift to him (Abu Musa). It is related of Abu Musa that he told four of the captives to dam the river and dig a grave in the middle, where he buried him. Then he beheaded the four captives in order for the secret to be kept from all except himself.

## Daniel's Ring

Ibn Abu Dunya also reported, by a chain of citations, that a ring was seen on the hand of Ibn Abu Barda Ibn Abu Musa. The gem was carved with two lions with a man between them, whom they were licking. Abu Barda said: "This is the ring of that man whom the people of this town say is Daniel. Abu Musa took it the day he was buried. The learned people of the town told Abu Musa that soothsayers and astrologers told the king in Daniel's time that a boy would be born who would destroy him and his kingdom. So the king swore to kill all the baby boys, except that they threw Daniel in the lions' den, and the lion and lioness began to lick him and did not harm him. His mother came and took him. Abu Musa said: "And so Daniel carved his image and the image of the two lions into the gem of his ring, for him not to forget Allah's blessing upon him in this.'"

# Prophet Uzair (Ezra)

Prophet Ezra (pbuh) was a saint and a wise man. He went out one day to his own farm, as was his custom. About noon he came to a deserted, ruined place and felt the heat. He entered the ruined town and dismounted his donkey, taking figs and grapes in his basket. He went under the shade of the khaiba tree and ate his food. Then he got up to look at what remained of the ruins. The people had long been lost, and he saw bones. "Oh! How will Allah ever bring it to life after its death?" [2:259]. He said this not out of doubt but out of curiosity. Allah sent the Angel of Death to take his life.

أَوْ كَٱلَّذِى مَرَّ عَلَىٰ قَرْيَةٍ وَهِىَ خَاوِيَةٌ عَلَىٰ عُرُوشِهَا قَالَ أَنَّىٰ يُحْىِۦ هَـٰذِهِ ٱللَّهُ بَعْدَ مَوْتِهَا ۖ فَأَمَاتَهُ ٱللَّهُ مِا۟ئَةَ عَامٍ ثُمَّ بَعَثَهُۥ ۖ قَالَ كَمْ لَبِثْتَ ۖ قَالَ لَبِثْتُ يَوْمًا أَوْ بَعْضَ يَوْمٍ ۖ قَالَ بَل لَّبِثْتَ مِا۟ئَةَ عَامٍ فَٱنظُرْ إِلَىٰ طَعَامِكَ وَشَرَابِكَ لَمْ يَتَسَنَّهْ ۖ وَٱنظُرْ إِلَىٰ حِمَارِكَ وَلِنَجْعَلَكَ ءَايَةً لِّلنَّاسِ ۖ وَٱنظُرْ إِلَى ٱلْعِظَامِ كَيْفَ نُنشِزُهَا ثُمَّ نَكْسُوهَا لَحْمًا ۚ فَلَمَّا تَبَيَّنَ لَهُۥ قَالَ أَعْلَمُ أَنَّ ٱللَّهَ عَلَىٰ كُلِّ شَىْءٍ قَدِيرٌ ۝٢٥٩

He remained dead for one hundred years. After one hundred years had passed and there had been changes in Israelite affairs, Allah sent an angel upon Ezra to revive his heart and his eyes in order for him to feel and see how Allah revives the dead. The angel said: "For how long did you sleep?" He said: "A day or part of a day." He said this because he knew he had slept early in the afternoon and woke up late in the afternoon. The angel said: "You remained asleep for 100 years." He ate and drank the food which he had prepared before he was overtaken by that long sleep. Then the angel revived his donkey. Almighty Allah said: "And look at your donkey!

Thus We have made of you a sign for the people. Look at the bones, how We bring them together and clothe them with flesh." When this was clearly shown to him he said: "I know now that Allah is able to do all things."

### Ezra Returns Home

He rode on his donkey and entered his native place, but the people did not recognize him, nor did his household, except the maid, now an old woman. He asked her: "Is this the house of Ezra?" She said: "Yes, but the people have long forgotten Ezra." He said: "I am Ezra, Allah had taken my life for a one hundred years and has now returned it to me." She said: "Ezra used to be answered when he prayed to Allah. Pray to cure me of blindness if you are Ezra." He prayed for her and massaged her eyes and took her by the hand. "Get up by the power of Allah," he said. The crippled woman stood up and walked; she opened her eyes and saw; her blindness was gone. She said: "I bear witness that you are Ezra."

### Ezra Finds and Copies the Torah

She rushed to the assembly of the Israelites. Ezra's son was one hundred eighteen years old, and his children's children now were lords of the assembly. She called out to them saying: "This is Ezra come to you." They accused her of lying. She said: "I am your old maid. He has just prayed to Allah for me, and here I am whole again, walking and seeing." The people stood up and looked at him. His son said: "My father had a mark between his shoulders, a black mole," and they discovered it. They said: "None among us memorized the Torah since Nabuchadnezzar burned it, except Ezra; and there was only one copy of the Torah, which was hidden by Sarukha. He buried it in the days of Nabuchadnezzar in a place none but Ezra knows." Ezra led the people to the hidden place and took out that copy of the Torah. Its leaves had rotted, and the book itself crumpled. Ezra sat under the shade of a tree surrounded by the children of Israel and copied out the Torah for them from that script. Henceforth, the Jews said that Ezra is the son of Allah, for two evidences which came down from Heaven and for his copying the Torah and for his fighting the cause of the Israelites. He had been copying the Torah for Ezekial in the land of darkness in the hermitage of Ezekiel. The village which was in ruins is said to be Sayrabadh. Ibn Abbas commanded: "So it is as Allah said: "We have made of you a sign for the people." [2:259] That is, for the Israelites, in that he was sitting among his children, the old men, and he a youth. He died as a forty year old, and Allah resurrected him at the same age on the day of his death."

# Prophet Zakariyah (Zechariah)

Prophet Zakariyah (pbuh) was now old and bent with age, in his nineties. Despite his feebleness, he went to the temple daily to deliver his sermons. Zakariyah was not a rich man, but he was always ready to help those in need. His one disappointment in life was that he had no children, for his wife was barren. This worried him, for he feared there was no one after him to carry out his work. The people needed a strong leader, for it they were left on their own, they would move away from Allah's teachings and change the Holy Laws to suit themselves. During one of his visits to the temple, he went to check on Mary, who was living in a secluded room of the temple. He was surprised to find fresh out of season fruit in her room. Besides him, no one had entry to her room. When he inquired, she told him that the fruit was from Allah. She found it every morning. But why was he so surprised, she asked him. Did he not know that Allah provides without measure for whom He wills? This noble girl had opened this eyes to a startling idea. Could he not ask his Lord to bless him with a child in his old age? Even if his wife was past childbearing age, nothing was impossible for his Gracious Lord!

## Zakariyah Asks for a Son - Quranic

Allah the Almighty revealed: 'Kaf, Ha, Ya, Ain, Sad, (These letters are one of the miracles of the Quran, and none but Allah Alone knows their meanings). This is a mention of the Mercy of your Lord to His slave Zakariyah. When he called out his Lord (Allah) - a call in secret, saying: "My Lord! Indeed my bones have grown feeble, and gray hair has spread on my head, and I have never been unblest in my invocation to You, O my Lord! And Verily! I fear my relatives after me, since my wife is barren. So give me from Yourself an heir, - who shall inherit me, and inherit also the posterity of Jacob (inheritance of the religious knowledge and Prophethood, not the wealth, etc.) And make him, my Lord, one with whom You are Well-pleased!" He said: "O my Lord! How can I have a son when I am very old, and my wife is barren?" Allah said: "Thus Allah does what He wills." He said: "O my Lord! Make a sign for me." Allah said: "Your sign is that you shall not speak to mankind for three days except with signals. And remember your Lord much (by praising Him again and again), and glorify Him in the morning and afternoon." [3:38-41]. Then he came out to his people from Al Mihrab (a praying place or a private room, etc.), he told them by signs to glorify Allah's Praises in the morning and in the afternoon. It was said to his son: "O John! Hold fast to the Scripture (The Torah)."

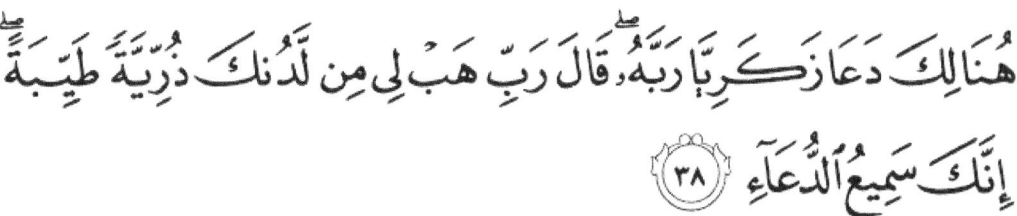

And We gave him wisdom while yet a child, and made him sympathetic to men as a mercy or a grant from Us, and pure from sins (John) and he was righteous, and dutiful towards his parents, and he was neither an arrogant nor disobedient (to Allah or to his parents). And Salamun (peace) on him the day he was born, the day he dies, and the day he will be raised up to life again! (Ch 19:1-15 Quran). Almighty Allah also said: "At that time Zakariyah invoked his Lord, saying: "O my Lord! Grant me from You, a good offspring. You are indeed the All-Hearer of invocation. Then the angels called him, while he was standing in prayer in Al- Mihrab (a praying place or a private room), saying: "Allah gives you glad tidings of John confirming (believing in) the Word from Allah ("Be!" - And he was! (i.e., the creation of Isa (Jesus), son of Mariam (Mary), noble keeping away from sexual relations with women, a Prophet, from among the righteous."

## Prophet Yahya (John)

Prophet Yahya (John) (pbuh) was born a stranger to the world of children who used to amuse themselves, as he was serious all the time. Most children took delight in torturing animals whereas, he was merciful to them. He fed the animals from his food until there was nothing left for him, and he just ate fruit or leaves of trees. John loved reading since childhood. When he grew up, Allah the Exalted called upon him: "O John! Hold fast to the Scripture (The Torah)." And We gave him wisdom while yet a child. [19:12]

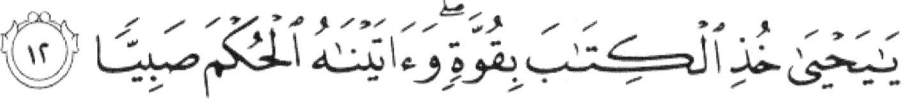

Allah guided Prophet John to read the Book of Jurisprudence closely; thus, he became the wisest and most knowledgeable man of that time. Therefore, Allah the Almighty endowed him with the faculties of passing judgments on people's affairs, interpreting the secrets of religion, and guiding people to the right path. John reached maturity. His compassion for his parents, as well as for all people and all creatures, increased greatly. He called people to repent their sins. There are quite a number of traditions told about John. Ibn Asaker related that one time his parents were looking for him and found him at the Jordan River. When they met him, they wept sorely, seeing his great devotion to Allah, Great and Majestic. Ibn Wahb said that, according to Malik, grass was the food of John Ibn Zakariyah, and he wept sorely in fear of Allah. A chain of narrators reported that Idris Al Khawlawi said: "Shall I not tell you he who had the best food? It is John Ibn Zakariyah, who joined the beasts at dinner, fearing to mix with men." Zakariayah did not see his son for three days. He found him weeping inside a grave which he had dug and in which he resided. "My son, I have been searching for you. Why are you are dwelling in this grave weeping?" "O father, did you not tell me that between Paradise and Hell is only a span, and it will not be crossed except by tears of weepers?"

He said to him: "Weep then, my son." Then they wept together. Other narrations say that John (pbuh) said: "The dwellers of Paradise are sleepless out of the sweetness of Allah's bounty; that is why the faithful must be sleepless because of Allah's love in their hearts. How far between the two luxuries, how far between them?" They say John wept so much that tears marked his cheeks.

## John's Love of Nature

He found comfort in the open and never cared about food. He ate leaves, herbs, and sometimes locusts. He slept anywhere in the mountains or in holes in the ground. He sometimes would find a lion or a bear as he entered a cave, but being deeply absorbed in praising Allah, he never heeded them. The beasts easily recognized John as the prophet who cared for all the creatures, so they would leave the cave, bowing their heads. John sometimes fed those beasts, out of mercy, from his food and was satisfied with prayers as food for his soul. He would spend the night crying and praising Allah for His blessings. When John called people to worship Allah, he made them cry out of love and submission, arresting their hearts with the truthfulness of his words. A conflict took place between John and the authorities at that time. A tyrant king, Herod Antipas, the ruler of Palestine, was in love with Salome, his brother's daughter. He was planning to marry his beautiful niece. The marriage was encouraged by her mother and by some of the learned men of Zion, either out of fear or to gain favor with the ruler. On hearing the ruler's plan, John pronounced that such a marriage would be wrong. He would not approve it, as it was against the Torah.

## John's Cruel Death

John's pronouncement spread like wildfire. Salome was angry. It was her ambition to rule the kingdom with her uncle. So she plotted to achieve her aim. Dressing attractively, she sang and danced before her uncle. Her arousing Herod's lust. Embracing her, he offered to fulfill whatever she desired. At once she told him: "I would love to have the head of John, because he has defiled your honor and mine throughout the land. If you grant me this wish, I shall be very happy and will offer myself to you." Bewitched by her charm, he submitted to her monstrous request. John was executed and his head was brought to Salome. The cruel woman gloated with delight. But the death of Allah's beloved prophet was avenged. Not only she, but all the children of Israel were severely punished by invading armies which destroyed their kingdom.

# Prophet Isa (Jesus)

In many verses in the Quran, Allah denied the claim of the Christians that He has a son. A delegation from Nagran came to the Prophet Muhammad (pbuh). They began to talk about their claim about the Trinity, which is that Allah is three in one, the Father, the Son, and the Holy Spirit, with some disagreement among their sects. That is why Allah affirmed in many verses of the Quran that Jesus is a slave of Allah, whom He molded in the womb of his mother like any other of His creatures, and that He created him without a father, as He created Adam without a father or a mother. Almighty Allah had chosen Isa to be one of his messengers to humanity.

### The Birth of Mary

Allah the Almighty said: "Allah chose Adam, Noah, the family of Abraham and the family of Imran above the Alamin (mankind and Jinns)(of their times). Offspring, one of the other, and Allah is All-Hearer, All-Knower. Remember when the wife of Imran said: "O my Lord! I have vowed to You what (the child that) is in my womb to be dedicated for Your services (free from all worldly work; to serve Your Place of worship), so accept this, from me. Verily, You are the All- Hearer, the All Knowing. Then when she delivered her (child Mary), she said: "O My Lord! I have delivered a female child," and Allah knew better what she delivered, - "and the male is not like the female, and I have named her Mary, and I seek refuge with You (Allah) for her and for her offspring from Satan, the outcast."

### Mary's Sustenance

So her Lord (Allah) accepted her with goodly acceptance. He made her grow in a good manner and put her under the care of Zechariah. Every time he entered Al-Mihrab (a praying place or a private room), he found her supplied with sustenance. As Allah recounted in the Quran: She said: "From Allah. Verily, Allah provides sustenance to whom He wills, without limit." (Ch 3:37 Quran)

### Mary's Family History

Allah declared that He had elected Adam (pbuh) and the elite of his offspring who obey Allah. Then He specified the family of Abraham (pbuh), which includes the sons of Ishmael (pbuh), and the family of Imran, the father of Mary. Muhammad Ibn Ishaaq stated that he was Imran Ibn Bashim, Ibn Amun, Ibn Misha, Ibn Hosqia, Ibn Ahriq, Ibn Mutham, Ibn Azazia, Ibn Amisa, Ibn Yamish, Ibn Ahrihu, Ibn Yazem, Ibn Yahfashat, Ibn Eisha, Ibn Iyam, Ibn Rahba am, Ibn David (Dawud).

## Mary's Birth - Longer Version

Prophet Zakariyah's (pbuh) wife's sister had a daughter named Hannah. She was married to Imran, a leader of the Israelites. For many years, the couple remained childless. Whenever Hannah saw another woman with a child, her longing for a baby increased. Although years had passed, she never lost hope. She believed that one day Allah would bless her with a child, on whom she would shower all her motherly love. She turned to the Lord of the heavens and the earth and pleaded with Him for a child. She would offer the child in the service of Allah's house, in the temple of Jerusalem. Allah granted her request. When she learned that she was pregnant, she was the happiest woman alive, and thanked Allah for His gift. Her overjoyed husband Imran also thanked Allah for His mercy. However, while she was pregnant her husband passed away. Hannah wept bitterly. Alas, Imran did not live to see their child for whom they had so longed. She gave birth to a girl, and again turned to Allah in prayer: "O my Lord, I have delivered a female child," and the male is not like the female, and I have named her Mary, and I seek refuge with You (Allah) for her and her offspring from Satan, the outcast." [3:36]

فَلَمَّا وَضَعَتْهَا قَالَتْ رَبِّ إِنِّي وَضَعْتُهَا أُنثَىٰ وَٱللَّهُ أَعْلَمُ بِمَا وَضَعَتْ وَلَيْسَ ٱلذَّكَرُ كَٱلْأُنثَىٰ وَإِنِّي سَمَّيْتُهَا مَرْيَمَ وَإِنِّي أُعِيذُهَا بِكَ وَذُرِّيَّتَهَا مِنَ ٱلشَّيْطَٰنِ ٱلرَّجِيمِ ﴿٣٦﴾

## Zechariah Becomes Mary's Guardian

Hannah had a big problem in reference to her promise to Allah, for females were not accepted into the temple, and she was very worried. Her sister's husband Zakariyah, comforted her, saying that Allah knew best what she had delivered and appreciated fully what she had offered in His service. She wrapped the baby in a shawl and handed it over to the temple elders. As the baby was a girl, the question of her guardianship posed a problem for the elders. This was a child of their late and beloved leader, and everyone was eager to take care of her. Zakariyah said to the elders: "I am the husband of her maternal aunt and her nearest relation in the temple; therefore, I will be more mindful of her than all of you." As it was their custom to draw lots to solve disagreements, they followed this course. Each one was given a reed to throw into the river. They had agreed that the reed's owner that remained afloat would be granted guardianship of the girl. All the reeds sank to the bottom except Zakariyah's. With this sign, they all surrendered to the will of Allah and made him the guardian.

## Mary's High Status

To ensure that no one had access to Mary, Zakariyah built a separate room for her in the temple. As she grew up, she spent her time in devotion to Allah. Zakariyah visited her daily to see to her needs, and so it continued for many years. One day, he was surprised to find fresh fruit, which was out of season in her room. As he was the only person who could enter her room, he asked her how the fruit got there. She replied that these provisions were from Allah, as He gives to whom He wills. Zakariyah understood by this that Allah had raised Mary's status above that of other women. Thereafter, Zakariyah spent more time with her, teaching and guiding her. Mary grew to be a devotee of Allah, glorifying Him day and night.

## Mary's High Status - Prophet Muhammad

Ali Ibn Abi Talib narrated that the Prophet Muhammad (pbuh) said: "The best of the world's women is Mary (in her lifetime), and the best of the world's women is Khadija (in her lifetime)." (Sahih Al-Bukhari). Abu Musa Al-Ashari also narrated that the Prophet Muhammad (pbuh) said: "Many among men attained perfection but among women none attained perfection except Mary the daughter of Imran, and Asiya the wife of Pharaoh, and the superiority of Aisha to other women is like the superiority of Tharid (an Arabic dish) to other meals."

## Mary Receives News of Jesus (pbuh)

While Mary was praying in her temple, an angel in the form of a man appeared before her. Filled with terror, she tried to flee, praying: "Verily! I seek refuge with the Most Beneficent (Allah) from you, if you do fear Allah." The angel said: "I am only a Messenger from your Lord, (to announce) to you the gift of a righteous son." She said: "How can I have a son, when no man has touched me, nor am I unchaste?" He said: "So (it will be), your Lord said: "that is easy for Me (Allah): And (We wish) to appoint him as a sign to mankind and a mercy from Us (Allah), and it is a matter (already) decreed, (by Allah).'" (Ch 19:18-21 Quran). The angel's visit caused Mary great anxiety, which increased as the months went by. How could she face giving birth to a child without having a husband? Later, she felt life kicking inside her. With a heavy heart, she left the temple and went to Nazareth, the city in which she had been born where she settled in a simple farm house to avoid the public. But fear and anxiety did not leave her. She was from a noble and pious family. Her father had not been an evil man nor was her mother an impure woman. How could she prevent tongues from wagging about her honor? After some months, Mary could not bear the mental strain any longer. Burdened with a heavy womb, she left Nazareth, not knowing where to go to be away from this depressing atmosphere. She had not gone far, when she was overtaken by the pains of childbirth. She saw down against a dry palm tree, and here she gave birth to a son.

Looking at her beautiful baby, she was hurt that she had brought him into the world without a father. She exclaimed: "I wish I had died before this happened and had vanished into nothingness!" Suddenly, she heard a voice nearby: "Grieve not, your Lord has placed a rivulet below, and shake the trunk of this tree, from which ripe dates will fall. So eat and drink and regain the strength you have lost; and be of good cheer, for what you see is the power of Allah, Who made the dry palm tree regain life, in order to provide food for you." For a while she was comforted by Allah's miracle, for it was a sure sign of her innocence and purity.

## Mary Returns to the City with Jesus

Mary decided to return to the city. However, her fears also returned. What was she going to tell the people? She began to worry. The baby then began to speak: "If you meet any person say: 'I have vowed to fast for The Beneficent and may not speak to any human today.'" With this miracle, Mary felt at ease. As she had expected, her arrival in the city with a newborn baby in her arms aroused the curiosity of the people. They scolded her: "This is a terrible sin that you have committed." She put her finger to her lips and pointed to the child. They asked: "How can we speak to a newborn baby?" To their total amazement, the child began to speak clearly: "I am Allah's servant. Allah has given me the Book, and has made me a prophet, and has blessed me wherever I may be, and has enjoined on me prayers and alms-giving as long as I live. Allah has made me dutiful towards she who had borne me. He has not made me arrogant nor unblessed. Peace unto me the day I was born, the day I die, and the day I shall be raised alive." Most of the people realized that the baby was unique, for it Allah wills something, He merely says "Be" and it happens. Of course, there were some who regarded the baby's speech as a strange trick, but at least Mary could now stay in Nazareth without being harassed.

## Mary Receives News of Jesus - Quranic

Allah the Exalted revealed: "And mention in the Book (the Quran, O Muhammad, the story of) Mary, when she withdrew in seclusion from her family to a place facing east. She placed a screen (to screen herself) from them; then We sent to her Our Ruh (angel Gabriel), and he appeared before her in the form of a man in all respects. She said: "Verily! I seek refuge with the Most Beneficent (Allah) from you, if you do fear Allah." The angel said: "I am only a Messenger from your Lord, (to announce) to you the gift of a righteous son." She said: "How can I have a son, when no man has touched me, nor am I unchaste?" He said: "So (it will be), your Lord said: "that is easy for Me (Allah): and (We wish) to appoint him as a sign to mankind and a mercy from Us (Allah), and it is a matter (already) decreed, (by Allah).'" [19:16-21]

وَاذْكُرْ فِي الْكِتَابِ مَرْيَمَ إِذِ انتَبَذَتْ مِنْ أَهْلِهَا مَكَانًا شَرْقِيًّا ﴿١٦﴾

فَاتَّخَذَتْ مِن دُونِهِمْ حِجَابًا فَأَرْسَلْنَا إِلَيْهَا رُوحَنَا فَتَمَثَّلَ لَهَا بَشَرًا سَوِيًّا ﴿١٧﴾

قَالَتْ إِنِّي أَعُوذُ بِالرَّحْمَٰنِ مِنكَ إِن كُنتَ تَقِيًّا ﴿١٨﴾

قَالَ إِنَّمَا أَنَا رَسُولُ رَبِّكِ لِأَهَبَ لَكِ غُلَامًا زَكِيًّا ﴿١٩﴾

قَالَتْ أَنَّىٰ يَكُونُ لِي غُلَامٌ وَلَمْ يَمْسَسْنِي بَشَرٌ وَلَمْ أَكُ بَغِيًّا ﴿٢٠﴾

قَالَ كَذَٰلِكِ قَالَ رَبُّكِ هُوَ عَلَيَّ هَيِّنٌ وَلِنَجْعَلَهُ آيَةً لِّلنَّاسِ وَرَحْمَةً مِّنَّا وَكَانَ أَمْرًا مَّقْضِيًّا ﴿٢١﴾

### The Birth of Jesus - Quranic

So she conceived him, and she withdrew with him to a far place (Bethlehem valley, about four to six miles from Jerusalem). And the pains of childbirth drove her to the trunk of a palm tree. She said: "Would that I had died before this, and had been forgotten and out of sight!" Then (the babe "Jesus" or Gabriel) cried unto her from below her, saying: "Grieve not! Your Lord has provided you a water stream under you; and shake the trunk of palm tree towards you, it will let fall fresh ripe dates upon you. So eat and drink and be glad, and if you see any human being, say: 'Verily! I have vowed a fast unto the Most Beneficent (Allah) so I shall not speak to any human being this day.'" [19:22-26]

$$\text{فَأَجَاءَهَا ٱلْمَخَاضُ إِلَىٰ جِذْعِ ٱلنَّخْلَةِ قَالَتْ يَـٰلَيْتَنِى مِتُّ قَبْلَ هَـٰذَا وَكُنتُ نَسْيًا مَّنسِيًّا ﴿٢٣﴾}$$

"Then she brought him (the baby) to her people, carrying him. They said: "O Mary! Indeed you have brought a thing Fariyya (an unheard mighty thing). O sister (the like) of Aaron (not the brother of Moses, but he was another pious man at the time of Mary)! Your father was not a man who used to commit adultery, nor was your mother an unchaste woman. Mary pointed to him. They said: "How can we talk to one who is a child in the cradle?" He (Jesus) said: "Verily! I am a slave of Allah. He has given me the Scripture and made me a Prophet; and He has made me blessed wheresoever I be, and has enjoined me prayer, and Zakat, as long as I live, and dutiful to my mother, and made me not arrogant, unblest. And Salam (peace) be upon me the day I was born, and the day I die, and the day I shall be raised alive!" (Ch. 19:27 – 33). Such is Jesus, son of Mary. (It is) a statement of truth, about which they doubt (or dispute). It befits not (the Majesty of) Allah that He should beget a son (this refers to the slander of Christians against Allah, by saying that Jesus is the son of Allah). Allah is above all that they associate with Him. When He decrees a thing, He only says to it, "Be!" - And it is.

Jesus said: "And verily Allah is my Lord and your Lord. So worship Him (Alone). That is the Straight Path. (Allah's Religion of Islamic Monotheism which He did ordain for all of His Prophets)." Then the sects differed (the Christians about Jesus), so woe unto the disbelievers (those who gave false witness saying that Jesus is the son of Allah) from the meeting of a great Day (the Day of Resurrection, when they will be thrown in the blazing Fire). How clearly will they (polytheists and disbelievers in the Oneness of Allah) see and hear, the Day when they will appear before Us! But the Zalimun (polytheists and wrong-doers) today are in plain error. And warn them (O Muhammad) of the Day of grief and regrets, when the case has been decided, while now they are in a state of carelessness and they believe not. [19:34-39]

## Some Stories about Mary's Pregnancy

It was said that Joseph the Carpenter was greatly surprised when he knew the story, so he asked Mary: "Can a tree come to grow without a seed?" She said: "Yes, the one which Allah created for the first time." He asked her again: "Is it possible to bear a child without a male partner?" She said: "Yes, Allah, created Adam without male or female!" It was also said that, while pregnant, Mary went one day to her aunt, who reported that she felt as if she was pregnant.

Mary in turn, said that she, too, was feeling as if she was pregnant. Then her aunt said: "I can see what is in my womb prostrating to what is in your womb." The Jewish priests felt this child Jesus was dangerous, for they felt that the people would turn their worship to Allah the Almighty Alone, displacing the existing Jewish tenets. Consequently, they would lose their authority over the people. Therefore, they kept the miracle of Jesus's speech in infancy as a secret and accused Mary of a great misdeed. As Jesus (pbuh) grew, the signs of prophethood began to increase. He could tell his friends what kind of supper waited for them at home and what they had hidden and where. When he was twelve years old, he accompanied his mother to Jerusalem. There he wandered into the temple and joined a crowd listening to the lecture of the Rabbis (Jewish priests). The audience were all adults, but he was not afraid to sit with them. After listening intently, he asked questions and expressed his opinion. The learned rabbis were disturbed by the boy's boldness and puzzled by the questions he asked, for they were unable to answer him. They tried to silence him, but he ignored their attempts and continued to express his views. Jesus became so involved in this exchange that he forgot he as expected back home. In the meantime, his mother went home, thinking that he might have gone back with relatives or friends. When she arrived, she discovered that he was not there, so she returned to the city to look for him. At last she found him in the temple, sitting among the learned, conversing with them. He appeared to be quite at ease, as if he had been doing this all his life. Mary got angry with him for causing her worry. He tried to assure her that all the arguing and debating with the learned had made him forgot the time.

## Jesus Does Not Observe the Sabbath

Jesus grew up to manhood. It was Sabbath, a day of complete rest: no fire could be lit or extinguished nor could females plait their hair. Moses (pbuh) had commanded that Saturday be dedicated to the worship of Allah. However, the wisdom behind the Sabbath and its spirit had gone, and only the letter remained in the Jews' hearts. Also, they thought that Sabbath was kept in heaven, and that the People of Israel had been chosen by Allah only to observe the Sabbath. They made a hundred things unlawful on Saturday even self-defense or calling a doctor to save a patient who was in bad condition. This is how their life was branded by such hypocrisy. Although the Pharisees were guardians of the law, they were ready to sell it when their interests were involved so as to obtain personal gains. There was, for example, a rule which prohibited a journey of more than one thousand yards on the Sabbath day. What do we expect of the Pharisees in this case? The day before, they transferred their food and drink from their homes two thousand yards away and erected a temporary house so they could travel a further thousand yards on the Sabbath day. Jesus was on his way to the temple. Although it was the Sabbath, he reached out his hand to pick two pieces of fruit to feed a hungry child. This was considered to be a violation of the Sabbath law. He made a fire for the old women to keep themselves warm from the freezing air, which is another violation.

He went to the temple and looked around. There were twenty thousand Jewish priests registered there who earned their living from the temple. The rooms of the temple were full of them.

## Jesus Receives His Prophethood

Jesus observed that the visitors were much fewer than the priests. Yet the temple was full of sheep and doves which were sold to the people to be offered as sacrifices. Every step in the temple cost the visitor money. They worshipped nothing but money. In the temple, the Pharisees and Sadducees acted as if it were a market place, and these two groups always disagreed on everything. Jesus followed the scene with his eyes and observed that the poor people who could not afford the price of the sheep or dove were swept away like flies by the Pharisees and Saducees. Jesus was astonished. Why did the priests burn a lot of offerings inside the temple, while thousands of poor people were hungry outside it?

On this blessed night, the two noble prophets John (pbuh) and Zakariyah (pbuh) died, killed by the ruling authority. On the same night, the revelation descended upon Jesus (pbuh). Allah the Exalted commanded him to begin his call to the children of Israel. To Jesus, the life of ease was closed, and the page of worship and struggled was opened. Like an opposing force, the message of Jesus came to denounce the practices of the Pharisees and to reinforce the Law of Moses. In the face of a materialistic age of luxury and worship of gold, Jesus called his people to a nobler life by word and deed. This exemplary life was the only way out of the wretchedness and diseases of his age. Jesus's call, from the beginning, was marked by its complete uprightness and piety. It appealed to the soul, the inner being, and not be a closed system of rules laid down by society. Jesus continued inviting the people to Almighty Allah. His call was based on the principle that there is no mediation between the Creator and His creatures. However, Jesus was in conflict with the Jews' superficial interpretation of the Torah. He said that he did not come to abrogate the Torah, but to complete it by going to the spirit of its substance to arrive at its essence. He made the Jews understand that the Ten Commandments have more value than they imagined. For instance, the fifth commandment does not only prohibit physical killing, but all forms of killing; physical, psychological, or spiritual. And the sixth commandment does not prohibit adultery only in the sense of unlawful physical contact between a man and a woman, but also prohibits all forms of unlawful relations or acts that might lead to adultery. The eye commits adultery when it looks at anything with passion.

## Jesus Denounces Materialism

Jesus was therefore in confrontation with the materialistic people. He told them to desist from hypocrisy, show and false praise. There was no need to hoard wealth in this life. They should not preoccupy themselves with the goods of this passing world; rather they must preoccupy themselves with the affairs of the coming world because it would be everlasting. Jesus told them that caring for this world is a sin, not fit for pious worshippers. The disbelievers care for it because they do not know a better way. As for the believers, they know that their sustenance is with Allah, so they trust in Him and scorn this world. Jesus continued to invite people to worship the Only Lord, Who is without partner, just as he invited them to purify the heart and soul.

## Jewish Priests Try to Embarrass Jesus

His teaching annoyed the priests, for every word of Jesus was a threat to them and their position, exposing their misdeeds. The Roman occupiers had, at first, no intention of being involved in this religious discord of the Jews because it was an internal affair, and they saw that this dispute would distract the Jews from the question of the occupation. However, the priests started to plot against Jesus. They wanted to embarrass him and to prove that he had come to destroy the Mosaic Law. The Mosaic Law provides that an adulteress be stoned to death. They brought him a Jewish adulteress and asked Jesus: "Does not the law stipulate the stoning of the adulteress?" Jesus answered: "Yes." They said: "This woman is an adulteress." Jesus looked at the woman and then at the priests. He knew that they were more sinful than she. They agreed that she should be killed according to Mosaic Law, and they understood that if he was going to apply Mosaic Law, he would be destroying his own rules of forgiveness and mercy. Jesus understood their plan. He smiled and assented: "Whoever among you is sinless can stone her." His voice rose in the middle of the Temple, making a new law on adultery, for the sinless to judge sin. There was none eligible; no mortal can judge sin, only Allah the Most Merciful. As Jesus left the temple, the woman followed him. She took out a bottle of perfume from her garments, knelt before his feet and washed them with perfume and tears, and then dried his feet with her hair. Jesus turned to the woman and told her to stand up, adding: "O Lord, forgive her sins." He let the priests understand that those who call people to Almighty Allah are not executioners. His call was based on mercy for the people, the aim of all divine calls.

## Jesus' Brings the Dead to Life

Jesus continued to pray to Allah for mercy on his people and to teach his people to have mercy on one another and to believe in Allah. Jesus continued his mission, aided by divine miracles. Some Qur'anic commentators said that Jesus brought four people back from the dead: a friend of his named Al-Azam, an old woman's son, and a woman's only daughter. These three had died during his lifetime. When the Jews saw this they said: "You only resurrect those who have died recently; perhaps they only fainted." They asked him to bring back to life Sam the Ibn Noah.

When he asked them to show him his grave, the people accompanied him there. Jesus invoked Allah the Exalted to bring him back to life and behold, Sam the Ibn Noah came out from the grave gray-haired. Jesus asked: "how did you get gray hair, when there was no aging in your time?" He answered: "O Spirit of Allah, I thought that the Day of Resurrection had come; from the fear of that day my hair turned gray."

## The Miracles of Jesus - Quranic

Allah the Almighty said: "Remember when Allah will say (on the Day of Resurrection): "O Jesus, son of Mary! Remember My Favor to you and to your mother when I supported you with Ruh-ul-Qudus (Gabriel) so that you spoke to the people in the cradle and in maturity; and when I taught you writing, Al Hikmah (the power of understanding), the Torah and the Gospel; and when you made out of the clay, as it were, the figure of a bird, by My Permission, and you breathed into it, and it became a bird by My Permission, and you healed those born blind, and the lepers by My Permission, and when you brought forth the dead by My Permission; and when I restrained the Children of Israel from you (when they resolved to kill you) since you came unto them with clear proofs, and the disbelievers among them said: 'This is nothing but evident magic.'" And when I (Allah) put in their hearts of the disciples (of Jesus) to believe in Me and My Messenger, they said: "We believe. And bear witness that we are Muslims." [5:110]

إِذْ قَالَ ٱللَّهُ يَٰعِيسَى ٱبْنَ مَرْيَمَ ٱذْكُرْ نِعْمَتِى عَلَيْكَ وَعَلَىٰ وَٰلِدَتِكَ إِذْ أَيَّدتُّكَ بِرُوحِ ٱلْقُدُسِ تُكَلِّمُ ٱلنَّاسَ فِى ٱلْمَهْدِ وَكَهْلًا وَإِذْ عَلَّمْتُكَ ٱلْكِتَٰبَ وَٱلْحِكْمَةَ وَٱلتَّوْرَىٰةَ وَٱلْإِنجِيلَ وَإِذْ تَخْلُقُ مِنَ ٱلطِّينِ كَهَيْـَٔةِ ٱلطَّيْرِ بِإِذْنِى فَتَنفُخُ فِيهَا فَتَكُونُ طَيْرًۢا بِإِذْنِى وَتُبْرِئُ ٱلْأَكْمَهَ وَٱلْأَبْرَصَ بِإِذْنِى وَإِذْ تُخْرِجُ ٱلْمَوْتَىٰ بِإِذْنِى وَإِذْ كَفَفْتُ بَنِىٓ إِسْرَٰٓءِيلَ عَنكَ إِذْ جِئْتَهُم بِٱلْبَيِّنَٰتِ فَقَالَ ٱلَّذِينَ كَفَرُوا۟ مِنْهُمْ إِنْ هَٰذَآ إِلَّا سِحْرٌ مُّبِينٌ ۝١١٠

## Jesus' Abilities and the Disciples - Quranic

Almighty Allah also revealed: "And He Allah will teach him (Jesus) the Book and Al Hikmah (the Sunna, the faultless speech of the Prophets, wisdom, etc.), (and) the Torah and the Gospel. And will make him (Jesus) a Messenger to the Children of Israel (saying): "I have come to you with a sign from your Lord, that I design for you out of clay, as it were, the figure of a bird, and breathe into it, and it becomes a bird by Allah's Leave; and I heal him who was born blind, and the leper, and I bring the dead to life by Allah's leave. And I inform you of what you eat, and what you store in your houses. Surely, therein is a sign for you, if you believe. And I have come confirming that which was before me of the Torah, and to make lawful to you part of what was forbidden to you, and I have come to you with proof from your Lord. So fear Allah and obey me. Truly! Allah is my Lord and your Lord, so worship Him (Alone). This is the Straight Path." Then when Jesus came to know of their disbelief, he said: "Who will be my helpers in Allah's Cause?" The disciples said: "We are the helpers of Allah; we believe in Allah, and bear witness that we are Muslims (we submit to Allah)." Our Lord! We believe in what You have sent down, and we follow the Messenger (Jesus); so write us down among those who bear witness (to the truth, La ilaha ill Allah - none has the right to be worshipped but Allah). And they (disbelievers) plotted (to kill Jesus), and Allah planned too. And Allah is the Best of the planners. [3:48-54]

## Allah Sends the Disciples a Feast

Jesus continued calling people to Almighty Allah and laying down for them what might be called "the law of the Spirit." Once when standing on a mountain surrounded by his disciples, Jesus saw that those who believed in him were from among the poor, the wretched, and the downtrodden, and their number was small. Some of the miracles which Jesus performed had been requested by his disciples, such as their wish for a "holy table" to be sent down from heaven. Allah said: "Remember when the disciples said: "O Jesus, son of Mary! Can your Lord send down to us a table spread (with food) from heaven?" Jesus said: "Fear Allah, if you are indeed believers." They said: "We wish to eat thereof and to be stronger in Faith and to know that you have indeed told us the truth and that we ourselves be its witnesses." Jesus, son of Mary, said: "O Allah, our Lord! Send us from heaven a table spread (with food) that there may be for us - for the first and the last of us - a festival and a sign from You; and provide us sustenance, for You are the best of sustainers." Allah said: "I am going to send it down unto you, but if any of you after that disbelieves, then I will punish him with a torment such as I have not inflicted on anyone among all the Alamin (mankind and jinn). And (remember) when Allâh will say (on the Day of Resurrection): "O'Esa (Jesus), son of Maryam (Mary)! Did you say unto men: 'Worship me and my mother as two gods besides Allah?'" "He will say: "Glory be to You! It was not for me to say what I had no right (to say). Had I said such a thing, You would surely have known it. You know what is in my inner self though I do not know what is in Yours, truly, You, only You, are the All-Knower of all that is hidden and unseen." [5:112-116]

It was related that Jesus commanded his disciples to fast for thirty days; at the end of it, they asked Jesus to bring food from heaven to break their fast. Jesus prayed to Allah after his disciples had doubted Allah's power. The great table came down between two clouds, one above and one below, while the people watched. Jesus said: "O Lord, make it a mercy and not a cause of distress." So it fell between Jesus's hands, covered with a napkin. Jesus suddenly prostrated and his disciples with him. They sensed a fragrance, which they had never smelled before. Jesus said: "The one who is the most devout and most righteous may uncover the table, that we might eat of it to thank Allah for it." They said: "O Spirit of Allah, you are the most deserving." Jesus stood up, then performed ablution and prayed before uncovering the table, and behold, there was a roasted fish. The disciples said: "O Spirit of Allah, is this the food of this world or of Paradise?" Jesus said to his disciples: "Did not Allah forbid you to ask questions? It is the divine power of Allah the Almighty Who said: 'Be,' and it was. It is a sign from Almighty Allah warning of great punishment for unbelieving mortals of the world. This is the kernel of the matter." It is said that thousands of people partook of it, and yet they never exhausted it. A further miracle was that the blind and lepers were cured.

## Those Worshipping Jesus and Allah's Questions to Jesus

The Day of the Table became one of the holy days for the disciples and followers of Jesus. Later on, the disciples and followers forgot the real essence of the miracles, and so they worshipped Jesus as a god. Almighty Allah asserted: "And remember when Allah will say (on the Day of Resurrection): "O Jesus, son of Mary! Did you say unto men: 'Worship me and my mother as two gods besides Allah?'" He will say: "Glory be to You! It was not for me to say what I had no right to say. Had I said such a thing, You would surely have known it. You know what is in my inner self though I do not know what is in Yours, truly, You, only You, are the All Knower of all that is hidden and unseen. Never did I say to them aught except what You (Allah) did command me to say: 'Worship Allah, my Lord and your Lord', And I was a witness over them while I dwelt amongst them, but when You took me up, You were the Watcher over them, and You are a Witness to all things. (This is a great admonition and warning to the Christians of the whole world). If you punish them, they are Your slaves, and if You forgive them, Verily You, only You are the All Mighty, the All Wise."

Allah will say: "This is a Day on which the truthful will profit from their truth: theirs are Gardens under which rivers flow (in Paradise) - they shall abide therein forever. Allah is pleased with them and they with Him. That is the great success (Paradise). To Allah belongs the dominion of the heavens and the earth and all that is therein, and He is Able to do all things." [5:116-120]

### The Plot to Kill Jesus

Jesus went on his mission until vice knew that its throne was threatening to fall. So the forces of evil accused him of magic, infringement of the Mosaic Law, allegiance with the devil; and when they saw that the poor people followed him, they began to scheme against him. The Sanhedrin, the highest judicial and ecclesiastical council of the Jews, began to meet to plot against Jesus. The plan took a new turn. When the Jews failed to stop Jesus's call, they decided to kill him. The chief priests held secret meetings to agree on the best way of getting rid of Jesus. While they were in such a meeting, one of the twelve apostles of Jesus, Judas Iscariot, went to them and asked: "What will you give me if I deliver him to you?" Judas bargained with them until they agreed to give him thirty pieces of silver known as shekels. The plot was laid for the capture and murder of Jesus. It was said that the high priest of the Jews tore his garment at the meeting, claiming that Jesus had denied Judaism. The tearing of clothes at that time was a sign of disgust.

### The Torture of Jesus

The priests had no authority to pass the death sentence at that time, so they convinced the Roman governor that Jesus was plotting against the security of the Roman Empire and urged him to take immediate action against him. The governor ordered that Jesus be arrested. According to the Book of Matthew, Jesus was arrested and the council of the high priests passed the death sentence upon him. Then, they began insulting him, spitting on his face and kicking him. It was the Roman custom for the condemned to be flogged before they were executed. So Pilate, the Roman governor, ordered that Jesus be flogged. The Mosaic Law stipulates forty lashes, but the Roman had no limit, and they were brutal lashes. After that, Jesus was handed to the soldiers for crucifixion. They took off his clothes, and kept them. They put a crown of thorns on his head to mock him. According to custom he carried his cross on his back to increase his suffering.

### Jesus's Crucifixion - Bible Version

Finally, they reached a place called Golgotha, meaning the Place of Skulls, outside the walls of Jerusalem. Instead of giving him a cup of wine diluted with scent to help lessen the pain on the cross, the soldiers gave Jesus a cup of vinegar diluted with gall. Then they crucified him and, as a further mockery, two thieves with him. So it is written in the Bible.

## Jesus's Crucifixion - Quranic

But the faith of Islam came with views quite different from that of the extend gospels with regards to both the end of Jesus and his nature. The Glorious Qur'an affirms that Allah the Exalted did not permit the people of Israel to kill Jesus or crucify him. What happened was that Allah saved him from his enemies and raised him to heaven.

They never killed Jesus, they killed someone else. Allah the Almighty declared: "And because of their saying (in boast), "We killed Messiah Jesus, son of Mary, the Messenger of Allah," but they killed him not, nor crucified him, but the resemblance of Jesus was put over another man (and they killed that man) and those who differ therein are full of doubts. They have no certain knowledge, they follow nothing but conjecture. For surely; they killed him not (Jesus, son of Mary): But Allah raised him (Jesus) up (with his body and soul) unto Himself (and he is in the heavens). And Allah is Ever All Powerful, All Wise. And there is none of the people of the Scripture (Jews & Christians), but must believe in him (Jesus, son of Mary, as only a Messenger of Allah, and a human being), before his (Jesus or a Jew's or a Christian's) death (at the time of the appearance of the angel of death). And on the Day of Resurrection, he (Jesus) will be a witness against them. (Ch 4:157-159 Quran). Almighty Allah also revealed: "And remember when Allah said: "O Jesus! I will take you and raise you to Myself and clear you (of the forged statement that Jesus is Allah's son) of those who disbelieve, and I will make those who follow you (Monotheists, who worship none but Allah) superior to those who disbelieve (in the Oneness of Allah, or disbelieve in some of His Messengers, e.g. Muhammad, Jesus, Moses, etc., or in His Holy Books, e.g. the Torah, the Gospel, the Qur'an) till the Day of Resurrection. Then you will return to Me and I will judge between you in the matters in which you used to dispute." [3:55]

إِذْ قَالَ ٱللَّهُ يَٰعِيسَىٰٓ إِنِّى مُتَوَفِّيكَ وَرَافِعُكَ إِلَىَّ وَمُطَهِّرُكَ مِنَ ٱلَّذِينَ كَفَرُوا۟ وَجَاعِلُ ٱلَّذِينَ ٱتَّبَعُوكَ فَوْقَ ٱلَّذِينَ كَفَرُوٓا۟ إِلَىٰ يَوْمِ ٱلْقِيَٰمَةِ ۖ ثُمَّ إِلَىَّ مَرْجِعُكُمْ فَأَحْكُمُ بَيْنَكُمْ فِيمَا كُنتُمْ فِيهِ تَخْتَلِفُونَ ﴿٥٥﴾

### Refutation of the Christians Claim

Allah disclaims begetting anyone - Surah 19, Almighty Allah refuted the claims of the Jews and the Christians in many verses of the Quran. And they say: "The Most Beneficent (Allah) has begotten a son (or offspring or children) (as the Jews say: Ezra is the son of Allah, and the Christians say that He has begotten a son (Christ), and the pagan Arabs say that he has begotten daughters (angels, etc.))." Indeed you have brought forth (said) a terrible evil thing. Whereby the heavens are almost torn, and the earth is split asunder, and the mountains fall in ruins, that they ascribe a son (or offspring or children) to the Most Beneficent (Allah). But it is not suitable for (the Majesty of) the Most Beneficent (Allah) that He should beget a son (or offspring or children).

There is none in the heavens and the earth but comes unto the Most Beneficent (Allah) as a slave. Verily, He knows each one of them, and has counted them a full counting. And every one of them will come to Him alone on the Day of Resurrection (without any helper, or protector or defender). [19:88-95]

Allah the Exalted also declared: "Yet, they join the Jinns as partners in worship with Allah, though He has created them (the Jinns), and they attribute falsely without knowledge sons and daughters to Him. Be He Glorified! And Exalted above (all) that they attribute to Him. He is the Originator of the heavens and the earth. How can He have children when He has no wife? He created all things and He is the All-Knower of everything. Such is Allah, your Lord! La ilaha illa Huwa (none has the right to be worshipped but He), the Creator of all things. So worship Him (Alone), and He is the Wakil (Trustee, Disposer of affairs, Guardian etc.) over all tings. No vision can grasp Him, but His Grasp is over all vision. He is the Most Subtle and Courteous, Well-Acquainted with all things. [6:100-103]

Almighty Allah commanded: "O people of the Scripture (Jews and Christians)! Do not exceed the limits in you religion, nor say of Allah aught but the truth. The Messiah Jesus, son of Mary, was (no more than) a Messenger of Allah and His Word, ("Be" - and he was) which He bestowed on Mary and a spirit (Ruh) created by Him; so believe in Allah and His Messengers. Say not: "Three (trinity)!" Cease! (It is) better for you. For Allah is the only One Ilah (God), Glory be to Him (Far Exalted is He) above having a son. To Him belongs all that is in the heavens and all that is in the earth. And Allah is All Sufficient as a Disposer of affairs. The Messiah will never be proud to reject to be a slave to Allah, nor the angels who are near (to Allah). And whosoever rejects His worship and is proud, then He will gather them all together unto Himself. So, as for those who believed (in the Oneness of Allah - Islamic Monotheism) and did deeds of righteousness, He will give their (due) rewards, and more out of His Bounty. But as for those who refuse His worship and were proud, He will punish them with a painful torment. And they will not find for themselves besides Allah any protector or helper. [4:171-173]

### Allah Disclaims Ezra as a Son

Almighty Allah also declared: And the Jews say: Ezra is the son of Allah, and the Christians say: Messiah is the son of Allah. That is a saying from their mouths. They imitate the saying of the disbelievers of old. Allah's Curse be on them, how they are deluded away from the truth! They (Jews and Christians) took their rabbis and their monks to be their lords besides Allah, (by obeying them in things which they made lawful or unlawful according to their own desires without being ordered by Allah) and (they also took as their lord) Messiah, son of Mary, while they (Jews and Christians) were commanded (in the Torah and the Gospel) to worship none but One Ilah (God- Allah) La ilaha illa Huwa (none has the right to be worshipped but He). Praise and glory be to Him, (far above is He) from having the partners they associate (with Him). [9:30-32]

## Allah Disclaims Begetting Anyone

Allah the Almighty also revealed: "Now ask them (O Muhammad): "Are there (only) daughters for your Lord and sons for them?" Or did We create the angels females while they were witnesses? Verily, it is of their falsehood that they (pagans) say: "Allah has begotten off-spring or children (angels are the daughters of Allah)" And, verily, they are liars! Has He (then) chosen daughters rather than sons? What is the matter with you? How do you decide? Will you not then remember? Or is there for you a plain authority? Then bring your Book if you are truthful! And they have invented a kinship between Him and the Jinns, but the jinn know well that they have indeed to appear (before Him) (i.e. they will be brought for accounts). Glorified be Allah! (He is free) from what they attribute unto Him! Except the slaves of Allah, whom He chooses (for His Mercy i.e. true believers of Islamic Monotheism who do not attribute false things unto Allah). [37:149-160] And Almighty Allah declared: "Surely, in disbelief are they who say that Allah is the Messiah, son of Mary. Say (O Muhammad): "Who then has the least power against Allah, if He were destroy the Messiah, son of Mary, his mother, and all those who are on the earth together?" And to Allah belongs the dominion of the heavens and the earth, and all that is between them. He creates what He wills. And Allah is Able to do all things. And (both) the Jews and Christians say; "We are the children of Allah and His loved ones." Say: "Why then does He punish you for your sins?" Nay, you are but human beings, of those He has created, He forgive whom He wills and He punishes whom He wills. And to Allah belongs the dominion of the heavens and the earth and all that is between them, and to Him is the return of all. O people of the Scripture (Jews and Christians)! Now has come to you Our Messenger (Muhammad) making (things) clear unto you, after a break in (the series of) Messengers, lest you say: "there came unto us no bringer of glad tidings and no warner." But now has come unto you a bringer of glad tidings and a warner. And Allah is Able to do all things. [5:17-19] Allah the Exalted warned: Surely they have disbelieved who say: "Allah is the Messiah, son of Mary." But the Messiah (Jesus) said: "O Children of Israel! Worship Allah, my Lord and your Lord." Verily, whosoever sets up partners in worship with Allah, then Allah has forbidden Paradise for him, and the Fire will be his abode. And for the Zalimun (polytheists, and wrong-doers) there are no helpers. Surely, disbelievers are those who said: "Allah is the third of the three (in a Trinity)." But there is no Ilah (god) (none who has the right to be worshipped) but One Ilah (God- Allah). And if they cease not from what they say, verily, a painful torment will befall the disbelievers among them. Will they not repent to Allah and ask His Forgiveness? For Allah is Oft-Forgiving, Most Merciful. The Messiah (Jesus), son of Mary, was no more than a Messenger; many were the Messengers that passed away before him. His mother (Mary) was a Siddiqah (she believed in the Words of Allah, and His Books. They both used to eat food, as any other human being, while Allah does not eat). Look how We made the Ayat (proofs, evidences, verses, lessons, signs, revelations, etc.) clear to them, yet look how they are deluded away from the truth. [5:72-75] Allah said: "All the praises and thanks be to Allah, Who has not begotten a son (nor an offspring), and Who has no partner in His Dominion, nor He is low to have a Wali (helper, protector, or supporter).

And magnify Him with all the magnificence, (Allahu-Akbar, Allah is the Most Great)." [17:111]

وَقُلِ ٱلْحَمْدُ لِلَّهِ ٱلَّذِى لَمْ يَتَّخِذْ وَلَدًا وَلَمْ يَكُن لَّهُۥ شَرِيكٌ فِى ٱلْمُلْكِ وَلَمْ يَكُن لَّهُۥ وَلِىٌّ مِّنَ ٱلذُّلِّ وَكَبِّرْهُ تَكْبِيرًۢا ۝

The pagans once asked the Prophet Muhammad (pbuh): "To whom is your Lord related, His original ancestors and His various branches of descendants?" It is also reported that the Jews said: "We worship Ezra, the Son of Allah," and the Christians said: "Jesus is the Son of Allah," and the Magians said: "We worship the sun and the moon," and the Pagans said: "We worship idols." In response to all of them Allah revealed some of His attributes: Unity, Uniqueness, and other substantives: Say: (O Muhammad): "He is Allah, the One. Allah As-Samad (The Self-Sufficient Master, Whom all creatures need, He neither eats nor drinks). He begets not, nor was He begotten; and there is none co-equal or comparable unto Him." [112:1-4]

الٓر ۚ تِلْكَ ءَايَٰتُ ٱلْكِتَٰبِ ٱلْمُبِينِ ۝

إِنَّآ أَنزَلْنَٰهُ قُرْءَٰنًا عَرَبِيًّا لَّعَلَّكُمْ تَعْقِلُونَ ۝

نَحْنُ نَقُصُّ عَلَيْكَ أَحْسَنَ ٱلْقَصَصِ بِمَآ أَوْحَيْنَآ إِلَيْكَ هَٰذَا ٱلْقُرْءَانَ وَإِن كُنتَ مِن قَبْلِهِۦ لَمِنَ ٱلْغَٰفِلِينَ ۝

إِذْ قَالَ يُوسُفُ لِأَبِيهِ يَٰٓأَبَتِ إِنِّى رَأَيْتُ أَحَدَ عَشَرَ كَوْكَبًا وَٱلشَّمْسَ وَٱلْقَمَرَ رَأَيْتُهُمْ لِى سَٰجِدِينَ ۝

# Prophet Muhammad

(Peace and Blessings Be Upon Him)

*And indeed, you are of a great moral character. [68:4]*

Prophet Muhammad (peace and blessing be upon him) was born in Mecca (Makkah), on Monday, 12 Rabi' Al-Awal (2 August A.D. 570). His mother, Aminah, was the daughter of Wahb Ibn Abdu Manaf of the Zahrah family. His father, 'Abdullah, was the son of Abdul Muttalib. His genealogy has been traced to the noble house of Ishmael, the son of Prophet Abraham in about the fortieth descend. Muhammad's father died before his birth. Before he was six years old his mother died, and the doubly orphaned Muhammad was put under the charge of his grandfather Abdul Muttalib who took the tenderest care of him. But the old chief died two years afterwards. On his deathbed he confided to his son Abu Talib the charge of the little orphan.

### Journey to Busra - Christian Monk merits Muhammad

When Muhammad was twelve years old, he accompanied his uncle Abu Talib on a mercantile journey to Syria, and they proceeded as far as Busra. The journey lasted for some months. It was at Busra that the Christian monk Bahira met Muhammad. He is related to have said to Abu Talib: 'Return with this boy and guard him against the hatred of the Jews, for a great career awaits your nephew."

### Muhammad's honest and honorable character

After this journey, the youth of Muhammad seems to have been passed uneventfully, but all authorities agree in ascribing to him such correctness of manners and purity of morals as were rare among the people of Mecca. The fair character and the honorable bearing of the unobtrusive youth won the approbation of the citizens of Mecca, and by common consent he received the title of "Al Ameen," The Faithful. In his early years, Propht Muhammad was not free from the cares of life. He had to watch the flocks of his uncle, who, like the rest of the Bani Hashim, had lost the greater part of his wealth. From youth to manhood he led an almost solitary life.

The lawlessness rife among the Meccans, the sudden outbursts of causeless and bloody quarrels among the tribes frequenting the Fair of Okadh (The Arabian Olympia), and the immorality and skepticism of the Quraish, naturally caused sad feelings in the heart of the sensitive youth. Such scenes of social misery and religious degradation were characteristic of a depraved age.

## Muhammad's marriage to Khadijah

When Muhammad was twenty five years old, he traveled once more to Syria as a factor of a noble and rich Quraishi widow named Khadijah; and, having proved himself faithful in the commercial interests of that lady, he was soon rewarded with her hand in marriage. This marriage proved fortunate and singularly happy. Khadijah was much the senior of her husband, but in spite of the disparity of age between them, the tenderest devotion on both sides existed. This marriage gave him the loving heart of a woman who was ever ready to console him in his despair and to keep alive within him the feeble, flickering flame of hope when no man believed in him and the world appeared gloomy in his eyes.

## Troubled, lawless times for the Makkans

Until he reached thirty years of age, Muhammad was almost a stranger to the outside world. Since the death of his grandfather, authority in Mecca was divided among the ten senators who constituted the governing body of the Arabian Commonwealth. There was no such accord among them as to ensure the safety of individual rights and property. Though family relations afforded some degree of protection to citizens, yet strangers were frequently exposed to persecution and oppression. In many cases they were robbed, not only of their goods, but even of their wives and daughters. At the instigation of the faithful Muhammad, an old league called the Federation of Fudul, i.e., favors was revived with the object of repressing lawlessness and defending every weak individual - whether Meccan or stranger, free or slave - against any wrong or oppression to which he might be the victim within the territories of Mecca. When Muhammad reached thirty-five years, he settled by his judgment a grave dispute, which threatened to plunge the whole of Arabia into a fresh series of her oft-recurring wars.

In rebuilding the Sacred House of the Ka'ba in A.D. 605, the question arose as to who should have the honor of raising the black stone, the most holy relic of that House, into its proper place. Each tribe claimed that honor. The senior citizen advised the disputants to accept for their arbitrator the first man to enter from a certain gate. The proposal was agreed upon, and the first man who entered the gate was Muhammad "Al-Ameen." His advice satisfied all the contending parties. He ordered the stone to be placed on a piece of cloth and each tribe to share the honor of lifting it up by taking hold of a part of the cloth. The stone was thus deposited in its place, and the rebuilding of the House was completed without further interruption.

## Kindness and generosity shown to the people

It is related that, about this time, a certain Usman, Ibn Huwairith, supported by Byzantine gold, made an attempt to convert the territory of Hijaz into a Roman dependency, but the attempt failed, chiefly through the instrumentality of Muhammad. These are nearly all the public acts related by historians in which Muhammad took part in the first fifteen years of his marriage to Khadijah. As for his private life he is described to have been ever helpful to the needy and the helpless. His uncle Abu Talib had fallen into distress through his endeavors to maintain the old position of his family. Muhammad, being rather rich at this time by his alliance with Khadijah, tried to discharge part of the debt of gratitude and obligation which he owed to his uncle by undertaking the bringing up and education of his son 'Ali. A year later he adopted 'Akil, another of his uncle's sons. Khadijah bore Muhammad three sons and four daughters. All the males died in childhood, but in loving 'Ali he found much consolation.

About this time, Muhammad set a good example of kindness, which created a salutary effect upon his people. His wife Khadijah had made him a present of young slave named Zaid Ibn Haritha, who had been brought as a captive to Mecca and sold to Khadijah. When Haritha heard that Muhammad possessed Zaid, he came to Mecca and offered a large sum for his ransom. Whereupon Muhammad said: "Let Zaid come here, and if he chooses to go with you, take him without ransom; but if it be his choice to stay with me, why should I not keep him?' Zaid, being brought into Muhammad's presence, declared that he would stay with his master, who treated him as if he was his only son. Muhammad no sooner heard this than he took Zaid by the hand and led him to the black stone of Ka'ba, where he publicly adopted him as his son, to which the father acquiesced and returned home well satisfied.

Henceforward Zaid was called the son of Muhammad. Muhammad was now approaching his fortieth year, and his mind was ever-engaged in profound contemplation and reflection. Before him lay his country, bleeding and torn by fratricidal wars that sunk in barbarism, addicted to the observation of rites and superstitions, were, with all their desert virtues, lawless and cruel. His two visits to Syria had opened to him a scene of unutterable moral and social desolation, rival creeds and sects tearing each other to pieces, carrying their hatred to the valleys and deserts of Hijaz, and rending the townships of Arabia with their quarrels and bitterness.

## Allah's Divine Inspiration touches Muhammad

For years after his marriage, Muhammad had been accustomed to secluding himself in a cave in Mount Hira, a few miles from Mecca. To this cave he used to go for prayer and meditation, sometimes alone and sometime with his family. There, he often spent the whole nights in deep thought and profound communion with the Unseen yet All-Knowing Allah of the Universe. It was during one of those retirements and in the still hours of the night, when no human sympathy was near, that an angel came to him to tell him that he was the Messenger of Allah sent to reclaim a fallen people to the knowledge and service of their Lord. Renowned compilers of authentic traditions of Islam agree on the following account of the first revelations received by the Prophet. Muhammad would seclude himself in the cave of Mount Hira and worship three days and nights. He would, whenever he wished, return to his family at Mecca and then go back again, taking with him the necessities of life. Thus he continued to return to Khadijah from time to time until one day the revelation came down to him and the Angel Gabriel (Jibreel) appeared to him and said: "Read!" But as Muhammad was illiterate, having never received any instruction in reading or writing, he said to the angel: "I am not a reader!" The angel took a hold of him and squeezed him as much as he could bear, and then said again: "Read!" Then Prophet said: "I am not a reader!" The Angel again seized the Prophet and squeezed him and said: "Read! In the Name of Your Lord, Who has created (all that exists), has created a man from a clot (a piece of thick coagulated blood). Read! And your Lord is the Most Generous, Who has taught (the writing) by the pen, has taught man that which he knew not." [96:1-4]

اقْرَأْ بِاسْمِ رَبِّكَ الَّذِي خَلَقَ ۞ خَلَقَ الْإِنسَانَ مِنْ عَلَقٍ ۞ اقْرَأْ وَرَبُّكَ الْأَكْرَمُ ۞ الَّذِي عَلَّمَ بِالْقَلَمِ ۞ عَلَّمَ الْإِنسَانَ مَا لَمْ يَعْلَمْ ۞

Then the Prophet repeated the words with a trembling heart. He returned to Khadijah from Mount Hira and said: "Wrap me up! Wrap me up!" She wrapped him in a garment until his fear was dispelled. He told Khadijah what had occurred and that he was becoming either a soothsayer or one smitten with madness. She replied: "Allah forbid! He will surely not let such a thing happen, for you speak the truth, you are faithful in trust, you bear the afflictions of the people, you spend in good works what you gain in trade, you are hospitable and you assist your fellow men. Have you seen anything terrible?" Muhammad replied: "Yes," and told her what he had seen. Whereupon, Khadijah said: "Rejoice, O dear husband and be cheerful. He is Whose hands stands Khadijah's life bears witness to the truth of this fact, that you will be the prophet to this people." After this experience Khadijah went to her cousin Waraqa Ibn Naufal, who was old and blind and who knew the Scriptures of the Jews and Christians, and is stated to have translated them into Arabic. When she told him of what she had heard, he cried out: "Holy! Holy! Verily, this is the Namus (The Holy Spirit) who came to Moses. He will be the prophet of his people. Tell him this and bid him to be brave at heart."

When the two men met subsequently in the street, the blind old student of the Jewish and Christian Scriptures spoke of his faith and trust: "I swear by Him in Who hand Waraqa's life is, Allah has chosen you to be the prophet of this people. They will call you a liar, they will persecute you, they will banish you, and they will fight against you. Oh, that I could live to those days. I would fight for these." And he kissed him on the forehead.

## Muhammad's Visions and struggle to fight depression

The first vision was followed by a considerable period, during which Muhammad suffered much mental depression. Only Almighty Allah knows what Muhammad must have been thinking and feeling at that time. He may have been worried about his visions, uncertain as to how the majority of the Makkans would treat Allah's blessing, since their own interests were at stake. The Makkans, at that time, relied heavily on trade that revolved around polytheistic and pagan rituals of false idols and statues and other things that they worshipped. One can't contemplate his future and responsibilities to the people of the world, as well as the challenges that Allah Almighty had chosen him for. The angel spoke to the grieved heart of hope and trust and of the bright future when he would see the people of the earth crowding into the one true faith. His destiny was unfolded to him, when, wrapped in profound meditation, melancholy and sad, he felt himself called by a voice from heaven to arise and preach. "O you (Muhammad) enveloped (in garments)! Arise and warn! And your Lord (Allah) magnify!" [74:1-3] He arose and engaged himself in the work to which he was called. Khadijah was the first to accept his mission. She was to believe in the revelations, to abandon the idolatry of her people and to join him in purity of heart and in offering up prayers to Allah the Almighty.

## The Companions

At the beginning of his mission, Muhammad - hereinafter called the Prophet - opened his soul only to those who were attached to him and tried to free them from the gross practices of their forefathers. After Khadijah, his cousin' Ali was the next companion. The Prophet used often to go into the desert around Mecca with his wife and young cousin that they might together offer thanks to the Lord of all nations for His blessings. Once they were surprised by Abu Talib, the father of 'Ali. He said to the Prophet: "O son of my brother, what is this religion you are following?" "It is the religion of Allah of His Angels, of His Messengers and of our ancestor Abraham," answered the Prophet. "Allah has sent me to His servants, to direct them towards the truth, and you, O my uncle, are the most worthy of all. It is meet that I should thus call upon you and it is meet that you should accept the truth and help in spreading it." Abu Talib replied: "Son of my brother, I cannot abjure the religion of my fathers; but by the Supreme Lord, while I am alive, none shall dare to injure you." Then turning towards Ali, the venerable chief asked what religion was his. Ali answered: "O father, I believe in Allah and His Prophet and go with him." Abu Talib replied: "Well my son, he will not call you to anything except what is good, therefore you are free to go with him." After 'Ali, Muhammad's adopted son Zaid became a convert to the new faith.

He was followed by Abu Bakr, a leading member of the Quraish tribe and an honest, wealthy merchant who enjoyed great consideration among his compatriots. He was but two years younger than the Prophet. His adoption of the new faith was of great moral effect. Soon after, five notables presented themselves before the Prophet and accepted Islam. Several converts also came from lower classes of the Arabs to adopt the new religion.

## Proliferation of Islamic Knowledge by our Prophet

For three weary long years, the Prophet labored very quietly to deliver his people from the worship of idols. Polytheism was deeply rooted among the people. It offered attractions, which the new faith in its purity did not possess. The Quraish had personal material interests in the old worship, and their prestige was dependent upon its maintenance. The Prophet had to contend with the idolatrous worship of its followers and to oppose the ruling oligarchy, which governed its destinies. After three years of constant but quiet struggle, only thirty followers were secured. An important change now occurred in the relations of the Prophet with the citizens of Mecca. His compatriots had begun to doubt his sanity, thinking him crazy or possessed by an evil spirit. Hitherto he preached quietly and unobtrusively. He now decided to appeal publicly to the Meccans, requesting them to abandon their idolatry.

For this he arranged a gathering on a neighboring hill and there spoke to them of their folly in the sight of Allah in worshipping pieces of stone which they called their gods. He invited them to abandon their old impious worship and adopt the faith of love, truth and purity. He warned them of the fate that had overtaken past races who had not heeded the preaching of former prophets. But the gathering departed without listening to the warning given them by the Prophet. Having thus failed to induce his fellow citizens to listen to him, he turned his attention to the strangers arriving in the city on commerce or pilgrimage. But the Quraish made attempts to frustrate his efforts. They hastened themselves to meet the strangers first on different routes, to warn them against holding any communication with the Prophet, whom they represented as a dangerous magician. When the pilgrims or traders returned to their homes, they carried with them the news of the advent of the bold preacher who was inviting the Arabs loudly - at the risk of his own life - to abandon the worship of their dear idols.

## Persecution perpetrated by the Makkan Tribe of Quraish

Now the Prophet and his followers became subject to some persecution and indignity. The hostile Quraish prevented the Prophet from offering his prayers at the Sacred House of the Ka'ba; they pursued him wherever he went; they covered him and his disciples with dirt and filth when engaged in their devotions; they scattered thorns in the places which he frequented for devotion and meditation. Amidst all these trials the Prophet did not waver.

He was full of confidence in his mission, even when on several occasions he was put in imminent danger of losing his life. At this time Hamza, the youngest son of Abdul Muttalib, adopted Islam. Hamza was a man of distinguished bravery, an intrepid warrior, generous and true, whose heroism earned for him the title of the "Lion of Allah." He became a devoted adherent of Islam and ever lost his life in the cause. The Prophet continued preaching to the Arabs in a most gentle and reasonable manner. He called the people, so accustomed to iniquity and wrong doings, to abandon their abominations. In burning words which excited the hearts of his hearers, he warned them of the punishment which Allah had inflicted upon the ancient tribes of 'Ad and Thamud who had obstinately disobeyed the teachings of Allah's messengers to them. He adjured them by the wonderful sights of nature, by the noon day brightness, by the night when it spreads its veil, by the day when it appears in glory to listen to his warning before a similar destruction befell them. He spoke to them of the Day of Reckoning, when their deeds in this world will be weighed before the Eternal Judge, when the children who had been buried alive will be asked for what crime they were put to death.


As the number of believers increased and the cause of the Prophet was strengthened by the conversions of many powerful citizens, the Prophet's preaching alarmed the Quraish. Their power and prestige were at stake. They were the custodians of the idols, which the Prophet had threatened to destroy; they were the ministers of the worship, which he denounced; in fact their existence and living wholly depended upon the maintenance of the old institutions. The Prophet taught that in the sight of his Lord all human were equal, the only distinction recognized among them being the weight of their piety. Allah said: "O mankind! We have created you from a male and a female, and made you into nations and tribes, that you may know one another. Verily, the most honorable of you in the Sight of Allah is that believer who has At Taqwa (one of the Muttaqun, pious and righteous persons who fear Allah much, abstain from all kinds of sins and evil deeds which He has forbidden), and love Allah much (perform all kinds of good deeds which He has ordained. Verily! Allah is All-Knowing, All-Aware." [49:13]


The Quraish would have none of this leveling of distinctions, as it reflected upon their long inherited privileges. Accordingly, they organized a system of persecution in order to suppress the movement before it became firmly established. They decided that each family should take upon itself the task of stamping out the new faith on the spot. Each household tortured its own members or adherents or slaves who were supposed to have connected themselves with the new religion. With the exception of the Prophet, who was protected by Abu Talib and his kinsmen, and Abu Bakr, and a few others who were either distinguished by their rank or possessed some influence among the Quraish, all other converts were subjected to different sorts of torture. Some of them were thrown into prison, starved, and then flogged. The hill of Ramada and the place called Bata thus became scenes of cruel torture.

## Quraish fear spread of Islam - Try in vain to blackmail Prophet

One day the Quraish tried to induce the Prophet to discontinue his teachings of the new religion, which had sown discord among their people. 'Utba Ibn Rabi'a, was delegated to see the Prophet and speak to him. 'Utba said: "O son of my brother, you are distinguished by your qualities; yet you have sown discord among our people and cast dissension in our families; you denounced our gods and goddesses and you charge our ancestors with impiety. Now we are come to make a proposition to you, and I ask you to think well before you reject it." "I am listening to you, O father of Walid," said the Prophet.

"O son of my brother, if by this affair you intend to acquire riches, honors, and dignity, we are willing to collect for you a fortune larger than is possessed by any one of us; we shall make you our chief and will do nothing without you. If you desire dominion, we shall make you our king; and if the demon which possesses you cannot be subdued, we will bring you doctors and give them riches until they cure you." When 'Utba had finished his discourse, the Prophet said: "Now listen to me, O father of Walid." "I listen." He replied. The Prophet, recited to him the first thirteen verses of Surah Fussilat, which may be interpreted as follows: "Ha Mim (These letters are one of the miracles of the Quran, and none but Allah Alone knows their meanings). A revelation from Allah the Most Beneficent, the Most Merciful. A Book whereof the Verses are explained in detail; - a Quran in Arabic for people who know. Giving glad tidings (of Paradise to the one who believes in the Oneness of Allah, Islamic Monotheism) and fears Allah much (abstains from all kinds of sins and evil deeds) and loves Allah much (performing all kinds of good deeds which He has ordained), and warning (of punishment in the Hellfire to be the one who disbelieves in the Oneness of Allah), but most of them turn away, so they listen not.

And they say: "Our hearts are under coverings (screened) from that to which you invite us, and in our ears is deafness, and between us and you is a screen, so work you (on your way); verily we are working (on our way). Say (O Muhammad): "I am only a human being like you. It is inspired in me that your Ilah (God) is One Ilah (God - Allah), therefore take the Straight Path to Him (with true Faith - Islamic Monotheism) and obedience to Him, and seek forgiveness of Him. And woe to Al-Mushrikeen; (polytheists, pagans, idolaters, and disbelievers in the Oneness of Allah, etc., those who worship others along with or set up rivals or partners to Allah etc.) Those who give not the Zakat and they are disbelievers in the Hereafter. Truly, those who believe (in the Oneness of Allah and in His Messenger Muhammad - Islamic Monotheism) and do righteous good deeds for them will be an endless reward that will never stop (Paradise). Say (O Muhammad): "Do you verily disbelieve in Him Who created the earth in two Days and you set up rivals (in worship) with Him? That is the Lord of the Alamin (mankind, jinn and all that exists).

He placed therein (the earth) firm mountains from above it, and He blessed it, and measured therein its sustenance (for its dwellers) in four Days equal (all these four days were equal in the length of time), for all those who ask (about its creation). Then He Istawa (rose over) towards the heaven when it was smoke, and said to it and to the earth: "Come both of you willingly or unwillingly." They both said: "We come, willingly." Then He completed and finished from their creation as seven heavens in two days and he made in each heaven with lamps (stars) to be an adornment as well as to guard (from the devils by using them as missiles against the devils).

Such is the Decree of Him the All Mighty, The All Knower. But if they turn away, then say (O Muhammad): "I have warned you of a Sa'iqa (a destruction awful cry, torment, hit, a thunder bolt) like the Sa'iqa which overtook 'Ad and Thamud (people)." [41:1-13] When the Prophet had finished his recitation, he said to 'Utba: "This is my reply to your proposition; now take what course you find best."

## Quraish increase Persecution - First Hijra of 615 C.E. to Abyssinia

Persecution by the Quraish grew fiercer every day and the sufferings of the Prophet's disciples became unbearable. He had heard of the righteousness, tolerance, and hospitality of the neighboring Christian king of Abyssinia. He recommended such of his companions who were without protection to seek refuge in the kingdom of that pious king, Al Najashi (Negus). Some fifteen of the unprotected adherents of Islam promptly availed themselves of the advice and sailed to Abyssinia. Here they met with a very kind reception from the Negus. This is called the first hijrah (migration) in the history of Islam and occurred in the fifth year of the Prophet Muhammad's mission, A.D. 615. These emigrants were soon followed by many of their fellow sufferers, until the number reached eighty-three men and eighteen women. The hostile Quraish, furious at the escape of their victims, sent deputes to the king of Abyssinia to request him to deliver up the refugees, that they might be put to death for adjuring their old religion and embracing a new one. The king summoned the poor fugitives and inquired of them what was the religion, which they had adopted in preference to their old faith. Ja'far, son of Abu Talib and brother of 'Ali, acted as spokesman for the exiles. He spoke thus: "O king, we were plunged in the depth of ignorance and barbarism, we adored idols, we lived in un-chastity, and we ate dead bodies, and we spoke abomination, we disregarded every feeling of humanity and sense of duty towards our neighbors, and we knew no law but that of the strong, when Allah raised among us a man, of whose birth, truthfulness, honesty, and purity we were aware. He called us to profess the Unity of Allah and taught us to associate nothing with Him; he forbade us the worship of idols and enjoined us to speak the truth, to be faithful to our trusts, to be merciful, and to regard the rights of neighbors; he forbade us to speak evil of the worship of Allah and not to return to the worship of idols of stone and to abstain from evil, to offer prayers, to give alms, to observe the fast.

We have believed in him, we have accepted his teachings and his injunctions to worship Allah alone and to associate nothing with Him. Hence our people have persecuted us, trying to make us forego the worship of Allah and return to the worship of idols of wood and stone and other abominations. They have tortured us and injured us until, finding no safety among them, we have come to your kingdom trusting you will give us protection against their persecution."

### Al-Najashi (Negus), King of Abyssinia protects Muslims

After hearing the above speech, the hospitable king ordered the deputies to return to their people in safety and not to interfere with their fugitives. Thus the emigrants passed the period of exile in peace and comfort. While the followers of the Prophet sought safety in foreign lands against the persecution of their people, he continued his warnings to the Quraish more strenuously than ever. Again they came to him with offers of riches and honor, which he firmly and utterly refused. But they mocked at him and urged him for miracles to prove his mission. He used to answer: "Allah has not sent me to work wonders; He has sent me to preach to you." Thus disclaiming all power of wonder working, the Prophet ever rested the truth of his divine mission upon his wise teachings. He addressed himself to the inner consciousness of man, to his common sense and to his own better judgment: "Say (O Muhammad): "I am only a human being like you. It is inspired in me that your Ilah (God) is One Ilah (God- Allah), therefore take the Straight Path to Him (with true Faith - Islamic Monotheism) and obedience to Him and seek forgiveness of Him. And woe to Al Mushrikeen; (polytheists, pagans, idolaters, and disbelievers in the Oneness of Allah etc., those who worship others along with Allah or set up rivals or partners to Allah etc. [41:6] Despite all the exhortation of the Prophet, the Quraish persisted in asking him for a sign. They insisted that unless some sign be sent down to him from his Lord, they would not believe. The disbelievers used to ask: "Why has Muhammad not been sent with miracles like previous prophets?" The Prophet replied: "Because miracles had proved inadequate to convince. Noah was sent with signs, and with what effect? Where was the lost tribe of Thamud? They had refused to receive the preaching of the Prophet Salih, unless he showed them a sign and caused the rock to bring forth a living camel. He did what they asked. In scorn they cut the camel's feet and then daring the prophet to fulfill his threats of judgment, were found dead in their beds the next morning, stricken by the angel of the Lord."

### The Holy Quran is a Miracle

There are some seventeen places in the Quran, in which the Prophet Muhammad is challenged to work a sign, and he answered them all to the same or similar effect: Allah has the power of working miracles, and has not been believed; there were greater miracles in nature than any which could be wrought outside of it; and the Quran itself was a great, everlasting miracle.

The Quran, the Prophet used to assert to the disbelievers, is a book of blessings which is a warning for the whole world; it is a complete guidance and explains everything necessary; it is a reminder of what is imprinted on human nature and is free from every discrepancy and from error and falsehood. It is a book of true guidance and a light to all. As to the sacred idols, so much honored and esteemed by the pagan Arabs, the Prophet openly recited: "They are but names which you have named - you and your fathers - for which Allah has sent down no authority." (CH 53:23 Quran). When the Prophet thus spoke reproachfully of the sacred gods of the Quraish, the latter redoubled their persecution. But the Prophet, nevertheless, continued his preaching undaunted but the hostility of his enemies or by their bitter persecution of him. And despite all opposition and increased persecution, the new faith gained ground. The national fair at Okadh near Mecca attracted many desert Bedouins and trading citizen of distant towns. These listened to the teachings of the Prophet, to his admonitions, and to his denunciations of their sacred idols and of their superstitions. They carried back all that they had heard to their distant homes, and thus the advent of the Prophet was made know to almost all parts of the peninsula.

## Makkans plea to Abu Talib to stop the Prophet

The Meccans, however, were more than ever furious at the Prophet's increasing preaching against their religion. They asked his uncle Abu Talib to stop him, but he could not do anything. As the Prophet persisted in his ardent denunciations against their ungodliness and impiety, they turned him out from the Ka'ba where he used to sit and preach, and subsequently went to Abu Talib. They urged the venerable chief to prevent his nephew from abusing their gods any longer or uttering any ill words against their ancestors. They warned Abu Talib that if he would not do that, he would be excluded from the communion of his people and driven to side with Muhammad; the matter would then be settled by fight until one of the two parties were exterminated. Abu Talib neither wished to separate himself from his people, nor forsake his nephew for the idolaters to revenge themselves upon. He spoke to the Prophet very softly and begged him to abandon his affair. To this suggestion the Prophet firmly replied: "O my uncle, if they placed the sun in my right hand and the moon in my left hand to cause me to renounce my task, verily I would not desist therefrom until Allah made manifest His cause or I perished in the attempt." The Prophet, overcome by the thought that his uncle and protector was willing to desert him, turned to depart. But Abu Talib called him loudly to come back, and he came. "Say whatever you please; for by the Lord I shall not desert you ever."

## Abu Talib protects his Nephew, the Prophet

The Quraish again attempted in vain to cause Abu Talib to abandon his nephew. The venerable chief declared his intention to protect his nephew against any menace or violence. He appealed to the sense of honor of the two families of the Bani Hashim and the Bani Muttalib, both families being kinsmen of the Prophet, to protect their member from falling a victim to the hatred of rival parties. All the members of the two families nobly responded to the appeal of Abu Talib except Abu Lahab, one of the Prophet's uncles, who took part with the persecutors.

## Omar Al-Khattab submits to Islam

During this period, Omar Al-Khattab adopted Islam. In him the new faith gained a valuable adherent and an important factor in the future development and propagation of Islam. Hitherto he had been a violent opposer of the Prophet and a bitter enemy of Islam. His conversion is said to have been worked by the miraculous effect on his mind of a Surah of the Quran which his sister was reading in her house, where he had gone with the intention of killing her for adopting Islam. Thus the party of the Prophet had been strengthened by the conversation by his uncle Hamza, a man of great valor and merit; and of Abu Bakr and Omar, both men of great energy and reputation. The Muslims now ventured to perform their devotions in public. Alarmed at the bold part which the Prophet and his followers were not able to assume, and roused by the return of the deputies from Abyssinia and the announcement of their unsuccessful mission, the Quraish determined to check by a decisive blow any further progress of Islam. Towards this end, in the seventh year of the mission, they made a solemn covenant against the descendants of Hashim and Muttalib, engaging themselves to contract no marriage with any of them and to have no communication with them. Quraish became divided into two factions, and the two families of Hashim and Muttalib all repaired to Abu Talib as their chief.

## Abu Lahab's hatred of Islam

Abu Lahab, the Prophet's uncle, however, out of his inveterate hatred of his nephew and his doctrine, went over to the opposite party, whose chief was Abu Sufyan Ibn Harb, of the family of Umayya. The persecuted party, Muslims as well as idolaters betook themselves to a defile on the eastern skirts of Mecca. They lived in this defensive position for three years. The provisions, which they had carried with them, were soon exhausted.

Probably they would have entirely perished but for the sympathy and occasional help received from less bigoted compatriots.

## Reconciliation of the Quraish

Towards the beginning of the tenth year of the mission, reconciliation was concluded between the Quraish and the two families of Hashim and Abdul Muttalib through the intermediation of Hisham, Ibn Omar, and Zobeir, Ibn Abu Umayya. Thus, the alliance against the two families was abolished, and they were able to return to Mecca. During the period the Prophet and his kinspeople passed in their defensive position, Islam made no progress outside; but in the sacred months, when violence was considered sacrilege, the Prophet used to come out of his temporary prison to preach Islam to the pilgrims.

## Death of Abu Talib and Khadijah

In the following year, both Abu Talib and Khadijah died. Thus the Prophet lost in Abu Talib the kind guardian of his youth who had hitherto protected him against his enemies, and in Khadijah his most encouraging companion. She was ever his angel of hope and consolation. The Prophet, weighed down by the loss of his amiable protector and his beloved wife, without hope of turning the Quraish from idolatry, with a saddened heart, yet full of trust, resolved to exercise his ministry in some of her field. He chose Taif, a town about sixty miles east of Mecca, where he went accompanied by a faithful servant Zaid. The tribe of Thakif, who were the inhabitants of Taif, received Muhammad very coldly. However, he stayed there for one month. Though the more considerate and better sort of men treated him with a little respect, the slaves and common people refused to listen to his teachings; they were outrageously indignant at his invitation to abandon the stones they worshipped. At length they rose against him, and bringing him to the wall of the city, obliged him to depart and return to Mecca. The repulse greatly discouraged his followers; however, the Prophet boldly continued to preach to the public assemblies at the pilgrimage and gained several new converts, among whom were six of the city of Yahtrib (later called Medina), of the Jewish tribe of Khazraj. When these Yathribites returned home, they spread the news among their people that a prophet had arisen among the Arabs who was to call them to Allah and put an end to their inquiries.

## Miraj (Ascension to the Heavens) on a creature called Buraq

In the 12$^{th}$ year of his mission, the Prophet made his night journey from Mecca to Jerusalem, and thence to heaven. His journey, known in history as Miraj (Ascension) was a real bodily one and not only a vision. It was at this time that Allah ordered the Muslims to pray the five daily prayers. Almighty Allah had said: "Glorified (and Exalted) be He (Allah) (above all that evil they associate with Him), Who took His slave Muhammad for a journey by night from AL-Masjid al Haram (at Makka) to the farthest mosque (in Jerusalem), the neighborhood whereof We have blessed, order that We might show him (Muhammad) of Our Ayat (proofs, evidences, lessons, signs, etc.). Verily, He is the All Hearer, the All Seer." (Ch 17:1 Quran). Abbas Ibn Malik reported that Malik Ibn Sasaa said that Allah's Messenger described to them his Night Journey saying:

"While I was lying in Al-Hatim or Al-Hijr, suddenly someone came to me and cut my body open from here to here." I asked Al-Jarud, who was by my side, "What does he mean?" He said: "It means from his throat to his public area," or said, "From the top of the chest." The Prophet further said, "He then took out my heart. Then a gold tray of Belief was brought to me and my heart was washed and was filled (with Belief) and then returned to its original place. Then a white animal which was smaller than a mule and bigger than a donkey was brought to me." (On this Al-Jarud asked: "Was it in the Buraq, O Abu Hamza?" I (Anas) replied in the affirmative. The Prophet said: "The animal's step (was so wide that it) reached the farthest point within the breach of the animals' sight. I was carried on it.

### Miraj - Muhammad's encounter with Prophet Adam (pbut)

Gabriel set out with me till we reached the nearest heaven. "When he asked for the gate to be opened, it was asked, 'Who is it?' Gabriel answered, 'Gabriel.' It was asked, 'Who is accompany you?' Gabriel replied, 'Muhammad.' It was asked, 'Has Muhammad been called?' Gabriel replied in the affirmative. Then it was said. He is welcomed. What an excellent visit his is!' The gate was opened, and when I went over the first heaven, I saw Adam there. Gabriel said to me: 'This is your father, Adam; pay him your greetings.' So I greeted him and he returned the greetings to me and said: 'You are welcomed, O pious son and pious Prophet.'

### Miraj - Muhammad's encounter with Prophets John and Jesus (pbut)

Then Gabriel ascended with me till we reached the second heaven. Gabriel asked for the gate to be opened. It was asked: 'Who is it?' Gabriel answered: 'Gabriel.' It was asked: 'Who is accompany you?' Gabriel replied, 'Muhammad.' It was asked: 'Has he been called?' Gabriel answered in the affirmative. Then it was said: 'He is welcomed. What an excellent visit his is!' The gate was opened. "When I went over the second heaven, here I saw John (Yahya) and Jesus (Isa), who were cousins of each other. Gabriel said to me: "these are John and Jesus; pay them your greetings.' So I greeted them and both of them returned my greetings to me and said, 'You are welcomed, O pious brother and pious Prophet.'

### Miraj - Muhammad's encounter with Prophet Joseph (pbut)

Then Gabriel ascended with me to the third heaven and asked for its gate to be opened. It was asked 'Who is it?' And Gabriel replied: 'Gabriel.' It was asked, 'Who is accompany you?' Gabriel replied, 'Muhammad.' It was asked, 'Has he been called?' Gabriel replied in the affirmative. Then it was said: 'He is welcomed, what an excellent visit his is!' The gate was opened, and when I went over the third heaven there I saw Joseph (Yusuf), Gabriel said to me: 'This is Joseph, pay him your greetings.' So I greeted him and he returned the greetings to me and said: 'You are welcomed, O pious brother and pious Prophet.'

## Miraj - Muhammad's encounter with Prophet Enoch (pbut)

Then Gabriel ascended with me to the fourth heaven and asked for its gate to be opened. It was asked 'Who is it?' Gabriel replied, 'Gabriel' It was asked: 'Who is accompany you?' Gabriel replied: 'Muhammad.' It was asked: 'Has he been called?' Gabriel replied in the affirmative. Then it was said: 'He is welcomed, what an excellent visit his is!' "The gate was opened, and when I went over the fourth heaven, there I saw Enoch (Idris), Gabriel said to me: 'This is Enoch; pay him your greetings.' So I greeted him and he returned the greetings to me and said: 'You are welcomed O pious brother and pious Prophet.'

## Miraj - Muhammad's encounter with Prophet Aaron (pbut)

Then Gabriel ascended with me to the fifth heaven and asked for its gate to be opened. It was asked: 'Who is it?' Gabriel replied: 'Gabriel.' It was asked: 'Who is accompany you?' Gabriel replied 'Muhammad.' It was asked: 'Has he been called?' Gabriel replied in the affirmative. Then it was said: 'He is welcomed, what an excellent visit his is!' So when I went over the fifth heaven, there I saw Aaron (Harun), Gabriel said to me: "this is Aaron; pay your greetings.' So I greeted him and he returned the greetings to me and said: "You are welcomed, O pious brother and pious Prophet."

## Miraj - Muhammad's encounter with Prophet Moses (pbut)

Then Gabriel ascended with me to the sixth heaven and asked for its gate to be opened. It was asked: 'Who is it?' Gabriel replied: 'Gabriel.' It was asked: 'Who is accompanying you?' Gabriel replied: 'Muhammad.' It was said: 'Has he been called?' Gabriel replied in the affirmative. It was said: 'He is welcomed. What an excellent visit his is!' "When I went over the sixth heaven, there I saw Moses (Musa). Gabriel said to me: "This is Moses; pay him your greeting. So I greeted him and he returned the greetings to me and said: "You are welcomed, O pious brother and pious Prophet." When I left him (Moses) he wept. Someone asked him: 'What makes you weep?' Moses said: 'I weep because after me there has been sent (as Prophet) a young man whose followers will enter Paradise in greater numbers than my followers.'

## Miraj - Muhammad's encounter with Prophet Abraham (pbut)

Then Gabriel ascended with me to the seventh heaven and asked for its gate to be opened. It was asked: 'Who is it?' Gabriel replied: 'Gabriel.' It was asked: 'Who is accompanying you?' Gabriel replied: 'Muhammad.' It was asked: 'Has he been called?' Gabriel replied in the affirmative. Then it said: 'He is welcomed. What an excellent visit his is!' "So when I went (over the seventh heaven), there I saw Abraham (Ibrahim). Gabriel said to me: 'This is your father; pay your greetings to him.' So I greeted him and he returned the greetings to me and said: 'You are welcomed, O pious son and pious Prophet.'

## Miraj - Sidrat-ul-Muntaha

Then I was made to ascend to Sidrat-ul-Muntaha (the Lote Tree of the utmost boundary). Behold! Its fruits were like the jars of Hajr (a place near Medina) and its leaves were as big as the ears of elephants. Gabriel said: "this is the Lote Tree of the utmost and boundary.' Behold! There ran four rivers, two were hidden and two were visible, I asked: 'What are these two kinds of rivers, O Gabriel?' He replied: 'As for the hidden rivers, they are two rivers in Paradise and the visible rivers are the Nile and the Euphrates.'

## Moses advises Muhammad to plea to Allah to lessen prayers

"Then Al-Bait-ul-Ma'mur (the Sacred House) was shown to me and a container full of wine and another full of milk and a third full of honey were brought to me. I took the milk. Gabriel remarked: 'This is the Islamic religion which you and your followers are following.' Then the prayers were enjoined on me: they were fifty prayers a day. When I returned, I passed by Moses, who asked me; 'What have you been ordered to do?' I replied: 'I have been ordered to offer fifty prayers a day.' Moses said: 'Your followers cannot bear fifty prayers a day, and by Allah I have tested people before you, and I have tried my level best with Bani Israel in vain. Go back to your Lord and ask for reduction to lessen your followers" burden.' So I went back, and Allah reduced ten prayers for me. Then again I came to Moses, but he repeated the same as he had said before. Then again I went back to Allah, and He reduced ten more prayers. When I came to Moses he said the same. I went back to Allah, and He ordered m to observe ten prayers a day. When I came back to Moses, he repeated the same advice, so I went back to Allah and was ordered to observe five prayers a day. "When I came back to Moses, he said: 'What have you been ordered?' I replied: 'I have been ordered to observe five prayers a day.' He said: 'Your followers cannot bear fear prayers a day, and no doubt, I have got an experience of the people before you, and I have tried my level best with Bani Israel, so go back to your Lord and ask for reduction to lesson your followers' burden.' I said: 'I have requested so much of my Lord that I feel ashamed, but I am satisfied now and surrender to Allah's Order.' When I left, I heard a voice saying: 'I have passed My order and have lessened the burden of My worshippers.'"

## Women's Oath - People of Yathrib (Madina) submit to Islam

In this year, twelve men of Yathrib, of whom ten were of the Jewish tribe of Khazraj and the other two of Aws, came to Meccan and took an oath of fidelity to the Prophet at Al-

Aqaba, a hill on the north of that city. This oath was called the Women's' Oath, not that any women were present at this time, but because a man was not thereby obliged to take up arms in defense of the Prophet or his religion, it being the same oath that was afterwards exacted of the women. This oath was as follows: "We will not associate anything with Allah; we will not steal nor commit adultery or fornication, nor kill our children (as the pagan Arabs used to do when they apprehended that they would not be able to maintain them), nor forge calumnies; we will obey the Prophet in everything that is reasonable, and we will be faithful to him in well and sorrow."

When they had solemnly engaged to do all this, the Prophet sent one of his disciples, Mus'ab Ibn Umair, home with them to teach them the fundamental doctrines and ceremonies of the religion. Mus'ab, having arrived at Yathrib by the assistance of those who had been formerly converted, gained several new converts, particularly Usaid Ibn Khudair, a chief of man of the city, and Sa'd Ibn Mu'adh, prince of the tribe of Aws. Islam spread so fast that there was a scarce a house that did not have some Muslims in it. The next year, being the thirteenth of the mission (A.D. 622) Mus'ab returned from Yathrib accompanied by seventy-three men and two women of that city who had adopted Islam, besides others who were as yet unbelievers. On their arrival, these Yathribites immediately sent to the Prophet and invited him to their city. The Prophet was not in great need of such assistance, for his opponents had by this time grown so powerful in Mecca that he could not stay there much longer without imminent danger. He therefore accepted their proposal and met them one night by appointment at Al Aqaba attended by his uncle Al-Abbas, who, though he as not then a convert, wished his nephew well.

Al Abbas made a speech to those of Yathrib wherein he told them that, as the Prophet Muhammad was obliged to quit his native city and seek shelter elsewhere, and they had offered him their protection, they would do well not to deceive him; and that if they were not firmly resolved to defend and not to betray him, they had better declare their minds and let him provide for his safety in some other manner. Upon their professing their sincerity, the Prophet swore to be faithful to them, on condition that they should worship none but Allah observe the precepts of Islam, obey the Prophet in all that was right, and protect him against all insults as heartily as they would their wives and families. They then asked him what would be their return, if they should happen to be killed in the cause of Allah; he answered: "Paradise," whereupon they pledged their faith to him and his cause.

## The Hijra and Makkans plot to kill Allah's Prophet

The Prophet then selected twelve men out of their number to act as his delegates. Thus was concluded the second covenant of Al Aqaba. The Yathribites returned home leaving the Prophet to arrange for the journey to their city. The Prophet directed his followers to seek immediate safety at Yathrib, which they accordingly did. About one hundred families silently disappeared from Mecca and proceeded to Yathrib, where they were received with enthusiasm and much hospitality. Finally, all the disciples had gone to Yathrib. The Prophet alone remained at Mecca, keeping with him only his young cousin, 'Ali, and his devoted friend Abu Bakr. The Meccans, fearing the consequence of this new alliance, began to think seriously of preventing Muhammad from escaping to Yathrib. They met in all haste. After several milder expedients had been rejected, they decided that he should be killed. They agreed that one man should be chosen out of every tribe and that each man should strike a blow at him with his sword so that responsibility of the guilt would rest equally on all tribes. The Bani Hashim, Muhammad's own tribe, were much inferior and therefore would not be able to revenge their kinsman's death. A number of noble youths were selected for the bloody deed.

As the night advanced, the assassins posted themselves round the Prophet's dwelling. They watched all night long, waiting to murder Muhammad when he should leave his house at the early dawn. By some the Prophet had warned of the danger, and he directed 'Ali to lie down in his place and wrap himself up in his green clock, which he did. The Prophet miraculously escaped through the window and he repaired to the house of Abu Bakr, unperceived by door. These, in the meantime, looking through a crevice and seeing 'Ali, whom they mistook for Muhammad himself, asleep, continued watching there until morning. When 'Ali arose, they found themselves deceived. The fury of the Quraish was now unbounded. The news that there would be assassins had returned unsuccessful and that Muhammad had escaped aroused their whole energy. A price of a hundred camels was set upon Muhammad's head.

### Narration Aisha Bint Abu Bakr (Prophet's Wife)

Narrated Aisha Bint Abu Bakr (the wife of the Prophet): "I never remembered my parents believing in any religion other than the true religion (Islam), and (I don't remember) a single day passing without our being visited by Allah's Messenger in the morning and in the evening. When the Muslims were put to test (troubled by the pagans), Abu Bakr set out migrating to the land of Abyssinia (Ethiopia), and when he reached Bark al-Ghimad, Ibn Ad-Daghina, the chief of the tribe of Qara, met him and said, O Abu Bakr! Where are you going?' Abu Bakr replied: 'My people have turned me out of my country, so I want to wander on the earth and worship my Lord.' Ibn Ad-Dhagina said: O Abu Bakr! A man like you should not leave his homeland, nor should he be driven out, because you help the destitute, earn their living, and you keep good relations with your kith and kin, help the weak and the poor, entertain guests generously, and help the calamity-stricken persons. Therefore, I am your protector. Go back and worship your Lord in your town.' So Abu Bakr returned and Ibn Ad-Daghina accompanied him. In the evening Ibn Ad-Dhagina visited the nobles of Quraish and said to them. 'A man like Abu Bakr should not leave his homeland, nor should he be driven out. Do you (Quraish) drive out a man who helps the destitute, earns their living, keeps good relations with his kith and kin, helps the weak and poor, entertain guests generously and helps the calamity-stricken persons?' So the people of Quraish could not refuse Ibn Ad-Dhagina's protection, and they said to Ibn Ad-Daghina: 'Let Abu Bakr worship his Lord in his house. He can pray and recite there whatever he likes, but he should not hurt us with it, and should not do it publicly, because we are afraid that he may affect our women and children." Ibn Ad-Dhagina told Abu Bakr all of that. Abu Bakr stayed in that state, worshipping his Lord in his house. He did not pray publicly, nor did he recite Quran outside his house.

## Abu Bakr builds Masjid

"Then a thought occurred to Abu Bakr to build a mosque in front of his house, and there he used to pray and recite the Quran. The women and children of the pagans began to gather around him in great number. They used to wonder at him and look at him. Abu Bakr was a man who used to weep too much, and he could not help weeping or reciting the Quran.

That situation scared the nobles of the pagans of Quraish, so they sent for Ibn Ad-Daghina. When he came to them, they said: 'We accepted your protection of Abu Bakr on condition that he should worship his Lord in his house, but he has violated the conditions and he has built a mosque in front of his house where he prays and recites the Quran publicly. We are not afraid that he may affect our women and children unfavorably. So, prevent him from that. If he likes to confine the worship of his Lord to his house, he may do so, but if he insists on doing that openly, ask him to release you from your obligation to protect him, for we dislike to break our pact with you but we deny Abu Bakr the right to announce his act publicly.' Ibn Ad-Dhagina went to Abu Bakr and said: 'O Abu Bakr! You know well what contract I have made on your behalf; now, you are either to abide by it, or else release me from my obligation of protecting you, because I do not want the Arabs hear that my people have dishonored a contract I have made on behalf of another man.'

Abu Bakr replied: 'I release you from your pact to protect me and am pleased with the protection from Allah.' At that time the Prophet was in Mecca, and he said to the Muslims: 'In a dream I have been shown your migration place, a land of date palm trees, between two mountains, the two stony tracts.' So, some people migrated to Medina, and most of those people who had previously migrated to the land of Ethiopia, returned to Medina. Abu Bakr also prepared to leave for Medina, but Allah's Messenger said to him: 'Wait for a while, because I hope that I will be allowed to migrate also.'

Abu Bakr replied: 'Do you indeed expect this? Let my father be sacrificed for you!' The Prophet said: 'Yes.' So Abu Bakr did not migrate for the sake of Allah's Messenger in order to accompany him. He fed two she camels he possessed with the leaves of As-Samur tree that fell on being struck by a stick for four months. "One day, while we were sitting in Abu Bakr's house at noon, someone said to Abu Bakr: 'This is Allah's Messenger with his head covered coming at a time at which he never used to visit us before.' Abu Bakr said: 'May my parents be sacrificed for him. By Allah he has not come at this hour except for a great necessity.' So Allah's Messenger came and asked permission to enter, and he was allowed to enter. When he entered, he said to Abu Bakr: "tell everyone who is present with you to go away.' Abu Bakr replied: 'There are none but your family, May my father be sacrificed for you, O Allah's Messenger!' The Prophet said: 'I have been given permission to migrate.' Abu Bakr said: 'Shall I accompany you? May my father be sacrificed for you, O Allah's Messenger!' The Prophet said: 'Yes.' Abu Bakr said, 'O Allah's Messenger! May my father be sacrificed for you, take one of these two she-camels of mine.' Allah's Messenger replied: 'I will accept it with payment.' So we prepared the baggage quickly and put some journey food in a leather bag for them. Asma, Abu Bakr's daughter, cut a piece from her waist belt and tied the mouth of the leather bag with it, and for that reason she was named 'Dhat-un-Nitaqain' (the owner of two belts). Then Allah's Messenger and Abu Bakr reached a cave on the mountain of Thaur and stayed there for three nights. Abdullah Ibn Abi Bakr who was an intelligent and sagacious youth, used to stay with them overnight. He used to leave them before daybreak so that in the morning he would be with Quraish as if he had spent the night in Mecca.

He would keep in mind any plot made against them and when it became dark he would go and inform them of it. 'Amir Ibn Fuhaira, the freed slave of Abu Bakr, used to bring the milch sheep (of his master, Abu Bakr) to them a little while after nightfall in order to rest the sheep there. So they always had fresh milk at night, the milk of their sheep, and the milk which they warmed by throwing heated stones in it. 'Amir Ibn Fuhaira would then call the herd away when it was still dark (before daybreak). He did the same in each of those three nights.

Allah's Messenger and Abu Bakr had hired a man from the tribe of Bani Ad-Dail from the family of Bani Abd Ibn Adi as an expert guide, and he was in alliance with the family of Al-As Ibn Wail As- Sahmi and he was in the religion of the infidels of Quraish. The Prophet and Abu Bakr trusted him and gave him their two she-camels and took his promise to bring their two she-camels to the cave of the mountain of Thaur in the morning after three nights later. And when they set out, Amir Ibn Futhaira and the guide went along with them and the guide led them, along the seashore." (Sahih Al-Bukhari). The nephew of Suraqa Ibn Ju'sham said that his father informed him that he heard Suraqa Ibn Jusham saying: "The messengers of the pagans of Quraish came to us declaring that they had assigned for the persons who would kill or arrest Allah's Messenger and Abu Bakr, a reward equal to their blood money. While I was sitting in one of the gatherings of my tribe, Bani Mudlij, a man from them came to us and stood up while we were sitting and said:

'O Suraqa! No, I have just seen some people far away on the seashore, and I think they are Muhammad and his companions.' I, too, realized that it must have been they. But I said: 'No, it is not they, but you have seen so-and-so and so-and-so, whom we saw set out.' I stayed in the gathering for a while and then got up and left for my home, and ordered my slave-girl to get my horse, which was behind a hillock, and keep it ready for me. "Then I took my spear and left by the back door of my house dragging the lower end of the spear on the ground and keeping it low. Then I reached my horse, mounted it and made it gallop. When I approached them (Muhammad and Abu Bakr), my horse stumbled and I fell down from it. Then I stood up, gold hold of my quiver and took out the divining arrows and drew lots as to whether I should harm them or not, and the lot which I disliked came out. But I remounted my horse and let it gallop, giving no importance to the divining arrows. When I heard the recitation of the Quran Allah's Messenger who did not look hither and thither while Abu Bakr was doing it often, suddenly the forelegs of my horse sank into the ground up to the knees, and I fell down from it.

Then I rebuked it, and it got up but could hardly take out its forelegs from the ground, and when it stood up straight again, its forelegs caused dust to rise up in the sky like smoke. Then again I drew lots with the divining arrows, and the lot which I disliked came out. So I called upon them to feel secure. They stopped, and I remounted my horse and went to them. When I saw how I had been hampered from harming them, it came to my mind that the cause of Allah's Messenger (Islam) would become victorious.

So I said to them: 'Your people have assigned a reward equal to blood money for your head.' Then I told them all the plans the people of Mecca had made concerning them. Then I offered them some journey food and goods, but they refused to take anything and did not ask for anything, but the Prophet said: 'Do not tell others about us.' Then I requested him to write for me a statement of security and peace. He ordered 'Amir Ibn Fuhaira, who wrote it for me on a parchment, and then Allah's Messenger proceeded on his way." (Sahih Al-Bukhari). "Narrated 'Urwa Ibn Az-Zubair: "Allah's Messenger met Az Zubair in a caravan of Muslim merchants who were returning from Sham. Az-Zubair provided Allah's Messenger and Abu Bakr with white clothes to wear. When the Muslims of Medina heard the news of the departure of Allah's Messenger from Mecca (towards Medina), they started going to the Harra every morning. They would wait for him till the heat of the noon forced them to return. One day, after waiting for a long while, they returned home, and when they went into their houses, a Jew climbed up to the roof of one of the forts of his people to look for something, and he saw Allah's Messenger and his companions, dressed in white clothes, emerging out of the desert mirage.

"The Jew could not help shouting at the top of his voice: 'O you Arabs! Here is your great man whom you have been waiting for!' So all the Muslims rushed to their arms and received Allah's Messenger on the summit of Harra. The Prophet turned with them to the right and alighted at the quarters of Bani Amr Ibn Auf, and this was on Monday in the month of Rabi ul Awal. Abu Bakr stood up, receiving the people, while Allah's Messenger sat down and kept silent. Some of the Ansar who came and had not seen Allah's Messenger before began greeting Abu Bakr, but when the sunshine fell on Allah's Messenger and Abu Bakr came forward and shaded him with his sheet, only then the people came to know Allah's Messenger. Allah's Messenger stayed with Bani Amr Ibn Auf for ten nights and established the mosque (Mosque of Quba) which was founded on piety. Allah's Messenger prayed in it and then mounted his she-camel and proceeded on, accompanied by the people till his she-camel knelt down at the place of the Mosque of Allah's Messenger at Medina. Some Muslims used to pray there in those days, and that place was a yard for drying dates belonging to Suhail and Sahl, the orphan boys who were under the guardianship of Asad in Zurara. When his she-camel knelt down, Allah's Messenger said: 'This place, Allah willing, will be our abiding place.' Allah's Messenger then called the two boys and told them to suggest a price for that yard so that he might take it as a mosque. The two boys said: 'No, but we will give it as a gift, O Allah's Messenger!' Allah's Messenger then built a mosque there. The Prophet himself started carrying unburned bricks for its building and while doing so, he was saying: 'This load is better than the load of Khaibar, for it is more pious in the Sight of Allah and purer and better rewardable.' He was also saying: 'O Allah! The actual reward is the reward in the Hereafter, so bestow Your Mercy on the Ansar and the Emigrants.' Thus the Prophet recited (by way of proverb) the poem of some Muslim poet whose name is unknown to me." (Ibn Shibab said, 'In the hadiths, it does not occur that Allah's Messenger recited a complete poetic verse other than this one.') (Sahih Al-Bukhari).

## Hijra - Islamic Calendar marks this date and "The Illuminated City"

Thus was accomplished the hijrah, or the flight of Muhammad as called in European annals, from which the Islamic calendar dates. When the Prophet Muhammad and his companions settled at Yathrib, this city changed its name, and henceforth was called, Al-Medina, Al-Munawara, the Illuminated City, or more shortly, Medina, the City. It is situated about eleven-day's journey to the north of Mecca. At that time it was ruled by two Kahtanite tribes, Aws and Khazraj. These two tribes, however, were constantly quarreling among themselves. It was only about that time when the Prophet announced his mission at Mecca that these tribes, after long years of continuous warfare, entered on a period of comparative peace. When the Prophet settled at Medina, the tribes of Aws and Khazraj forgot entirely their old feuds and were united together in the bond of Islam. Their old divisions were soon effaced and the Ansar", the Helpers of the Prophet, became the common designation of all Medinites who had helped the Prophet in his cause. Those who emigrated with him from Mecca received the title of "Muhajereen" or the Emigrants. The Prophet, in order to unite both classes in closer bonds, established between them a brotherhood, which linked them together as children of the same parents, with the Prophet as their guardian.

## Allah's Apostle Settles in Madina

The first step the Prophet took, after his settlement at Medina, was to build a mosque for the worship of Allah according to principles of Islam. Also, houses for the accommodation of the emigrants were soon erected.

## Muhammad's Charter - Jews and Muslims unite to defend against enemies

Medina and its suburb were at this time inhabited by three distinct parties, the Emigrants, the Helpers, and the Jews. In order to weld them together into an orderly federation, the Prophet granted a charter to the people, clearly defining their rights and obligations. This charter represented the framework of the first commonwealth organized by the Prophet. It started thus: 'In the name of the Most Merciful and Compassionate Lord, this charter is given by Muhammad, the Messenger of Allah to all believers, whether of Quraish or Medina, and all individuals of whatever origin who have made common cause with them, who shall all constitute one nation." The following are some extracts from the charter: The state of peace and war shall be common to all Muslims; no one among them shall have the right of concluding peace with, or declaring war against, the enemies of his co-religionists. The Jews who attach themselves to our commonwealth shall be protected from all insults and vexations; they shall have an equal right with our people to our assistance and good offices. The Jews of the various branches and all others in Medina shall form with the Muslims one composite nation; they shall practice their religion as freely as the Muslims. The allies of the Jews shall enjoy the same security and freedom. The guilty shall be pursued and punished. The Jews shall join the Muslims in defending Medina all enemies. The interior of Medina shall be a sacred place for all who accept this charter.

All true Muslims shall hold in abhorrence every man guilty of crime, injustice or disorder; no one shall uphold the culpable, though he be his nearest kin. After dealing with the interior management of the State, the charter concluded as follows: "All future disputes arising among those who accept this charter shall be referred, under Allah to the Prophet." Thus this charter put an end to the state of anarchy that prevailed among the Arabs. It constituted the Prophet Muhammad as chief magistrate of the nation.

### The Charter faces Mutiny (Inside enemies)

The party of the Ansars, or Helpers, included some lukewarm converts who retained an ill-concealed predilection for idolatry. These were headed by Abdullah Ibn Ubai, a man with some claims to distinction. They ostensibly joined Islam, but in secret were disaffected. They often were a source of considerable danger to the newborn commonwealth and required unceasing watchfulness on the part of the Prophet. Towards them he always showed the greatest patience and forbearance, hoping in the end to win them over to the faith, which expectations were fully justified by the result. While the death of Abdullah Ibn Ubai, his party which were known as the party of the "Munafiqeen" (the Hypocrites) disappeared. The Jews who constituted the third party of the Medinites were, however, the most serious element of danger.

No kindness or generous treatment on the part of the Prophet would seem to satisfy them. They soon broke off and ranged themselves with the enemies of the new faith. They did not hesitate to declare openly that they preferred idolatry, with its attendant evils, to the faith of Islam. Thus, the Prophet had to keep an eye on his enemies outside Medina, on the one hand, and those within the city on the other. The Meccans who had sworn Muhammad's death were well acquainted, thanks to the party of the Hypocrites and of the Jews at Medina, with the real forces of the Muslims. They also knew that the Jews had accepted Muhammad's alliance only from motives of temporary expedience and that they would break away from him to join the idolaters a s soon as the latter showed themselves in the vicinity of Medina.

The safety of the state required the proscription of the traitors who were secretly giving information to the common enemy. About six men were executed for high treason of this nature. Towards the second year of the hijrah, the idolaters of Mecca began a series of hostile acts against the Muslims of Medina. They sent men in parties to commit depredations on the fruit trees of the Muslims of Medina and to carry away their flocks. Now came the moment of severest trial to Islam. It became the duty of the Prophet to take serious measures to guard against any plot rising from within or a sudden attack from without.

## Battle of Badr - Makkan Troop formations approaching Madina

Allah's Prophet put Medina in a state of military discipline. He had to send frequent parties to guard against any sudden onslaught. No sooner did the Prophet organize hi state than a large well-equipped army of the Meccans was afield. A force constituting of one thousand men marched under Abu Jahl, a great enemy of Islam, towards Medina to attack the city. The Muslims received timely notice of their enemies' intention. A body of three hundred adherents, of whom two thirds were citizens of Medina, was gathered to forestall the idolaters by occupying the valley of Badr, situated near the sea between Mecca and Medina. When the Prophet saw the army of the infidels approaching the valley, he prayed that the little band of Muslims might not be destroyed. The army of the Meccans advanced into the open space which separated the Muslims from the idolaters. According to Arab usage, the battle was began by simple combats. The engagement that became general. The result of the battle was that the Meccans were driven back with great loss. Several of their chiefs were slain, including Abu Jahl. A large number of idolaters remained prisoners in the hands of the Muslims. They were, contrary to all usage and traditions of the Arabs, treated with the greatest humanity.

The Prophet gave strict orders that sympathy should be shown to them in their misfortune and that they should be treated with kindness. These instructions were faithfully obeyed by the Muslims to whose care the prisoners were confided. Dealing with this event, Sir William Muir, in his book Life of Muhammad, quotes one of the prisoners saying: "Blessing be on the men of Medina; they made us ride, while they themselves walked; they gave us wheaten bread to eat, when there was little of it, contenting themselves with dates." The remarkable circumstances, which led to the victory of Badr, and results, which followed from it, made a deep impression on the minds of the Muslims; the angels of the heaven had battled on their side against their enemies. The division of the spoils created some dissension between the Muslim warriors. For the moment, the Prophet divided it equally among all. Subsequently, a Qur'an revelation laid down a rule for future division of the spoils. According to this rule, a fifth was reserved for the public treasury for the support of the poor and indigent, while the distribution of the remaining four fifths was left to the discretion of the Chief of the State.

## Makkan Avenge Loss in Badr - Battle of Uhud

The next battle between the Quraish and the Muslims was the battle of Uhud, a hill about four miles to the north of Medina. The idolaters, to revenge their loss at Badr, made tremendous preparations for a new attack upon the Muslims. They collected an army of three thousand strong men, of whom seven hundred were armed with coats of mail, and two hundred horses. These forces advanced under the conduct of Abu Sufyan and encamped at a village six miles from Medina, where they gave themselves up to spoiling the fields and flocks of the Medinites. The Prophet, being much inferior to his enemies in number, at first determined to keep himself within the town and to receive them there; but afterwards, the advice of some of his companions prevailing he marched out against them at the head of one thousand men, of whom one hundred were armed with coats of mail; but he had no more than one horse, besides his own, in his whole army. With these forces he halted at Mount Uhud. He was soon abandoned by Abdullah Ibn Ubai, the leader of the Hypocrites, with three hundred of his followers. Thus, the small force of the Prophet was reduced to seven hundred. At Mount Uhud the Muslim troops passed the night, and in the morning, after offering their prayers, they advanced into the plain. The Prophet contrived to have the hill at his back, and, the better to secure his men from being surrounded, he placed fifty archers on the height in the rear, behind the troops, and gave them strict orders not to leave their posts whatever might happen. When they came to engage, the Prophet had superiority at first. But afterward, his archers left their position for the sake of plunder, thus allowing the enemy to attack the Muslims in the fear and surround them. The Prophet lost the day and very nearly lost his life. He was struck down by a shower of stones and wounded in the face by two arrows, and one of his front teeth was broken. Of the Muslims, seventy men were killed, among whom was the Prophet's uncle Hamza. Of the infidels, twenty-two men were lost.

Quraish were too exhausted to follow up their advantage, either by attacking Medina or by driving the Muslims from the heights of Uhud. They retreated from the Medinite territories after barbarously mutilating the corpses of their dead enemies. Narrated Al-Baraa' Ibn Azib: "The Prophet appointed Abdullah Ibn Jubair as the commander of the infantry men (archers) who were fifty on the day (of the battle) of Uhud. He instructed them: 'Stick to your place, and don't leave it even if you see birds snatching us, till I send for you; and if you see that we have defeated the infidels and made them flee, even then you should not leave your place till I send for you.' Then the infidels were defeated. By Allah I saw the women fleeing lifting up their clothes revealing their leg bangles and their legs. So, the companions of Abdullah Ibn Jubair said: "The booty! O people, the booty! Your companions have become victorious, what are you waiting for now?" Abdullah Ibn Jubair said: "Have you forgotten what Allah's Messenger said to you?" They replied: "By Allah! We will go to the people (the enemy) and collect our share from the war booty." But when they went to them, they were forced to turn back defeated. At that time Allah's Messenger in their rear was calling them back. Only twelve men remained with the Prophet, and the infidels martyred seventy men from us.

"The Prophet and his companions caused the Pagans to lose one hundred and forty men, seventy of whom were captured and seventy were killed. Then Abu Sufyan asked three times: 'Is Muhammad present among these people?' The Prophet ordered his companions not to answer him. Then he asked three times: 'Is Ibn Abu Quhafa present amongst these people?' He asked again three times: 'Is Ibn Al Khattab present among these people?' He then returned to his companions and said: 'As for these (men), they have been killed.' Omar could not control himself and said to Abu Sufyan: ' You told a lie, by Allah! O enemy of Allah! All those you have mentioned are alive, and the thing which will make you unhappy is still there.'

Abu Sufyan said: 'Our victory today compensates for yours in the Battle of Badr, and in war (the victory) is always undecided and is shared in turns by the belligerents. You will find some of your killed men mutilated, but I did not urge my men to do so, yet I do not feel sorry for their deed.' After that he started reciting cheerfully: 'O Hubal, be superior!' On that the Prophet said (to his companions): 'Why don't you answer him back?' They said: 'O Allah's Messenger! What shall we say?' He said: 'Say, Allah is Higher and more Sublime.' Then Abu Sufyan said: 'We have the idol of Al-Uzza, and you have no 'Uzza.' The Prophet said (to his companions): 'Why don't you answer him back?' They asked: 'O Allah's Messenger! What shall we say?' He said: 'Say Allah is our Helper and you have no helper.'" (Sahih Al Bukhari). The moral effect of this disastrous battle was such as to encourage some neighboring nomad tribes to make forays upon the Medinte territories, but most of these were repelled.

## More Mutiny as Charter members cause dissent

The Jews also were not slow to involve in trouble the Prophet and his followers. They tried to create disaffection among his people and slandered him and his adherents. They mispronounced the words of the Qur'an so as to give them an offensive meaning. They also caused their poets, who were superior in culture and intelligence, to use their influence to sow sedition among the Muslims. One of their distinguished poets, called Ka'b, of the Bani An-Nadir, spared no efforts in publicly deploring the ill success of the idolaters after their defect at Badr. By his satires against the Prophet and his disciples, and his elegies on the Meccans who had fallen at Badr, Ka'b succeeded in exciting the Quraish to that frenzy of vengeance which broke out at Uhud. He then returned to Medina, where he continued to attack the Prophet and the Muslims, men and women, in terms of the most obscene character. Though he belonged to the tribe of Bani An Nadir, which had entered into the compact with the Muslims and pledged itself both for the internal and external safety of the State, he openly directed his acts against the commonwealth of which he was a member. Another Jew, Sallam by name, of the same tribe, behaved equally fiercely and bitterly against the Muslims. He lived with a party of his tribe at Khaibar, a village five days' journey northwest of Medina. He made every effort to excite the neighboring Arab tribes against the Muslims. The Muslim commonwealth with the object of securing safety among the community, passed a sentence of outlawry upon Ka'b and Sallam. The members of another Jewish tribe, namely Bani Qainuqa', were sentenced to expulsion from the Medinite territory for having openly and knowingly infringed the terms of the compact. It was necessary to put an end to their hostile actions of the sake of maintaining peace and security. The Prophet had to go to their headquarters, where he required them to enter definitively into the Muslim commonwealth by embracing Islam or to leave Medina. To this they replied in the most offensive terms: "You have had a quarrel with men ignorant of the art of war. If you are desirous of having any dealings with us, we shall show you that we are men." They then shut themselves up in their fortress and set the Prophet and his authority at defiance. The Muslims decided to reduce them and laid siege to their fortress without loss of time. After fifteen days they surrendered.

Though the Muslims at first intended to inflict some severe punishment on them, they contented themselves by banishing the Bani Qainuqa'. The Bani An-Nadir had now behaved in the same way as Bani Qainuqa'. They had likewise, knowingly and publicly, disregarded the terms of the Charter. The Prophet sent them a message similar to that which was sent to their brethren, the Qainuqa'. Then, relying on the assistance of the Hypocrites' party, returned for a defiant reply. After a siege of fifteen days, they sued for terms. The Muslims renewed their previous offer, and the Jews of An Nadir chose to execute Medina. They were allowed to take with them all their movable property, with the exception of their arms. Before leaving Medina, they destroyed all their dwellings in immovable property and arms which they could not carry away with them were distributed by the Prophet with the consent of the Ansar and the Emigrants. A principle was henceforth adopted that any acquisition not made in actual warfare should belong to that state and that its disposal should be left to the discretion of the ruling authorities.

The expulsion of the Bani An-Nadir took place in the fourth year of the hijrah. The remaining portion of this year and the early part of the next were passed in repressing the hostile attempts of the nomadic tribes against the Muslims and inflicting punishment for various murderous forays on the Medinite territories. Of this nature was the expedition against the Christian Arabs of Dumat Al Jandal (a place about seven days' journey to the south of Damascus), who had stopped the Medinites traffic with Syria and even threatened a raid upon Medina. These marauders, however, fled on the approach of the Muslims, and the Prophet returned to Medina after concluding a treaty with a neighboring chief, to whom he granted permission of pasturage in the Medinite territories.

## Enemy's Army (headed by Abu Sufyan) march towards Madina

In the same year, the enemies of Islam made every possible attempt to stir up the tribes against the Muslims. The Jews also took an active, if hidden, part in those intrigues. An army of ten thousand well-equipped men, marched towards Medina under the command of Abu Sufyan. They encamped near Mount Uhud, a few miles from the city. The Muslims could gather only an army of three thousand men. Seeing their inferiority in numbers on the one hand, and the turbulence of the Hypocrites within the town on the other, they preferred to remain on the defensive. They dug a deep moat round the unprotected quarters of Medina and encamped outside the city with a trench in front of them. They relied for safety of the other side upon their allies, the Quaraiza, who possessed several fortresses at a short distance towards the south and were bound by the compact to assist the Muslim s against any raiders. These Jews, however, were induced by the idolaters to violate their pledge and to join the Quraish. As these Jews were acquainted with the Hypocrites within the walls of the city were waiting for an opportunity to play their part, the situation of the Muslims was most dangerous. The siege had already lasted for 20 days.

The enemy made great efforts to cross the trench, but every attempt was fiercely repulsed by the small Muslim force. Disunion was now rife in the midst of the besieging army. Their horses were perishing fast, and provisions were becoming less every day. During the night, a storm of wind and rain caused their tents to be overthrown and their lights extinguished. Abu Sufyan and the majority of his army fled, and the rest took refuge with the Quraiza. The Muslims, though they were satisfied with the failure of their enemies, could not help thinking that the victory was unsatisfactory so long as the Quraiza, who had violated their sworn pledge, remained so near. The Jews might at any time surprise Medina from their side. The Muslims felt it their duty to demand an explanation of the violation of the pledge. This was utterly refused. Consequently, the Jews were besieged and compelled to surrender at discretion. They only asked that their punishment should be left to the judgment of Sa'd Ibn Mu'adh, the prince of the tribe of Aws. This chief, who was a fierce soldier, had been wounded in the attack and died of his wounds the following day. Infuriated by the treacherous conduct of the Bani Quraiza, he gave judgment that the fighting men should be to death and that the women and children should become the slaves of the Muslims.

### The Prophet protects the Christians of Madina

It was about this time that the Prophet granted to the monks of the Monastry of St. Catherine, near Mount Sinai, his liberal charter by which they secured for the Christians noble and generous privileges and immunities. He undertook himself and enjoined his followers, to protect the Christians, and to defend their churches. They were not to be unfairly taxed; no bishop was to be driven out of his diocese; nor Christian was to be forced to reject their religion; no pilgrim was to be stopped from his pilgrimage; nor were the Christian churches to be pulled down for the sake of building mosques or houses for the Muslims.

Christian women married to Muslims were to enjoy their own religion and not to be subjected to compulsion or annoyance of any kind. If the Christians should stand in need of assistance for the repair of their churches or monasteries, or any other matter pertaining to their religion, the Muslims were to assist them. This was not to be considered as supporting their religion, but as simply rendering them assistance in special circumstances. Should the Muslims be engaged in hostilities with outside Christians, no Christian resident among the Muslims should be treated with contempt on account of his creed. Any Muslim violating any clause of the charter should be regarded as a transgressor of Allah's commandments, a violator of His testament and neglectful of His faith.

## The Treaty of Hudaibiya

Six years had already elapsed since the Prophet and his Meccan followers had fled from their birthplace. Their hearts began to yearn for their homes and for their Sacred House the Ka'ba. As the season of the pilgrimage approached, the Prophet announced his intention to visit the holy center, and numerous voices of his disciples responded to the call for the journey to Mecca. The Prophet, accompanied by seven or eight hundred Muslims, Immigrants and Ansars, all totally unarmed, set out on the pilgrimage. Quraish gathered a large army to stop them from entering Mecca and maltreated the envoy whom the Prophet had sent to ask permission to visit. After much difficulty, a treaty was concluded by which it was agreed that all hostilities should cease for ten years; that anyone coming from the Quraish to the Prophet without the permission of the guardian or chief should be given back to the idolaters; that any Muslim persons going over to the Meccans should not be surrendered; that any tribe desirous of entering into alliance, either with the Quraish or with the Muslims, should be at liberty to do so without disputes; that the Muslims should go back to Medina on the present occasion and stop advancing further; that they should be permitted in the following year to visit Mecca and to remain there for three days with the arms they used on journeys, namely, their scimitars in sheaths. The Treaty of Hudaibiya thus ended, the Prophet returned with his people to Medina.

## Prophet Muhammad dispatches envoys

About this time it was revealed to the Prophet that his mission should be universal. He dispatched several envoys to invite the neighboring sovereigns to Islam. The embassy to the king of Persia, Chosroes Parvis, was received with disdain and contumely. He was haughtily amazed at the boldness of the Mecca fugitive in addressing him on terms of equality. He was so enraged that he tore up into pieces the Prophet's letter of invitation to Islam and dismissed the envoy from his presence with great contempt. When the Prophet received information on this treatment, he calmly observed: "Thus will the Empire of Chosroes be torn to pieces."

## Heraclius submits to Almighty God and embraces Islam

The embassy to Heraclitus, the Emperor of the Romans, was received much more politely and reverentially. He treated the ambassador with great respect and sent the Prophet a gracious reply to his message. Another envoy was sent to an Arab price of the Ghassanite tribe, a Christian feudatory of Heraclius. This prince, instead of receiving the envoy with any respect, cruelly murdered him. This act caused great consternation among the Muslims. Narrated Abdullah Ibn Abbas: Abu Sufyan Ibn Harb informed me that Heraclius had sent a messenger to him while he had been accompanying a caravan from Quraish.

They were merchants doing business in Syria, Palestine, Lebanon, and Jordan, at the time when Allah's Messenger had a truce with Abu Sufyan and Quraish infidels. So Abu Sufyan and his companions went to Heraclius at Ilya (Jerusalem). Heraclitus called them in the court and he had all the senior Roman dignitaries around him. He called for his translator who, translating Heraclius's question, said to them: "Who among you is closely related to that man who claims to be a Prophet?" Abu Sufyan replied: "I am the nearest relative to him (amongst the group)." Heraclius said: "Bring him (Abu Sufyan) close to me and make his companions stand behind him." Abu Sufyan added: "Heraclius told his translator to tell my companions that he wanted to put some questions to me regarding that man (The Prophet) and if I told a lie they (my companions) should contradict me. By Allah! Had I not been afraid of my companions labeling me a liar, I would have not have spoken the truth about the Prophet." Abu Sufyan's narration continues: "The first question he asked me about him was; what is his family status among you?" "I replied: "He belongs to a good noble family amongst us." Heraclius further asked: "Has anybody among you ever claimed the same (to be a Prophet) before him?" I replied: "No." He said: "Was anybody amongst his ancestors a king?" I replied: "No." Heraclius asked: "Do the nobles or the poor follow him?" I replied: "It is the poor who follow him." He said: "Are his followers increasing or decreasing (day by day)?" I replied: "They are increasing." He then asked: "Does anybody amongst those who embrace his religion become displeased and renounce the religion afterwards?" I replied: "No." Heraclius said: "Have you ever accused him of telling lies before his claim (to be a Prophet)?" I replied: "No." Heraclius said: "Does he break his promises?" I replied: "No. We are at truce with him but we do not know what he will do in it." I could not find opportunity to say anything against him except that.

Heraclius asked: "Have you ever had a war with him?" I replied: "Yes." Then he said: "What was the outcome of the battles?" I replied: "Sometimes he was victorious and sometimes we." Heraclius said: "What does he order you to do?" I said: "He tells us to worship Allah and Allah alone and not to worship anything along with Him, and to renounce all that our ancestors had said. He orders us to pray, to speak the truth, to be chaste and to keep good relations with our kith and kin."

Heraclius asked the translator to convey to me the following: "I asked you about his family and your reply was that he belonged to a very noble family. In fact, all the Messengers come from noble families among their respective peoples. I questioned you whether anybody else among you claimed such a thing; your reply was in the negative. If the answer had been in the affirmative, I would have thought that this man was following the previous man's statement. Then I asked you whether anyone of his ancestors was a king. Your reply was in the negative, and if it had been in the affirmative, I would have thought that this man wanted to take back his ancestral kingdom.

I further asked whether he was ever accused of telling lies before he said what he said and your reply was in the negative. So I wondered how a person who does not tell a lie about others could ever tell a lie about Allah. I then asked you whether the rich people followed him or the poor. You replied that it was the poor who followed him. And, in fact, all the Messengers have been followed by this very class of people. Then I asked you whether his followers were increasing or decreasing. You replied that they were increasing, and, in fact, this is the way of true faith, till it is complete in all respects. I further asked you whether there was anybody, who, after embracing his religion, became displeased and discarded his religion. You reply was in the negative, and, in fact this is (the sign of) true faith, when its delight enters the hearts and mixes with them completely. I asked you whether he had ever betrayed. You replied in the negative, and likewise the Messengers never betray. Then I asked you what he ordered you to do. You replied that he ordered you to worship Allah and Allah alone and not to worship anything along with Him, and forbade you to worship idols, and ordered you to pray, to speak the truth and to be chaste. If what you have said is true, he will very soon occupy this place underneath my feet and I knew it (from the scriptures) that he was going to appear but I did not know that he would be from you, and if I could reach him definitely, I would go immediately to meet him and if I were with him, I would certainly wash his feet."

Heraclius then asked for the letter addressed by Allah's Messenger which had been delivered by Dihya to the Governor of Busra, who forwarded it to Heraclius to read. The contents of the letter were as follows: "In the name of Allah, the Beneficent, the Merciful. (This letter is) from Muhammad, the slave of Allah and His Messenger to Heraclius the ruler of Byzantine. Peace be upon him who follows the right path. Furthermore, I invite you to Islam, and if you become a Muslim you will be safe, and Allah will double your reward, and if you reject this invitation of Islam, you will be committing a sin by misguiding your subjects. And I recite to you Allah's Statement: SAY (O Muhammad): 'O People of the Scripture (Jews & Christians): Come to a word that is just between us and you, that we worship none but Allah, and that we associate no partners with Him and that none of us shall take others as lords besides Allah.' Then, if they turn away, say: 'Bear witness that we are Muslims.' " Abu Sufyan then added: When Heraclius had finished his speech and had read the letter, there was a great hue and cry in the Royal Court. So we turned out of the court. I told my companions that the question of Ibn- Abi-Kabsha (the Prophet Muhammad) had become so prominent that even the King of Bani Al-Asfar (Byzantine) was afraid of him. Then I started to become sure that he (the Prophet) would be the conqueror in the near future till I embraced Islam (Allah guided me to it). The sub narrator added that Ibn An-Natur was the Governor of Ilya (Jerusalem) and Heraclius was the head of the Christians of Sham.

Ibn An-Natur narrated that once while Heraclius was visiting Ilya (Jerusalem), he got up in the morning with a sad mood. Some of his priests asked him what was wrong. He replied: "At night when I looked at the stars, I saw that the leader of those who practice circumcision had appeared (become the conqueror). Who are they who practice circumcision?" The people replied: "Except the Jews, nobody practices circumcision, so you should not be afraid of them (Jews). Just Issue orders to kill every Jew present in the country.' While they were discussing it, a messenger sent by the king of Ghassan to convey the news of Allah's Messenger to Heraclius was brought in.having heard the news, he (Heraclius) ordered the people to go and see whether the messenger of Ghassan was circumcised. The people, after seeing him, told Heraclius that he was circumcised. Heraclius then asked him about the Arabs.

The messenger replied: "Arabs also practice circumcision." After hearing that Heraclius remarked that sovereignty of the Arabs had appeared. Heraclius then wrote a letter to his friend in Rome who was as good as Heraclius in knowledge. Heraclius then left for Homs (a town in Syria) and stayed there till he received the reply of his letter from his friend, who agreed with him in his opinion about the emergence of the Prophet and the fact that he was a Prophet. On that, Heraclius invited all the heads of the Byzantines to assemble in his palace at Homs. When they assembled, he ordered that all the doors of his palace be closed. Then he came out and said: "O Byzantines! If success is your desire and if you seek right guidance and want your empire to remain, then give a pledge of allegiance to this Prophet (embrace Islam)." (On hearing the views of Heraclius) the people ran towards the gates of the palace but found the doors closed. Heraclius realized their hatred towards Islam and when he lost the hope of their embracing Islam, he ordered that they should be brought back in audience.

(When they returned) he said: "What was already said was just to test the strength of your conviction and I have seen it." The people prostrated before him and became pleased with him, and this was the end of Heraclius's story (in connection with his faith). (Sahih Al-Bukhari).

## Attack from the Jews of Khaibar thwarted

In the same year the Jews of Khaibar, a strongly fortified territory at a distance of four days' journey from Medina, showed implacable hatred towards the Muslims. United by alliance with the tribe of Ghatfan, as well as with other cognate tribes, the Jews of Khaibar made serious attempts to form a coalition against the Muslims. The Prophet and his adherents were apprised of this movement and immediate measures were taken in order to repress any new attack upon Medina. An expedition of fourteen hundred men was soon prepared to march against Khaibar.

The allies of the Jews left them to face the war with the Muslims all alone. The Jews firmly resisted the attacks of the Muslims, but eventually all their fortress had to be surrendered, one after the other to their enemies. They prayed for forgiveness, which was accorded to them on certain conditions. Their lands and immovable property were secured to them, together with the free practice of their religion.

## Allah's Messenger and the Muslims perform Hajj

Before the end of the year, it being the seventh year of the hijrah, the Prophet and his adherents availed themselves of their armistice with the Quraish to visit the holy Ka'ba. The Prophet, accompanied by two hundred Muslims, went to Mecca to perform the rites of pilgrimage. On this occasion the Quraish evacuated the city during the three days which the ceremonies lasted. Sir William Muir, in his book, Life of Mohammed Vol. III comments on the incident as follows: It was surely a strange sight, which at this time presented itself at the vale of Mecca, a sight unique in the history of the world. The ancient city is for three days evacuated by all its inhabitants, high and low, every house deserted, and as they retire, the exiled converts, many years banished from their birthplace, approach in a great body accompanied by their allies, revisit the empty homes of their childhood, and within the short allotted space, and fulfil the rites of pilgrimage. The outside inhabitants, climbing the heights around take refuge under tents or other shelter among the hills and glens; and clustering on the overhanging peak of Abu Qubeis, thence watch the movements of the visitors beneath, as with the Prophet at their head, they make the circuit of the Ka'ba and rapid procession between Essafa and Marwah, and anxiously scan every figure, if perchance they may recognize among the worshippers some long lost friend or relative. It was a scene rendered only by the throes, which gave birth to Islam. In accordance with the terms of the treaty, the Muslims left Mecca at the end of three day's visit. This peaceful visit was followed by important conversions among the Quraish. Khalid Ibn Al-Walid, known as the Sword of Allah, who, before this, had been a bitter enemy of Islam and who commanded the Quraish cavalry at Uhud; and Amr Ibn Al' As, another important character and warrior, adopted the new faith.

## Retribution for the Murder of the Muslim Envoy

When the Prophet and his followers returned to Medina, they arranged in expedition to exact retribution from the Ghassanite prince who had killed the Muslim envoy. A force of three thousand men, under the Prophet's adopted son Zaid, was sent to take reparation from the offending tribe. Khalid Ibn Al-Walid was one of the generals chosen for the expedition. When they reached the neighborhood of Muta, a village to the southeast of the Dead Sea, they met with an overwhelming force of Arabs and Romans who were assembled to oppose them. The Muslims, however, resolved resolutely to push forward. Their courage was of no avail and they suffered great losses. In this battle Zaid and Ja'far, a cousin of the Prophet, and several other notables were killed.

Khalid Ibn Al- Walid, by a series of maneuvers, succeeded in drawing off the army and conducting it without further loses to Medina. A month later, however, Amr Ibn Al-' as marched unopposed through the lands of the hostile tribes, received their submission, and restored the prestige of Islam on the Syrian frontier. About the end of the seventh year of the hijrah, the Quraish and their allies, the Bani Bakr, violated the terms of the peace concluded at Hudaibiya by attacking the Bani Khuzaah, who were in alliance with the Muslims.

Bani Khuzzah appealed to the Prophet for help and protection. The Prophet determined to make a stop to the reign of injustice and oppression, which had lasted so long at Mecca. He immediately gathered ten thousand men to march against the idolaters and set out on January, 630. After eight days the Muslims army halted, and alighted at Marr Az-Zahran, a day's journey from Mecca. On the night of their arrival, Abu Sufyan, who was delegated by the Quraish to ask the Prophet to abandon his project, presented himself and besought an interview. In the morning it was granted. "Has the time not come, O Abu Sufyan," said the Prophet, "for you to acknowledge that there is no deity save Allah and that I am His Messenger?" Abu Sufyan, after hesitating for a while, pronounced the prescribed formula of belief and adopted Islam. He was then sent back to prepare the city for the Prophet's approach. With the exception of a slight resistance by certain clans headed by Ikrima and Safwan, in which many Muslims were killed, the Prophet entered Mecca almost unopposed. The city which had treated him so cruelly, driven him and his faithful band for refuge among strangers, the city which had sworn his life and the lives of his devoted adherents, now lay at his mercy. His old persecutors were now completely at his feet. The Prophet entered Mecca on his favorite camel Al Kaswa, having Usama Ibn Zaid sitting behind him. On his way he recited Surah Al Fath (Victory): "Verily! We have given you (O Muhammad) a manifest victory. That Allah may forgive you your sins of the past and future, and complete His Favor on you, and guide you on the Straight Path; and that Allah may help you with strong help. (Ch 48:1-3 Quran)

## Prophet Muhammad (pbuh) orders the destruction of the idols

The Muslim army entered the city unpretentiously and peacefully. No house was robbed, no man or woman was insulted. The Prophet granted a general amnesty to the entire population of Mecca. Only four criminals, whom justice condemned, were proscribed. He did however, order the destruction of all idols and pagan images of worship, upon which three hundred and fifty idols which were in the Sacred House of Ka'ba were thrown down. The Prophet himself destroyed a wooden pigeon hung from the roof and regarded as one of the deities of the Quraish. During the downfall of the images and idols he was heard to cry aloud: "Allah is great. Truth has come and falsehood has vanished; verily falsehood is fleeting." The old idolaters observed thoughtfully the destruction of their gods, which were utterly powerless.

After the Prophet had abolished these pagan idols and every pagan rite, he delivered a sermon to the assembled people. He dwelt upon the natural brotherhood of man in the words of the Qur'an: "O Mankind! We have created you for a male and a female, and made you into nations and tribes, that you may know one another. Verily, the most honorable of you in the Sight of Allah is that (believer) who has At-Taqwa (one of the Muttaqun, pious, and righteous persons who fear Allah much, abstain from all kinds of sins and evil deeds which He has forbidden), and love Allah much (perform all kinds of good deeds which He has ordained.) Verily Allah is All-Knowing, All-Aware. (Ch 49:13 Quran). Narrated Hisham's father: When Allah's Messenger set out (towards Mecca) during the year of the Conquest (of Mecca) and this news reached (the infidels of Quraish), Abu Sufyan, Hakim Ibn Hizam and Budail Ibn Waraqa came out to gather information about Allah's Messenger. They proceeded on their way till they reached a place called Marr-az-Zahran (which is near Mecca).

Behold! There they saw many fires as if they were the fires of Arafat." Budail Ibn Waraqa' said: "Banu' Amr are less in number than that." Some of the guards of Allah's Messenger saw them and took them over, caught them, and brought them to Allah's Messenger. Abu Sufyan embraced Islam. When the Prophet proceeded, he said to Al' Abbas: "Keep Abu Sufyan standing at the top of the mountain so that he would look at the Muslims. SO Al-Abbas kept him standing (at that place) and the tribes with the Prophet started passing in front of Abu Sufyan in military batches. A batch passed in front of Abu Sufyan and said: "O 'Abbas who are these?" 'Abbas said: "They are Banu Ghaifar." Abu Sufyan said: "I have got nothing to do with Ghifar." Then a batch of the tribe of Juhaina passed by and he said similarly as above. Then a batch of the tribe of Sa'd Ibn Huzaim passed by and he said similarly as above. Then came a batch, the like of which Abu Sufyan had not seen. He said: "Who are these?" Abbas said: "They are the Ansar headed by Sa'd Ibn 'Ubada, the one holding the flag." Sa'd Ibn 'Ubada said: "O Abu Sufyan! Today is the day of a great battle and today (what is prohibited in) the Ka'ba will be permissible."

Abu Sufyan said, "O Abbas! How excellent the day of destruction is!" Then came another batch of warriors which was the smallest of all the batches, and in it there was Allah's Messenger and his companions, and the flag of the Prophet was carried by Az-Zubair Ibn Al-Awwam. When Allah's Messenger passed by Abu Sufyan, the latter said to the Prophet: "Do you know what Sa'd Ibn Ubada said?" The Prophet said: "What did he say?" Abu Sufyan said: "He said so-and-so." The Prophet said: "Sa'd told a lie, but today Allah will give superiority to the Ka'ba and today the Ka'ba will be covered with a cloth covering." Allah's Messenger ordered that his flag be fixed at Al-Hajun. Narrated Urwa: Nafi' Ibn Jubair Ibn Mut'im said: "I heard Al-Abbas saying to Az-Zubair Ibn Al- Awwam, 'O Abu Abdullah! Did Allah's Messenger order you to fix the flag here?' "Allah's Messenger ordered Khalid Ibn Al-Walid to enter Mecca from its upper part from Kadaa' while the Prophet himself entered from Kudaa.

Two men from the cavalry of Khalid Ibn Al-Walid named Hubaish Ibn Al Ashar and Kurz Ibn Jabir Al-Fihri were martyred on that day. (Sahih Al Bukhari) Now great multitudes came to adopt Islam and take the oath of allegiance to the Prophet. For this purpose an assembly was held at As-Safa Mountain. Omar, acting as the Prophet's deputy administered the oath, whereby the people bound themselves not to adore any deity but Allah to obey the Prophet to abstain from theft, adultery, infanticide, lying and backbiting. Thus was fulfilled the prophecy embodied in the Surah Al Fath in the Quran. During his stay at Mecca, the Prophet dispatched his principal disciples in every direction to preach Islam among the wild tribes of the desert and call them to the true religion of Allah. He sent small detachments of his troops into the suburbs who destroyed the temples of Al Uzza, Suwaa, and Manat, the three famous idols in the temples of the neighboring tribes. The Prophet gave strict orders that these expeditions should be carried out in a peaceable manner. These injunctions were obeyed in all cases, with one exception. The troops under Khalid Ibn Al-Walid, the fierce newly-converted warrior, killed a few of the Bani Jazima. When the news of this wanton bloodshed reached the Prophet, he was deeply grieved and exclaimed: "Oh, my Lord, I am innocent of what Khalid has done." He dispatched a large sum of money for the widows and orphans of the slain and severely rebuked Khalid. At this time the tribes of Hawazin and Thakif showed unwillingness to render obedience to the Muslims without resistance. They formed a league with the intention of attacking the Prophet, but he was vigilant enough to frustrate their plan. A big battle was fought with this new enemy of Islam near Hunain, a deep and narrow defile nine miles northeast of Mecca. The idolaters were utterly defeated. One body of the enemy, consisting chiefly of the Thakif tribe, took refuge in their fortified city of Ta'if, which eight or nine years before had dismissed the Prophet from within its walls with injuries and insults. The remainder of the defeated force, consisting principally of the Hawazin, sought at a camp in the valley of Autas. This camp was raided by the Muslim troops.

The families of the Hawazin, their flocks and herds with all their other effects, were captured by the troops of the Prophet. Ta'if was then besieged for a few days only, after which the Prophet raised the siege, well knowing that the people of Ta'if would soon be forced by circumstances to submit without bloodshed. Returning to his camp where the prisoners of Hawazin were left safely, the Prophet found a deputation from this hostile tribe who begged him to set free their families. The Prophet replied that he was willing to give back his own share of those captives and that of the children of Abdul Muttalib, but that he could not force his followers to abandon the fruits of their victory. The disciples followed the generous example of their teacher. The hearts of several members of the Thakir tribe were so influenced by this that they offered their allegiance and soon became earnest Muslims. The Prophet now returned to Medina fully satisfied with the achievements of his mission.

The ninth year of the hijrah is known as the Year of Embassies, as being the year in which the various tribes of Arabia submitted to the claim of the Prophet and sent embassies to render homage to him. These tribes had been awaiting the issue of the war between Muhammad and the Quraish; but as soon as the tribe - the principal of the whole nation and the descendants of Ishmael, whose prerogatives none offered to dispute - had submitted, they were satisfied that it was not in their power to oppose Muhammad. Hence their embassies flocked into Medina to make their submission to him. The conquest of Mecca decided the fate of idolatry in Arabia. Now deputations began to arrive from all sides to render the adherence to Islam of various tribes. Among the rest, five princes of the tribe of Himyar professed Islam and sent ambassadors to notify Muhammad of the same. These were the princes of Yemen, Mahra, Oman, and Yamama. The idolaters of Ta'if, the very people who had driven the Messenger of Islam from their midst with violence and contempt, now sent a deputation to pray forgiveness and ask to be numbered among his followers. They begged, however, for temporary preservation of their idols. As a last appeal they begged for one month of grace only. But even this was not conceded. The Prophet said Islam and the idols could not exist together. They then begged for exemption from the daily prayers. The Prophet replied that without devotion, religion would be nothing. At last they submitted to all that was required of them. They, however, asked to be exempted from destroying the idols with their own hands. This was granted.

The Prophet selected Abu Sufyan and Mughira to destroy the idols of Ta'if, the chief of which was the notorious idol of Al-Lat. This was carried out amidst cries of despair and grief from the women of Ta'if. The conversion of this tribe of Ta'if is worthy of notice. This tribe, which hither to had proved hostile to the new faith, was noted among the Arabs for its idolatrous priesthood. A small detachment under Ali was sent to reduce them to obedience and to destroy their idols. The prince of the tribe was 'Adi, the son of the famous Hatim, whose generosity was spoken of all over Arabia.

On the approach of the Muslim force, Adi fled to Syria, leaving his sister with his principal clansmen, to fall into the hands of the Muslims. These were conducted by Ali with every sign of respect and sympathy to Medina. When the daughter of Hatim came before the Prophet, she addressed him in the following words: "Messenger of Allah, my father is dead; my brother, my only relation fled into the mountains on the approach of the Muslims. I cannot ransom myself; I count on your generosity for my deliverance. My father was an illustrious man, the prince of his tribe, a man who ransomed prisoners, protected the honor of women, fed the poor, cothed afflicted, and was deaf to no appeal." The Prophet replied: "Your father had the virtues of a true Muslim; if it were permitted to invoke the mercy of Allah on any whose life was passed in idolatry, I would pray to Allah for mercy for the soul of Hatim." Then, addressing the Muslims around him, he said: "the daughter of Hatim is free, her father was a generous and humane man;

Allah loves and rewards the merciful." With the daughter of Hatim, all her people were set at liberty. She proceeded to Syria and related to her brother the generosity of Muhammad. 'Adi, touched by gratitude, hastened to Medina, where he was kindly received by the Prophet. He professed Islam and returned to his people and persuaded them to abandon idolatry. They all submitted and became devoted Muslims.

Hitherto no prohibition had been enforced against idolaters entering the Holy Ka'ba, or performing their abominable rites within the sacred precincts. Towards the end of the ninth year of the hijrah, during the month of pilgrimage 'Ali was delegated by the Prophet to read a proclamation that ran as follows: "No idolater shall after this year perform the pilgrimage; no one shall make the circuit of the Ka'ba naked (such a disgraceful custom was practiced by the pagan Arabs); and treaty with the Prophet shall continue in force but four months are allowed to every man to return to his territories; after that there will be no obligation on the Prophet, except towards those with whom treaties have been concluded."

The vast multitude who had listened to the above declaration returned to their homes, and before the following year was over the majority of them were Muslims. During the tenth year of the hijrah, as in the preceding one, numerous embassies continued to pour into Medina from all parts of Arabia, to testify to the allegiance of their chiefs and their tribes. Teachers were sent by the Prophet into the different provinces to teach the new converts the principles and precepts of Islam. These teachers were invariably given the following injunctions when they were about to depart on their mission: "Deal gently with the people, and be not harsh; cheer them, and do not look down upon them with contempt. You will meet with many believers in the Holy Scriptures, who will ask you: 'What is the key to heaven?' Answer them it (the key to heaven) is to bear witness to the divine truth and to do good."

Thus, the mission of the Prophet Muhammad was now accomplished; the whole work was achieved in his lifetime. Idolatry with its nameless abominations was entirely destroyed. The people who were sunk in superstition, cruelty, and vice in regions where spiritual life was utterly unknown were now united in one bond of faith, hope and charity. The tribes which had been from time immemorial engaged in perpetual wars were now united together by the ties of brotherhood, love, and harmony. Henceforth, their aims were not confined to this earth alone; but there was something beyond the grave - much higher, purer, and diviner - calling them to the practice of charity, goodness, justice, and universal love. They could now perceive that Allah was not that which they had carved out of wood or stone, but He is the Creator of the Universe.

## Prophet Muhammad's last Sermon, mount Arafat

On the return of the sacred month of pilgrimage, the Prophet, under the presentiment of his approaching end, determined to make a farewell pilgrimage to Mecca. In February 632, he left Medina with a very considerable concourse of Muslims. It is stated that from ninety thousand to one hundred and forty thousand people accompanied the Prophet. Before completing all rites of the pilgrimage, he addressed the assembled multitude from the top of Mount Arafat in the following words: "O people! Listen to my words, for I know not whether another year will be vouchsafed to me after this year to find myself among you. Your lives and property are sacred and inviolable among one another until you appear before the Lord, as this day and this month are sacred for all; and remember, you will have to appear before Allah Who will demand from you an account for all your actions. O people, you have rights over your wives, and your wives have a right over you. Verily you have taken them on the security of Allah and have made their people lawful unto you by the words of Allah. And your slaves, see that you feed them with such food as you eat yourselves, and clothe them with the stuff you wear, and if they commit a fault which you are not inclined to forgive, then part with them; for they are the servants of the Lord and are not to be harshly treated. O people, listen to my words and understand them. Know that all Muslims are brothers. You are one brotherhood; but no man shall take anything from his brother, unless by his free consent. Keep yourselves from injustice. Let him who is present tell this to him who is absent. It maybe that he who is told this afterward may remember better than he who has now heard it." The Prophet concluded his sermon by exclaiming: "O Lord, I have fulfilled my message and accomplished my work." The assembled multitude, all in one voice, cried: "Yea, verily you have." The Prophet again exclaimed: "O Lord, I beseech You, bear witness to it."

## The Prophet returns to Madina

Having rigorously performed all the ceremonies of the pilgrimage, that his example might be followed by all Muslims for all succeeding ages, the Prophet returned with his followers to Medina. The eleventh year of the hijrah, being the last year of Muhammad's life, was spent at Medina. There he settled the organization of the provincial and tribal communities which had adopted Islam and become the component parts of the Muslims federation. More officers had to be deputed to the interior provinces for the purpose of teaching their inhabitants the precepts of the religion, administering justice, and collecting Zakat. Muadh Ibn Jabal was sent to Yemen. On his departure to that distant province the Prophet enjoined him to use his own discretion in the event of his being unable to find express authority in the Quran. Ali was deputed to Yamama in the southeast of the peninsula. To him the Prophet said: "Never decide between any two parties who come to you for justice unless you first hear both of them."

## Murders and false claims of Prophethood arise

A force was being prepared under Usama Ibn Zaid, whose father was killed at Muta, against the Byzantines, to exact the long-delayed reparation for the murder of the envoy to Syria. However, the news of the Prophet's sickness and failing health caused that expedition to be stopped. This news was soon noised abroad and produced disorder in some districts. Three pretenders had arisen who gave themselves out as prophets and tried by all kinds of imposture to win over their tribes. The most dangerous of these pretenders was known as Al Aswad. He was a chief of Yemen and a conjurer. He soon succeeded in gaining over his tribesmen and, with the help, reduced to subjection many of the neighboring towns. He killed Shahr, whom the Prophet had appointed as Governor of Sana in the place of his father Bazan, who had just died. Bazan had been the viceroy of Yemen under Chosroes of Persia; after he had adopted Islam he was allowed by the Prophet to remain as Governor of Yemen. He was able to convert to Islam all the Persian colony in that province. Al-Aswad, the conjurer, had now killed Shahr, but soon after he was massacred by the Persians of Yemen. The other two pretenders, Tulayha and Haroun by name, were not suppressed until after the death of the Prophet, during the reign of Abu Bakr. Haroun, better known as Mussaylamah, addressed to the Prophet a letter which ran as follows: "From Mussaylamah the Prophet of Allah, to Muhammad the Prophet of Allah. Peace be to you. I am your partner. Let the exercise of authority be divided between us. Half the earth will be mine, and half will belong to your Quraish. But the Quraish are too greedy to be satisfied with a just division." To this letter the Prophet replied as follows: "From Muhammad the Messenger of Allah to Mussaylamah the liar. Peace be to those who follow the right path. The earth belongs to Allah. It is He Who makes the reign whomsoever He pleases. Only those will prosper who fear the Lord."

## Prophet Muhammad's last days

The health of the Prophet grew worse. His last days were remarkable for the calmness and serenity of his mind. He was able, though weak and feeble, to lead the public prayers until within three days of his death. He requested that he might be permitted to stay at 'Aisha's house close to the mosque during his illness, an arrangement to which his other wives assented. As long as his strength lasted, he took part in the public prayers. The last time he appeared in the mosque he addressed the congregation, after the usual prayers were over, in the following words: "O Muslims, if I have wronged anyone of you, here I am to answer for it; if I owe anything to anyone, all I may happen to possess belongs to you."

A man in the crowd rose and claimed three Dirhams which he had given to a poor man at the request of the Prophet. They were immediately paid back with these words: "Better to blush in this world than in the next." The Prophet then prayed and implored Allah's mercy for those who had fallen in the persecution of their enemies.

He recommended to all his followers the observance of religious duties and the leading of a life of peace and goodwill. Then he spoke with emotion and with a voice still so powerful as to reach beyond the outer doors of the mosque: "By the Lord in Whose hand lies the soul of Muhammad as to myself, no man can lay hold on me in any matter; I have not made lawful anything excepting what Allah has made lawful; nor have I prohibited anything but that which Allah in His Book has prohibited."

Then turning to the women who sat close by, he exclaimed: "O Fatimah, my, daughter, and Safia, my aunt, work you both that which procure you acceptance with the Lord, for verily I have no power to save you in any wise." He then rose and re-entered the house of Aisha.

## The death of Prophet Muhammad, peace be upon him

After this, the Prophet never appeared at public prayers. A few hours after he returned from the mosque, the Prophet died while laying his head on the bosom of Aisha. As soon as the Prophet's death was announced, a crowd of people gathered at the door of the house of Aisha, exclaiming: "How can our messenger be dead?" Omar said: "No, he is not dead; he will be restored to us, and those are traitors to the cause of Islam who say he is dead. If they say so let them be cut in pieces." But Abu Bakr entered the house at this moment, and after he had touched the body of the Prophet with a demonstration of profound affection, he appear at the door and addressed the crowd with the following speech: "O Muslims, if anyone of you has been worshipping Muhammad, then let me tell you that Muhammad is dead. But if you really do worship Allah then know that Allah is living and will never die. Do you forget the verse in the Quran?

"Muhammad is not more than a Messenger, and indeed (many) Messengers have passed away before him. If he dies or is killed, will you then turn your back on your heels (as disbelievers)? And he who turns back on his heels, not the least harm will he do to Allah, and Allah will give reward to those who are grateful." [3:144]

$$\text{وَمَا مُحَمَّدٌ إِلَّا رَسُولٌ قَدْ خَلَتْ مِن قَبْلِهِ الرُّسُلُ أَفَإِيْن مَاتَ أَوْ قُتِلَ انقَلَبْتُمْ عَلَىٰ أَعْقَابِكُمْ وَمَن يَنقَلِبْ عَلَىٰ عَقِبَيْهِ فَلَن يَضُرَّ اللَّهَ شَيْئًا وَسَيَجْزِي اللَّهُ الشَّاكِرِينَ ﴿١٤٤﴾}$$

Upon hearing this speech of Abu Bakr, Omar acknowledged his error, and the crowd was satisfied and dispersed. Al-Abbas, the Prophet's uncle, presided at the preparation for the burial, and the body was duly washed and perfumed. There was some dispute between the Quraish and the Ansars as to the place of burial; however, Abu Bakr settled the dispute by affirming that he had heard the Prophet say that a prophet should be buried at the very spot where he died. A grave was accordingly dug in the ground within the house of Aisha and under the bed on which the Prophet died. In this grave the body was buried, and the usual rites were performed by those who were present.

Thus ended the glorious life of that Prophet Muhammad. May the peace and blessings of Allah be upon him.

## The Legacy of the Prophet (Peace be upon him)

"The Messenger of Allâh (Peace and blessings be upon him), whenever he is given the opportunity to choose between two affairs, he always chooses the easiest and the most convenient. But if he is certain that it is sinful, he will be as far as he could from it. He has never avenged himself; but when the sanctity of Allâh is violated he would. That would be for Allâh's not for himself. He is the last one to get angry and the first to be satisfied. His hospitality and generosity were matchless. His gifts and endowments manifest a man who does not fear poverty."

Ibn'Abbas said: "The Prophet (Peace and blessings be upon him) was the most generous. He is usually most generous of all times in Ramadan, the times at which the angel Gabriel (Peace and blessings be upon him) comes to see him. Gabriel used to visit him every night of Ramadan and review the Qur'ân with him. Verily the Messenger of Allâh (Peace and blessings be upon him) is more generous at giving bounty or charity than the blowing wind."

Jabir said:

"The Prophet (Peace and blessings be upon him) would never deny anything he was asked for."

His courage, his succour and his might are distinguishable. He was the most courageous. He witnessed awkward and difficult times and stoodfast at them. More than once brave men and daring ones fled away leaving him alone; yet he stood with full composure facing the enemy without turning his back. All brave men must have experienced fleeing once or have been driven off the battlefield at a round at a time except the Prophet (Peace and blessings be upon him) 'Ali said: "Whenever the fight grew fierce and the eyes of fighters went red, we used to resort to the Prophet (Peace and blessings be upon him) for succour. He was always the closest to the enemy."

Anas said: "One night the people of Madinah felt alarmed. People went out hurriedly towards the source of sound, but the Prophet (Peace and blessings be upon him) had already gone ahead of them. He was on the horseback of Abu Talhah which had no saddle over it, and a sword was slung round his neck, and said to them: 'There was nothing to be afraid for.'"

He was the most modest and the first one to cast his eyes down. Abu Sa'îd Al-Khudri: "He was shier than a virgin in her boudoir. When he hates a thing we read it on his face. He does not stare at anybody's face. He always casts his eyes down. He looks at the ground more than he looks sky-wards. His utmost looks at people are glances. He is willingly and modestly obeyed by everybody. He would never name a person whom he had heard ill-news about — which he hated. Instead he would say: 'Why do certain people do so....'"

Al-Farazdaq verse of poem fits him very much and the best one to be said of:

"He casts his eyes modestly but the eyes of others are cast down due to his solemnity, and words issue out of his mouth only while he is smiling."

The Prophet ﷺ is the most just, the most decent, the most truthful at speech, and the honestest of all. Those who have exchanged speech with him, and even his enemies, acknowledge his noble qualities. Even before the Prophethood he was nicknamed Al-Ameen (i.e. the truthful, the truthworthy). Even then — in Al-Jahiliyah — they used to turn to him for judgement and consultation. In a version by At-Tirmidhi, he says that 'Ali had said that he had been told by Abu Jahl that he (Abu Jahl) said to the Messenger of Allâh (Peace and blessings be upon him): "We do not call you a liar; but we do not have faith in what you have brought." In His Book, Allâh, the Exalted, said about them "It is not you that they deny, but it is the Verses (the Qur'ân) of Allâh that the Zalimûn (polytheists and wrong-doers) deny." [6:33]

Even when Heraclius asked Abu Sufyan: "Have you ever accused him of lying before the ministry of Prophethood?" Abu Sufyan said: "No."

He was most modest and far from being arrogant or proud. He forbade people to stand up at his presence as other people usually do for their kings.

Visiting the poor, the needy and entertaining them are some of his habits. If a slave invited him, he would accept the invitation. He always sat among his friends as if he were an ordinary person of them. 'Aishah said that he used to repair his shoes, sew or mend his dress and to do what ordinary men did in their houses. After all, he was a human being like others. He used to check his dress (lest it has some insects on). Milking the she-sheep and catering for himself were some of his normal jobs. The Prophet (Peace and blessings be upon him) was the most truthful to his pledges, and it is one of his qualities to establish good and steady relationship with his relatives — 'Silat-Ar-Rahim'. He is the most merciful, gentle and amiable to all people. His way of living is the simplest one. Ill-manners and indecency are two qualities completely alien to him.

He was decent, and did not call anybody names. He was not the sort of person who cursed or made noise in the streets. He did not exchange offences with others. He pushed back an offence or an error by forgiveness and overlooking. Nobody was allowed to walk behind him (i.e. as a bodyguard). He did not feel himself superior to others not even to his slaves (men or women) as far as food or clothes were concerned.

Whoever served him should be served by him too. 'Ugh' (an utterance of complaint) is a word that had never been said by him to his servant; nor was his servant blamed for doing a thing or leaving it undone. Loving the poor and the needy and entertaining them or participating in their funerals were things the Prophet (Peace and blessings be upon him) always observed. He never contempted or disgraced a poor man for his poverty. Once he was travelling with his Companions and when it was time to have food prepared, he asked them to slaughter a she-sheep. A man said: I will slaughter it, another one said: I will skin it out. A third said: I will cook it. So the Messenger of Allâh (Peace and blessings be upon him) said: I will collect wood for fire. They said: "No. We will suffice you that work." "I know that you can do it for me, but I hate to be privileged. Allâh hates to see a slave of his privileged to others." So he went and collected fire-wood.

Let us have some of the description of Hind bin Abi Halah: "The Messenger of Allâh (Peace be upon him) was continually sad, thinking perpetually. He had no rest (i.e. for long). He only spoke when it was necessary. He would remain silent for a long time and whenever he spoke, he would end his talk with his jawbone but not out of the corners of his mouth, i.e. (snobbishly). His speech was inclusive. He spoke inclusively and decisively. It was not excessive nor was it short of meaning. It was amiable. It was in no way hard discoroning. He glorified the bounty of Allâh; even if it were little. If he had no liking for someone's food, he would neither praise nor criticize.

He was always in full control of his temper and he would never get seemed angry unless it was necessary. He never got angry for himself nor did he avenge himself. It was for Allâh's sanctity and religion that he always seemed angry.

When he pointed at a thing he would do so with his full hand-palm, and he would turn it round to show surprise. If he were angry he would turn both his body and face aside. When he was pleased, he cast his eyes down. His laughter was mostly smiling. It was then that his teeth which were like hail-stones were revealed.

He never spoke unless it was something closely relevant to him. He confirmed the brotherhood relationship among his Companions; and thus he made them intimate and did not separate them or implant enmity among them. Those who were honourable with their peoples, were honoured and respected by him and were assigned rulers over their own peoples. His cheerfulness was never withdrawn at anyone's face; even at those whom he warned his people from or those whom he himself was on the alert of. He visited friends and inquired about people's affairs. He confirmed what was right and criticized the awful and tried to undermine it. He was moderate in all affairs. He was equal to others and was not privileged. He would never act heedlessly, lest the others should get heedless. Each situation was dealt with in its proper due.

Righteousness was his target; so he was never short of it nor indifferent to it. People who sat next to him were the best of their people and the best of them all were — for him — those who provided common consultations. For him, the greatest ones and the highest in ranks were the best at providing comfort and co-ordination and succour. Remembrance (of Allâh) was a thing he aimed at and established whenever he sat down or stands up. No certain position was assigned for him to sit on. He sits at the end of the group, seated next to the last sitter in the place. He ordered people to do the same. He entertained his participants in social gatherings alike so that the one addressed would think that there was no one honoured by the Prophet (Peace and blessings be upon him) but himself. He whoever sat next to him or interrupted him in order to ask for his advice about an affair of his, would be the first to start the talk and the one to end it. The Prophet (Peace and blessings be upon him) would listen to him patiently till he ended his speech. He never denied a request to anyone, if unapproachable, then few gratifying words would work, instead.

His magnanimity, broad mindedness his tolerance could embrace all people and entitled him to be regarded as father for them all. In justice, all of them were almost equal. Nobody was better than another except on the criterion of Allâh fearing. A favoured one, to him, was the most Allâh fearing. His assembly was a meeting of clemency, timidness, patience and honesty. Voices were not raised in rows or riots. Inviolable things were never violable. Fearing Allâh and worship were their means to sympathy and compassion. They used to esteem the old and have mercy on the young. They assisted the needy and entertained strangers.

The Messenger of Allâh (Peace and blessings be upon him) was always cheerful, easy, pleasant-tempered and lenient. He was never rude or rough nor clamorous or indecent. He was neither a reproacher nor a praiser. He overlooked what he did not desire, yet you would never despair of him. Three qualities he disposed of: hypocrisy, excessiveness, and what was none of his concern. People did not fear him in three area: — for they were not qualities or habits of his —: He never disparaged, or reproached nor did he seek the defects or shortages of others. He only spoke things whose reward was Divinely desirable. When he spoke, his listeners would attentively listen casting down their heads. They only spoke when he was silent. They did not have disputes or arguments about who was to talk. He who talked in his presence would be listened to by everybody till he finished his talk. Their talk would be about the topic discussed or delivered by their first speaker. The Messenger of Allâh (Peace and blessings be upon him) used to laugh at what they laughed at and admired what they used to admire. He would always show patience with a stranger's harshness at talk. He used to say:

"When you see a person seeking an object earnestly, assist him to get his need. And never ask for a reward except from the reward-Giver, i.e. Allâh."

Kharijah bin Zaid said: "The Prophet (Peace and blessings be upon him) was the most honoured among the people with whom he sat. His limbs could hardly be seen. He was often silent and rarely talked when speech was not a necessity. He turned away from those whose speech was rude or impolite. His laughter was no more than a smile. His speech, which was decisive, it was neither excessive nor incomplete. Out of reverence and esteem and following the example of their Prophet (Peace and blessings be upon him), the Companions' laughter at his presence — was smiling, as well."

On the whole the Prophet (Peace and blessings be upon him) was ornamented with peerless attributes of perfection. No wonder to be like that for he was brought up, educated and taught (the Qur'ân) by Allâh. He was even praised by Allâh:

"And verily, you [O Muhammad (Peace and blessings be upon him) ] are on an exalted standard of character." [68:4]

Those were the attributes and qualities that the Prophet (Peace and blessings be upon him) enjoyed which made the hearts of souls of the people close to him, draw near to him and love him. Those traits made him so popular that the restraint and enmity of his people grew less and they started to embrace Islam in large crowds.

This description is in fact no more than a rapid review or rather short brief lines of Muhammad's (Peace and blessings be upon him) aspects of full perfection. Trying to encompass the whole perfect picture of the Prophet (Peace and blessings be upon him). No one can ever claim to be possessed of full knowledge or complete mastery of the great attributes of the greatest man in this universe. No one can ever give this man, the top of perfection, his due descrpition. He was a man who always sought Allâh's light, to such an extent that he was wholly imbued with the Qur'ânic approach.

O Allâh! send your blessings (and the Holy Words of Yours) upon Muhammad and the family of Muhammad, as You have send blessings upon Ibrâhim and the family of Ibrâhim. You are worthy of all praise, All Glorious.

O Allâh! bless Muhammad and the family of Muhammad as You have already blessed Ibrâhim and the family of Ibrâhim. You are worthy of all praise, All Glorious.

The complete story of the Prophet, peace be upon him, is continued in
Stories of the prophets by Ibn Kathir (Book 2)


International Books Publishing House


www.al-Qarni.com

www.ingramcontent.com/pod-product-compliance
Lightning Source LLC
Chambersburg PA
CBHW082200070526
44585CB00020B/2218